Shadow Strategies
of an
American Ninja Master

Shadow Strategies of an American Ninja Master

by

Glenn J. Morris, Ph.D., D.Sc.

Shidoshi and hachidan, Togakure Ryu Bujinkan Ninpo
Oshihan, Bunbu Ichi Zendo Budo Bugei Remmei
Soke, Hoshinroshiryu

Frog, Ltd.
Berkeley, California

Published by Frog, Ltd.

Frog, Ltd. books are distributed by
North Atlantic Books
P.O. Box 12327
Berkeley, California 94712

Cover art by Wayne Oliver
Book design and production by Catherine E. Campaigne
Printed in the United States of America

Library of Congress Cataloging-in-Publication Data
Morris, Glenn, 1944–
    Shadow strategies of an American ninja master / Glenn Morris.
        p.   cm.
    ISBN 1-883319-29-3
    1. Ninjutsu.   2. Martial arts—Japan.   I. Title.
GV1114.73.S53   1996   95-923
796.8'15—dc20   CIP

    3   4   5   6   7   8   9   /   02   01   00

This book is dedicated to Aree Marquis and Sara Glenn Mariko; to Buyu that keep going; to Bujin that keep coming back; and to spiders everywhere. Additional thanks to Wayne Oliver for cover design, to shihan Kevin Millis for Bujinkan kanji brushwork, and to tai chi Shi Gong Y. C. Chiang for sculpting my personal chop shown on the cover. New hoshin black belts include Robin Martin, Leo Langwith, and Bill Little.

Table of Contents

Foreword

The cry is often "Follow me!" or "Still they come."
Yet at zero, Doctor Morris has added more,
Describing steps, side trails, and how they sum.

A view seldom shared, but sound ...
Where many claim to have gone before,
He plants a lonely flag in fertile ground.

This adventurer's journey that Dr. Morris takes you on is unique. He takes you to the mountain top where you can view, below, the entire panorama of the hidden valley of the Martial Arts. A breathtaking and exhilarating view.

He takes you on an experiential, empirically researched guided tour of the way of life he teaches—and lives to the best of his ability. He practices every day living with full attention. He focuses on the fact that our greatest battles lie within ourselves, within our own psyche. Under his direction, you take a creative approach to learning. The multicultural experiences that he has enjoyed over the years while studying the philosophy and psychology of the art make Dr. Morris uniquely qualified to present this map of the mind of the strategist. He stresses the "joy of mastery," but also makes you realize that no one can know everything.

Richard Kim, Ph.D., D.Sc.
Hanshi, Shorenji Karate
Soke, Zen Bei Dutoku Kai
California, 1995

Introduction

The combat martial arts of Asia have a history and philoso-phy that encourage distance from the act of war. Though these arts excel in the arena of strategy, their emphasis on virtue seems to contradict Western concepts of the good as being non-violent. Yet *Budo* (martial way) postulates that one on this path might achieve not only virtue, but at the highest level, enlight-enment. To the conventional American, studying violent tech-niques useful in personal combat seems a mockery of religious and ethical principles. Yet from gentle Christianity we had the Crusades, as well as the warm and friendly fires of the Inquisi-tion. Islam is better known in the West for Holy Wars than Mohammed's *Koran*. The Shaolin monks of China and muscu-lar Buddhas of Japan with striking fists, binding chains, and burning swords stir our curiosity.

Just as there are many different religions, there are many different martial arts. There can be a variety of martial arts in one country. The Japanese record eight hundred plus *ryu* (schools) of jujutsu alone. In China 382 recognized schools of *wushu* (military art) exist. Under pressure from the military gov-ernment eight of the nine major Korean martial arts (with moo do kwon tang soo do refusing) were unified as tae kwon do in the early 1950s. These are differences of degree more than kind. The arts' similarities in nonsport applications on the higher planes are the spiritual corps that parallels religion.

True *Budo* has an overwhelming emphasis on the devel-opment of moral character. It teaches respect for order and harmony, articulates the defensive rather than the offensive nature of the arts, and reveres the teachers. The right practice of certain breathing forms, postures, and attitudes allows the practitioner to enter profound transcendent meditative states. Today in the West, and for the most part in the East, sport and competition have replaced the moral basis and ethical training evolved in esoteric practice *(vajramukti)* of the martial arts associated with Buddhist Chuan Fa, the Shaolin monks of China, the Kshatriya of India, and the Sennin of Japan. For the modern practitioner to discover "religious feeling" in his or her martial art, the quest can be the equivalent of the Grail searches of Arthurian mythology.

The hardest teacher is one possessed by a love of truth and the need to speak it as seen through his or her own eyes. Such people are fiery mirrors of reality. The hardest science teacher I ever had at Penn State was Dr. Alice Beatty from Texas, who taught zoology at the DuBois Campus. She probably knew more about shrimp than anyone in the world. She introduced me to the harsh realities of flunking one quiz after another. I studied twenty-six hours straight for her final exam, which consisted of classifying twenty-five pieces of anonymous critter according to genus, species, ecological niche, function, and utility to man to wrest a C. I will never forget looking down into her microscopes to watch tiny organisms rape, pillage, and devour one another. Life at the bottom of the food chain is not all that different from the top. Evolution is a constant, and constants should not surprise.

She would say in her soft Texas drawl (that until then I had associated with being ill-educated), "You seem like such a nice boy, Mr. Morris. I can't understand why you are not doin' well in m' class." I couldn't either. She was killing me with kindness. I wasn't used to being challenged by a true master that lived her work. She spent her summers with the ocean-going fishing fleets. Her lab critters came from the sea, which mountain boys like myself had only briefly visited. I'd never even eaten shrimp at that point in my life. In my mind I can still hear her soft, dry voice resonating south of the Panhandle: "This is a horseshoe crab," as she would lift some poor dead exotic armored sea beastie out of her treasure chests.

On the arts side at Penn State, Ms. Janette Burns gave me a wealth of experience in Theatre and Speech that eventually resulted in a Ph.D. in Communication. The doorways that knowledge opens lead into countless interesting fields of study and endeavor. Life does not cease while you are in school, nor does a degree guarantee meaningful work. But, it is a good door opener.

These may seem odd starting points for both a martial artist and someone recommending a path of spiritual development. Reflect a moment. The harshest reality of ignorance is dependence. Knowledge is power. The unexamined life is not only not worth living—it is boring, boring, boring. You know what I mean. A life without a foundation in awareness is often limited to a single spectrum of experience, resulting in unpleasant surprises as the reward of ignorance. This breeds fear, which leads to hostility. The martial artist parvenu answers hostility with hostility.

Since I wrote my first book on these topics, *Path Notes of an American Ninja Master* (North Atlantic Books, 1993), I travel in more rarefied circles and return to the basics of my fundamental practices to re-examine them from a higher perspective. This is a good exercise. I've found that a strong foundation is the mother of many opportunities. We tend to leap after an opportunity before we can handle what is offered. You still have to leap, but a little more grace, if you please.

In the present book I cover basic secrets of balance and alignment; results of seeing with the mind and eyes of god, or the divine; energy applications for healing, warfare, and sexual fulfillment; the care and feeding of *Bujin* (warding spirits) across cultures and time zones; characteristics of saints, martial artists, and seekers of spiritual truth across cultures; real American values and their common shadow perversions; teaching of children, adults, and demons; and some poetry. Like the first book I prefer not to use standard academic footnotes, but will give you enough info to go hunting. Useful books and studies will be noted in the text, and I expect you to read them all, not just look up a quote out of context. Perhaps best of all, I include an expert bibliography ranked by topic and utility rather than alphabet. This is supposed to be an interesting guide not a dissertation. The secrets of the shadow are seldom discussed in the West, as the study of emotions *(nin)* is considered slippery science and difficult. For many this will not be an easy read.

The Ninja as Enlightened Warrior, Ancient and Modern

*P*ath Notes of an American Ninja Master discussed the lighter side of Bujinkan Ninpo, an ancient Japanese martial lineage that many martial art experts claim does not exist anymore. Ninjutsu is sometimes referred to as "the art of assassination," "the way of stealth," "the art of winning," and "the art of endurance." It was immortalized in the novel and popular TV movie, *Shogun*, as a "death cult." Nicolas Linnear, the hero of Eric Lustbader's ninja novels, continually searches for a teacher to help him complete what he senses is missing from his spiritual training. In most martial art B movies, particularly the ones made in Asia, the ninja are the bad guys. One exception, Tiger Tanaka, a character developed in the James Bond novels was represented positively, as was his fictional clan.

In the 1980s Stephen Hayes as a shodan began to publish practical and instantly useable handbooks of Togakure Ryu combat techniques leavened with pragmatic information concerning self-protection, and self-development. Hayes inadvertently launched the "ninja craze." To quote Ronald Holt, Ph. D., writing in *The Journal of Asian Martial Arts* (Vol. 3, No. 3, 1994), "... fake ninjutsu schools have erupted like teenage mutant

1

ninja acne.... Somewhere between the Terminator and Obi-wan Kenobi, the ninja emerged as a new American mythic hero and generic villain."

The ambiguous ninja ways, mysticism, magic, strategy, war-riorship, *qi qong* (chi kung), easily learned and effective combat techniques, exotic weaponry, and artistic creation were together a heady stew to sort for the average American palate. Stephen Hayes' seminars, books, and the annual Shadows of Iga Festival served as an introduction to most American ninja enthusiasts who weren't siphoned off by phony imitators. Steve continues his rationalized interpretation of traditional ninja training through the establishment of the Kasumi-An dojos, the Nine Gates Institute, and Blue Lotus Assembly. Many of us started off studying under Steve, then moved on to study with expert teachers of Bujinkan Budo Taijutsu in the States, Europe, and Japan, or we became personal students of Masaaki Hatsumi. Once your foundation is in place, you should seek deep and varied experience.

To understand ninja ways requires a knowledge of history, an inquiring mind open to new experience, attention to detail, and a reverence for the esoteric as well as the pragmatic. Actual combat experience is helpful, but not necessary. In this chapter I'll define some Japanese terms, relate a little history, identify some key historical figures and religious concepts, and compare the traditional and the modern ninja of the Togakure (pronounced toe-GAWK-uh-ray) Ryu (pronounced rue and meaning a stream of consciousness, or school).

The guiding principles of Bujinkan Ninpo can be illustrated by the words of Toshitsugu Takamatsu-*soke* (suffix indicating Grandmaster), the thirty-third linear Grandmaster of the Togakure Ryu: "The essence of all martial arts and military strategies is self-protection and the prevention of danger. Ninpo deals with the protection of not only the physical body, but the mind and spirit as well. The way of the ninja is the way of enduring, surviving, and prevailing over all that would destroy one. More than simply defeating or outwitting an enemy, Ninpo is the way of attaining that which we need to live happily, while making the world a better place." The ninja behavior is exemplified by my occasional teacher and friend, Masaaki Hatsumi-soke, thirty-fourth linear Grandmaster and an artist of the twenty-first century. Writing in his newsletter or densho *(Sanmyaku)*, Hatsumi-soke occasionally quotes Toda Shinryuken-sensei of Shinden Fudo-ryu (one of Takamatsu's teachers) as saying the essence *(gokui)* of taijutsu is the basis of peace. Toda (in 1890) postulated five rules for achieving the unshakable heart: (1) "Know that endurance is simply one puff of smoke. (2) Know that the way of human beings is justice. (3) Forget the heart of greed, ease, and favoritism (relying on others). (4) One should regard both sadness and malice as natural laws, and gain the enlightenment of an unshakable heart. (5) In your heart never leave the ways of loyalty and filial piety, and aspire greatly for the ways of the pen and the sword *(Bunbu)."*

According to its own legends, Ninpo has its roots in ancient Taoist China. In Japan, it is loosely associated with two Buddhist sects: Tendai Mikkyo *(Vajrayana),* and Shingon. Ninpo is also associated with the ancient indigenous religions of *Shugendo* (mountain mystics), and Shinto (The Way [Tao] of the Gods [spirit, energy, or heart], or spirit sword, or spirit of China), which is the indigenous religion that, typical of Japanese syncretism, greatly resembles some aspects of Taoism. Mikkyo can be linked to Tibet.

These were the predominant religions in the Iga and Koga mountain areas of Japan. South of Iga was the Kumano Sea. Its coast produced the sea-going *Kuki Suigun* (boat samurai, traders, and pirates) and remains a Shinto sanctuary today. During the Tang Dynasty (AD 618–907) many Chinese religious and military leaders emigrated to Japan to flee oppression or lack of opportunity in their homeland. These Taoist warriors and monks brought with them martial and mental techniques which were learned, developed, and refined by the families who accepted and inter-married with them in the rocky, forested, remote highland valleys that hold the heart of the island fortress that is Japan. Spider Kung Fu, which was once the secret royal fighting art of Imperial China, contains *kamae* (fighting postures) similar to Ninpo, as are the self-defense techniques of the boxing *(chuan fa)* and grappling *(chin-na)* kung fu arts. ("Kung fu" actually means hard work, and like "chi kung" is usually limited to Western terminology.). *Gyokko Ryu Koshijutsu* has Chinese antecedents that extend back to the eighth century. Given the chaotic history of Japan before the age of unity, which particularly applies to the pirate coasts of Kumano and the bandit haven mountains of Iga and Koga, tracing exact lineages is impossible. We rely on legends, but can feel the truth through the experience of taijutsu. Although *koshijutsu* (combat skills of working with energy points on the body) is derived from Chinese medical applications, the various ancient ryu completely identify with Japanese applications and terminology.

The people of the mountains, even today, seem close to their Shinto roots. Shinto is in some ways very similar to what we call shamanism in the West. Mikkyo, the sect most closely associated with the martial arts in general (due to many samurai retiring to become monks) is considered the most tantric/magical of the Buddhist belief systems. It is not necessary to become a Buddhist to study Ninpo, but the study and experience of religions is considered part of ninja skill training, as ninja often passed as priests or monks as part of their training in intelligence gathering. Throughout Japanese history the religious were able to travel anytime, and anywhere. The ninja as well as the mountain warrior priests *(yamabushi)* of Shugendo are associated with the *tengu* (crow-like mountain demons associated with superhuman swordsmanship) and tengu may have been a joking pejorative for the indigenous people of an area (like the Ainu) used by the conquering samurai.

Until 894, which ended the Nara Period, there was considerable trade and interaction with China. China was the dominant culture, and much imitated by the Japanese of that period. Chinese concepts of religion and warfare were taught as a major part of the education of nobles and traders, and were absorbed into everyday life. Lao Tzu and Sun Tzu (In Mandarin Chinese, Lao-tse, author of *The Way of Power,* and Sun-tse, *The Art of War*) were required reading in the Nara court. Later historians quoted by Stephen Turnbull in his history of the ninja even referred to the families of this region as Chinese bandits who had memorized Sun Tzu.

Taoist concepts oppose the conduct of war as economically wasteful of wealth and lives, and Sun Tzu recommends cutting off the head of the snake before it can grow dangerous. When a people are outnumbered by a superior force which holds their ground, assassination and terror become a pragmatic choice for those with no desire to be owned by the conqueror. During the Gempei Wars in the twelfth century, Iga was overrun by the samurai of the Northern emperor (creating a new underclass of former nobles and indigenous people to be exploited), as well as by the Tokugawa shogunate of the sixteenth century. These events contributed to the "disappearance" of the ninja *ryuha* (martial traditions).

The ninja of Koga were renowned as samurai skilled in small-group tactics and the cracking of fortresses. The ninja of Iga were samurai greatly respected for personal combat skills, the gathering of intelligence, and strategy. The ninja of Kumano were sea-going warriors, whalers, and traders. The women had skills that were seldom recorded in a patriarchal society, and like those who pledged allegiance to the Southern emperor and lost their places in the new social order during the Gempei Wars, historical references to *kunoichi* (female ninja) are difficult to find. Togakure Ryu mythology indicates that the kunoichi used disguises similar to their male counterparts, finding the roles of priestess, actress, and geisha particularly useful for gathering intelligence. The men occasionally disguised themselves as women.

Shinobi (spirit belt or ninja) warriors were regarded as supermen by the more conventional warriors of their time, and jealousy is a common reaction to excellence in the insecure or poorly led. The "winning" families seldom rewarded the ninja with acceptance and recognition, but they were quick to pay for their services when men of valor were needed for individual or small-group tactics. Ishakawa Goemon is regarded by the people of Iga in the same way Robin Hood is by the people of Nottingham. Goemon was boiled to death as a bandit when he was finally captured. The ninja, like the dragon/tree kings of Wales and Cornwall in pre-Roman-invasion England, were devoted more to the land they served than any upstart family. Selling knowledge was simply another strategy for holding their mountain keeps.

Ninpo (the Way of the emotions as a guide to preserving life), which subsumes *ninjutsu* (the physical skills that can be learned to win fights), deals with strategy, moral development, and ethics, as well as what we in the West would consider sorcery, shamanism, and healing. The Japanese—and probably the Chinese—version of shamanism more closely resembles some aspects of yoga, human alchemy, and manipulation of subtle energy. The religious practice of Ninpo is sometimes referred to as *nindiki,* according to Richard Kim-hanshi in conversation, and was primarily followed by women. (The men were in hiding or dead.) Ninpo is mentioned respectfully in Zen scrolls as far back as the thirteenth century. Its symbols and methodology reflect a religious syncretism as well as scientific empiricism predating the Scientific Method by hundreds of years. The spider is a creativity symbol of destruction, removal, and renewal across cultures as well as a nature symbol for the wheel of dharma. Its eight legs represent pathways. The rat is associated with the subjection of demons in Hindu theology. The Teenage Ninja Turtles' *sensei* (teacher) is appropriately a rat. Turtle shell shields were supposedly used by the coastal ninja (unkindly referred to by samurai as the pirates of Kumano), and the turtle is revered in many Asian and Native American cultures for courage and longevity derived from its low profile, tough shell, and speed at covering up. Turtle breathing is a little-known Taoist esoteric technique for building chi through the expansion and contraction of the total skeleton. When you do it correctly, the third eye phosphenes look like a tortoise shell viewed from above.

Togakure Ryu Ninpo, initially named *Togakure Ryu Happohiken* and considered a branch of *koshijutsu* (energy point skills or dim mak). It was founded by Daisuke (Nishina) Togakure, a vassal of Kiso Yoshinaka who lost in a revolt against the Heike regime nearly nine hundred years ago. That predates Columbus and coincides with European history's William the Conqueror. Similar lifestyle, different skin color. Daisuke Togakure could be compared to Hereward the Wake of Saxon fame, who fought a losing guerrilla war against the invading Franks in the bogs of Anglia. The founder of this ancient ryu was a backwater rural prince with responsibilities to his people. He barely escaped, losing everything but life to the conquering horde of the Northern emperor's samurai, as did the Celts to the Saxon/Vikings, and to the Franks on another island much further West.

In post-Nara Period Japan, the losers in a war against the state were supposed to commit *seppuku* (ritual suicide). Nishina didn't do that. He ran in terror back to his mountain keep, and like Robin Hood took to the woods. What he learned from watching most of his friends being hunted down and slashed to pieces by the new world order became the basis of a school that teaches how to survive both spiritually and physically in a harmonious manner against overwhelming odds, when every hand is turned against you, and those in positions of authority consider you an outlaw. The ninja of Iga, influenced by Taoism, had already decided the samurai practice of seppuku was a con of indescribable proportion and evil, as all experience and life are to be lived to the fullest. One does not end one's life over matters of face. The act of suicide carried out by cutting a half-moon across the bottom of the rib cage with a knife requires a certain amount of commitment, and a great deal of pain control. A friend could serve as a helper to send you on your way once you spoke your death poem praising nature in three or five lines of haiku and actually began the cut (see Clavell's *Shogun* movie). The way one arranged and sat on one's clothing prevented untidy thrashing about, but there is little difference between gut shot and gut stabbed in a world without antibiotics. When you made the first thrust, you were probably successful in achieving your goal. The friend who lifted your head with his or her sword was only speeding the process to save you the embarrassment of being a three-day wonder if you missed hacking the aortic arch while you were sawing through the small intestines, which contain the spirit or *hara.* Cutting open the guts, while lifting the head may also provide a faster route for releasing the contents of *Ida* and *Pingalla* (major energy routes) into the atmosphere without the filter of the socially learned self residing in the cortex. (Do you buy that? The samurai did!)

The samurai practiced *seppuku* as a demonstration of determination and a means of redemption by showing through their actions that "life as it now stands before me is not worth living. I have screwed up so badly that only my murder of this body can stand as my apology for my actions, or for serving such a fool. I have failed miserably in my attempt to learn compassion, and hope by this act of supreme will power to gain entry to that purer land to come, as spiritual life is precious beyond material gain." There was a long list of acceptable reasons for one to commit suicide. The samurai belief was by taking this irreversible act that required considerable exercise of the will, the individual would be generating enough energy to drop-kick his spirit into the upper reaches of the Void, spirit world, or Pure Land.

The samurai families on the losing sides of conflict were no longer considered samurai by the winning shogun, and they were forced to forfeit their property and holdings, resulting in an impoverished class of former warriors and administrators. This practice may have created the *Yakuza* (crime families), which are sometimes associated with the ninja, as well as ultra-conservative right wing politics. Those families wishing to live had to adjust to the new social system. As it had a very rigid structure and social expectations, those conquered were begrudgingly given "the dirty work." From the perspective of transpersonal psychology, clinging to life under such conditions is hardly a sin, and giving it up can be of great value. (Remaining separate from your self, reality, and others divorces you from your true connective feelings. This rejected baggage eventually grows into self-destructive grief, or the deeper shadow known as death-wish resulting from the experience of feelings that come from living a life of thwarted desire.)

Some Western comparisons may help explain the "art of invisibility's" nine-hundred-year underground existence. The fate of the "Good People" or Cathars of twelfth-century France, whose benevolent and spiritual practice of heretical Christian selflessness (no ego) attracted the attention of the Roman Catholic Church, is one example. The Church's response to their gentility developed into the Inquisition. I spent a great deal of time in France as a young soldier and never met a Cathar or anyone who had even heard of Catharite Christianity. A little practice of stealth on the Cathars' part might have resulted in four, rather than three, major manifestations of Christianity, but no... The Good People were burned on thousands of stakes, and their mountain fortresses were pulled down, leaving only empty ruins on the peaks to titillate historians and archeologists nine hundred years later.

If someone were to ask modern Americans about life in the original thirteen colonies, you can be pretty certain they would leave out the Six Nation Indian confederation that served as a model for our famous Constitution. Where are the Six Nations now? Or you might ask what happened to the nomad plains confederations. Crazy Horse, visionary warrior of the traditional Lakota, led his people as a "shirt wearer" over thirty years against all comers. His only mistake was joining with Sitting Bull to cream Custer at the Little Big Horn. Two years later he was bayoneted to death at peace negotiations, and his people's place on the Earth was appropriated by "white eyes" who spoke of ownership. The desert and mountain Apache are faintly memorialized by the cry "Geronimo!" when we leap out of airplanes. The little kingdoms of very ancient Japan shared a similar fate, and in my opinion, the shinobi samurai or ninja are their only legacy.

Knowing the Past Helps One Understand the Present

Dr. Masaaki Hatsumi-soke, known to his American students as "The Boss" and who defers to Mrs. Hatsumi as "Super Boss," is the head of nine ryu or martial traditions. That is soke times nine. The power and knowledge of these particular lineages and what he has acquired from the ryu after nearly forty years of study might be speculated upon by considering the number of generations. "The Boss" is thirty-fourth Soke of Togakure Ryu Ninpo; twenty-eighth Soke of Kukishinden Ryu Happo Hiken; fifteenth Soke of Gikan Ryu Koppojutsu; fourteenth Soke of Kumogakure Ryu Ninpo; seventeenth Soke of Takagi Yoshin Ryu Jutaijutsu; twenty-eighth Soke of Gyokoshin Ryu Ninpo; eighteenth Soke of Koto Ryu Koppojutsu; twenty-sixth Soke of Shinden Fudo Ryu Daken Taijutsu; and twenty-first Soke of Gyokko

Ryu Koshijutsu. He holds an earned Ph.D. for his studies, books, and videos. He is a medical doctor (Japanese traditional bone specialist), writer, researcher, television actor, and painter of considerable renown (earning up to $50,000 a pop in his own land). I have seen martial artists get all puffy about being able to trace their lineage back to the 1920s. Dr. Hatsumi carries the weight of his tradition with a light heart and no arrogance. The schools and lineages of the Togakure Ryu fade into the shadowy mysteries of legend and mythology, yet are as real and existent today as a blow to the heart. Three of the ryu are considered ninjutsu and the other six are samurai traditions. The whole of the above nine essential *kobudo ryuha* (martial traditions of the heart) is referred to as Bujinkan Ryu Ninpo Taijutsu, or in the generic by the practitioners as Budo Taijutsu.

Baby-talk analysis of the names of the above ryu indicates a major emphasis on *shin* or spirit, *ku* or Void, and *ko* or heart. The emphasis obviously suggests to the discerning eye that one might pick up something useful from these schools beyond the proper way to make a fist, swing a sword, or butcher a predator. When you jump in one of these streams, the water will change you.

To in Japanese can be translated as "Chinese" as well as "straight sword." Takamatsu-sensei (Hatsumi's teacher) said you have to follow the Silk Road to get the complete history of Ninpo and that thread spins out of China and goes all the way to India through Tibet. The straight-sided two-handed sword often associated with the ninja is remarkably similar to the sword favored by cavalry in the late Han dynasty of ancient China, and the Jin dynasty of Tibet (*Swords and Hilt Weapons*. Barnes & Noble, 1993). Modern ninja use the battle-proven techniques of "Warring States Period" rather than modern kenjutsu. The flowing body movement and attitudes developed are more like tai chi than karate or judo. Flow, speed, surprise, and power are necessary survival traits for living through a melee comprised of thousands of berserks wearing armor and swinging yard-long razor blades.

The classic Iga (home province of Togakure Ryu) ninja worked at developing a deep and accurate self-knowledge, and from that mystical perspective of universality granted by *satori* (kensho, or enlightenment), he or she only engaged in combat when motivated by discovery, love, or reverence. Spiritual refinement, which can be translated as energy skill or chi kung, was the primary goal for the traditional ninja of the Togakure Ryu. *Taijutsu* (body combat skills) involving striking, kicking, avoiding, blocking, grappling, choking, throwing, and escaping the holds of others as the primary skills; leaping, rolling, silent movement, and tumbling, were all secondary skills. Tertiary knowledge of the sword and a whole slew of other skills, including knowledge of weapons, medicine and healing, land and animal stewardship, and pharmacopoeia, continue the list.

Ninpo is a living art with an awe-inspiring reputation as a route to enlightenment as well as a system of self-protection par excellence. Hatsumi-soke has brought together nine schools of esoteric warrior arts under his lineage Bujinkan. One of the more famous is the Takagi Tree Felling School *(Takagi Yoshin Ryu Jutaijutsu),* mentioned with humorous chagrin in the Kurosawa film, *The Seven Samurai.* The techniques of this school are constantly surprising as well as overwhelming. They are particularly useful for the smaller warrior when faced with an inescapable, armed, and larger opponent. Hatsumi-soke has said that "true martial arts are not for the strong, but are the salvation of the weak and the meek."

According to *shihan* (senior master instructor) Koryu Muramatsu of Noda-shi, Japan, who told the story to Greg Kowalski, who told it to me, Setsuemon (Oriemon) Shigetoshi Takagi lived during the mid-1600s, making him a near contemporary of Miyamoto Musashi. He was a master teacher of *jutaijutsu* (soft body skills similar to tai chi). It was common in those days to accept challenges from visiting masters or duelists, as duels keep a senior practitioner honest. They are particularly beneficial when the survival of a student depends directly on the effectiveness of the practice learned from one's teacher. Duels were often fought with practice weapons, as death is a harsh reward for age or ignorance. (Teachers tend to live longer than duelists.) Takagi fought a duel with a teacher of Masaki Ryu Jutaijutsu and was so thoroughly thrashed that it shook him to his very soul. Out of this painful lesson came the realization of the vulnerability he had passed on to his students. He left his school, and his comfortable living, and humbly set out to search for a truer martial way.

Takagi had a scientific frame of mind. As he traveled, he observed what others were doing. When he saw a teacher who impressed him or had skills he desired to acquire, he stayed for a while to study and then moved on, reflecting on what he had experienced. He had an eclectic spirit and thus avoided confusing a specific teaching with its vast and undifferentiated subject. (This trap has caught several tigers, past and present.) No ryu or teacher he encountered in his search for a better way appealed enough to him to be considered a resting point. Takagi searched for basic principles and eventually came to the realization that to survive without harm he had to first avoid and then upset his opponent's way of moving and thinking. He also realized that this rule applied to his own personal development. He had to personalize his jutsu, lifting skilled technology into spiritual art.

These principles derived from experience of the unexpected elevated his skills at survival to new heights. Takagi became recognized as a great teacher. He won over many challengers, and students flocked to his teaching in the hope of picking up some of his skills. He gladly shared with his students what worked for him. Several generations later, the senior students, realizing the power of the methods they practiced, named their school after him. In the seventeenth century the head of this ryu and the head of Kukishinden Ryu Happobiken became good friends after a match and merged their schools. Masaaki Hatsumi accepted the leadership of these ancient schools of self-protection from Takamatsu-sensei and integrated their beneficial teachings as part of Bujinkan Ninpo. Much that was known of these schools was destroyed in the fire bombing of World War II. Takamatsu-sensei restored that knowledge from memory after the war.

Similar stories exist concerning other founders of the schools subsumed under the Togakure Ryu Bujinkan Budo Taijutsu. In his book *Ninja Submission,* Hatsumi-soke states to the awestruck interviewer impressed by the age of the lineages, "To be honest with you, we don't know much about the things that happened in ancient times" (Keibunsha, 1991, printed in Japanese). The heritage that the modern student assumes is legendary in the East, as well as the West.

Hatsumi often quotes Chinese *heiho-sho* (works on strategy), and I have seen him demo for two hours straight showing variations of one "push hand" technique without once making an offensive move. Every one of his responses resulted in the total incapacitation of his *uke* (training partner who receives) without injury but enormous pain. He used up five uke during this period of instruction. He is an artist of the highest order. When he says in his densho, "People who do not know the essence of Budo or Ninpo will stray into unhappiness in spite of themselves," he is making an observation on the attraction of shadow *Bugei* (art of combat mainly concerned with the use of weapons). Although a great deal is conjectured and rumored concerning the ninja's weapon skills and arsenal of tools, the concept of *kaname* or "divine eyes" is the most powerful of the weapons in the ninja array. The use of kaname requires purity of intention and accounts for the ninja concern with the study of religion for guidance in spiritual development.

Hatsumi-soke has said to me in conversation, "The true Budo man must find religious feelings."

The first priority of the Togakure Ryu ninja is spiritual integration. The samurai equivalent is called *haragei* (internal development) and is considered the most important study in the practice of karate. (I have never met a karate master who could actually teach it, though quite few manifest to some degree.) Hatsumi-soke has said the ninja is expected to have "religious feelings," meaning an experiential knowledge of religions, which means a return to innocence for most adults. The mirror of the soul must be examined layer by layer, for it holds great treasures. The spiritual quest of the ninja is a personal adventure into the depths of his or her own innermost being to integrate mind, body, and spirit with the universal. It requires a merging of the opposites: *omote* (outer or shown, yang, light) and *ura* (inner or hidden, yin, shadow) in terms of martial technique; *in* (yin) and *yo* (yang) in terms of energy use; understanding the opponent which is your learned self or superego; and male (yang) and female (yin), or androgyny. One then uses these integrated perspectives to eliminate dualism and strategically act without thought in harmony with one's basic nature of bringing light to shadow *(mushin)*. Few accomplish their primary task, as it requires great humility to recognize our failings as human beings in the material world. We would rather operate from our strengths, putting physical skill above philosophy and strategy. When Hatsumi-san says a particular ninja's taijutsu skills "are a gift from God," he usually means the individual hasn't been able to figure out the true feeling of the art but has great technical skill regardless. The upper-class Japanese are very polite.

Takamatsu-soke was a spy in China for the Japanese during World War II, and previously in dealings with the court of the last Chinese emperor. He was president of the outlawed *Busen* (war college) branch in Shanghai. He was a friend of Morihei Ueshiba, the founder of aikido, and knew Jigoro Kano, who revolutionized jujutsu into judo. A ninja joke that Kano and Takamatsu-sensei were having a conversation concerning the difficulty of finding people to participate in learning real martial arts finishes with the line, "Well, Jigaro, why don't you turn it into a sport?" There is a well-documented story concerning an assassination attempt during the Japanese Occupation of Shanghai where Takamatsu-soke fled (or lured) his six attackers into a dark, multi-storied, building. He appeared unarmed. They were armed with swords, knives, and bludgeons. (Samurai do not allow captive people to carry modern weaponry.) Six men fell on their weapons, or leapt to their death. Takamatsu-sensei was acquitted in the Chinese court. He testified that his attackers were clumsy and he just tried to get away from them by climbing the walls and stairwells. This could establish his skills at *muto dori* (unarmed against the sword techniques), *kyojitsu* (weird airs), or to the innocent, his superb climbing and gymnastic skills. Takamatsu-sensei may have hid out in the temple (Mikkyo Buddhism) after the war, (like Colson when caught, turning to Jesus) but to my knowledge didn't seek a congregation. He was a spy, he wanted their secrets. He passed what was useful to the Ryu. Like Hatsumi, he was a genius, and saw little need for perpetuating middlemen when the source is the self. For those who were hunting him, the rumors of his very sudden death at Hiroshima with other highly ranked members of the China Busen (*Kokuryukai* or Black Dragon or Amur River secret society devoted to annexing Manchuria from 1901) were enough to direct their attention to the more immediate and politically useful goal of stamping out Communist sympathizers with the help of the Yakuza. Takamatsu-sensei's spirit at the time of his teaching Hatsumi-soke had experienced both the false glory of offensive war and the value of Ninpo's survival strategies.

Hatsumi-san said at the Atlanta Tai Kai in 1994 that Takamatsu-soke is the only man he ever feared, and that he was so virtuous a teacher that his goodness still influences his behavior. During the last fifteen years of Takamatsu's life he had only one student, though many falsely claim to have had the privilege. Hatsumi-soke told Kevin Millis that in the fifteen years of training with Takamatsu-soke, they only trained indoors twice. Ninja remain close to their nature and seek to learn from the Earth. Tai chi masters also recommend training outdoors, particularly under large trees close to water.

The ancient ninja specialized in using a wide variety of weapons (which definitely goes against classical Buddhist Dharma, but not Taoism, Mikkyo, Shugendo, or Shinto). The modern ninja learns how to use contemporary weaponry, but traditional practice weapons are emphasized in the dojo. Many of the American members of the ryu are war veterans. Ninjutsu is often associated with Special Forces, British SAS and Royal Marines, SEAL team training, and the Israeli counter-terrorist strike teams, but the Budo Taijutsu tradition for most ninja is to avoid government work. Ninpo may be training to preserve the mind and spirit, but ninjutsu preserves the body. Japanese gun laws resemble those of Britain, where you aren't allowed the protection from government oppression offered by the Second Amendment to the USA's Constitution. Thus the Japanese work on the skills necessary for adept use of edged weapons, empty-handed techniques against opponents with and without weapons, and various fighting tools that extend one's reach or power. Americans take those same survival principles and apply them pragmatically to the modern environment.

Seminars in the USA are occasionally offered in electronic security techniques, meditation, HALO (high altitude, low opening insertions), UDT (underwater demolition training, and water infiltration), booby trapping, sniper and automatic weapons training, escape and evasion, incendiaries, tracking and survival, bodyguarding, combat driving, camouflage, identity assumption, handguns, and archery. A nervous white belt at the 1987 Shadows of Iga Festival questioned Hatsumi-soke as to what a ninja would do if attacked by a pit bull. He silently replied by miming the action of a pump shotgun. Ninjutsu adapts skillfully to the modern environment of guerrilla and technological warfare, terrorism, urban violence, and street crime. The teachings of Sun Tzu and Lao Tzu have not lost their power over the centuries.

The *Bujin* (warding spirits) flow through Hatsumi. In *Bujin Tetsuzan* (God-like weird spirits at the top of the mountain, or titular head of the ryu, or iron mountain) Masaaki Hatsumi, we are able to see it, and them, come together. Hatsumi-san has become so casual about his interaction with the spirit world that he offers it as an ordinary experience to be shared. He talks coyly of his chi sickness and mentions that after his "intestines healed, and he could stand upright, his body became lighter." He says that "Budo is a physical process and to talk about an experience that one has not had only confuses the student, as it is better for them to figure it out for themselves." Endurance or the ability to keep playing is the heart of Ninpo. *Shinken-gata* (spirit sword techniques sometimes translated as real combat skills) or "ki" transcends male or female as the desirable end product. Those who cannot see or feel the spirits can still observe the flow.

As understanding of the *ura* (the hidden) increases, the taijutsu practitioner's use of body movement and energy become more subtle. *Godan* (fifth-degree black belts) and above in Budo Taijutsu focus primarily on refining their skills in softness and distance weapons. There are fifteen *dan* (black belt) degrees rather than the usual five (combat systems) or ten (sport or tournament systems) in the Bujinkan system. Soke or grandmaster is not a rank, but a place in nature, and is a title that only applies to the head of the lineage, or The Boss. As the ninja's life work was often that of a spy, or gatherer of intelligence, visible indications of strength and power could be a warning to the enemy. Though kata is never emphasized, the basic body dynamics are learned through the *sanshin* (Relaxed body dynamics and fighting postures that are often taught as an aerobic warm up. Muramatsu-sensei—who is famous for his fighting abilities—told me sanshin were very important for developing chi), and the *kihon happo* which are a series of fight scenarios that teach battle-proven techniques, and *henka* (variations) that flow out of the combat situation. I might also add that many of the moves are surprisingly funny in order to take advantage of conventional methods of fighting. People often crack up when training with the real ninja. In Japan, Togakure Ryu Bujinkan Ninpo (Budo Taijutsu) is considered real ninjutsu.

Upon entering the ryu one seldom realizes that it is a still evolving process that can take up to forty years to master. The basics differ from year to year, depending on what century The Boss is emphasizing, as the armor and weapons of the enemy forces change. Every ninja master has a unique body dynamic. When I came into the system *koppo jutsu* (breaking bones) was emphasized; now it is middle-distance weapons like the spear and *naginata* (sword on a pole), and in a few years it might be archery.

Hatsumi-soke has increased his teaching around the world as he becomes more aware of the mortality of the flesh and acts to ascertain the survival of his legacy. His skill in making contact can easily be seen in the much greater success rate in the *godan* test (fifth-degree black belt sword avoidance) necessary for shidoshi licensing (described in *Path Notes*). At the Baltimore testing Kevin Millis and I were rocking in our chairs every time he cut at a student, and we were sitting thirty feet off to the right side. Some of the kids looked like they had been struck by lightning and were knocked right out of their roll. (Some seem to think it has something to do with their own prowess. They tend to be the most fun to watch over time.) At the Tucson Tai Kai in 1995 the feeling was much more subtle and one of the new shidoshi told me, "It was very strange. I felt I was pushed over by a sudden breeze." The gift of the master is endless.

None of the movie ninja even come close to the grace, speed, and power of the Togakure Ryu higher-level practitioner. What is usually shown is karate or tae kwon do in black or colored night suits with rather awkward weapon work and *shuriken* (throwing blades) to identify the ninja. In my travels around the world, I have run into people claiming to be Korean ninja who might be better served by studying hwarang do, or Chinese ninja, who should really go find a good kung fu instructor. The nasty books with sillier pictures put out by Ashida Kim (an interesting name for an obvious round eye), Katsumi Toda (not too likely given the content), and Death Touch Master Long (tae kwon do in funny clothes) are popular examples of duping the ignorant. They are like quotes out of context. It never fails to amaze me how some people manage to get into print with such obviously contrived and fraudulent backgrounds. Sometimes there is useful information presented, but in comparison to the real knowledge they are food for the moon. The faking techniques for chi kung frauds are similar to the tricks one substitutes for magic in the ninja art of *genjutsu* (skills one exhibits for money). These include walking fire, or broken glass, feats of strength, like suspending oneself between two chairs, or sending someone sailing with a two-inch punch which only require knowledge of body dynamics, escape from bondage similar to Harry Houdini's famous stunts, and the breaking of boards and stones with focus rather than strength.

Hatsumi-soke claims that he has been exposed to at least seventy-five theories concerning the true origins of the mythic ninja. (I gave you mine in the Spider Prince chapter in *Path Notes of an American Ninja Master.*) It is interesting to note that "the art of assassination," as ninjutsu is often designated by its detractors, forbids the taking of your opponent's life unless your own is in jeopardy. Most of what is in the popular literature concerning ninja practices (and for that matter samurai) is militaristic hogwash. The Japanese treat the gathering of intelligence as a heroic activity best conducted through secret societies. Espionage is usually best conducted by civilians or military personnel who can appear as civilians (Richard Deacon. *Kempei Tai: The Japanese Secret Service Then and Now,* Charles Tuttle, 1990). Regardless of its history, the modern Togakure Ryu or Bujinkan Budo Taijutsu has two primary roles. (1) Preservation of traditional and historical techniques of self-protection, and (2) development of a worthwhile and wholesome international organization that is beneficial for its members and their families.

Taking a Peek at the Bujinkan Organizational Chart

There is a vast ignorance concerning the expectations (or rules) of Bujinkan Dojo. People don't know how to identify a real ninja or (God help us) find their way through the maze of misinformation and misunderstanding when East meets West and warrior/shamans meet warrior/businessmen. Neither is certain of the identity of the other. The Bujinkan is finally becoming organized to the point where there is enough structure and competent teachers for a beginner to study on the martial path without falling prey to frauds. I am certain that if I had the opportunity to begin study in this art as a young person, I would be a wiser and better man.

First, The Boss (Masaaki Hatsumi-soke) is the boss. You can study where and with whom you wish, but eventually, if you intend to become a teacher of Budo Taijutsu, you will have to kneel before the sword. You will find your path smoothed if you study in Japan. Some instructors say you can get all you need studying in the USA, but that only reflects their insecurity. The Japanese masters have more experience and are glad to share it, if approached with an open heart. Bujinkan is an international organization. In any large organization there will be differences of opinion, but a newcomer would be wise to focus on the directions of Hatsumi-soke and leave the petty politics, disinformation, and power playing to those who enjoy that sort of thing. Such people tend to "go away" around sixth or seventh dan, if not earlier.

The various Bujinkan Dojo directly support and have access to Hatsumi-sensei. Bujinkan is the name of Hatsumi-soke's manifestation of the art of Ninpo. Any additions to that word should be regarded with suspicion. If it ain't Bujinkan, it ain't Ninpo. Legitimate dojo are usually identified with the senior instructor's name, Japanese attitude, or local feature tied to Bujinkan. Bujinkan Nagase Dojo. Bujinkan Millis Dojo. Woodlands Bujinkan Dojo. Kokusai Bujinkan Dojo. Its that simple.

There is an organization called the *shidoshi-kai* (Master Teachers Guild) which has certain rules and expectations. Take a moment and peek into my mail and my commentary in the parens. Hatsumi-san is very *laissez faire* (French for type-B personality administrator) and usually forgives or ignores rule breakers, as he dislikes forcing his will on the members of the ryu. There are twenty expectations, but following are the ten that have general application. The rest can jokingly be considered "oral tradition," as you will get them when you get there.

1. Our purpose is to live a healthy life, without harming society, enculturing the mutual relationships of nature and encouraging mankind through the martial ways. (This is referred to as a vision statement in organizational development. Its meant to briefly and succinctly inform the stranger of our ways or what we are all about. It is a statement of intent from which all behavior is shaped and flows.)

2. All members must have a membership card for the year issued by the *Hombu* (headquarters in Japan). There are two types of membership card: General Membership and shidoshi-kai Membership.

a. The general membership card applies to members of the Bujinkan Dojo, whether ungraded, kyu-graded, or dan-graded. (You can join without becoming a ryu member.)

b. The shidoshi-kai membership card applies to those of fifth dan and above who have teaching licenses (called shidoshi), and those from first to fourth dan, under the supervision of a shidoshi as interns (called shidoshi-ho). Members who are teaching Bujinkan Budo Taijutsu should possess one of these cards. Non shidoshi-kai members are not recognized as teachers and cannot grade students. (If you want to teach and promote, you have to pay your professional dues. The grading of students can be fairly lucrative. People like to learn the real thing from a legitimate master or licensed teacher.)

4. Members over fourth dan are promoted personally by Hatsumi-soke, who judges their technique, character, and integrity. (The Boss can see into your heart.) Those who are unable to visit the Hombu in Japan may request consideration by mail, enclosing a videotape for Soke's reference. Requests for consideration for promotion may also be made at the annual regional gatherings for training under Hatsumi and the shihan called *Tai Kai*. (The Boss personally supervises the executive ranks and owns the selection procedure. Eighth dan and above are decided by committee. Requests and payment are no guarantee of promotion.) Those with criminal records, serious psychological problems, or mental abnormalities need not apply. (Hatsumi-soke's standards and definition of neurosis or "abnormal" are somewhat more compassionate than mine coming from different cultural expectations. See Lao Tzu 49.)

5. Members of the shidoshi-kai will be informed of Soke's activities, such as new Hombu videos and other publications. Videos can be purchased direct from Bujinkan Dojo Hombu, 636 Noda, Noda-Shi, Chiba-Ken, 278 Japan. Average video cost including shipping and handling is less than eight thousand *yen* (Japanese basic monetary unit) and can be purchased by any

Bujinkan member. It is recommended that students purchase individually from the available listing and pay in yen. Soke's newsletter *Sanmyaku*, which is distributed internationally in fifteen languages, is treated as a *densho* (personal transmission of the fundamental and authentic stuff) and is available from WIN Publishing, PO Box 30338, Stockton, CA. 95213, for $45.00 a year.

6. Only membership cards and licenses issued by the Bujinkan Dojo Hombu will be recognized as valid. People issuing fake membership cards and/or certificates will face expulsion from the Bujinkan Dojo. (I have yet to issue a certificate of ninja training or promote anyone in Bujinkan Budo. I have made suggestions when I thought someone was being unfairly treated or too humble. The Boss seems to think I'm a good judge of character.)

7. The "Bujin" symbol is copyrighted. If planning to use it, you must first contact the Hombu for permission.

8. Members must follow *Bufu Ikkan* (the martial ways as a principle of everyday strategy makes living easy) for the sake of protecting natural justice, and happiness without turning to personal profits and desires. (And there's the rub. We are protectors, not predators. Ninpo is treated as a hobby rather than a cash cow profession. The techniques are easy to learn, but the principles of balance take years to master. As with all physical arts, it is difficult to teach what you cannot do.)

9. Members are responsible for their own dojo/community and should contact the Hombu directly on important matters or grievances. Hatsumi-soke has appointed a four-man staff consisting of Noguchi-sensei, Seno-sensei, Nagase-sensei, and Mark Lithgow-sensei.

There are also the very senior Japanese practitioners who serve as the *Juyushi* (knights of wisdom, or flexible friends and teachers of good intent) who have been *deshi* (disciples) to Hatsumi-soke's abuse more than thirty years. Eight men hold this rank of honor—all Japanese—and along with The Boss, they have the responsibility of creating the next grandmaster. They usually stay in Japan. The Juyushi Guardians comprise Hatsumi-soke's preferred uke, who are familiar to most non-Japanese practitioners, as we have all trained with Noguchi Yukio-shihan, Oguri Koichi-shihan, Seno Hideo-shihan, and Tanaka Hiroshi-shihan in seminars over the years. In ancient times these people would be considered the elders or clan heads. After eighth dan, ranking is usually decided by a committee of the tenth dan or at least three of the Juyushi.

10. Communication with the Hombu is best done in Japanese. (Noda City is not Tokyo.) Please check the time difference before calling. (If your skills do not include Japanese, contact Ben Jones in England [tel. 448-434-7701] who can translate five different languages professionally, Regina Brice is also a professional translator, lawyer, and shidoshi [tel. 216-774-4807], or one of the other shidoshi who is fluent.) Members of the shidoshi-Kai have Soke's telephone and fax numbers.

Understanding The Difference between Budo and Bugei

Where the Japanese look to the ancestors for wisdom by reading the *gunki-mono* (war tales of the samurai), Westerners of religious persuasion look to the Bible (tales concerning ancient Judaism and Christianity). The stories of Saul, David, and Solomon from the Old Testament contain elements worthy of enduring legend and illustrate the difference between *Bugei* (martial studies appropriate for warfare) and *Budo* (martial arts appropriate for self-development). After David slew Goliath with a surprise distance-weapon tactic, he was groomed by Saul to become a king. Saul eventually fell on his own sword (like a Roman officer or samurai) to avoid being captured. Before his death Saul grew jealous of David and used his innocence and drive to strengthen his kingdom. He told David to marry his daughter Melah, as descent is matriarchal in Judaism. His bride price was one hundred foreskins of Saul's enemies. This task took a while. The foreskins were not taken as a sign of religious conversion, but a simple proof of martial prowess less showy than the ear collecting of the Turks (and some perverts in American combat units) or the head collecting of the Mongols, Jivaro, and Samurai. They are also a lot easier to carry about once dried. David collected his bride price happily—in fact, doubled it to show his loyalty as he proceeded to consolidate Saul's holdings. It's in the Book of Samuel, King James version.

The skills of conquest (Bugei) are not the same as development (Budo). Where Saul and David were warrior/nomad kings wresting a homeland (Bugei) in an unforgiving environment held by the Philistines, David's son Solomon had the advantages of being raised in relative security and peace bought by the power of his ancestors. Solomon was a great poet, judge, and builder of networks (Budo). He is the only man in the Bible with the appellation "wise." The mind of the subtle strategist (an expert in all aspects of suasion) is deadly in the conduct of war, creative when turned toward art, just when bent to the application of law, steadfast in the preservation of family and friends, and clever in the accumulation of power and wealth. In modern terms this is called "transfer of training."

The shadow side of Budo is Bugei and having to use it. Given the historical record, there is no reason to expect that the dark life-preserving strategies of Bugei will ever lie fallow long enough to be totally supplanted by the life-enhancing practices of Budo, which lead to the light. The *kanji* (Japanese graphic writing) that represent *Budo* can mean "stopping the spear." This indicates the peaceful nature of the warrior practitioners. *Bugei* is usually translated as the "art of combat" or "using the spear," *Bujutsu* refers to the basic warrior skills that can be taught, and *Bujin* at its simplest means warrior, but can also mean divine or immortal. *Bushi* means warrior or knight. As

Musashi posits in *The Book of Five Rings,* both the samurai and the ninja are expected to develop *Bunbu,* a knowledge of all the arts, as they are an essential element in humanizing the individual. Musashi, though sainted for his duel-winning swordsmanship and written works on strategy, was a talented sculptor, wrote poetry, and practiced *sumi-en* brush painting. Most samurai studied penmanship, dance, and flower arranging and were expected to compose a death haiku (short three- or five-line poem capturing a feeling) if requested to die. The semantic loading of Japanese terminology clearly indicates the spiritual nature and status of traditional strategists in their social hierarchy. What I have found fascinating about Budo Taijutsu is that the Bugei applications of the art have not been lost or modified as is often reported concerning other forms of Japanese Budo (Donn Draeger and Robert Smith. *Asian Fighting Arts,* Berkley Books, 1969).

The collection of written concepts of *Bushido* (the way of knights) best known in the USA is the *Hagakure,* from the pen of Yamamoto Tsunetomo, a scribe who served the House of Nabashima in the later seventeenth century. Tsunetomo lived in a time of peace, was not a martial artist, and had never experienced battle. At the time of its publication the *Hagakure* was considered "overly harsh" and "empty theory, unaccompanied by practice." This might serve as a warning to those who use it as their guide for the samurai path. It does contain some very useful commentary, and is well worth reading, but falls into the category of what modern scientists call "armchair research" or "cocktail anthropology," and in a court of law would be considered "hearsay." *The Code of the Samurai* by Daidoji Yuzan (see bibliography, A.L. Sadler under "Strategy and Hieho") is considered a far better text concerning the manners and morals of Japanese knighthood, as Yuzan actually lived what he wrote about in the sixteenth century surviving the rule of six different shogun.

Conventional wisdom seldom reflects the reality of the long years of work that go into becoming a true professional. The willingness to endure hardship for the achievement of some greater good is a character trait valued both East and West. The Japanese ninja with their motto of "keep going" tend not to pay too much attention to someone who is learning their art until he or she has kept showing up for about five years. They like to get to know you. They want to see how you react to hardship as well as over-promotion. (Of course those who have been over-promoted only recognize the incompetence of the other guy.) After ten years or so they begin to share the secrets of the art that have been shared with the shihan. Ninpo has gone through a long process of shaking out the people who really should be doing some other martial art.

A modern ninja who is proud of his relation to the established military, his religion, his mercenary butchering ability, or even his belt rank is far from assuming his proclaimed art's mantle of benevolent protective authority, which extends from the cosmic emptiness of peaceful infinity resting within the self. The person who has achieved emptiness expresses this freedom in everyday life, and the actions are identifiable in spirit and character. Often their words and actions resonate their deepest experience. Open acceptance of intention can only be achieved through endurance. The kanji for Ninpo can be interpreted as endurance, or more lightly as "keep playing." *Bujinkan* can be translated as "the school of the divine warriors" as well as "war spirit building." *Shidoshi* can be translated as "knight of the four ways" or "teacher of the ways of life and death." *Kyoshi* can mean "death knight" and "four centers" and Tokyo could be translated in very old kanji as China center, or capital, or noble straight sword. Learning Japanese well requires a subtle mind with a sense of history.

Hatsumi-sensei has now begun the cycle of training drawn from peaceful times for building character and inner strength, and for preserving weapon mastery associated with the Japanese concepts of Budo. The doors of Bujinkan will narrow as the route and climb to the shidoshi-Kai become harder and higher. For example, The Boss expects his instructors to gain a formal education to support their physical skills. He asked the higher-level instructors to put more emphasis on their medical training in 1988 when I was in Japan for the celebration of his sixtieth birthday and thirtieth year of his sokeship.

The Boss says "the subtleties of human behavior are difficult to understand." The modern practitioner of this ancient and tricky art may have great physical skills but is expected to learn the *omote* from his teachers, and the *ura* from his own study and experience. When Hatsumi shares the Bujin with the initiate during the sword test for godan, their instruction in the ways of the ura escalates into the ways of shamanism and sorcery if they can handle it. This little bit of rank can create questions in the minds of those who know them well, if the newly promoted think they no longer have to keep playing. Even the experience of awakening the kundalini is only a benchmark on the ninja path of self-protection.

The bad ninja eventually find that gentility and purity of intention can indeed be a way to salvation, or they go screaming off on their own into St. John of the Cross's dark night of demonic paranoia. Paranoia is caused by the adrenal release that is a side effect of increasing the body's energy through meditation or transfer from someone who is more advanced (shaktipat). If one cannot let go of one's fear, or learn to think objectively, one cannot solve the *koan* (riddle/problem). Hatsumi-san recommends such people seek solace in the shelter of a good religion based in love. Good intention is only recognized when supported by good behavior. Good behavior is that which selflessly furthers the development of all human beings, which is the core concept underlying most major religions. The ethical system of Budo requires sincere absorption of eight concepts.

(1) *Jin*—to develop a compassionate understanding of other people or *hodoku.* (2) *Gi*—to observe ethical behavior. (3) *Chu*—to show loyalty to one's teacher or superior. (4) *Ko*—to respect and care for one's parents. (5) *Rei*—to treat others with respect. (6) *Chi*—to enhance wisdom by broadening one's knowledge. (7) *Shin*—to be truthful at all times. (8) *Tei*—to care for the aged and those of humble station. It is an eight-fold test most people fail when observed by the multi-faceted, eidetic, spider eyes of the demon gods.

Commentary

The most popular Asian concept of the divine begins with the One. The great soul split in two: one part remained in wholeness while the other incarnated to experience existence. The unfolding of the One took the universal form of paired opposites: light/darkness, male/female, good/evil, omote/ura, spirit/matter, Psyche and Eros, etc. Eventually this manifestation resulted in the "ten thousand things." The gods exist and you must get through them to reach the One. To traverse this holy terrain requires the marriage of ego and soul. Mikkyo Buddhism teaches that this can be accomplished in this lifetime through the embracing of opposites. *Mikkyo* (hidden meanings or secret teachings) is the most magical and tantric of many Japanese sects of Buddhism. Mikkyo, like *Zen* (the best known sect in the USA), is historically associated with the ninja, as is ancient *Shinto* (the indigenous Japanese religion that contains geomancy and spirit worship) and *Shugendo,* the art of the warrior mountain monks. The mental part of Budo Taijutsu, which subsumes Bujinkan Ninpo, appears as a form of secular Shinto similar to esoteric Taoism as one gets deeply into subtle influence. A formal relationship with any of these established religions is *not* recommended by Hatsumi-soke for his *deshi* (disciples).

Hatsumi-san recently chastised the Mikkyo monks on Mt.

Hiei by saying he understood why Oda Nobunaga wanted to burn them out. I'll tell you why... When people become too goody-goody they begin to falsify their stories and behavior. Hypocrisy becomes easily institutionalized by the insecure, and the shadow begins to grow in those who are disenfranchised. The shadow of the rejected seeks revenge, as it is denied opportunity and endures a neglected environment to become stronger (only the fittest survive), as its struggle for recognition is real rather than part of a social and material illusion. When the rejected makes its move, the rejecter is often destroyed by the excessiveness of the shadow's demands. We say in the West, "Pride goeth before a fall." Children recognize that pride is the reaction pattern of the insecure wishing to create an impression of competence. Recognizing the shadow requires humility and a child-like viewpoint.

The ninja concepts concerning shadow *(kage)* warriorship are deeper than Jungian psychology and require a working relationship with both the archetypes of sky and land (*kami* and *oni*). Fujibayashi, writing about Iga Ryu ninja practice in his *Bansenshuka* (1696) referred to the work as "a hundred thousand rivers." The journey is primarily within, but the results are sometimes external. Accepting the rejected shadow can be a fierce struggle. Learning to use the god-given tools of the subconscious to ride the wave of living energy requires a fearless imagination controlled with impeccable intent. Surfing the wave has little to do with formal religion but does require, as Hatsumi-soke has posited, an understanding of "religious feeling." Its best to relax into it, but that does not make the journey any easier. However, you are less prone to paranoia, panic, or heart attacks.

I suspect calling out the million names of God has as much effect as calling out one of the many Buddhas' names. Even those who seek the Pure Land (or the Happy Hunting Ground) must do it in faith. Faith requires intention or internalized spirit, not blind ignorant repetition of a word that represents something you do not understand. *Mea culpa.* Visiting a friend's house doesn't make you like the friend. Imitating the friend might convince others that you are similar, but you'd be hard-pressed to fool his wife. Going to church on Sunday hardly corresponds with healing the blind or teaching children to be loving. Evil is most associated with the crowded path that appears easy to the near-sighted. *Experto credite* (trust me).

The men and women I have come to respect and love as exemplars of humanity have invariably suffered to attain their higher knowledge. Jesus was crucified. Franklin was exploited by his older brothers. Lincoln was executed by a political assassin. Moses was raised as a priest/king/mage adopted into the royal family of Egypt and rejected this power to purge his people of their slave mentality in the burning forge of the Sinai for forty years. He died as they, properly prepared by his guidance, entered the Promised Land. Gautama Siddhartha walked away from great wealth so he could study for twenty years that which he feared. My sister, Janet, was given cerebral palsy by a clumsy doctor at birth. She went on to cheerfully and successfully coach women's basketball and World Championship cheerleading teams from her braces. She taught me much about observation, as she could never do what she was capable of teaching. She was driven from her teaching job in Alaska by Mormons on the school board who felt a crippled woman should not coach sport.

Hatsumi-soke told shihan Kevin Millis, "Dr. Morris is the fiercest human being I have ever met." I always thought that was a pun on my tantrism, not a comment on my behavior for my friend to correct. Tantra yoga (the fierce path) is usually thought of in the West as sexual practice. The essence of tantra is life energy or kundalini associated with the nervous system and environment. The goal of tantra, as with most true spiritual practices, is the achievement of unity of consciousness. However, tantric yoga is considered a rapid path to that goal, which has implicit dangers. I once read an essay by a war correspondent commenting on what he perceived as "the ferocity of medics" in Vietnam. He was surprised by how fiercely they reacted to the carnage and stupidity of war. Medics are selected for their intelligence. How would you react if you had their job in that situation? Rage is too small a word to describe the horror one feels when watching the destruction of countless lives to no real purpose beyond upholding the corrupt and defending the incompetent. I was very fortunate in my period of enlistment and saw very little combat outside of bars. Like Abraham Lincoln commenting on his service in the "Indian Campaigns" against Tecumseh, "I killed as many of the enemy as they killed of me."

Evil is only a problem to those who do not understand that to refrain from evil is a choice that must be experienced as a choice, or no learning has taken place at a meaningful level. As a human being's highest purpose seems to be learning to serve as a Good Shepherd, evil would be all the obstacles on that path. My perception of evil does not attach it as a prefix to *-lution*. I define it as the domination of others to prevent their natural ascent to a meaningful life and death. When we prevent others from learning enough to take their shot at immortality in either realm of being, we sin. The keys to the energy kingdom are loving kindness, meditation, visualization, and a strong heart and stomach. There is no mind/body/spirit separation. Nor can one, except through faulty logic, separate oneself from the cultural and ecological niche, which is the Earth in this universe. All is one. In 1917 Lord Bertrand Russell, the British philosopher and mathematician, commented, "The oneness of the world is an almost undiscussed postulate of most metaphysics... Yet I believe ... that the apparent oneness of the world is merely the oneness of what is seen by a single spectator or apprehended by a single mind" ("On Scientific Method in Philosophy," *Mysticism and Logic and Other Essays*, George Allen and Unwin,

London, 1963). Lord Berty was a brilliant man, but wrong on this one. He did the best that he could with the tools of his time.

Budo is sometimes described as a warrior's religion, but the reality is closer to a simple recognition of the power of natural selection raised beyond biology to a strategy for social survival. The principles of Budo are "survival mechanisms that sustain life, consciousness, and morality demonstrating the value of the sacred regardless of the econiche" (Daniel C. Dennet, *Darwin's Dangerous Idea: Evolution and the Meaning of Life*, New York: Simon & Schuster, 1995). Internalizing the concepts and practice of Budo may develop in one an appreciation of the religious.

Grandmaster
by Richard Moran, a student of Karim abu Shakra's

I used to feel too tall for my height,
Now I seem to fit.

I feel my hands with my feet,
The coming of the wind.
I see animals for their beauty,
And my feet with my hands,
And life—the world turns,
Bringing night to day, wind with rain, life with death.

Nature, for we are all animals, brings a greater power.

Suddenly, I understand the world,
Living our life on earth with love and kindness.

Two

Exercises for Greater Sensitivity

Walking in complete harmony is the fundamental physical practice of the school of the divine warriors. It requires balance. The techniques are easy to learn but may take years to master. The ancient Taoists proclaimed that moving meditation is a million times more effective than sitting meditation. The effectiveness is derived from the movement of the spine. The ninja combines knowledge of breathing techniques, sensing of subtle energy through observation, affirmations that increase acuity, and techniques for moving silently. Sensitivity, which is often thought of only as a characteristic of weepy, whining, sniveling, do-gooders who purport to feel everyone's pain and suffering, is necessary for distinguishing subtle differences in the human environment. You see and feel more when you walk with awareness. Slow movement while observing allows one to attract less attention, and to appear harmless or guiltless. Increasing one's ability to see approaching danger requires familiarity with one's natural environment and neighborhood, as well as the ability to see into darkness. Exercises for increasing visual ability can be as crucial to survival as a network of friends. Being able to face danger calmly is an advantage when the primate body is stressed to the point of panic, or the adrenals are asking you to crush the insulting presence. The ninja use affirmations to ingrain and sustain equanimity. People learn a skill better and more quickly when they are told not just how to do something, but why it is done a particular way to have the most benefit. Try the following exercises out and then adapt them to your situation.

Walking

The much-vaunted ninja stealth walk is an easily learned natural way of perambulating the body through rough terrain without sustaining injury. If practiced consistently for a short period of time, it becomes the way you walk. Some Americans refer jokingly to their Japanese counterparts as "Scufflers" because of the odd characteristics of the walk which increase its efficacy. As Musashi states quite clearly in *The Book of Five Rings,* you should "make your everyday walk your warrior's walk," which has meanings beyond shaping your aggressive attitude. The warrior's walk can only be mastered if you soften your neck, knees, and ankles by stretching, as well as free your shoulders. The ura of the technique is moving your consciousness down into your feet, increasing their sensitivity while rooting or lowering your burden.

The nerves in the feet are the longest and most sensitive in the human body. The brain devotes a considerable part of its capacity to handling messages from the feet. People who work with the body's bioelectrical system universally indicate that the feet can project energy as well as draw. We tend to enclose our feet in hard leather boxes with the thick hide of dead animals specially treated to protect us from the gentle ministrations of Mother Nature. We tend not to take very good care of our feet and consider them ugly. The cultural denigration of this part of the body desensitizes one's ability to feel with and use the feet effectively. Often *taiso jutsu* (shiatsu massage) is necessary to awaken the holographic mirror of the body that resides in the feet and hands. (A firewalk will wake them up, big time. How to do a firewalk is described in Chapter Nine.)

The ninja walk itself looks slightly bow-legged and penguin-footed—exactly how a baby walks. The *hakama* (skirt-like trou donned by kenjutsu and aikido players) is worn to conceal the footwork, not to show off a graceful twirl. The head is erect, the shoulders are back and down, the rib cage is tilted slightly up to free the spine for easy movement. The breath is soft and prolonged through abdominal control at the groin—Musashi's "wedging in." The coccyx is tucked under with the exhale pumping energy up the spine. The pelvis is held slightly forward of the ankles, perhaps an inch farther to the front than tai chi practitioners' balance point, which centers over the ankles. The pelvic girdle, like the skull, is often too rigidly fused and the bones must be loosened to act as effective chi pumps. Walking can speed that process. With practice the legs and hips reinforce the bone energy pump. Hatsumi-soke remarks on this in his densho, *Sanmyaku* Vol 1, No 3. The knees are turned slightly outward so the toes are covered but the big toe can be seen when you look down, allowing you to easily drop to the ground to either side at a slant. This makes dodging, rolling, leaping, or retaliation a simple matter of shifting your hip. As Musashi wrote, "Move the hips and the arms and legs will follow," which also refers to control of the emotions, opening the base chakras, and the freeing of the pelvic girdle.

If you've been around real ninja or Chinese masters you may have noticed they tend to like walking. Hatsumi-soke spends two hours every night walking in his neighborhood in Noda City, Japan. He particularly likes the hours after the bars close, as that is when a martial artist may get to practice protective skills while moving with the predators. I have no idea how many dojo owners follow this practice. Small-town Japan tends to be very quiet at night.

Walking while you meditate allows you to subtly maneuver the psoas muscle across the pelvis as well as rotate the spine and pelvis. While walking you practice using these structures as energy pumps, as you stretch your ligaments and work your fascia. The subtle side-to-side rocking of the knees and ankles while standing, stretching, or walking keeps the movement fluid, and immediate, and seems to greatly slow the aging process, which makes life more enjoyable. Often ninja practice different types of walking, and Kevin and I used to joke about belonging to the Japanese equivalent of Monty Python's Ministry of Silly Walks. I found I could spot many of the ninja heading for Tai Kai through observing their walk in the Houston and Tucson airports.

The stride is shortened approximately by half for Americans, creating much better balance. Many long striders look like the legendary golem, Frankenstein, as they totter and crash along at great speed. The shorter stride when walking with relaxed knees and ankles results in a flat, smooth movement beloved of drill instructors everywhere; when stretched out for running, one looks a bit like Groucho. Steven Seagal is the only movie martial artist who has spent the time to get most of the walk. He has yet to master the talk, or feelings. I have never seen Seagal perform a technique above what I consider eighth kyu, but what he does, he does well. If you don't have anyone to watch walking properly, take in a few of his flicks. His physical fundamentals are very good.

In the placement of the foot, the body's center is sent to the stationary foot, which grips the surface. The moving foot is without weight and feels the air for obstacles as it moves forward to seek a safe repose. As the strongest part of the foot, the heel makes weightless contact first, then the side of the foot comes down lightly, as there may be broken glass or caltrops for the unwary. (This lightness also applies when kneeling.) Once the edge of the foot is firmly placed, the toes are brought into contact, little to big, in a flattening movement. This is silent. The center is then shifted to the stepping knee as the hip moves forward, then to the down foot as the rear knee is brought forward and up by the shifting of the hip as in a kick. The knee and foot check the air and then drop to permit the footwork. The weight is all in the grounded foot, or all moving into the free foot as one breathes softly through the nose. The movement is completely integrated.

When you begin this practice, the walk is exaggerated. It takes concentration and focus to get the bones and muscles to return to the natural movement of the baby. However, just shortening your stride and turning your feet out as you walk, while placing the heels first, will do wonders for your energy and balance. You may then integrate your breath with the walk, and once you have mastered that, begin to play with energy as well. You may be pleasantly surprised at how sensitive your feet really are once you begin paying attention to them. The kinesiology massage with which many ninja begin their workout, before or after meditation, encourages the foot to regain its grace. If you don't like your feet you will never move with economy or grace. When your friends continue to be startled by your sudden presence, your stealth walk has become natural to you.

Melee applications call for sticking closer to your attacker, allowing you to meddle in his next move as well as easily retaliate in a harder-to-see-coming manner. Intelligence is based on the same principle. Distance and timing are very important. Working around your opponent with short balanced strides allows you to apply your techniques with weight and power.

It is always advisable to humbly place your *obi* (belt) or hips beneath your opponent's. Lowering techniques require a mobile center. Many techniques in tai chi, ninjutsu, and *kenjutsu* (sword skills) require walking through your opponent, but they are done most efficaciously from an angle or the side. Musashi refers to it as "treading him down" in the Fire chapter *(The Book of Five Rings)*. The really skilled use the opponent's rush and their own body dynamic to disappear and reappear at the back of their opponent. Wasted movement is death to a ninja or anyone else, even an economy. Think about it.

Speed and surprise defeat strength and power, just as distance and timing can wreak havoc with speed. Surprise is always useful, so it becomes important to appear to know nothing. It is sometimes wise to appear stupid, helpless, or old, as it makes the predator over-confident and easier to manipulate into the trap. Showing off with your skills is an invitation to an enemy to find your weakness. If your enemy has higher intelligence, rest assured that your weaknesses will be very visible. The Native Americans from my neck of the woods have a saying, "The flying hawk hides its talons." Hatsumi-soke recommends rising above kata so that one's survival skills become invisible and natural.

Staying active is important. What you don't use, you lose. Stretching is sometimes called the way of strength. If you're not stretching, you had better be walking, swimming, or bicycling. Take every opportunity to stretch and twist your spine and fingers. It may even reverse arthritis, as it did in me. Stretching most certainly helps prevent injury as you age. When I have slipped on ice or fallen through floors, the ability to turn a fall into a roll saved me from a lengthy recuperation and amazed the bystanders. "Did you see that guy go down and roll back to his feet? He didn't even drop his briefcase."

The Wind Walk, which is sometimes improperly shown in the movies, is an interesting variation used for slipping through narrow corridors, covering the distance of a broad jump in two quick steps to close suddenly with an opponent, or used in situations where the ninja does not wish to be tracked. It has the advantage of allowing the Wind Walker a 180-degree field of vision, and when done in a group with members facing out, a full 360-degree range. The ura is lifting your center upward to be lighter in weight, or at least have less attraction for the ground. The omote is a cross-step with the point of contact more often the toes than the heel. As the practitioner is leaping, running, or falling sideways, the weight is going to the crossed foot.

The arms are swung across the body with the steps to aid in balance. Because the feet point outward, a particular advantage of the walk is that a tracker will not be able to tell which way the ninja party is going, unless he or she is very skilled.

The ancient Mikkyo monastery that I stayed in on Mount Koyasan had hallways with floors purposely made to creak loudly. I think they are called mockingbird floors and were part of most Japanese castles' security system. They served as an early warning for the sentries. About three in the morning, I stole out of my room to see if I could Wind Walk down the hall without setting off the creaks. I was having a good time testing my silent entry skills when Kuboda, a Zen monk, came around the corner and spotted my stealthy exercise. He cracked up, and then joined me on the opposite wall. We whipped up and down the corridor a couple of times while restraining our laughter and then he went back to whatever monkish duties had him up and about at that hour. I went back to bed. No creaks, and Kuboda seemed to find my exercise quite amusing. He would laugh and tiptoe every time he saw me during the rest of my stay at the monastery. He was staying with the Mikkyos to give our group a lesson in the Rinzai techniques of Zen meditation.

Musashi's dislikes as listed in the Wind chapter include "hard hands and stiff wrists." He also comments on walking styles that use up too much energy to be useful in a prolonged fight. The warrior prizes supple feet as well as hands. A thinner sole is necessary to receive useful data when engaged in travel through enemy territory in those hours that guarantee safety, because few are willing to learn the skills of stealth, or stealing in, or even staying awake. Most American ninja love *tabi* (split-toed canvas boots) once they've worn them a while. They're like kung fu shoes with better traction and balance. You can't kick them off, yet you can still pick up dirt and sticks to throw with your toes. A human being's feet are prehensile. Some people can pick up and throw quite accurately with their toes,

41

as it can be quite an advantage to deliver a load of dirt to the opponent's eyes ahead of your incoming foot. This takes time and practice. Short-term thinking is dangerous to one's health as well as one's wallet. The same goes for memory, meditation, sensory enhancement, and physiological skill building.

Warrior Meditation

In religious meditation, it is often thought valuable to allow the crossed legs to simply fall asleep. In manners of balance and longevity you would probably rather increase the efficiency of your perineum as an energy pump by gently massaging it with your heel while in The Position (*fudosa* or the Sage Seat). This provides the double benefit of reducing your chances of cancer of the prostate while also—if you have mastered the Secret Smile meditation in *Path Notes of an American Ninja Master* deepening the potency of your grin. This works best while raising your hips on a *zafu* (special hard round pillow used for Zen meditation), resting both knees on the ground or a soft mat, and tucking one foot, usually the right, under your groin with the sole up and the heel resting against the area between the genitals and the rectum described by the materialistic and health-oriented Chinese as "the million-dollar point" and by most Americans as "the taint"! Its efficacy when pressed as a birth control method during the male orgasm is well documented, and its name reflects its value. A jab there can resurrect the unconscious, and in dim mak *(koshijutsu)* and in karate, a hard blow is considered a slow kill. The other foot is pulled into sole press against the shin of the tucked leg. The back is straight and balanced from the hips and shoulders, and the head is lifted from the ears while preserving the natural curve of the neck. Subtly shift your knees or press with your foot to increase your control of the movement of the heel. Learn to coordinate the resulting energy bursts with your breath and move it back to and up your spine. Watch with your eyes on the back of your eyelids what the phosphenes (or light) begin to do. The Seat of the Sages is not the full lotus, which is a show-off position for those who have missed the need for running energy and have to deaden their legs. Stretching and rubbing the meridians of the hands and feet before as well as after meditation can increase your pleasure in this exercise for the brain.

This Sage Seat can also be a means of achieving the legendary reversed orgasm, which goes on for as long as the practitioner can stand it. Usually you get to laughing so hard you have to give it up. Once you have control of the perineum and want to send a squirt of love juice to the poor benighted gin-soaked and dehydrated kidneys, the medical applications for self-healing become apparent. We learn better when we experience pleasure. The medical sex manuals of the ancient Taoists are quite complete and well translated and widely dispersed, as even the politically correct Confucians who replaced the Taoists with a more rule-bound social system weren't going to give that up.

This is approximately the same position that in Tibetan tantric lore shows hundreds of Buddhas locked in *yab yum* (Tibetan tantric manifestation of yin and yang, or androgyny of the spirit) with their fierce spiritual consorts. It's a great way to reduce anger and fear. It appears to be for adventurers. Some faint from ecstasy, but being locked into a searcher of the opposite sex will prevent you taking any serious damage if you have fused your micro-cosmic orbits. If you keep the temperature down through meditation while practicing you should not have to contend with scorched organs. Drink a lot of water. Be happy. Visit a massage therapist. Avoid chi sickness through acupuncture, shiatsu, and other methods of freeing up blocks in the meridians. Keep going.

Shikantaza (the highest form of *zazen*, or sitting meditation) requires that the sitter empty the mind of all supportive beginning techniques, like counting breath, and face into the shadow brightly alert with no expectations, and with attention that is free of thoughts, directed to no object, and attached to no particular object. It is considered the mind of someone properly approaching death. Sustaining this meditative attitude in all activities of one's life is a result of, and/or contributes to *satori* (enlightenment). Learning to breath seamlessly and deeply from the *dan tien* (point below the navel) is essential to meditation. Learning to exhale as you strike and inhale as you pull is a lesser skill for fighting. The skilled ninja teacher of taijutsu claims, "No breath, no intent. Only taijutsu." The vampire modifies this dictum to fit the situation.

Chogyam Trungpa, a rather famous modern and much quoted teacher of Tibetan Buddhist Dharma, states, "The practice of meditation is **the** and **only** way. Without that, there is no way out and no way in." Meditation training in Ninpo focuses on four levels of awareness: first, getting in touch with the body; second, learning to control emotions; third, shaping of intention; and fourth, exploring realities of being.

Intentional Meditation
or Total Affirmations or Kuji

Once you have mastered emptying your mind in meditation, you might like to incorporate the following attitudes in entering your meditation cave (Chapter Five in *Path Notes*), or just make them part of your everyday approach to life. These have been researched by the Hoshinroshiryu (my school, recognized by the World Head of Family Sokeship Council) and are most often practiced as part of the belt system associated with the exercise of the corresponding chakra. The assumption of attitudes with fighting postures (kamae) is one of the more challenging and interesting aspects of traditional Ninpo training. The ancient ninja warriors discovered certain physical techniques worked better when you assumed a particular attitude. The attitudes that worked best were related to levels of enlightenment associated in Chinese medicine and Hindu tantric practice with the opening of the four main body chakras leading to the eventual opening of the intuitive chakras of the brain. In Mikkyo Buddhism the exercises are referred to as the *Go Dai* (five attitudes or principles).

Hatsumi-soke mentioned to me in 1995 that he was making a new set of training videos for shodan and above that would include the appropriate attitudes to be assumed with each skill. These will be available from the Bujinkan Hombu soon. I requested that he do the new tapes with an English translator, but The Boss often insists that he can only express some ideas in Japanese. Below is my interpretation of the first two traditional applications of the Go Dai for warriors, and one for twentieth- century business people. You may think of these as active affirmations to assume as attitudes as you go about your daily activities.

The first is a stabilizing activity similar to the Earth practices in higher-level Ninpo. It is a Westernized description of the feelings that develop as the base chakra, or biological energy source resulting from regenerating hormonal influences, is activated. In ninjutsu this attitude is assumed when attacked by someone you do not perceive to be particularly dangerous. If you are able to internalize the attitude, the phosphenes behind your eyes will become red, and if the practitioner has been meditating properly, his or her aura will also turn bright candy-apple red. The colors of the aura in most people reflect mood changes, not permanent attitudes. You might be surprised by how much your physical strength and sense of well-being increase as you assume an affirmative attitude. This is an important psychological distinction that few master. In Ninpo the use of affirmations as a form of self-hypnosis prepares the individual for dealing with various stress-laden situations with aplomb. The Ninpo affirmations are practiced with "triggering" actions known as *mudra* (Sanskrit) or *kuji* (Japanese) to speed their assumption subconsciously. One can bang the teeth together twice, rock down hard on the heels, or touch the little finger and the thumb together to connect the affected meridian to the brain. The affirmation and triggering device are first developed as part of one's meditation, adding it to the Secret Smile.

Affirmations are worthless if you do not internalize the exact meaning of the words through behavior. Martial applications that are enhanced include holding your ground, shrugging off or deflecting your opponents' attacks, blows, throws, and treading them down.

An Earthy Attitude

1. The Stabilizing Posture (Earth kamae) is calm and relaxed with the shoulders down, the back straight, the head back and erect, and the chin pulled slightly in. The knees are turned slightly out, as are the toes. The pelvis rocks imperceptibly with your breath and shifts with your stride so your spine is always supported and balanced. The chakra being opened is called in Sanskrit the *muladhara* (the basal center) and is located at the sex center below the genitals. Its color is red. When you move, you move your whole body with the action coming from the hips. When you walk, you place your heel on the ground first and then shift your weight forward along the side of the foot. Your shoulders and arms swing in a rolling motion as you walk and rotate your spine. Your knees and ankles should be relaxed, soft, and flexible. Practice making this your everyday walk—it will do more than just benefit your fighting style. You will become centered, smooth, and flowing.

The positive side of the thinking/feeling attitude of Stability is the relaxed, happy acceptance of the universe or situation as it is. There is no fear, as you are confident in your strength and experience. You are steady, loving, and confident. You are uninhibited, practical, and enjoy a good laugh. You smile at others and make eye contact. You reward service and kindness with praise and reciprocity. You are careful with the truth of your words. You are honest and reliable. If there were still kings and queens worthy of the name you would be their peer. You enjoy the way your body feels and study how it reacts to the world and people around you. You do not use your strength to intimidate others, but to help those who are weaker to find their own source of strength. You use your anger to right wrongs and punish those who attack you, but do not initiate, only retaliate in an appropriate manner. You are a teacher of the way as well as a warrior. The negative side, which you work on eradicating through silencing your social mind, is conventionality, rule-boundedness, anger, and unbridled sexuality.

The Second Step in Getting Wet

2. The key to Adapting (Water kamae) is learning to use the power of emotional reaction in any situation. The chakra being opened is the point above your pelvis, two finger-widths below the navel, referred to as the *hara* by the Japanese, *svadhishthana* in Sanskrit, or *dan tien* (seat of the soul) in Chinese. We usually refer to this power as having guts, or doing something even when you're afraid. The endocrine tie-ins include the adrenal glands, so this exercise teaches your body how to channel the energy of reactive terror into power. The emotional reaction colors the phosphenes bright orange when the set of the mind is positive. The trigger might be touching the ring finger to the thumb, combined with a quick and deep intake of breath. These techniques work particularly well for correcting and restoring courage in the abused as well as protecting the meek.

The posture is one of moving away but maintaining the ability to retaliate from a safer position. The posture of *Ichimonji no kamae* of Togakure Ryu Ninpo Taijutsu—the result of 800 years-plus of empirical combat research—best represents the physical manifestation of this attitude. The legs are spread wide for balance, one back in a lazy L rather than a T as in cat stance. The hips are lowered and the knees are relaxed. One arm loosely covers the center line of the upper body—throat and solar plexus. The other is extended loosely to strike and ward off grabbing attacks. The L back angling step of the legs away from the attacker allows the individual using this posture to be completely safe from attack even though he or she appears vulnerable. The back is straight and the angling foot points away from the opponent, so you can bail out. The movements of the Water or adaptive attitude are flowing, using the natural body movement of the attacker to direct you out of his or her way. They are like a wave smoothing down a rock by flowing out and crashing back. You will learn to move circularly like water sucking someone down into a whirlpool, or like a stream flowing round your opponent and filling every opening with your presence to unbalance and wear him down. You can attack a number of points at the same time with your body, while avoiding your opponent's strikes with clever angling footwork. Study on this.

The thinking/feeling attitude of Adapting/Water, or the positive side of fear, is enjoying the challenge, using every trick you've studied to defeat the attacker. The water person is a good listener and enjoys clever conversation and artistic achievement. You are responsive to others and focused on "getting the job done." You like to try new things and tend to be sensual and seductive, as well as strong. You're optimistic. Ambitious for yourself and others, you're a good friend and a feared enemy. The negative side is paranoia, being hung up on competition and needs for approval, which can be eradicated by seeking mushin. The negative side of this attitude can be considered a pandemic perversion in America and keeps most psychotherapists working. Characteristics of people who adapt negatively include manifesting a brownish aura, thinking primarily in terms of winning and losing, having little or no control over emotional responses, manipulating others, and lying and cheating with ease.

Applying the Principle Outside the Dojo

3. The thinking style or attitude of the successful business person interested in long-term growth and accomplishment is similar to the warrior or inner adventurer, but turns the focus more outward. Business, Heiho, and Budo have been intertwined in Japanese strategy for centuries. Working on improving one's self while improving one's skills is the spiritual basis of success that can transfer to any activity. The following affirmation is basic to business and requires an upright posture.

"Like the warrior who understands the self and the opponent, you are confident that you will achieve success in your field of endeavor. You have learned the skills necessary for competence and are willing to take the time and make the sacrifices necessary to reach your goals. The successful business person is prepared and organized for effectiveness, and works confidently to become more efficient. You are disciplined and tenacious in your resourceful research into the needs of your customer and organization. You are polite, humble, and kind. You work well with others and never lose your sense of humor. You carefully establish your reputation for integrity and solid values. When representing others, you work to achieve functional elegance in appearance. You remain intensely focused on being not just responsive, but empathically anticipative, increasing the value of your expertise. You are a careful listener and like to help solve problems." The negative side is that few people have the discipline to learn to be this way.

Seeing

To increase the depth and width of your visual field of perception, stand with a friend eye-to-eye about ten feet apart. As you stare into his or her eyes, have another friend approach from the rear and sides to test your peripheral vision. As the person moves up and down at your sides, check him or her out for weapons, without looking away from the person in front of you. Have your training partners start slow and then speed up the exercise. This will increase your ability to get useful information from the sides. When you are comfortable with this skill, try it again with your eyes closed and pay attention to what happens to the phosphenes. Really lazy ninja practice extending their peripheral vision by watching television from the corners of their eyes, or using the reflections in mirrors and windows to check toward the rear. You may also want to engage the hearing and listening by focusing your attention.

When you've all had a turn or three at each task, try silently walking up to one another focusing on the face, but seeing the whole body from the top of the head to the feet. Move closer together until you can still see all of the other person from a distance of a foot to six inches. If he or she starts to move a foot or hand, step on it or tap it without removing your gaze from his or her face. Once you are able to do that, have them raise their hands above their heads, or to the side. When Musashi ranks perception over seeing, he is discussing, among other things, a higher and wider view. Some Native Americans used a similar exercise called "soft eyes" in the training of their medicine men. If you can see your opponent's hands and feet while looking into their eyes in melee or negotiation, it gives you a considerable advantage. Looking at someone in this manner allows you to pick up subtle nuances that most others miss, as they are not free to explore their material world or observe things both horizontal and vertical in a strategic perspective. This exercise is particularly interesting at night, when the spirit is more visible.

Soft eye practice is particularly valuable when watching your sensei demonstrate techniques, as you have a better chance of picking up the subtle nuances such as multiple points of attack and energy use. Too often students only watch what the hands or feet are doing. Taijutsu involves the whole body.

Commentary

If you work only on these sensitivity exercises while you practice some other art, you will soon surpass your compadres if you pay attention. Slow down to learn, then speed it up. If your fundamentals are sound, your advanced techniques will amaze you.

The stealth walk will even protect you when walking through fire. That is not enemy fire. The Simba Lion Men found at the battle of Stanleyville in the former Belgian Congo that their witch doctor's blessing was rebuked by .30 caliber. Many Chinese masters of kung fu quit teaching fighting applications when handguns became easy to acquire. Chi kung is not effective against hot lead, but stealth techniques might get you into or out of range. Research this carefully.

These exercises for greater sensitivity are fundamental to using chi in martial arts. Many claim to develop chi in their ryu names, but the secrets have been lost while the kata were preserved, or the past teacher cheated his or her student and the new teacher is ignorant. Usually these skills are not taught until the student has spent four or five years with the teacher. It is probably why many schools only offer punching, blocking, and kicking without any modification of the shown kata. Practice that emphasizes strength and rigidity very seldom results in flow. Many American instructors of the martial arts were never exposed to these techniques, as they weren't in Japan, China, or Korea beyond their tour of military duty. Often the ura is not taught until the student has reached *sandan* (third-degree black belt) in traditional Japanese systems. Most American *shodan* (first-degree black belt) rush into teaching and competition with little knowledge of the subtler aspects of the martial arts. I have seen young shodan claiming to teach tae kwon do, aikido, kendo, jujutsu, ninjutsu, and wing chun from a master's perspective. Fat chance. Most traditional Japanese schools require as many years in grade as the dan belt level before promoting. Bujinkan promotes by skill level, service to the ryu, and spiritual accomplishment, as well as Hatsumi-soke's whims, and in order to see how people react. Most of the higher-level practitioners spent many years in other systems, which The Boss sometimes takes into consideration.

If you are interested in surviving the development of chi, or a strong spirit, using researched descriptions for culturally supported success provides a winning recipe when you are baking your own cake. Use affirmations when you meditate. Attempt to visualize the behavior. As your vision is absorbed into your behavior, the strength of the shadow needs can be harnessed to productive rather than destructive results. The ninja use of actual desired attitudes and behaviors rather than a symbolic mantra as their focus in meditation is a major contributing factor to their reputation as the ultimate warriors. They use affirmations and body movement to open each of the chakras, eventually resulting in the kundalini. As each chakra is opened, it links up with the next chakra until the cosmic orbit is complete. I will discuss the other three chakra openings in Chapter Nine. This affirming practice also accounts for the ninja ability to move through the dual mandalas, or to enter the spirit world. They keep playing. Ninja focus on the process of becoming rather than the outcome, as they are more concerned with quality than immediate desire, the process or path is the goal, and the end is but a beginning. These are the primary themes of Dr. Masaaki Hatsumi's teaching and natural behavior as I have absorbed and understand them.

Lessons of the Heart
by Glenn J. Morris

Love is learned, it cannot be taught

You can be loving, and lovely is in the eye as seen by the
    lover
You can be a lover to those who love you
Without loving them, but it is hard
It requires discipline; its a job; it gets old
It deadens the soul and the soul is the heart
And the heart hardens and forgets

You can love those who don't love you
But the service is empty
The devotion is wasted
And if the loved one is callous or cruel
It wounds the soul and the soul is the heart
And the heart hardens and forgets

You can love with a small "l" as small "l" love is better than
    no love
But it requires being false to your self
Which isn't all bad
You learn to live with other people
But the soul doesn't grow
And the soul is the heart
And the heart withers and forgets

You can live with a handicapped heart mistaking dependence
    for devotion, approval for love
You can try to force yourself to forget what it is to be
    complete
Put your passion into your work
Or material status/wealth/muscles/whatever

So the soul doesn't forget passion
And the soul is the heart
And the heart hungers and almost forgets

You can find with electric recognition the love of your soul
Soul mate (What a shock to find the concept is real!)
Who feels you at a distance
Whose touch electrifies your blood
Whose eyes hold you locked
Whose voice delights your ears
Whose laughter awakens your heart
Awakens the heart
And the soul is the heart
And the heart softens
And will not

WILL NOT FORGET

Three

Balance Points

A real martial artist devotes a great deal of study to the concept of balance. Homeostasis, harmony, *wa,* and *te* are all metaphors for stress destruction, and a first step in "the thousand-mile pathway" that brings one to *satori, kensho,* or enlightenment. One of the fundamental features of all esoteric systems is the study of structure to find those places where a figure may be strengthened or weakened with the least possible effort. "Pride goeth before a fall." Subtle influence can be magnified by a push at the right moment. Understanding balance is a requisite for creating a pleasant home, a work of lasting art, or surviving a struggle. A certain confidence is developed when you begin to realize that a light shove in the right direction at the right time can fell the largest opponent. "Push Hands" of tai chi conceals the fundamentals of devastating attacks in taijutsu to both the bone and tissue structure as well as the body's electrical system. The rooting and one-pointedness must become instantaneous with the natural movement of chi, with no interference from the critical mind.

Where the yogi seeks balance in the most incredible positions, the trickster ninja enjoys the grappling art of disrupting balance in the aggressively egocentric. The possibility of *wa* (being in harmony) increases when one balances intellectual power (cultural learning) with intuitional perception (animal feelings). Our culture tends to treat perception and intuition as genetic luck in the male and a frivolous gift in the female. In Ninpo intuitive perception is a developed skill augmented by meditation and training experiences. Balancing one's nature by being in tune with the econiche (the immediate neighborhood eventually encompasses the universe) opens the individual to understanding subtle influence by continuously improving one's ability to process information in non-ordinary ways. In this chapter you'll find concepts concerning balance and exercises to try out with your friends and acquaintances.

Unbalancing the Opponent

The balance points of hoshinjutsu, wei shen kung fu, ninjutsu, karate-jujutsu, and karate are fundamentally the same. They are just attacked in different manners. Great minds think alike regardless of culture, particularly in regard to a human body. In *hoshin* (true spirit, weapon heart, or demon master at the most primitive), the enraged primate is viewed as standing stiffly erect, usually as a reaction to the very painful technique you just applied to his or her fingers or some other part of the body. If the head is pushed or pulled past the hips or the hips past the heels, the body begins to fall. When the "fellee," out of fear reaction stiffens to prevent the fall, rather than continues the offensive attack, he or she is easiest to slam to the ground, which teaches humility to the arrogant. Keeping an opponent off balance, with a couple of minutes of pain while you reason with them, can be a very effective teaching tool.

Most people in pain tend not to think too clearly and respond slowly. When you are bending and folding another human being in unusual directions, the ligaments scream in shock. You can feel their vibration in the fascia. The body reacts with fear when bones begin to grate out of their joints or normal housing. Irregular beating is an ordinary reaction to shocks to the heart. The body has little love for pain that damages, and it is rude to damage your training partner beyond stretching or shallow bruises in an art where the strikes are often dim mak points. It requires great skill to practice the Shaolin maxim of "Avoid, rather than harm; harm, rather than injure; injure, rather than kill; kill, rather than be killed." All those choices are available to the well-balanced practitioner of Ninpo in practically every one of the *kihon* (standardized responses for training fight scenarios) following the flow of an attack.

Balance can also be disrupted if the shoulders are pushed or pulled past the hip without the feet moving. There are many ways to keep the feet from moving, such as standing on them. When the hips are outside the knees in any direction, the opponent is easy to dump. Moving the center across the ankle of a stabilized foot invariably results in a fall. Following the classic set-up of the sucker punch—"Look over there!"—the body will follow where the head leads. By making the opponent look up and to the rear (seeing the past as good) you negate his future. There are many ways to bring these principles to bear on those in need of instruction. Ninjutsu, jutaijutsu, or Budo Taijutsu for the very learned polite precisely reduces some complex diagrams to simple principles that add more direction to the above generalizations.

The ninja make the angles more explicit than the Chinese did creating an even safer attack by angling into position as a natural consequence of moving away from the strike into *Ichimonji* (first response that makes one safe). I had never seen the movement used defensively until my first Stephen Hayes seminar. It opens up marvelous possibilities to a free thinker. What a great position to be in—just lying back and picking out your target. Safe as houses! If you were to draw a line between your opponent's heels and cross it with a line from your shoulder, you would be looking at a T. This gives you a shot, with all your power, going into the opponent's greatest weakness. If you understand pyramidal balance points, it is a target that is hard to let pass; and you have probably crippled his outflung arm if you understand acupuncture meridians. The electric fields flow down, and up the center line of the body, and they can be easily disrupted by the sensitive.

Master Sherm Harrill's throwing art of jutedo, derived from the basic kata of isshinryu karate through *bunkei* (artistic searching for combat methods), requires not only understanding the balance points, but hitting them in precisely timed sequences that send the opponent sailing in seizure if your chi kung is good. I particularly like his technique of lifting the rib cage with one blow while slamming down on the shoulder or clavicle (depending on mood and opportunity) to send the opponent smashing to the ground. This move takes advantage of two balance points. The head is moved backward by the painful lifting of the ribs, which also shifts the hips past the knees in a forward direction. The downward-angled blow, if done in a small circle strike, speeds the opponent's fall.

Striking and gripping pressure (or release points) as you disrupt your opponent's balance from as many points of contact as possible increases their confusion. I like to maintain at least three to five points of contact when grappling. Grandmaster Jim Hopkins of the Dragon Wind system of offensive gung fu actually maintains five to seven points in close combat. Like me, he spent a lot of time with good catch-as-catch-can wrestlers and football players—sports that emphasize strength, speed and balance. If you can keep your opponent off balance physically, it rattles his confidence. While he focuses on Khe Sahn, you carry out a Tet Offensive. Vietnamese kung fu distinctly models Sun Tzu, with the perceptive multi-faceted eye of an intelligent enemy.

If you don't have a ninja master to share with you all the exciting nuances of surviving rough-and-tumble close combat, "Judo Gene" LeBell's book *Grappling Master* (Pro-Action

Publishing, 1992) may give you some useful unarmed techniques for control and capture. Then there's *Judo in Action* (Japan Publications Trading Company, 1967), written in English by Kazuzo Kudo, Kodokan ninth dan which really gets into the angles, but it was published years ago and is now a collector's item. I remember reading it in the early seventies and being very impressed. I no longer own it, but I remember the chapters on strangles were awesome, and the pictures left little to the imagination.

The falling away techniques of taijutsu also rely on balance points to speed or soften a fall. The use of triangles in ninjutsu is similar to the use in wu shu and judo, but the footwork is wider than in aikido. Dim mak or koshijutsu skills are greatly enhanced by a knowledge of balancing. The skilled practitioner can heal as well as harm, according to how he uses chi in grappling and striking. The truly skilled can be a mirror for their training partners, and the lessons are not always pleasant.

Having unshakable balance and harmony in one's life requires right action as part of being natural. Right action that is learned but not internalized requires thought and is slower. This is a universal principle which is poorly imitated by conscientious repetition of kata. Ninpo is taught through the interpretation of feelings, rather than exact positioning as in most martial arts. Chozan Chissai (writing circa 1716–1735), a famous samurai strategist associated with Taoism, Bugei, and bujutsu, discusses this in *Tengu Geijutsuron (Discourse on the Art of the Mountain Demons)*. Trevor Leggett in *Zen and the Ways* (Tuttle, 1987) intersperses Chissai's commentary with pictures of exercises drawn from Taoist Esoteric Yoga that improve the body's ability to project chi. Reinhard Kammer published a complete translation of Chissai's work with Arkana paperbacks in 1986, entitled *The Way of the Sword*. Chissai's preservation of the cheerful commentary concerning swordsmanship as presented by the visionary mountain demon birds (*tengu*) of ancient Japan is remarkably similar to modern practice in Bujinkan where the emphasis is on natural action and reaction rather than stylized postures of attack and defense. Spontaneous movement flowing from fear or joy has great power, and it is only predictable in the stupid or overly assertive. An aging expert usually has little trouble defeating the enthusiastic youthful amateur if his basics disrupt balance and are powerful, subtle, and intelligent. The fact that many good people will not help or rescue a victim out of fear for their own safety should keep you working to improve your skills.

Attention

Chi kung meditation as an adjunct to martial arts or the practice of strategy requires regular practice of particular movements with the realization that everything changes and improvement must be ongoing. When the body is stretched to its limits through breathing techniques, natural resources tend to appear and if recognized can become part of the practitioner's normal repertoire. Resuscitation from death, starvation, dehydration, suffering, and torture are all associated with visions of God and are often part of the training for those seeking religious experience. The techniques of the accidentally transcendent beginner are extended and refined by practice into the spontaneous grace of the seasoned veteran. You will have to research this deeply.

As the neophyte opens his or her perceptions through relaxed concentration, he or she becomes more able to respond to the realities of the environment. This state of clarity is achieved most easily through immersion in the present moment without desire for outcome. If we have no preconceptions, we are better able to respond with appropriate speed and accuracy to the challenges that others present, if our basic skills (kihon) are natural. This awareness is often difficult to remember. Although it was what carried us through the confusion of childhood, it generally becomes hidden under layers of socially learned self-images and concepts that inhibit natural and free behavior.

The ability to fantasize action can be applied to external reality to facilitate outcomes, but when your life is on the line, be willing to relinquish limiting patterns to intuitional command when the strategy begins to fail. This requires attention as well as sensitivity. Occasionally I have visualized throws that worked beautifully in mental rehearsal but failed to pass the test of mugging by a dangerous twenty-year-old. As you become more detached from results, the lessons of endurance allow you to develop gifts beyond the standards of conventional ranking. Simple exposure to more and more bodies in training can become an encyclopedia of pain to the astute and focused practitioner. Empathy prevents *hubris* (Greek: endangering pride) and *schadenfroid* (German: malicious enjoyment of the pain of others). Meditate on this.

The integrated self takes advantage of that spontaneity in *mushin* (no intellect; also empty spirit—sometimes referred to as the Void). The Void is another term for the subconscious, as well as the spirit world. As one learns to use the body's strengths, the subconscious becomes more functional. Moderation in diet as well as expression becomes more desirable as the emotions—which are seated in the organs of the body—provide more and more information to the adventurer through the medium of feelings. As one becomes more sensitive, more able to draw information from feelings (also referred to as intuition), one gains skill with energy work. The world appears more magical as one comes to regard feelings as legitimate sources of information as well as motivation. Because feeling precedes thought, body movement becomes more efficient and responses more appropriate to the situation. William James, the first great American psychologist, tried to explain this back at the turn of the twentieth century. It has been a subject of debate ever since in the halls of academic psychology. My experiences in the martial arts lead me to respect the elder James.

The struggle for dominance does not have to be at the

expense of others, regardless of the historical record. From the child's perspective violence is exciting, until one is injured irreparably. The ninja know that their techniques kill when applied properly by the defenseless, aged, or infirm. Sport techniques are for the young and exceptionally gifted. If your fundamentals kill, practice leads to the development of many options, so that application of your art can be part of your everyday life. All of us have a loving heart, but to bring its power to fruition can be like peeling away the layers of an onion. One tends to weep. Where the family has failed, we can hardly expect the local public school to accept the burden of socializing the violent. The dojo can serve reluctantly as a temple of correction for the demon that requires discipline.

When you are handicapped by a vicious and hostile attitude because your spider eyes reveal no justice, it does you little good to interact with others until you can appear harmless and helpful. Then if you are attacked you are just a righteous citizen delivering a lesson where it is obviously needed. As mothers resent mutilation to their children regardless of their shortcomings, it's probably better to stick with training a more mature perspective. Prison is so lonely, the food is bad, and the company worse.

Feeling

The overly intellectual are hampered in the use of the intuition. Those unschooled in the use of feelings as a guide for intuitional response remind those who observe them of why the ancient Greek rhetors referred to the study of emotions as "pathetics." The following exercises help develop skill in reading emotions. They are enhanced by the ability to see into the infrared, or "see" or "feel" auras (the body's energy fields).

Blindfold one member of the dojo. Have the other members stand in a line or surround the blindfolded one at a distance of about eight feet. Designate one of the members to act as the geek. The geek's job is to project hatred and a desire to harm the blindfolded one. The other members think only loving thoughts. You may be surprised to discover how many blindfolded people can easily pick out the geek. Feeling love and hate is relatively easy among the powerful. Feeling the emotions of those with normal levels of chi is more difficult. The body reacts to emotion. In some people it may only cause a twitch; others may be drawn to or repelled by danger. This exercise can be varied by emotion. Accuracy can be increased by giving appropriate feedback. Once the subject finds the right wavelength, they can begin to explore both projection and reception. Relaxation is a great aid to opening oneself to subtle influence.

Most people have to think to attack, and an attack is usually driven by anger. Hostility is an easily felt emotion similar to fear. The feelings you begin to read in your instructor may send you in search of another as proof positive of your avoidance skills. Conversely, a Ninpo teacher's refusal to accept you may correlate with his or her empathetic abilities. Some people become quite accurate at measuring the depth of another's commitment; some become telepathic with practice. Study softly on this.

I had to laugh when a young black belt friend of mine commented on how many of the attendees at the Washington/Baltimore Tai Kai '93 seemed to completely miss the point of Hatsumi's remarks concerning inner space and balance. The Boss wasn't inscrutable to him, nor were some of the senior instructors. He regaled me with his objective analysis of the few who are still grappling with their demons of arrogance, bitterness, and lack of human compassion. He obviously felt they were flunking "The School Wrested from the Nine Demon Gods." It's no big thing. He should have seen them five or six years ago. Hatsumi has been miraculously therapeutic for some of these wild men and women. I say that with a tip of my psychologist hat. The people who are attracted to the ultimate warrior art seldom realize that their major battle will be learning how to tame the social self by conquering their experience and learning to love their original nature. It's tough when you enter the game from a Western perspective. All the same, when it comes to hard times, I want those people on my side. Late in the training at the '95 Tucson Tai Kai, when The Boss asked the shidoshi to use more of their feminine side when demonstrating techniques, the command created mostly confusion. We all grow from rubbing on each other. It's part of the fun of becoming a balanced member of the Togakure Ryu. Endurance is the secret of Bujinkan.

Ben Franklin pithily wrote, "Experience keeps a dear school, yet fools will learn in no other"(under "Wisdom & Foolishness," *Selections from Poor Richard's Almanac,* Avanel Books, 1982). I remember dancing with a young woman in a Longview, Texas, honkytonk who became defensive when I asked her how many times she had been married. She couldn't have been more than twenty-two, was physically very beautiful, and ignorant as dirt. After a little gentle prodding she said, "O.K. I've been married three times. The first lasted eighteen months. The second, five. The third lasted seven an' a half hours. I ain't got much of a selection system, but let me tell you, Doc, I'm on one hell of a learning curve." Life unaware can be like running an obstacle course blindfolded.

We all have acquaintances we can't trust. We know people we are better off avoiding. Once you have some practice in reading intention (shaped emotions), you should spend some time with people who have characteristics that you find hard to stomach, and pay attention to exactly what they make you feel. What goes on in your body, what happens behind your eyes? What is their energy like? Once you have a catalog of experientially based characteristics of people you dislike, spend some time with people you really trust and enjoy. Go through the same process with these people. As most people don't have a clue to the "vibrations" they put out, it may help you to winnow out the chaff. The violent, the crazed, the cons, and the beautiful put out a feeling, and you should be conscious of how it affects you. Having the ability to perceive these feelings, with some practice, you can also moderate what you project. Sometimes it is useful to put out a real scary "vibe" to slow down the aggressive, or a beautiful one to attract the same. The contemplation of beauty has beneficial effects, particularly when it balances the humdrum or horror of our daily lives.

When one can feel emotions and energy and "see" auras, it tends to improve the selection system for discovering friends. Being able to read the sample helps one to select harmonious partners. Harmonious partners make the learning of this skill pleasant and fun. Compatible and passionate partners can make it earth-shaking. Energy is fueled by the emotions of the organism, and an exchange can be said to resemble osmosis. (I think of it as "awakening your inner paramecium," with a trickster ninja wink and tip of the hat toward Dr. Alice Beatty, my old Penn State zoology professor who taught me the meaning of failure.) The skilled try to maintain neutrality during an exchange, but there is always some leakage. Those who have the talent as a biogenetic gift but not the awareness often find themselves reacting to others' intentions to the detriment of their decision-making ability. Integrated individuals are so rare, and so beautiful in their harmony. It takes a lot of work to develop a soul that is fragrant as a rainbow.

Skin-breathing meditation is part of the practice of high-level chi kung and Budo Taijutsu practitioners who follow a spiritual or meditative path. As you inhale, feel the pores of your skin open, and as you exhale, push energy toward the soles of your feet, toes, and fingers. You might envision this practice as pulling energy out of the air into your body like a vacuum and then spinning it through your bone marrow as you fire it out your fingertips or feet. This is just an exercise to clean the filtering system for energy withdrawal. Chinese enthusiasts in the healing or chi-developing arts call this technique "bone and marrow washing." Some people make it part of their Secret Smile or add in the six healing sounds. Martial applications can be developed. When you put your arm around someone and inhale, you can rip off a goodly sample of energy, and as you exhale you can light them up. Staying attached while you are draining the life force from a sentient, fighting being requires athletic ability, singular skill to avoid damage, and can hardly be classified as a good time. It is easier to overload them. It is better to give than receive. With practice, energy exchange is as simple as breathing. With skill, touch is no longer necessary. Hatsumi-soke recommends soft weapons.

Skin-breathing, or marrow-washing, is a most useful augment to therapeutic touch. Healing applications become readily apparent. There is not a great demand for *Yidam* (protective vampire spirits regarded by Tibetan Buddhists as wrathful deities) in our materialistic democratic economy, so you are free to create your own job description if you want to actualize your hobby. The few bodyworkers and massage therapists I've managed to lure into the higher-level energy-conscious martial arts have loved their new powers. They often are not too interested in the combat arts, as they perceive themselves as healers and usually have a lifestyle that keeps them out of harm's way, but once into the web they enjoy the trap.

Gender Balance

Empathetic skills tend to improve as people become more in touch with their feelings. People literally seem to become smarter, if only because they make better choices in their companions. They not only treat themselves with more kindness, but extend their self-acceptance to others. However, in those who do not accept their shadow selves and potentials in terms of sexuality, violence, and power, the imbalance creates tendencies toward psychosis as the rejected shadow grows stronger.

For the macho male, the realization that the female side holds the keys to grace, healing, and outrage is often frightful. For the conventional dependent female, the realization that assertive behavior and independent thought may lead to inner strength can present a serious challenge. For the intellectual who realizes that the brain extends to the tail and not all useful knowledge is between the ears and behind the eyes, this can force a greater emphasis on strengthening the body. Those who are physically gifted can be shattered by the realization that strength, beauty, and attractiveness have limits that are quickly reached in a complex society. The humble search for balance when one has been graced with great gifts, prevents being eaten by hubris.

Contemporary American psychologist Carl Rogers' acceptance practice leads to harmonious relationships and mutually beneficial interventions. This practice involves courageously facing and accepting all aspects of oneself—good, bad, or indifferent. This principle when applied to the self and others allows one to realistically formulate strategy and tactics with a high probability of avoiding surprise and defeat. It also results in greater amiability. Acceptance helps one learn to understand the ineffable (C. R. Rogers, *A Way of Being*, Houghton Mifflin, 1980). You can only face the demon gods naked in your humility and ignorance for having missed their stealthy presence thus far. The rejected grow strong, if they survive. It's a crude school for the challenged that repeats and repeats unless the student learns the lesson and escapes through graduation into greater balance.

First Lesson
by Phyllis McGinley

The thing to remember about fathers is, they're men.
A girl has to keep it in mind.
They are dragon-seekers, bent on improbable rescues.
Scratch any father, you find
Someone chock-full of qualms and romantic terrors.
Believing change is a threat;
Like your first shoes with heels on, like your first bicycle
It took such months to get.

Walk in strange woods, they will warn you about the snakes
     there.
Climb, and they fear you'll fall.
Books, angular boys, or swimming in deep water,
Fathers mistrust them all.
Men are the worriers. It's difficult for them
To learn what they must learn;
How you have a journey to take and very likely,
For a while, will not return.

Four
_____

Crime, Conventionality, Women and Weapons

Historically, politically, and socially, Taoism existed as a counter to Confucianism in both China and Japan. In China Taoism is steeped in social protest. The practices of Taoism precede the writing of the Yellow Emperor, Huang tsi, as well as predate Lao Tzu. There is a surviving Taoist religion that bears little resemblance to what is recommended by ancient Taoist sages. In Japan, Taoism is hidden in symbolic use of esoterica in Mikkyo and Shinto. For instance, the five elementals (Go Dai) that figure so prominently in Ninpo and Mikkyo as a central device for organizing energy are associated prehistorically in Chinese legends of the Tao with a shamanistic female tribal leader who "patched the sky with five colored stones." The Golden Mother of the Tortoise Pedestal, also called The Queen Mother of the West (or Death) in Japan, is often designated as the female spirit guide of the founders of various ancient and modern martial arts. China is west of Japan, and the feminine has always been recognized as the primal equal to the order-bringing masculine in Taoism. It is recorded that a female Taoist adept informed the Emperor Wu of the militaristic Han dynasty, "You were born licentious, extravagant, and violent; you live in the midst of blood and force—no matter how many Taoist sages you bring here in hopes of achieving immortality, you will only wear yourself out." It is amazing that this rebuke was preserved in conventional Confucian history which seldom attacked the heads of state. If the rule-bound conventional Confucianism of the samurai social system can be considered the ultimate in bureaucratic masculine administrative authoritarianism, then Taoism represents feminine nurture in the guise of the mysterious female. (See Cleary, *Immortal Sisters,* in Bibliography for a discussion of the above women and Taoism in ancient China.)

Followers of the Tao, as well as Chan Buddhism (Zen in Japan) were expected to develop the art of invisibility or subtle influence and revere the statements "A skilled artisan leaves no traces" and "She enters the water without making a ripple." Warrior women did not confuse their social status of disenfranchised daughters in a patrilineal system with their personal worth as human beings. *Kunoichi* (female practitioner of Ninpo) can be translated as "one who suffers." The spirit women of Japan *(kuchiyose,* or *miko* "a woman through whose mouth a god or spirit speaks") were also called *shinikuchi* (mouth of the dead when summoning spirits) or *ikikuchi* (mouth of a living one) if summoning the spirit of a living person over distance.

Samurai warriors were almost always male, and unless a household had been through some murderous defeats, women were not expected to take the warrior role. However, there are a few legends concerning remarkable warrior women similar to our Western war queens. One concerns the widow Chiyome Mochizuki, who, rather than retire as a nun after Moritoki Mochizuki was killed at the Battle of Kawanakejime in 1561, set up one of the most effective and undetected networks of kunoichi agents to aid Daimyo Shingen Takeda during the Shengokujidai Warring Period.

Taoist adepts commonly hid within the constraints of mainstream society. They also concealed their spiritual connections from attempted suppression by ignorant authorities and petty tyrants. It is difficult to achieve internal harmony when you are attacked by the external establishment. Taoism upholds the concept of the benign sage who works with natural principles and remains hidden from society. To quote the *Wen-Tzu,* "The skilled appear to have no abilities, the wise appear to be ignorant." Muramatsu-sensei is very open about showing techniques and discussing how to work with feelings. He is described by Hatsumi-soke as being the modern ninja most like the ancient ninja. I find him to be a highly intelligent, gentle, man who exudes power, and when not showing the fighting techniques, casually discusses healing, massage, and meridian work from the viewpoint of a scholar/therapist. When acting as his uke, I found myself envying the few Americans he has taken on as students. I had to laugh when he corrected another ninja using one of my favorite techniques "as being very good but something only used by beginners." (I can see that it will take me a couple of years to master "eight leaf willow palm hand" so it is back to the drawing board for Dr. Death.)

Hiding energy work and subtle influence skills appears to be the norm for the modern ninja. I have surprised a number of high-level Ninpo practitioners by being able to feel their subtle energy healing attempts. (I've taken some fairly severe damage over the years.) When caught they reacted with embarrassment, with the exception of Hatsumi-san, who seemed to think it was interesting and funny that he wasn't subtle to me. Using subtle influence to benefit others requires an understanding of some of the darker aspects of one's social system. Conventionality, gender roles, crime and criminality, all reflect the need for and development of a true spiritual path.

Crime

A number of anthropological studies (Turnbull, Meade, Robertson, Conrad, Nettler, and so on) indicate that the greater the authoritarianism in a society, the greater the incidence of theft

71

and criminality. When a strategist looks at our society from a shadowy perspective it can be rather frightening. According to government figures published in *Newsweek* in 1994, it is estimated that six million violent crimes occur in the USA per year. Less than two million are reported. While the attacker and victim of most rapes, assaults, and murders are people who know each other, eighty percent of the robberies are carried out by strangers. Less than fifty percent of these are ever solved. Only seven percent of U.S. burglaries result in an arrest. Of those convicted, only twenty-five percent are sent to prison (National Center for Policy Analysis figures). The violent perpetrator of a crime usually serves less than two years, and the average incarceration for murder is seven. The average age of the criminal is in the teens. The recidivism rate is well over sixty percent. The cost of all crime in our kinder, gentler society is estimated at seven hundred billion dollars a year. That's some major boodle. Crime must be paying for somebody. There are a third less police on our streets per citizen than in the 1950s, and neighborhood foot patrols, which have been shown to reduce crime, are rare in our major cities. The person who feels secure in his or her household without a knowledge of self-defense and security techniques may be living in a dream house where the stairs don't reach the attic.

Criminals

Twenty-six studies of violent crime and offenders were presented at the American Association for the Advancement of Science convention in 1990. I include here the commonalities that emerge from the research on violent perpetrators. The results are chilling but there is hope from Canadian studies concerning the effect of non-competitive, everybody-gets-to-play sport studies. Garth Clarke's *A Coach's Kit for Modified Soccer* (see bibliography) with its tips on how to organize soccer for communities, could aid quite a few neighborhoods in need of help. Baylor's College of

Medicine did a study of convicted murderers in Texas in the late 1960s and discovered that ninety percent of them either did not play as children or displayed abnormal behavior when attempting to participate in sports, such as bullying, sadism, and cruelty. Soccer, boxing, wrestling, and martial arts are all low-overhead ways to teach discipline. Music and art are more difficult but have greater long-term utility. The scientific study of violent criminals across cultures reveals the following profiles:

When young: Concentration problems, little athletic skill, abused as children, depression, shyness, low verbal IQ, need for excitement, lower self-image, vulnerable to peer pressure, and alcohol/drug abuse. They can be identified by violent behavior in grade school. The ones who continue to be social problems are perceived as leaders of their lowlife groups, and often have schizo parents who may abuse them sexually or violently. The followers usually do not create problems if they begin to get some academic success. The leaders who continue are socially rewarded for getting the best of their more sheepish peers. They can feed their egos through the appearance of danger.

When older: Polydrug user, with alcohol and cocaine predominant, sporadic work record, minimal education, few friends, violence associated with social instigation particularly when drinking, past history of arrests, relatives who are also criminals, attention defects (short attention span and/or inability to perceive long-term gratification), low self-esteem tied to the belief that they can be "charmers," low income (suppressed economics and high-risk neighborhoods). Getting scared yet? Sound familiar?

Interventions that worked: Athletic training for kids *where the coaches would go and get them to make sure they played.* Play regardless of skills, let 'em learn not benchwarm, make sure they experience success and learn that 80 percent of success is showing up. Police leagues in Canada resulted in a 30 percent drop in vandalism and kid crimes by introduction of team sports for the juvies in high-risk neighborhoods. Control neighborhoods showed no change. Crime rate returned to normal two years after the program was dropped for lack of funding. The work of one criminal at large, especially over several years, can cost a community a lot more than a soccer team.

Older criminals responded to age (older = less violent), marriage, job training, and education. This strongly suggests making job training or school diploma attainment with no discipline problems a part of all sentencing. Prison, work gangs, or boot camp as forfeit. Literacy, detox, and Alcoholics Anonymous might be combined as an effective intervention, with part of the sentence being a requirement to teach after completing the program, and early release based on your success rate and/or community service directed by local institutions or parole officers. You don't get out until they punch your ticket. There are some interesting anecdotal studies concerning the beneficial effects of teaching yoga and meditation in prison. Conventional thinking suggests deterrence and punishment as the logical solution to crime, but the scientific data do not support that politically popular solution. If that were the solution to the problem of crime, we would have no two-time losers.

Conventionality

For serious glorification of perfectionism and conventionality leading to a no-growth, xenophobic, totalitarian state, it's hard to find a better example than Japan under the samurai. One of the translations of the word *samurai* is "one who serves." (An interesting reverse on self-esteem, necessary for servant mentality.) "The way of the samurai is death" is a famous maxim usually interpreted to mean that the samurai were willing to die for honor; to serve their feudal master to the death, take their own lives if they betrayed their master, or even to commit suicide to get his attention when he seemed bent on destruction. Sometimes the samurai was willing and able to kill others who did not particularly care to share those same benefits of a life of service to his *daimyo* (warlord). If you are able to read between the lines, a long-term interpretation of this famous samurai maxim could be, "If you are really going to live this set of rules to the hilt, it will result in your violent death. It will kill you spiritually, economically, culturally, and physically. Don't do this unless you want to die, as most sane people will eventually attempt to kill you, because the way of the samurai is death. It's less than democratic and furthermore doesn't seem to result in much change or general creativity. You have a job and the boss gets the rest. Smile and know your place. If you do well, you will be rewarded. As we have a population problem on this island, failure to do well will be punished by death." American colonists tried to leave this sort of thinking in Europe for very good reasons. If you know your history from an adult perspective, you know what I mean. Freedom, democracy, escape from religious persecution and irrational wars—a chance to build a new life far from the old rulers.

The literal translation of this way of the samurai resulted in eight hundred years of civil war in Japan. The rationale is similar to the inability on the part of some people to recognize the metaphors in the Bible. Concrete thinking is associated with conventionality, societal stagnation, and stupidity. We had a civil war in the USA that lasted only four years, and people are still aggravated nearly five generations later. I've often had my friends of Southern extraction point out the resting place of heroes and villains of the War Between the States. We had stimulating discussions as to who was which, as my viewpoint was tainted by a "Gawddam Yankee" perspective. Interesting what you don't learn in the history books written by the winners.

One of the reasons the Japanese martial arts are so prolific and efficient is they are based on profound and profuse experience. People there used to kill each other with great regularity, thus getting to practice what they were studying. To quote

Musashi, "The Way is in Practice!" Every time the samurai managed to gain power, which was often because of their arrogance and aggressiveness, it resulted in wars of extermination, culminating in Hiroshima and Nagasaki.

In-your-face assertiveness, coupled with the need to dominate or exploit, will eventually attract the attention of those who will kill you. It is one of the reasons most combatic martial artists include the teaching of fundamental politeness, or etiquette. Reality can be harsh, and manners serve to smooth the path of social intercourse. The soft *ryuha* (martial schools) of Osaka and Kyoto described in the *Hagakure* as "weak" were life-giving arts *(Budo)* of self-protection as opposed to the death-bringing samurai arts *(Bugei)* for warfare. The samurai are gone now, except in visions of cherry blossoms wafted on a divine wind. Their lifestyle is summed up by the Western saying, "Those who live by the sword die by the sword." Bruce Lee, creator of Jeet Kune Do, a very practical martial art, often quoted the Taoist maxim "Soft defeats hard." In the West we say, "A soft answer turneth away wrath."

A life-giving martial art is necessary to protect against the pathology of morbidity. Or in recognizing the inevitability of death, one pursues it for a greater feeling of control and choice. Choosing death over life is generally regarded as a sin, or missing the mark, by all major religions and philosophies. Parting with the material world appears a tragedy for the young, but there are times when the transition to the next stage is a blessing for the aged or exhausted. Dying for a concept has always been regarded by the ninja as one of the more stupid aspects of samurai culture. As human beings with Taoist/Shinto forefathers, they did not embrace the concept of *seppuku* (ritual suicide) impolitely referred to as *hara-kari* (cutting the guts). They earned the samurai contempt by not playing by the samurai rules. The ninja thought going home to Momma was more important than the honor of dying gloriously for your Overlord.

A careful reading of Musashi makes it clear he had no desire to die for his honor and was *ronin* (independent warrior or wave man) nearly all his life. In fact, he was on the losing side in his first fixed battle and spent the next few years running and hiding from the victors. He was one of the greatest duelists in Japan's war-torn history, killing more than sixty men and boys in face-to-face recorded duels and as many or more in unrecorded challenges and melee. He was a much better artist than swordsman, and is greatly misunderstood by most of his modern interpreters who have never seen a heavy thirty-inch razor blade coming at them, do not have the smooth foreheads of meditators, and have no conception of strategy beyond charging to glory.

Conventionality develops out of living without examining the values that motivate those immersed in a particular social system. The unexamined life has its own dangers, and values important to Americans will be discussed later, as one must understand one's self as well as one's enemy (i.e., one's social conditioning) to prevail.

Women in the Martial Arts

Women in the martial arts face a similar problem of dealing with silly codes of honor and conventional behavior if they like the sweat and contact of sport and want to compete in the same arenas as men. Just dealing with human physiology creates some interesting advantages and handicaps. On a scale of one to ten when it comes to upper body strength, men might be sevens and women threes. If we examine spirit, women would be sevens and men threes. Most sports are structured to the advantage of men, and most men fight with an awareness of sport rules regardless of the situation. I mean squaring off and trading head and body shots like boxers, or grappling like wrestlers so that the stronger, faster, or more athletic person usually wins. What is even more important is understanding that sport has nothing to do with winning under combat conditions where fire-power, trickery, and deceit usually prevail. The conventions of sport will result in the death of a woman in a real fight. It is conventionally stupid to teach a woman, or anyone else for that matter, to square off with an opponent and trade blows and blocks as if there were constraints to movement and fighters don't use weapons. It is even stupider to allow her to think that high snap kicks will deter a determined rapist, or that throws can be accomplished with the ease one experiences with the well-trained *uke*.

I have a policewoman friend who was improperly taught aikido wrist techniques that might have resulted in her death if she had ever tried to apply them in that manner. She had a lot of help from a cooperative uke and had never learned to apply the grips properly with full-bodied taijutsu. A policewoman has a high probability of having to use her art and being seriously harmed if it fails her under street conditions. The aikido "teacher" who showed her those techniques misled her to believe she could do them effectively. To teach a woman to trust a technique that works only under specific conditions is the same as killing her, particularly when you know she will be facing danger. Teachers of sport often do not realize that the self-defense applications of what they are teaching pale in comparison to the well-applied boot, knife, sword, club, or handgun.

Most women are aware that the incidence of rape increased enormously during the chauvinistic Reagan and Bush years. According to FBI figures, reported rapes doubled from 1990 to 1991. One out of seven women is raped by the age of eighteen, and a large percentage in their preteens by older acquaintances and relatives. About half of all rapes involve serious violence to the victim. These are American statistics! The woman who rejects the opportunity to train in a life-giving martial art may not be facing reality. The situation is even more frightening when unwanted pregnancy and sexually transmitted diseases that kill are added to the equation. One out of four college women report being raped. In ninety percent of reported rapes alcohol or drugs were involved. Date rape is considered a sport on some college campuses, as it is seldom reported, and if it is, the incident is often covered up to avoid bad publicity (Robertson, *Sociology* and my own experience of observing how the administration handled complaints against fraternity houses and athletes at Hillsdale College). Dr. Jon Kayne, a forensic psychologist, and *buyu* (martial arts friend), did a study of jailed rapists in the early eighties and found that in every case, they believed masturbation was a bad thing, and rationalized that the sex drive in the male could not be controlled. There is a problem here that goes deeper than saying, "Rape is a bad thing, and you shouldn't do it." I've known lots of guys who say things like, "If I don't get it at least once a week, I get mean." It may be an unfair generalization to say so, but these men were usually conservative, pretty good athletes, and Roman Catholic to boot. On the liberal side of the Catholic question we have JFK, who complained of migraines when Jackie or Marilyn were not in town. Sexual response is learned behavior in primates.

Japan has a very low incidence of reported rape (my editor suggests shame is an issue), but then prostitution is legal, and concubinage is socially encouraged. It remains a very patriarchal society. Historically a woman of the samurai class who was raped or taken advantage of was expected to commit seppuku. She could eradicate the shame by killing the rapist. There is an old samurai saying that goes: "The rapist and the man who beats his wife are both cowards" (Daidoji Yuzan, circa 1710). Cowardice in most militaristic societies is punishable by ostracism, banishment, or death.

Hatsumi-san treats his wife Mariko-sensei with great respect for a Japanese man, who for the most part do not practice much equality in gender, having fairly strict role expectations. The woman is expected to be subservient, at least in public. This is common throughout most of Asia and Africa. The Boss takes his wife with him wherever he goes, and sends me photos of them walking hand in hand down the Champs Élysées in Paris, dragged out in King and Queen costumes at the England Tai Kai, or riding on a tandem bike in Germany. Most Japanese men don't like to expose their wives or daughters to the freer Western lifestyle out of fear that it might be (and invariably is) catching. Most Japanese corporations do not like to have their women or wives live in the USA longer than two years out of fear they will become too Americanized.

In Japan, women are permitted to wear a purple *dogi* (training suit) with a red belt regardless of rank. In America they usually train in the same dogi colors as the men (black). The purple dogi are considered prettier and more feminine by Super Boss, who feels women wearing the black indicates sloppiness. Even fewer women train in Japan in ninjutsu than in the USA. Hatsumi, coming from his cultural background, downplays the role of the kunoichi historically, but any woman who likes the martial arts, recognizes instantly that this is an art that works for women. Budo Taijutsu for women emphasizes legwork, avoidance, and catching the attacker off guard from an unexpected angle, with a heavy emphasis on psychology and intuition. I wouldn't be surprised to find the *Kumogakure Ryu* (Spider Doorway or Hidden Cloud School, depending on how translated) was a favorite among kunoichi who had to pass as geisha or holy women, as well as those who wanted climbing, rope techniques, and halberd *(naginata)*. I suspect this particular school of Ninpo is much older than its documented fourteen generations. Women in Ninpo have a tradition that extends at least as far back as the eleventh century. The thirteenth-century Zen nun teacher at Tokeiji, Yoshihime (daughter of General Kanazawa Sada), is described as a student of Ninpo. Her nickname was "devil girl."

Japanese samurai training for women, after the fourteenth century, primarily focused on *naginata* as the weapon of choice when the men screwed up enough that the women were forced to fight for their lives or freedom. Women in the Ninja clans sometimes fought alongside their men, similar to the women of the Cheyenne and Sioux of the American Plains. Mariko-sensei often demonstrates the use of long corded weights for tangling and striking from a distance. *Tanto* (long wedge-shaped chisel-pointed fighting knife that can pierce armor) were concealed in flower arrangements that allowed the kunoichi to get close to their target. The Chinese regarded the naginata as superior to the sword on the battlefield. It was a good last-ditch weapon for women, and a favored weapon of professional people who had better things to do than practice with swords all day. Think of the *bo* staff with a twenty-four-inch curved razor attached to one end. It provided more distance to create timing. Distance and timing, as well as setting up your opponent to think he or she is getting what they want, are critical for preserving most female flesh. Bullies deserve to meet the great mother.

Once women get past the social expectations of their training partners and learn the basic movements of taijutsu, they can even take advantage of ingrained attitudes and expectations. It's all fair in Ninpo. She can take advantage of the gentleman's hesitation to go full bore on a woman. She can feign weakness to lure him into a false sense of security that he probably wouldn't allow facing a male, and then deck him. Feminine wiles have dropped more than one budding Samson in the dojo and on the street. As ninjutsu training includes weaponry, she can find tools to increase her powers. Because the bone-breaking dynamics come from weight shifting and footwork rather than muscular strength, most women find themselves physically competent quite quickly. Because the art is customized to each player's body by a skilled teacher, they gain in confidence and decision-making skills. The techniques for avoiding and absorbing blows without harm reduce the fear of being hit.

The rolling techniques confuse the average opponent and will loosen the grip of even the strongest male. The heightened awareness brought by the training of intuition is often attained more quickly by the female than the male and adds to her avoidance techniques.

Women in the dojo—particularly older women with some experience beneath their belts like education and raising children—have a civilizing effect that is beneficial to the dojo climate, as they tend to be very pragmatic. For a hundred-and-twenty-pound, five-foot-four female to figure out how to drop and incapacitate a two-hundred-and-fifty-pound, six-foot-plus male is a serious exercise in balanced problem-solving, requiring the development of considerable good humor in her male experimental subject. It usually takes a while to learn how to do the process without killing or injuring the opponent. Killing and injuring the opponent is relatively easy. Taking a prisoner or making a friend is much more difficult and requires great sensitivity to your opponent's range of movement. Often the close contact of many of the techniques in Budo Taijutsu is disturbing to the male practitioner, but as women are socialized to accept greater intimacy, they pick it up with ease.

The female's greater hand/eye speed and coordination give her an advantage once she grasps the balance points. Her lower center of gravity paired with leg strength equal to men can develop considerable knock-down power and throwing skills. If you've ever seen Kathy Long, former world kickboxing champion and author of a good book on women's self-defense (No, No, No!), tread her movie opponents down in Knights, you know what I mean. Don't pay too much attention to the movie high kicks. When we were developing the belt system in hoshin we would show the techniques to "the girls" and then watch them figure out how to do them, as they would discover the secrets of no strength. The hardbodies, and most female athletes today, can run rings around the average male and may choose to close with a male opponent, but—Sun Tzu recommends never engaging in conflict until the issue is already decided in your favor. Too many people carry weapons for any of us to carry chips.

Some Female Practitioner Profiles

Rumiko Hayes convinced me I should take ninjutsu more seriously during a training exercise in which I was doing my best to eviscerate her with a mock Western Bowie—she stretched me out, slammed me to the dirt, dragged me around, captured my weapon, and took me prisoner. She was eight months pregnant at the time and used the leverage from her rounded belly to lock my elbow between her thighs. She was astounding. Her taijutsu gave her complete control whenever I tried any of the attacking methods I'd studied in the army. I outweighed her by a good hundred pounds in those days.

Dr. Lee Buesking is the highest-ranked woman in the honest Korean martial art of Moo Duk Kwan, Tang Soo Do. She is also highly ranked in tae kwon do and is Grandmistress of her own school, Jion Jee Do Kwan. This remarkable woman told me she had to learn early on how to avoid and control the men, as it certainly wasn't part of the traditional kata. She has fought, dodged, and taught her way to sixth dan (Senior Master) in a culture that has little respect for warrior women. She looked pretty hot in a spangled gown at the Hall of Fame. She told me at a seminar in Trinidad that aside from her teacher, she has never been accepted by the other male masters as a friend in her preferred martial art. The men even tried to injure her when she was the first woman tested for master in Korea. That is a sad commentary on being macho. She is an excellent teacher. She dropped a few people in Trinidad and gave a good showing at fighting multiple assailants. She has more male students than female in her Clawson, Michigan, *dojang* (Korean for dojo). I saw her girls fight at the North American Mixed Martial Art Championships. They took some trophies. They like to win.

Shannon Kubiak, of Shaolin Kempo—who was inducted the same year as me into the World Martial Arts Hall of Fame—won three world championships before she was eighteen. She's a fierce competitor who stands out in an arena usually dominated by males. She does tournament-winning weapon kata with the steel whip or long fighting chain. She told me her next goal is to win the world men's point sparring. This will take some doing, as most tournaments don't allow cross-sex fighting. She will severely damage some masculine egos, as she is the pretty blonde girl next door. She is in the Air Force Reserve officer training program. Her female teacher, Simu Vivian Mayle, came out of retirement to win the gold in the middleweight masters' division open point sparring, and a bronze medal in masters' division weapons kata at the Australian Goodwill Games in 1995.

The Martin twins, Merry and Dolly, didn't have to work too hard to pass the Bujinkan sword test for telepaths. I've had a number of female friends mention that they picked up valuable lessons from the Martin sisters. Their older sister has trained in Japan on and off for years, and Hatsumi-soke thinks highly enough of her techniques to use her photograph in one of his books demonstrating *sanshin.*

Sharon Presley, an Air Force Academy cadet who trains in Ninpo, spent an afternoon as my uke at the 1993 Tai Kai and told me afterward that "it is a wonder that another human being will attack someone after being exposed to what aggression can lead to." She was smart, fast, and the most polite human being I've thrown around in years. She was obviously the leader in the group from the Academy that year. I was honored that she chose me to mug.

Abigail Allen, who passed the sword test when I did, teaches near Albuquerque, New Mexico. She runs her own construction company and recently began building her own dojo in Bernalillo. She teaches from a traditional Japanese perspective, and quite a few families study with her.

Regina Brice, a Harvard graduate, passed her godan test with style in 1993 and is the first black woman to achieve that rank. She had to search through some Ninja frauds before she located Bujinkan. She has a gritty sense of humor, and like some white men, doesn't jump. She speaks Japanese, has a Michigan law degree, and translates for senior instructors. She lived in Japan for three years. A year or so before she took the godan test, Hatsumi suddenly threw a hidden spear at her backwards over his shoulder. She dodged it. She and Hatsumi share many a giggle. She gave me some excellent advice when I wrote *Path Notes*.

Female masters are treated with respect in Budo Taijutsu and the Shaolin-derived martial arts, from my observation. The feminine perspective may differ. Some informants felt respect came more from male fear of the senior instructors they were training with or associating with, than from people being willing to physically train with them, or from being nice when they didn't feel like it. One said, "I'll live with it, but some of the girls are having a hard time." Kunoichi in the modern sense might be translated as one who suffers some chauvinism to reach her goals.

Weapons

Most martial arts weapons that are taught in the dojo are about as useful on the street as tits on a hog. These days the police will arrest you before you can administer a simple beating with a bo staff or nunchaku, and though there are few laws concerning the carrying of swords in public, they tend to enforce the three-inch blade regulation in most states. Gun laws allow the criminal to beef up to Uzi submachine guns, but you as a law-abiding citizen are allowed hunting rifles, shotguns, and varmint pistols of whatever caliber and barrel length you fancy. Given the odds, I would take the time to learn about kitchen explosives, but that's how I look at things and I don't even belong to the Michigan Militia or the NRA! For you, the perfect weapon would probably be the *hanbo* (walking stick), or *yawara.* Regina Brice has published *A Martial Artist's Guide to American Law* and *Martial Arts Law,* a newsletter which will inform you on what you can get away with (Sanshin Consulting Int'l. P.O. Box 87, Oberlin, Ohio 44074).

The *yawara,* short stick, or *vajra* (three names for the same basic tool) has both esoteric and exoteric uses and meanings. On one level it is nothing more than the most primitive of hand axes with which our Neolithic ancestors gathered their daily bread. It can be seen as a phallus and is usually grasped between the two globes by the index and middle finger for striking in what kenjutsu, chi kung, and *chin-na* (Chinese grappling art) practitioners call "Buddha Hand." Its spike tips can be used to smash through bone as well as adjust meridian *ko* (energy points). I prefer the wooden variation with a finger loop that can easily be taken anywhere that five inches of ³/₄-inch dowel can be taken. You know, airplanes, theaters, even the dojo. Some people like to put lead into the wood to create the same effect as weighting your fist with a roll of coins.

Short stick *(eda koppo)* techniques can be used against the sword if you are slick enough. They add pain as well as ferocity to most throws, blows, and chokes. It's a great self-defense weapon that is a specialty area in hoshinjutsu and one of the basic weapons of the Togakure Ryu Bujinkan. The kubotan techniques used as a key chain are crude by comparison. Taking out a swordsman with a five-inch piece of wood requires a bit of practice and a lot of stealth technique for a young woman, an old man, or a ninja master. It will engage your attention for a good while, as well as your imagination, if you can't dodge the sword. The short stick is used to attack *koshijutsu* points to swiftly weaken the opponent. Knowledge of the fifty most useful striking points *(kyusho)* on the body is a ninja study. In hoshin we focus on thirteen, and in dim mak they can thrill you with over three hundred and sixty points of fright and blight.

The vajra, or thunderbolt, is also treated as a religious icon by the Tibetans and more magical Buddhists. The double-spike version represents yang or male energy striking out imaginatively to heal the world. You heal the world by first healing yourself, and then begin mastering the techniques of psychic surgery. The two-globed vajra represents androgyny and a bridge between circles of influence. The Tibetans call it *dorje*, or Lord of Stones. This metal vajra is usually carried by priests or sages. As a weapon it gives striking, lifting, and throwing an excitatory expansion to the carrier. As an icon it represents yin and yang as it is two headed. The center grip is often shaped like a two bowled grail emptying out the four elementals as prongs, which support the spike (which represents the Void, as it extends through both sides), as well as prevent it from going too deep. This implement is better at pulling than piercing. It is grasped in the middle, showing that the way lies between good and evil. The good man or woman seeks moderation but understands the extremes of the dualistic world. I'll bet you were never told that about a yawara. Yawara can even be translated as "martial art."

The hanbo is any straight staff of approximately cane length, or a meter long. Its a little longer than what we used to call a cudgel when stick fighting was popular. I think of it as a cane or walking stick. It is acceptable at any gathering, if you work on your limp and tremble slightly, giving the appearance of injury. A cane is even more acceptable, but the crook somewhat limits your options, though it adds a few fun throws and trips, that are more difficult to accomplish without the hook. Masaaki Hatsumi and Quintin Chambers wrote *Stick Fighting* (Kodansha International, 1971) on the *Kukishinden* (Kukoshindo in the book) Ryu stick fighting techniques. They are hard to learn from the pictures and diagrams but the feeling is there if you have the imagination. Chambers is still a little miffed that Hatsumi-soke chose not to discuss the techniques as coming from Ninpo, but at that time he was being more secretive, as well as testing his interpretation of the system. There is also a book on stick fighting that Hatsumi-soke wrote in Japanese that includes great moves with golf clubs and other fun things you might have around the house. A stick is such a sweet weapon. It gives you the full range of retaliation, capture, attack, or injury options to any opponent you can lure within thirty feet. The hanbo is good training for the sword as well.

Hanbo work is not like Filipino *Kali* (double two-foot-long short stick fighting). The philosophy and movement are in no way similar. (For that matter, ninja bo fundamental techniques are far superior to any karate style's bo kata that I've seen, and very similar to yari and Chinese spear.) The hanbo techniques rely heavily on smooth, well-oiled taijutsu and footwork. The stick fighter does not square off against his opponent unless he or she is setting the opponent up. In hoshin we tend to use the cane due to its illusory appearance as an aid to the challenged, but I must admit I have stolen liberally from ninjutsu in this area. I've had many students who studied the forms of kali, made popular through recent movies, but they get easily blown away by the simplest of hanbo or ninja sword techniques. The ninja no-strength body dynamics (jutaijutsu) are perfect for the protection of the elderly as well as the lightweight. Hwarang-do and hapkido both have extremely useful cane techniques as part of their system.

The thuggee of India used a scarf, or even his loincloth, as a fighting and strangling weapon. This tactic was extremely effective, as the thugs were able to conceal their dark and criminal activities under the guise of religion for centuries. The ninja *tennugui* (head towel often utilized like a mask) was used as a water filter as well as a weapon. You can easily sew some lead shot into a cloth belt to make an extremely useful weapon, or weight the bottom fringe of your stylish big coat like the French riot police. Lead and brass will not set off most metal detectors.

The coat can also be used like a net, as can a sheet if you have studied bedroom escapes, which are a hoshin specialty popular among the college crowd. (Window leaping, ledge hanging, stealth walking, tree climbing ... you remember what it was like to be young and in love with the wrong person. Scary sometimes what one does for a tight squeeze or a stiff thrill when the dorm entrance is guarded.) A belt or a fighting chain is used exactly like a hanbo. It's all angling and footwork, with the advantage of being able to tangle up the opponent and drag him or her around. Dragging someone around by the neck tends to shorten their life expectancy while stretching their breathing experience to new limits. The Biblical injunction to make the serpent straight and the staff crooked is pointing toward a little-known secret of stick fighting familiar to Moses from his Egyptian training to be a prince, as well as a metaphor for the kundalini and energy use. The *kusari-fundo* (short weighted chain) is an easily concealed scarf-type weapon developed by the Japanese police of by-gone age for capturing unruly swordsmen. It is a favorite ninja study and far more useful than *nunchaku* (karate stick weapons connected by a short chain or cord—illegal in most states). A kusari-fundo is carried by Fudomyo (the Japanese warrior representation of the god of enlightenment) in his left hand in order to bind evil spirits for judgment.

Serious Business

I personally think that women have to be their own bodyguards. Those that emancipate themselves from socialized expectations of frailty display a heroic fortitude worthy of the bravest of men. I have always taught the women with whom I've lived how to combat shoot and gave them small-bore pistols to hide at their discretion, just in case they decide to go for me. It is a good confidence and trust builder. I taught my daughters to shoot, along with other self-defense skills, and joked with their boyfriends about their skills with poison. They took after their mothers and were more feminine types—not terribly interested in my madness beyond occasional observation of class to check out the new crop of young men. After I'd been divorced from my second wife for a few years, she took a lover. She made the mistake of telling him about the hideout gun. He wanted to know where she kept it. She said that I had told her to never reveal that information to anyone, not even me, as it was meant to save her life. He didn't stick around too long after that. Not knowing where the gun was, but knowing Linda, seemed to make him unsettled.

You should examine the art you are learning to decide if you will be able to do it when your strength and speed are reduced by age or injury, or your opponent has the strength and youth advantage. Until I trained with ninja I had little faith in any unarmed techniques I'd seen when used against weapons, unless the weapon-bearer was inept and clumsy. I always recommended the carrying of Sam Colt's equalizer for serious business. However, I haven't felt a serious need to use distance weapons in years, except for food gathering. Once you start empathizing with animals, hunting and fishing may fall into the category of something you used to do, unless you are hungry. I eat what I kill. Hunting with a camera is still a lot of fun.

Now this is a little dark and pessimistic, but you really should learn how to shoot—no matter what anybody tells you about how they might take it away from you and use it on you. The pistol can be regarded as a modern variation of the *shuriken* (throwing stars and spikes). If you've followed my logic this far you will probably shoot the perp right down the center until the gun is empty. If the gun is empty it can still be used similar to the yawara to harden the hand. The center is easiest to hit and holds the vital organs and meridians, making the center line the weakest part of the enemy. I take it for granted you will not be shooting at the police or military, who usually wear body armor.

Hatsumi-soke says "Weapons are for the weak!" You can

explain how in your terror and panic you kept squeezing the trigger as the loud noise just kept scaring you. Multiple holes from a .22 or .25, which doesn't kick and shoots straight for ten feet regardless of load, are just as effective as one whopping slap from a .45 or .357 magnum, which are difficult to shoot without flinching, unless you practice. (If you are reasonably sane, you have better things to do with your time.) The slug of a small caliber is much harder to trace as its rifling is invariably destroyed, one of the reasons the little guns are favored by assassins. They are also thought of as "girl guns" for plinking, so owning one does not set off alarm bells in the minds of the investigating officers, the way a Glock 10 mm. will. Be certain the crime scene reflects the facts of your story. Learning to shoot well from a cross-bodied, modified Weaver stance can be challenging and fun, as well as life-preserving. If you can get consistent two-inch groups without using the sights at three, ten, and twenty feet, with either hand you are as competent as you'll ever have to be. Go for it.

A shotgun is a wonderful little alley sweeper for the truly nervous. A semi-auto twenty-gauge, or .410, hardly kicks at all and can be rigged to hold five rounds of heart-stopping No. 2 shot, or buck shot. A twenty-two-inch barrel is legal in most states. There are many interesting loads to be purchased at your local hardware or gun shop. Doc Holiday, a consumptive American dentist who felt OK in corrals, was said to load his double barrel with carpet tacks, though he is not recognized as the inventor of the flechette. When an American-built assault rifle can cost up to three thousand dollars, it is probably a good idea to examine the Chinese SKS (based on the AK 47), which can usually be had for about a hundred. Since ownership of semi-automatics may soon disappear as a collector's privilege, you might be interested to know that you can do anything that an assault rifle can do with a "cowboy" brush rifle, or lever action saddle gun, and more. The nineteenth-century Remington and

Browning designs are in some ways superior in terms of mobility, handling, and accuracy. The cheap .30 caliber load which can be had all over the world fits both rifles and handguns and easily penetrates class II body armor. As long as you refrain from harming others, who gives a rap what your hobby happens to be!

An art that is smart has evasion and deceit built into its *kihon* (fundamentals). A woman should train with men but may want to fight smarter. Our nation was founded on the principles of ambush, and our greatest military heroes were masters of movement and surprise. A woman should never tell her opponent what she is going to do if she expects to win. Surprise defeats strength and speed. Study on this. Many conventional women are afraid to study martial arts, as they do not think they will be welcome in the dojo. This is not true of Bujinkan. If you fall into that hesitant category, try visiting to watch how the local shidoshi teaches. Ask questions. If you need recommendations, tell him or her Dr. Morris sent you.

"Crook and Flail"
by Glenn Morris

Behind every word is a picture.

When words were pictures
And meaning was writ large,

The Pharaohs crossed arms to protect the heart,
Held in the forehand a crook, and in the backhand a flail.

A pictograph portrays the reality of the word,
An angel with an animal spirit.

Spirit is a stick figure holding fire.

Gossip is two women close and one farther out—
Some people talk, others are talked about.

Eureka is a man kneeling humbly, his arms flung wide in joy.

The crook is a tool of the good shepherd,
Helpful to the flock.

The flail is a scourge for those who need to discipline desire.

A picture is worth a thousand words to the Child.

Benevolence becomes a threat.
Beauty is mindful of the beholder.

All times are dangerous to the ignorant.

Five

The Shadow Book of Busato Morris

The life of a martial artist is not one that many people choose. Having to match your physical and mental abilities against the standards of a true master is invariably humbling. It often results in the love of a very dark angel indeed. To begin, one must accept the fact that one knows nothing, and in this state of abject and objective humility begin to learn once again as a child. It is helpful to have kind but honest teachers who challenge your thinking with their presence.

In ancient Japan and China, those who wanted to better their social position or who aspired to greatness were expected to develop leadership characteristics, and leadership was best taught and tested by the warrior schools of swordsmanship. Leadership was associated with the "Ten Perfections." The ten perfections were determination, patience, objectivity, truthfulness, energy, generosity, kindness, equanimity, ethics, and wisdom. The sword and staff are ancient symbols of power. The single-edged sword allows one to shelter behind the shield of choice, where the more masculine double-edged sword cuts both ways. The strongest power stands behind the blade's edge. The sword is safest locked in stone, as those who draw it into the light often come face to face with their death if their intentions are not pure. Those who live by the sword do indeed die by it, whether by violence, exhaustion, or venereal disease, as death is an equal opportunity reiver. The staff of wisdom can be as deadly as the sword in skilled hands.

The need for a spiritual quest into one's deepest and most secret self is felt by many who begin to develop a profound dislike for the consequences of unbridled desire (casually identified as greed). We feel emptiness in our churches. We see avarice and lack of principle in our politicians, and we hear defiance and longing in our music. The spiritual warrior is faced with a journey that forces transcendence of the material world to become a bridge to alternative realities. Living the dual mandala means being able to exist both as a spirit and a human being. Following the short path (tantra) to this historically well-documented transcendental state is sometimes called "The Fierce Way." Taming one's demons often is a matter of coming to grips with the effects of parenting and the culture in which one is immersed, and recognizing that the goals one pursues may well result in the death of cherished egoistic viewpoints. To transcend one's culture and socially learned self requires critically examining one's values. Jungian and strategic principles are particularly valuable in analyzing the subtle influence of social patterns. Understanding and accepting the rejected (the shadow) is far more important than simple avoidance. In this chapter I'll talk about some of the darker aspects of our cultural values that cast a shadow on one who would pursue the warrior path. I attempt to illustrate my points with examples drawn from contemporary culture, including those in leadership positions. Thrown in are contrasting or parallel concepts from Zen or Ninpo appropriate to my discussion.

Psychologists and The Shadow

Intuition—the mysterious female, the shadowy valley—is both the most powerful and most neglected of our mental faculties.

"Its [intuition's] reach extends beyond the expectations of conventional wisdom—even beyond the usual sensory boundaries of time and space... It is essential that we learn to cultivate and apply our deepest intuitional gifts. Intuition can guide us to a future based on both compassion and innovation." (Jeffrey Mishlove, Ph. D. Director, Intuition Network in discussing *intuition* magazine, 1995) This positive view is shadowed by the identification of intuition with the darker side of human nature as a close cousin of the irrational animal id *(Nin)*. The id reveals itself through emotional attachment, or what and who we value. An extremely useful concept was recently identified in psychology as "self-serving bias," which is pandemic in human beings and is defined as our readiness to regard ourselves favorably. It is against this universal perception that religion and literature so often warn concerning the perils of pride.

Until the last twenty years or so, Western psychology worked very little with emotions, and little scientific work has focused on mapping the unconscious mind. The identification as "unconscious" may give you a clue to the paucity of understanding. The shadow is usually described in terms of rejected potentials, as things we would never do or ways we would never be. Behavior exists on a continuum, and in reality all points on the line can be activated at any given moment. Good or bad is most often regarded as social judgment by those who understand cultural relativity. In Budo the principles that motivate good or eliminate bad behavior are survival mechanisms tested under combat conditions. In Asia, the shadow is also discussed as the Void, and is regarded as both a mental state where a martial artist can release all of his or her potentials, and a place where spirits dwell. Esotericists believe that the psyche (spirit or soul) is multidimensional and exists across different realities. This could be a metaphor for reincarnation, but when you travel in the astral, the esoteric description gains validity. Regardless of the metaphor, all of your bodies are connected through the shadow by emotion. The unrecognized shadow is regarded as the Id—wild, primal nature, and uncontrollable by those whose concern is restraint rather than use.

The recognized shadow, on the other hand, is a horse of a gentle nature. It is that part of us that is the learning child, the mother of creativity, and will give you the ride of your life if embraced in understanding and acceptance. Carl Rogers, a great psychologist, felt acceptance was the basis of personal growth education and love (*On becoming a person,* Houghton Mifflin, 1961). To reject our shadow or animal nature is to lock ourselves into a false reality where neither goodness nor people's proclivity to sin are recognized, and thus reality can be manipulated by those in power. Sigmund Freud, pioneering psychologist and hypno-therapist, had great difficulty recognizing the shadow side of lust, and feared the id even though he was quite creative in some of his more erroneous explanations. He failed to recognize the truth of child rape from some of his informants, as he knew their fathers, and rationalized their neurosis into penis envy. The adventurer learns to ride his nightmare even when the truth is horrific. Pure Freudian therapists have only a thirty percent success rate—about the same as being interred in an insane asylum. Given the expense and time requirements of psychiatric therapy with your odds of successfully integrating, you are probably further ahead to enter a dojo.

Understanding Your Greatest Enemy

To-iri no jutsu (the ninja art of entering from a remote or distant vantage point) offers guidelines for the intelligence gatherer moving into enemy territory, preferably long before actual warfare. Part of the training is to know what the opponent values in order to effectively manipulate, or weaken their ability to fight. In anthropology one is asked to attempt to rise above being immersed in the culture one is studying and assume the viewpoint of "being an observer from Mars." Carl von Clausewitz, a

Western philosopher and strategist, suggests that warfare is failed diplomacy, and winning diplomacy requires a knowledge of what is valued. Two twentieth century scholars, Edward D. Steele and W. Charles Redding were curious to see if there were a relatively unchanging cluster of values that make up the American cultural concept of the good ("The American Value System: Premises for Persuasion," *Western Speech*, 26, 1977, p. 169). Following are the roots of the American Way in order of their strength. I add the shadow of the value as seen by a strategist and the relation to levels of enlightenment from a Zen or Ninpo perspective.

Ideal Morality. Americans like to see the world in terms of black or white, good or bad, ethical or unethical. They often carry this duality into all forms of competition, seeing the winners as good, the losers as bad. The ideal American does not cheat or lie, and practices what he or she preaches. Some credit this to Puritan morality, but valuing truth is common across racial, social, and religious spectrums. The shadow of unrealistic, idealistic moralism (Puritanism or Calvinism) is a government too pure to do dirty work, or even more frightening, a theocracy run by Fundamentalists eager to purge the "dirt" as they define it. There ought to be a law that takes drugs off the street and regulates dangerous substances like alcohol and tobacco. Because we cannot legislate morality is no reason not to regulate vice. Alcohol and tobacco have proven far more destructive than many of the restricted drugs we leave to criminal distribution. This is an area where we could look to England or Denmark as a model. In our inner cities, crack has won the War on Drugs. However, when England decriminalized addictive drugs, the crime rate in her major cities dropped significantly (Ray Oakley, *Drugs, Society, and Human Behavior*, Mosby, 1983). I remember readings studies of Danish crime rates that indicated a seventy percent reduction of theft and violent crime in some cities. That was twenty some years ago and I don't remember the citations, but they were convincing. Belief in non-existent ideals has a rigid shadow that relates to the "mind of everyman" in Zen *(Bonpo-no-joshiki)*, which does not believe that things can change and only reacts to past experience as a guide to the present. *Zembyo* (Zen sickness) occurs when one becomes egocentric and attached to his meditative practice and attempts to push them off on others as "the only way."

Individual Sovereignty. Every person, regardless of sex, education, race, religion, or wealth, is valued as "an autonomous, unique, decision-making personality worthy of concern and possessing intrinsic dignity" (Steele and Redding, above). Private and government policy are supposed to boost the individual's opportunities to seek happiness and protect his or her welfare. Your home is your castle. We are all God's children. The shadow is exclusivity of sovereignty to one's particular group or belief system. *Jiriki* (one's own spiritual practice) is the belief that only through one's own effort can realization be accomplished.

Achievement. Occupational achievement is a measure of success and status in America. Achievement motivation can be taught and used to encourage entrepreneurial activity and creativity right down to the village level, as was demonstrated by Dr. David McClelland and other members of the Ivy League research teams introducing entrepreneurship to impoverished villages in India back in the early sixties. The US government and Harvard used up a lot of time and money to measure the results of a historical study based on the impact of achievement themes in children's literature in another project. (An example would be Little Toot, the train that thought he could. When the achievement theme faded in American children's literature around 1860, about thirty years later when the children were adults in positions of power, they tried to close the U.S. Patent Office, as everything had been invented.) The themes were taught to the villagers and within five years, the villages which had been economic disaster areas for hundreds of years became hotbeds of expanding economic activity at all levels. McCleland was a famous man; you can look up the studies in most basic texts of psychology.

There are certain themes that resonate in the behavior of legendary people that do not have to be learned young, but must be learned at some point to achieve harmony and balance in yourself, while preparing and waiting for the right opportunity to have the greatest effect, or receive the greatest reward for your effort. The key components of achievement motivation are: feeling that your effort makes a difference— this is also called having a personal locus of control; willingness to take moderate risk, 50/50 chances, not high risk or low risk; and intense interest in the area in which one wants to excel, usually to the point of letting other things slide (which often results in a rather sloppy academic performance). Usually the greatest recognized success is achieved in legitimate business, manufacturing, and service. The American view of wealth is that its accumulation is a by-product of serving the general good. Entrepreneurs are regarded as social heroes in the business sector. *Jiriki* in the material world. The music industry, sports, and entertainment media have become avenues to wealth, second only to the socially unacceptable illegal drug industry. The common shadow is the psychological tie of success with competitive needs, which often causes confusion of financial reward with personal merit. (Winners are rich and losers are poor.)

Change or Progress. Human nature can be improved and society is moving toward a better way of life. Nothing is impossible when you can get to the moon. Everything changes over time. The shadow of this value is the generation gap, and the poorly schooled and unemployed. *Bonpu-no-joshiki* (everyman's consciousness as opposed to the enlightened consciousness) Zen process changes ordinary thinking or "everyman's consciousness" that is filled with aggression, desire, and ignorance to *kensho,* which is identified by acceptance, peace, and experiential knowing.

Ethical Equality. All individuals are spiritually equal in the sight of God! All people have the opportunity for personal achievement and status. Americans believe in the principle of equal rights before the law. Law is to preserve the rights of the individual—the few from the many, as well as the many from the few. The shadow of this value is criminal manipulation of prejudice and legalities to gain unfair advantage. Ours is the most litigious society in the world. The wealthy and unscrupulous use lawyers like pit bulls to bully. The legal profession polices its own with the same selfishly shoddy arrogance exhibited by the American Medical Association. Buddhism is essentially democratic and demands that its practitioners relinquish aversion toward any human being. *Ahimsa* (Sanskrit for no death-taking, or pain-giving, or no harming) extends equality to the treatment of all living things. Taoism is more elitist, but the Japanese are notorious for their syncretism, and like Bruce Lee stated in *The Tao of Jeet Kune Do,* "Take what is useful."

Equal Opportunity. Americans accept the belief that no matter what the birth, an individual can rise in the economic and social system. Free public education is a means of helping people rise and a responsibility of the government. The shadow is allowing the government to remove freedom of thought, and the shadow of that is ignorant, unscientifically trained members on the school boards or cronyism in hiring when expertise is required. The family-and-friends systems do not guarantee the same quality of life as continuous improvement, which always requires new ideas to test. When we fail to support our public school system, we fail the next generation. This is the most complex society in the world. A newcomer, or child, must learn the language, catch up in education, learn the basic social skills and generally accepted laws, and make himself or herself useful by finding employment. The competition is fierce. It is not over until you quit or die. *Tenjo tenge yuiga dokusan* (working your way to transcendence and completion by facing your own devils). The Way of Endurance is similar. When you are dealing with a ninja master who only focuses on the taijutsu, you may experience what one of my gatherers-of-intelligence calls "the imprudent teachings of the redneck ninja from hell."

Effort and Optimism. Work is a way of realizing God's grace. No problem is too big, or too complicated. Americans are always busy, even when relaxing. This action orientation sometimes fails to reward deep thought in the young. The shadow is imagination and creativity are often seen as laziness by those who have little of it. *Tariki* ("power of the other") is the belief that through associating with good people of similar belief, doing good works, and reciting Buddha's name (like doing the Jesus Prayer), realization will be accomplished. *Ikkan* (pleasure in integrity) can be translated as keep going or keep playing; it is a favorite ninja expression attached to a number of mottoes, such as *Ninpo Ikkan* or *Bufu Ikkan.*

Pragmatism, Practicality, and Efficiency. Americans believe in getting things done in the most efficient way. The shadow is they often mistake speed for efficiency, and quantity for quality. Short-term thinking rewards partial solutions to complex problems—curing symptoms as opposed to addressing causes. Abstract thinking, long-term planning, and creativity are thought to be the realm of eggheads and intellectuals. In the rush to be doing something constructive, people will often neglect the value that broad practical experience can bring to problem-solving ability. *Jiriki* again. *Sennin* (devotion to what works over time) is the the name of the Japanese mountain mystics' version of yoga that emphasizes chi kung breathing techniques.

Rejection of Authority. Americans feel a deep hatred of restraints by social organizations and hierarchical personal authority, which is supported by history. They believe in freedom from unwarranted authority. Americans believe in freedom of choice and generally respect that right in others—abortion and gay rights being notable exceptions. They think of protecting rights rather than enforcing duties. Government is expected not to hinder free enterprise. Free enterprise is expected not to harm employees, customers, or the environment. The shadow is rules are made to be broken. If laws are not seen to benefit in the short term or too difficult to enforce, they are largely ignored. Prohibition is an easy example. Americans usually recognize that you cannot legislate morality but can tax the hell out of vices. Failure to control some vices is disastrous to the body politic or biologic. Criminals should not be allowed to accumulate great wealth when they adversely affect the common good. The stupidity of moralizing drug laws has destroyed many of our inner cities. *Jiriki* again. Art and creativity require breaking free from the old to grasp the new. Ninpo as a martial art teaches creativity through a physical medium that allows endless choices for the practitioner evolving from a traditional base of combat-proven techniques. There is no right or wrong way to do a technique beyond discovering what works. Benjamin Franklin wrote in *Poor Richard's Almanac,* "Laws too gentle are seldom obeyed; too severe, seldom executed."

Science and Secular Rationality. For Americans, even chaos has natural laws. Americans believe in an ordered universe where evolution and change allow for prediction and control. Through science, technology, and problem-solving, the people "can continually improve both themselves and the external conditions" (Steele and Redding, above). The shadow is positivist rationalism. Over-emphasis on rationality weakens the ability to use intuition. Americans mistrust "their guts." That action speaks louder than words is a belief that carries the short-term thinker into entry-level jobs with cognitive skills that keep them there. McDonald's is a trap for the unwary whose communication skills have to be developed to ask "Hold the pickle?" as well as a great place to enter the market economy. "Ideas have consequences" is a rhetorical truism that when viewed as a negative statement—rather than an encouragement to problem-solving—is an interpretation with severe social consequences, according to both the psychologist and the strategist. When we only show the "good," our children fall easy prey, first to the censors, and then to excess. Disestablishmentarianism or separation of Church and State was a fundamental value of the American founders, fifty out of the fifty-six signers of the Declaration of Independence belonged to the Scottish Rite of Free Masonry which emphasizes freedom of religion. James Madison, an ultraconservative, wrote a lengthy treatise on religious liberty. Buddhists recommend deep study before committing to any belief system, and to be very skeptical of scripture and "armchair research." *Kokoro* (total commitment of being) is manifested by using all the powers of consciousness—mind, heart, and spirit.

Sociality. People who are attractive with outgoing, friendly personalities are rewarded in American society. The shadow is beautiful people may succeed by standing around. Modeling pays extremely well. Peer pressure and needs for approval compete with personal growth, often creating a fear of being alone. Name recognition quotients are hardly a measure of quality. Americans dislike a facile surface and fear being "taken" by a smooth talker. The wavering rationality of Bill Clinton was made to appear "slick" to appeal to this shadow value. Kindness is perceived as weakness by the predatory. *Amae* (acceptance of others) is the core value of Japanese socialization, demanding compassion for all human beings. *Yako Zen* (wild fox Zen), the Zen of those who pretend to be enlightened, is similar to the money-grubbing Christianity we see evoked by television evangelists, or the wisdom of politicians displayed in media sound bites, or the humor of Rush Limbaugh.

Material Comfort. Americans believe that a high standard of living reflects work and leads to happiness. The richest class in America inherited from their ancestors and the once-bountiful resources of the continent, or work in established organizations. They tend to forget that happiness is a by-product of doing well. Material comfort often creates unlimited desire for more. "More, Mommy. Give me more!" casts a hard shadow over limited resources. People should develop a realistic appreciation of their real worth in a competitive society. Musashi in the Earth chapter of *The Book of Five Rings* posits nine principles to be internalized by the strategist. The fifth is, "Distinguish between gain and loss in worldly matters." Compassion is the hardest social skill to learn, but experience of poverty can be a helper on this one. That is why monks are sent out to beg for their meals. My older sister suggests strongly that politicians who cut funds from adult education should have the opportunity to practice their survival skills on the typical welfare payment of four or five thousand a year, and see how they do at keeping their family and friends. *Hakushi* (white paper mind) is the absence of desire that manifests through emptying the mind of expectations, and is useful to viewing reality without emotional coloring.

Quantification. Americans like measurement. They're competitors. They think in terms of bigness. Bigness is good. Big cars, big bombs, big muscles, often leading to big mouths and hungry spirits. Quantity is usually stressed over quality. Get 'em out. Keep 'em moving. Get ahead of the Joneses. Beat the Russians. The shadow of this value is not paying attention to many of the small details that encourage quality of life. Spirit is subtle and moves in mysterious ways, not always following a standard convention. Competition with others sometimes prevents close examination of the self. Many small moves can equal one large one. The shadow of competition is jealousy. The emphasis for the jealous is the end, not the means. The darkest shadow is believing that your own way, or winning, is everything. Those who participate in silly events like the Ultimate Fighting Championship prove nothing but their hubris. The most common winning move in no-holds-barred open tournaments is pulling down your opponent's head and kneeing him in the face. Not what I would call a skill move, though effective. *Hen-chu-sho* (the second level of enlightenment) manifests as non-distinction, or not perceiving things or events through judgment but accepting their existence as a neutral process. Study on this. *Ken-chu-shi* (entering the two aspects, or in Ninpo "living the dual mandala") recognizes the uniqueness of all, which requires acceptance of differences and learning to use them wisely.

External Conformity. The shadow of the powerful drive to individuation is the desire to please in order to conform to or be accepted by some group. We are, after all, social animals. Separatism is not the American Way. Some groups have very low standards for acceptance. Groucho Marx found great humor in social situations. He said he wouldn't want to join a club that would actually seek him for a member. The ninja assumes identity with the group he or she is associating with, or spying on, to avoid discovery. *Ken-chu-to* (living in the midst of both realities) is spontaneous but correct reaction to any situation. The *Wen-Tzu* says the sages "have no strange clothing or weird behavioral patterns. . . They are different, but not strange."

Humor. Americans are funny. Their humor is egalitarian in nature. They poke fun at arrogance, stupidity, most human folly, their selves, their sexual practice, their spouses, children, ethnic differences, their work, their bosses, their intellectuals, their leaders, their religions—whatever strikes their sense of the absurd. Americans like to put everyone on the same level. The shadow of this value is the negative joke that reduces one's humanity. Sarcasm and knocking others' success is an easy way to pretend authority. People in power regard a critic with suspicion. Cassandra of Troy would not reach many ears here, either. Those who advance by knocking others do not contribute to growth. Happy Ho Tai (the Shinto god usually shown as a middle-aged, big-bellied, grinning man doing an overhead chi kung shoulder stretch) is the Buddha of laughter.

Generosity and Considerateness. Americans are genuine humanitarians, especially materially. Americans believe in sharing their way of life as if they were missionaries of Democracy. They have literally rebuilt the economic, social, and political systems of their defeated enemies to reflect more closely their own model. It's a good thing, for the most part. Our friends go to war almost as often as we do, but traditionally we come to the rescue. Columbia prefers trade to warfare. Athena prefers education to warfare. Liberty cherishes the refugee. The shadow is applying the solution inappropriately. It does no good to provide welfare without training, education, and accountability, whether on a national or local scale. Aesop's fable concerning the fate of the grasshopper who played and fiddled all summer and the ants who worked and stored their grain may strike a chord as winter approaches. To quote Ben Franklin, "He that would catch fish must venture his bait" (*Selections from Poor Richard's Almanac,* Avenel, 1982). Compassion for all sentient beings is the end result of satori. Hatsumi says often, "A true martial artist does not lose kindness." The *Wen-Tzu* offers this commentary, "The higher the status, the humbler one should be. The greater the office, the more careful one should be. The larger the income, the more generous one should be. One who follows these three principles will not be resented."

Patriotism. Americans are loyal to their traditions and values. They exhibit a willingness to be good citizens, to be proud of the United States, to defend it from external aggression. When American ninja at the Hawaiian Tai Kai stopped practice to salute the flag of a passing marching band, Hatsumi-soke was surprised and impressed. He liked that. He later remarked to Kevin, "It is no wonder the Americans cannot be defeated."

Gorgias, that florid Greek rhetorician who was scorned by Socrates, opens his humorous *Encomium to Helen* with "A city is adorned by good citizenship, the body by beauty, the soul by wisdom, acts by virtue, and speech by truthfulness. But, the opposites of these values are a disgrace. Man and woman, word and deed, city and government, we ought to praise if praise worthy, and blame if blame worthy, for it is equally wrong and stupid to censure what is commendable and to commend what is censurable" (James J. Murphy, ed., *A Synoptic History of Classical Rhetoric,* Random House, 1972). It would seem even the doughty and cynical Greeks did not let their patriotism rank above their good sense.

Americans sometimes fail to recognize aggression that does not appear warlike, as they are individualists and allow strangers a great deal of rope. This also applies to government folly. When the government truly disgusts them and makes it hard to believe in the sanctity of their chosen land, citizens protest, march on Washington, and burn effigies and flags to attract the attention of unheeding politicians, who forget their place at the trough is at the will of the people. During election years bum listeners are voted out. "Freedom from" even extends to patriotic fervor. Outsiders often mistake this behavior as not loving, or being unwilling to serve the flag. Americans willingly serve the blind beauty Justice and her sister Liberty with a vengeance that is awesome to behold and terrifying to those who have tread upon them. The shadow is knee-jerk jingoism. The American Legion, to which I belong, labored to pass an amendment to the Constitution "protecting" Old Glory. I think that was a well-intended mistake. Freedom of behavior is more important than symbols. In 204 years there have been only seventeen changes to the Constitution after the Bill of Rights. All of these but the eighteenth (Prohibition) extended individual freedom or democratic process. This flag amendment should also be repealed. It is simply an opportunity for politicians to wrap themselves in the flag, and with an average of six flag burnings a year, it makes no sense beyond creating a media event. It would be wiser to create an

amendment barring amendments to a document that has preserved the vision of the men who created it for over two hundred years. This is a necessary protection from obvious
scoundrels whose vision barely extends past the results of the
latest poll.

Flag-wavers and false enthusiasm are regarded in a more
dangerous category than false advertising. No president of the
United States, except Richard Nixon, has flagrantly attempted
to cheat the will of the people. Even George Washington refused
to become king when given that role by Congress. This way of
life is unique and serves as a burning torch for the enlightenment of the rest of the world, even when we forget and fail to
sustain our moral obligations as human beings and Americans.
Ninja were political advisors to some of the shogun and emperors of Japan because of their understanding of human nature
and esoteric skills. If you are not paying attention to the political scene and exercising your rights, you are missing part of
your training concerning living well in both realities. The weaker
the central government, the safer you are as a citizen. The Taoists
of old would consider many of our present elected leaders as
little more than robber barons ravishing the environment. The
advisers may be skilled in wresting income, but the trickle-down
has obviously failed to bear fruit when creativity is stifled and
expectations do not fit the reality of a changing market or simple greed of the Boesky stripe. You do not wait for the invisible
hand when it seeks quality. States with unemployment as high
as fourteen percent find it difficult to feed the few at the top
when the middle class is disappearing. When junior politicians
can feed at the public trough to the tonnage of over a hundred
thousand a year in a city that seems to be growing because of
special interests, they find it difficult to understand the plight
of a single mother abandoned by family struggling to pull six
or seven thousand together. A new form of GI Bill is needed.
Bushido (the way of the warrior) posits that one should be loyal

to one's country first, leader second, family third, and self last. The American Constitution wisely reverses this order to protect the individual. Bushido is the way of death.

Shadow Values in the Martial Arts

Miyamoto Musashi, in the *Go Rin No Sho (The Book of Five Rings)* Wind chapter, discusses which martial behaviors he thinks do not add luster to the Way. His commentary seems directed toward much of what I see prevalent in the teaching of many so-called martial artists today. One should very carefully read and think about what this man had to say. He is considered *Kensei* (a sword saint)—the human equivalent of Saint George or the Archangel Michael to millions of intelligent people. I have read him cover to cover at least once a year in various translations for fifteen years. I often look up what he has to say about a technique or situation. He won more than sixty recorded duels, many to the death (Some historians suggest there may have been as many more unrecorded), and participated in six wars.

Musashi had a terrible reputation for disconcerting his opponents by unexpected behavior. He was even accused of cheating when his opponents were seventy to one. He was a generalist, and in touch with his shadow such that his words translate easily into modern strategy for the intelligent reader. He was dark enough to put traps into his directions for swordsmen, so only the experienced and intelligent would understand and avoid—a form of reverse psychology so effective with the aggressive, oppositional, competitive, and approval-seeking. These directions are probably responsible for many aggressive anal retentives achieving their beloved samurai death over the centuries. Musashi early on states that he does not like oaths, which establishes his ronin status. It also establishes his honesty for someone who knows that oaths invariably lead to lies. Musashi was a follower of the heart. I would want to be certain that a son or daughter of mine were familiar with Musashi's book on strategy, even if they never took up the sword. His criticism of the schools of his time could be directed toward many of the "hothouse flowers" prevalent in these peaceful times supposedly ruled by law and order. (There have been more than one hundred and twenty wars since I was born in 1944, and few major cities have not seen their poor riot in the street, or felt the curse of gangs.)

In the foreword to the Wind chapter, Musashi states his complaints about other martial arts schools, such as getting carried away with display, and overly rewarding political and business acumen. These attitudes are relevant today. Shoddy self-defense systems perpetuate the greed of both instructor and student by how the belt licensing is structured. The more colored belts you see, the more cautious you should be. A big warning is seeing a belt other than black with stripes and hashmarks like a Marine lifer's sleeve. When you see a black belt with a bunch of stripes, it should be topped by a lot of gray hair. Some systems allow the practice of "time in grade" belts, which is a bit like Union feather-bedding, as one seems to be rewarded for standing around rather than working on the self or the appointed task. The instructor has a paying student who doesn't take up much time. The student has friends who don't respect him or the system. A little self-study outside the shelter of the temple might be more appropriate. When belts are given without an appreciable standard of physical or mental accomplishment, or simply sold in a primarily physical system, it is a political and economic trifle that contributes little to character or spirit. Paying for what you have not earned destroys the reputation of the school and renders your instructor's license and student certificates worthless. Paying for what you cannot use is like paying for a steel sword and getting one made from tin.

I seriously have no idea what has led so many high-level martial artists in different systems to regard my work with such favor. I was actually awarded Instructor of the Year 1992 at the North American Karate and Kenpo Championships. It's a small plaque, but a great honor, and with seventy-five cents will get me a cup of coffee in this economy. I have noticed that the techniques I share from Ninpo consistently surprise and work against senior-level practitioners from most other martial arts. They were probably grateful for being taught something that works. I continually force myself to return to the fundamentals of white belt teaching and painstakingly examine myself and the new client to draw out the secrets—whether physical, mental, or spiritual— he or she must teach me so that we both can learn to be most effective in our lives. The basic postures and movements of Budo Taijutsu and hoshin are filled with useful variations and tricks that work best from a stable, balanced, yet pliable platform, directed by a quick mind that understands the consequence of letting your feelings make the choice. Intuitional feeling comes before intellectual thought, and both precede action.

Theocracy and The Shadow

Sogyal Rinpoche in *The Tibetan Book of Living and Dying* (Harper San Francisco, 1992), a book that has many valuable ideas concerning meditation, points out that for too many of us, our lives are like housekeeping in a dream, and the external distractions of modern civilization seem a celebration of all those things that lead away from the essential joys of internal, personal development. His discussion of living life with an understanding of death is critical to real spiritual development. It is important to be able to look into the mind of a person from another culture and see what might be missing from your own. Great minds think alike on many issues, but the differences are where the fun starts. As we tend not to believe that the soul is immortal, we fear death of any type and treat death as an awful event to be feared, rather than a termination of this body and an escape into a different existence. It is the fear of death that allows religion to have such a pervasive and authoritarian hold on the minds of many. When the spiritual side of living is mostly ignored in a material culture, death is regarded as an end rather than a change or a part of the process of living. *Sho-chu-hen* (the first level of enlightenment in Zen) manifests as a realization that the true self resides in the body as spirit. The spirit communicates with the socialized mind through intuition.

Governments, large business organizations, and religions share similar strategies for controlling those living under their restrictions. Governments that side with religion tend to be authoritarian, as God is on their side. This situation has been associated with extreme economic decline after the industrial revolution. It is only necessary to glimpse the effects of Old Shinto and Buddhism on Japan, Roman Catholicism across South America, and Fundamental Baptists and Evangelicals in the US of A's Deep South, or to walk the streets of Beirut, Amman, Jerusalem, Rome, or Calcutta to realize there is a problem or shadow to all religious perspectives that demand governmental authority. When a scientist looks at religion, he or she may assume the viewpoint of a rhetorician, psychologist, or sociologist as being far safer and saner than that of a theologian. Below I cite the root or core principle of the seven most popular religions in the world listed by age of existence or primacy. Analysis of root principles reveals interesting similarities:

Hinduism: "This is the sum of duty: Do naught unto others which would cause pain if done to you." Mahabharata 5:1517.

Taoism: "Regard your neighbor's gain as your own gain, and your neighbor's loss as your own." Tai-Shang Kan-Ying P'ien.

Judaism: "What is hateful to you, do not to your fellow man. That is the entire Law; all the rest is commentary." Talmud, Shabbat 31a.

Buddhism: "Hurt not others in ways you yourself would find hurtful." The Book of Nature.

Christianity: "All things whatsoever ye would that men should do to you, do ye even so to them; for this is the Law and the Prophets." Matthew 7:12. King James Version

Confucianism: "Is there one maxim that should be acted on one's whole life? Surely it is the maxim of loving kindness. Do not unto others what you would not have them do unto you." Analects 15:23.

Islam: "No one of you is a believer until he desires for his brother that which he desires for himself." Sunan.

As you look at this list you can see the emphasis on fairness, balance, and reciprocity that stands as the core of how one is to act when dealing with another human being. These are rules which will sustain one through most social situations. The only problem is that historically these behaviors were only extended to those perceived as one's "own kind." There is a shadowy psychological problem that exists in many people which derives from inability to generalize the feeling of love or open acceptance of others. I refer to it as the "Love Is Pie Syndrome." When love is pie, once you give a slice it is gone. If you give a slice to Fred, then you can't give a slice to Mary. One must carefully ration love, so as not to waste what is a precious commodity. Love as pie results in jealousy and is a sign of poor parenting and limited understanding of the nature of love. If God is love as the mystics in every major religion opine, then love is not a commodity but an undying, universal presence which cannot be exhausted by use or the Second Law of Thermodynamics. Love is the learned result of kind behavior in the intelligent. It can grow, or it can wither, but you can never have too much or give too much away, particularly to a child. If you have ever been adored by someone you respect, you will know of what I write. Love is not pie. Study on this.

I have no problem with Sinead O'Connor singing "War" and tearing up a picture of the Pope. Her viewpoint is enraged Taoist. Gaelic Bards have oft been troublesome to those who pay for the privilege of listening to their siren songs. Her spirit remembers a less regimented time; her methods harm no one and may cause some to think in a more constructive manner. The Popes have a history of being consistently political since the third century. If you need a real horror story concerning the power of Popes, get a historian to describe what actually happened during the Crusades. There were two Popes, one French and one Italian, pissing on each other and thoroughly screwing up Europe during the fourteenth century. At that time robber barons literally ruled after The Hundred Years War. Our current Polish prince of the papacy is slow to recognize change. Jews should remember well the cleansing flames of first the Inquisition and later the Holocaust. The locations of most of the Nazi death camps were east of Germany. In 1992, Rome decided to recant Galileo's persecution for noticing the Earth was not the center of the universe after four hundred years. Mary, mother of Jesus, was not canonized until the twentieth century. Ms. O'Connor has a right to complain about Papal tradition. When a religion claims absolute authority over its herd, it's supposed to be right. The Roman Catholic Church has failed miserably in its evocation of love, primarily by avoiding the reality of feminine spirituality.

Catholic-bashing is easy, as the Church often seems to act as the educational and political arm of the Holy Roman Empire, but Protestants have little to be proud of, if recent and historical political behavior mirror spiritual accomplishment. A discussion in Chapter Nine of charismatic attributes associated with Budo, Ninpo, Christianity, Islam, Buddhism, Native American shamanism, and Hindu yoga demonstrates quite clearly that they have little to do with religion or saintliness, if by that we are talking about "the good" as a collection of rules passed down by the elders concerning worship.

The Shadow Revealed through Selection of Heroes and Villains

The values of people are revealed by how they describe the actions of others in prose, poetry, legend, or simple conversation. In communication this is called rhetoric, an ancient study similar to modern psychology mixed with marketing. The selection of heroes and villains reveals the aspects of the desired ideal self. Cultural heroes and heroines are held up as exemplars of possible behavior for the community. The stuff of legends. The individual immersed in his or her particular culture may have little awareness of the power of the vision of the self one is becoming—the rich self, the thin self, the brave and daring self, the wise and knowing self, the loved and admired self. The reality also includes the shadow self you fear becoming—the unemployed self, the alcoholic self, the cowardly and fearful self, the fat and flabby self, the academically failed self, the hated and despised self. Such possible selves motivate us to make choices that avoid the latter and work toward the former (Inglehart, Markus, and Brown, *Recent Advances in Social Psychology: An International Perspective,* North-Holland: Elsevier Science Publishers, 1989). Who are your heroes? What do they tell you about your self? Cultural heroes and media heroes tell us what is valued. Below are some heroes and villains to test your shadow skills of identification.

The natural skills of the mountain people used in the hunting and poaching of the white-tailed deer allowed an American WW I hero, Sergeant York, to easily capture a terrified company of Teutonic city dwellers when he began his sniper's stalk in the muddy trenches and blasted horror of No Man's Land. He did not fix bayonet and call out a champion; he cut the blonde haired beauties down from a distance under cover. When the war was over, York returned to his beloved mountain valleys and lived to a ripe old age with a clear conscience, for his enemy was tyrannical.

Musashi finally retired under the protection of a samurai lord and died of old age. When he died, lightning split the sky. Lightning goes up, not down. I've had conservative friends throw up Nazi architect Albert Speer as an example of a clever organization builder. Speer served Adolph Hitler, an insane Jew- and Gypsy-murdering tyrant molded from the hell of WW I and the harsh treaties typical of European chauvinism, which is second only to the barbaric, comic opera cruelties of the less sophisticated Balkans. Audey Murphy was rejected by the Marines and Navy to become the most decorated officer in World War Two which he followed by a brief movie career to become a successful business mogul. Speer died in an Allied prison for war criminals.

Capitalist Bernard Baruch built a better war machine and ate the Nazis' lunch. Now we have Serbs to admire as war criminals instead of freedom-fighters in the Balkans, as history does repeat itself to those who can't learn and change. The Serbs started WW I by assassinating Archduke Ferdinand of Austria. The United Nations and our allies treated these ethnic-cleansing barbarians to the spectacle of super-powers wringing their hands like distressed chamberlains. The recent Gulf War, which involved hundreds of thousands of US troops and allies, is beginning to be treated as a police action, when in reality it was a major war. Schwarzkopf, with admirable brilliance and intelligence showed the utility of Sun Tzu to a tyrant attempting to fight WW III with a WW I mentality. I use these examples as they represent clear choices, where Korea, Vietnam, and Grenada still confuse me. Ambrose Bierce, a Yankee hero from our War Between the States, who became a controversial writer depicted war in his collection of short stories *Tales of Soldiers and Civilians* as that arena where the best and worst are trapped in the same location.

War heroism is writ large in our history. However, just creating a worthwhile life for yourself and others can require heroic action. Many are unsung who labor in thankless positions to feed their households, raise their children to be good in a decaying social environment, and labor to improve their skills. The heroes and heroines that one chooses as a source of inspiration need not be recognized as such by others. When times are difficult and one has to run against the wind, the image of the hero who endured strengthens one's will to keep going. True heroism is making a difference in how people want to live. Lao Tzu points out that "When horses are used to pull war chariots out of the city gates, rather than market goods in, the leaders have lost the Way." Sport occasionally provides valuable lessons. For a psychologist, the Houston Rockets' struggle to repeat winning the NBA Championship in 1995 showed clearly that teamwork, accepting the challenge of opportunity, and maintaining integrity are more the characteristics of champions than greed, hostility, egocentrism, youth, talent, and unbridled competitiveness. The spirit is eternal.

The conservatives claim that our children have no heroes. They are wrong. Today's heroes emerge as media events and posters in a million adolescent bedrooms. The heroes of the next generation may not be who we would choose, but they are just as real and influential.

The Shadow in Big Business

Failure to recognize and downsize its shadow made General Motors easy pickings for the Japanese, as Rome was to the Goths and Huns. In their arrogance, GM's ruling executives refused to collect intelligence, ignored the screams of the customer for too long, and were content to rest in their confidence before the battle was enjoined. Sun Tzu's maxim "The best sword is never drawn" has three meanings. The decade of the 1980s was commonly called the "Era of Greed," as if that were the equivalent of the "Era of Swing." Greed can be defined as the taking of what is not your own on a consistent basis. It is theft through dominance of the weaker. I was amazed, as a Leadership consultant, at the number of twits who could not make a connection between their behavior and the economic situation. The quality and acceptance formula discussed in the last chapter helps one to understand the effect of people on performance. A more complex world needs leaders and teachers who can impose elegant solutions to complex problems. When a major corporation hits the wall, it can create as well as destroy legends. Think of this as a cautionary bed-time tale for the children of stockbrokers.

In a time not so long ago, or far away, it was evident that the vision of leadership was blurred and no longer directed to benefit the marketplace or those who served it. The hard men who had fought long years to wrest their positions of power, created by their fathers who had conquered the known world in a fight against the most monstrous tyrannies of the slave-killing ultra-right, were content to exploit and defend their holdings. They rode the highways of their wealthy and heavily forested land on huge iron steeds of many colors, and failed to notice the hordes of smaller, plainer, fish-like steeds circling their borders, or when they did, they only laughed at their small pretensions to economy and quality. The voice of the turtledove (read customer) had not been heard in the land between the great once-clear waters for many years.

The blue-shirted workers bowed their heads in shame and humiliation, as their managers flailed at shadows. Their beloved children were not following them into the plants, but faced a readier death in the streets of a financially raddled, corrupt, and crack-possessed Detroit, where even the fortress Ren Cen and inner city universities—havens of learning for the urban dwellers—felt the rough touch of drug dealers, murderers, and rapists. Surely God's face was turned from them.

Small yellow men with strange names like Taichi Ohno, following the ideas of Weaver Watcher Toyoda, wrested trade and sustenance from the Americans. The Michiganders' blonde, blue-eyed women looked askance at the scantiness of their fur offerings. One of their great Sellers of Ideas and Chryslers, like Machiavelli begging from the Medici, was forced to go on welfare from the Great Fathers in Washington. Detroiters could feel a cold wind ripping across Lake Michigan from the financial districts of Chicago, which withered the flowers in Grosse Pointe.

The Year of Our Lord 1987 was as harsh as a notice of foreclosure to the auto industry. It reeked of the loss of goodwill from a customer too often treated with the uneven hand of the arrogant. It was fishy with carrion. For customers to turn the cheek once again and accept a "promise of excitement" for their hard-earned and shrinking supply of money was increasingly a fantasy nurtured only by the ethnocentric, the car executives, and the UAW. Apple pie and motherhood no longer drew the buyers to Chevrolet. Beautiful Dinah was too old to blow for youth worshippers with short attention spans. The big smooth ride and slide was crumbling and crashing into the rocky shores of international competition.

When people don't buy cars, or do buy cars made in other countries, it takes a major hunk of the future out of Michigan. As their slice of the medium-price and luxurious big-car market share shrank, and their bonuses increased, the executives of General Motors watched in disbelief as Ross Perot and Roger Smith wrangled above them on the fourteenth floor. The small yellow men stealthily applying Miyamoto Musashi's famed sword strategy of "attacking the corners" followed by "rat's head to ox neck" ripped competitively into GM's share of the marketplace for a chunk of gold that tilted Tokyo.

There were experiments to see if American workers could be organized under Japanese management techniques—which they learned from us, strangely enough—making the question of can Japanese methods apply to the American workplace moot to anyone who understood human beings. Somehow the "scrolls of higher knowledge" written by Deming and Maier were passed to the financial people, who are not known for physical creativity, and the knowledge of process manufacturing with a human face was lost.

Skip LeFauve was putting together the Saturn team, which the barterers of General Motors' conventional knowledge hoped and expected to go belly up. They felt it a waste of time to re-enter the small-car market where they had been so thoroughly thrashed. (Conservatives look to the past for leadership, as vision is a creative process.) It bodes well for the future that Skip ignored the prophecies of the elders. Skip admirably set a new standard for excellence through total continuous improvement, including the dealership practices and advertising. (Working for him was always more interesting than working for anyone else. He is one of General Motors' few surviving great men. It takes tremendous flexibility and engineering know- how to do a start-up right.)

The Engine Division, where I labored for Arv Mueller, a creative engineer, was fighting constantly to get funding for the Northstar System, based on Quad 4 technology. The corporate fiscal wizards in leadership positions at that time wanted to stick with a low-tech, aluminum block engine that leaked oil. Arv had me put together a Leadership training seminar to prepare the supervisors and union leadership for changes to come. The program I developed with Ed Purchis and Bob Simpson and a lot of line supervisor and worker "input" included: Deming statistical methodology; personality and stress evaluation; meditation; teamwork; firewalking; board breaking; problem-solving; communication skills; sharing the business plan; and strategy. Within six months the program's accountability system revealed more than five hundred quality improvements in the manufacturing process, which saved the division millions of dollars as well as raised quality standards significantly as measured by the customer. We ran 4000 supervisors, managers, union officers, and employees through this program over a three year period.

After Arv was moved to Chevrolet and my protector on the fourteenth floor left the corporation in disgust, the program was dropped (a victim of the not-invented-here syndrome), as it did not conform to the corporate headquarters' sponsored program. Their concept of positive leadership was mostly training in sucking up to your boss while presenting a positive image to outsiders.

Electronic Data Systems, with GM's wealth, had become the largest privately owned electrical data service and telephone company in the world. EDS was charged with unifying GM under one communication system. The reorganization of General Motors into platform groups to break the power of the car lines was only a small part of this culture war. EDS has performed far better with Ross Perot out of the picture. I find it interesting that the Motor Division went in five years from what a headquarters executive described to me "as an obscure collection of plants under Buick-Oldsmobile-Cadillac" to the "heart and soul" of the corporation. Eventually GM's Board, reacting to stock declines, retired the politicians and accountants who mostly protected their fiefdoms. Northstar and Saturn represent the heroic strategists opposed to the entrenched bureaucracy.

The Shadow in the Classroom

The classrooms of the community college where I taught psychology, sociology, and speech part-time after fleeing General Motors were filled with single mothers on Pell grants hesitantly learning the skills to wrest the kind of lives they missed for lack of a real education in their earlier years. There were older men wanting to learn new skills to better their chance at promotion, and many younger students who wanted to get better jobs but could not afford the local private schools with their high tuition.

It's a heady brew to teach where you can be a service to the community and have colleagues who love the art of teaching. (Like the combatic martial arts, higher education does not pay well, particularly on a part-time basis. It offers an economic choice only a fool or lover would accept, considering the sacrifice.) The students as a whole have short attention spans. They are not well read and have problems applying what they read to their own lives. Transfer of training requires imagination, and their passive schooling by network television has created an interesting inability to exercise critical thinking. Many discover to their shock that education guarantees neither employment nor higher wages when the economy is stagnant and unemployment is high. The marketplace only consistently rewards acceptable quality.

Excess appears normal to such people, and apathy or violence are the most common ways to solve problems, as thousands of hours of passively watching poorly performed soaps, sitcoms, and snippets of news have hampered their ability to critically think for themselves. The more they are lost in illusion, the more they see actors as heroes (rather like their grandfathers buying the tales of Ned Buntline, or people who perceive John Wayne as a military hero). They follow the "Soaps" and talk about the characters as if they were neighbors. Yet they can smoke, sip a drink, or put on lipstick at seventy miles an hour while driving, hearing music, and talking to a friend.

These students learn fast when they recognize advantage and get past the short-term rewards of their chosen lifestyle. They have great courage and possibility for flow. They are more fun to train than lions. (Even an alcoholic's brain begins to recover and grow back from the horrors of dehydration, if kept from the sauce for a few years.) I make them write questions on each chapter, on anything they want to know, and that usually eats up an hour or so every night. We call it "stump the prof!" I make them write essays on how the reading material can apply to their lives—most fail, and some tell the most glorious lies. I give open-book tests on multiple- guess abstracts and they go nuts trying to find the answers in the time limit, learning that research is not easy. Their reading and writing improve, because not only are they involved, but they fear returning to the world they have left. The streets are meaner than when I was a boy. Vietnam is only one of many recent betrayals of public trust by our government.

When I taught at Wayne State University in Detroit the school experimented with an open admissions policy. The students that entered the university under this policy had an eighty percent drop-out rate. I was given three sections of these uninitiated to inculcate into the ways of academe. In addition to course content (Speech) I taught them through role-playing where to sit, how to stay awake, how to ask questions, how professors identified "good" and "bad" students, and how to make positive impressions. My sections carried a 3.0 or better in their other classes. All the students, but one older woman, made it through their first year, and all the rest returned the next. They were smart enough, but no one had ever shown them how to act, or that success in a classroom could be strategized like street-smarts. The other sections of street-savages which did not receive my inoculation concerning scholarly expectations maintained the eighty-percent drop-out rate. The failure rate reinforced the faculty expectations.

The Individual Whose Shadow Has Awakened

As the use of the intuitive or shadow results in deeper perception, one becomes different from those who are not as aware. The perceptive human being becomes more in tune with nature, and as skill grows through paying attention one finds that there is a loneliness associated with higher consciousness, as most people do not share your abilities. Friendship and compassion become important to maintaining a stable existence in common society. It is as if one has truly become "a wolf in sheep's cloth-ing." Knowing is both an advantage and a barrier in conven-tional social situations. Discretion does become the better part of valor. Lao Tzu says there are times when the animal and ancestor spirits must be felt, but ignored. Sun Tzu recommends making the dark your friend through intelligence. Ninja rule the night. The best teachers of Budo Taijutsu don't put much empha-sis on rank, but have been hanging out for quite a long time. They are the ones who say, "I'm just here to train," and do just that. You must research this carefully.

"The Way," and "Other Thoughts,"
by Steve Noonkesser, strategist lurking in Manokotak, Alaska

The Way
To him untrained—a new power arises,
Bubbles, boils, invigorates, and confounds,
The rainbow rises—colors dance.

Understanding approaches,
First the mechanics—use of this new thing—Power.
The one becomes two,
One Dark, quick, cutting, of telling effect, or so it would
    seem . . .
One Light, slow, benign, power of the old and patient, staying
    power . . .

Untrue assumptions,
The dark is enticing: flesh, speed, the gleaming blade.
Quick gain, iron dominion,
The fall unseen—the long fall . . .

The quiet path
The Light dawns slowly
Encompasses completely
Built of Earth and Wind foundations

The source of the Light is true power
Benevolent strength—caring, protective . . .
Which is chosen?

The gleaming scythe? The oaken staff?

Other Thoughts

That which is touched—might be . . .
That which is heard—could be . . .
That which is seen—may be . . .
That which is sensed—is.

The gut outsmarts the rational brain.
The eye tricks the mind.
The ear fools the heart.
The hand often fumbles.

The spirit does not lie—learn this and believe.

The Way is not in the rules, nor how the game is played.
The Way is not heard, nor seen, nor snared by the intellect.
The Way is in the journey.
The Way is the quest of the spirit.

Six

Using the Force

If you've familiarized yourself with Chinese medicine and particularly the knowledge associated with acupuncture, acupressure, chi kung, koshijutsu, or dim mak, you will find that
there are points on the body that serve as crossroads for its
energy fields, controlling the function of muscles and organs.
Frequent use of the Secret Smile meditative technique strengthens these fields and can rejuvenate the endocrine glands as well
as organs, particularly if used with the Six Healing Breaths or
Sounds. When ninja say things like "the stronger spirit wins,"
they are often referring to the higher energy developed through
chi kung meditative practice, which is more beneficial than Zen
or Vipassana as they are typically taught.

Ninja often discuss the effects of *haragei* (Japanese for belly
breathing) as if they were sounds or vibrations, rather than fields
of energy. This may be due to archaic symbolism relating the five
elements to sound vibrations used in mantra meditation to vibrate
the bones in the head. Most modern research indicates that the
ancient sound "seed" *Aum,* or any other sustained "MMMMM"
sound, will have a similar effect (Ellen J. Langer, *Mindfulness,*
Addison-Wesley, 1989). Subtle Influence or Energy Techniques
have applications beyond breaking bricks or walking on fire,

which are simply focusing techniques to reduce fear. Healing and empathy are far more sophisticated applications and require deep study, true prayer (shaped intention), and meditation.

In Ninpo, *kyojitsu* (weird airs, working with intent, lies that appear as truth, and avoidance techniques) and *shinken-gata* (spirit sword techniques or true combat skills) are considered "great abilities" and are taught through physical techniques, sensitivity drills, and subtle energy confrontations between players as problems to be solved. The beginner is usually impressed by the physical combat skills of the players, and as knowledge of the art deepens, awareness of subtle energy manipulation is first met with amazement or incredulity. Then they realize that if The Boss is showing it, with practice they might be able to learn how to do it. In most martial arts these skills are not taught or even known about—only occasionally mentioned as something some long-dead master was able to do, or discussed as end products without filling in the steps necessary for attainment of the skills. Even in Ninpo, the teaching of kyojitsu is considered (incorrectly by some) to be the exclusive privilege of the soke (Masaaki Hatsumi), and most of the shidoshi and senior teachers only present the taijutsu skills, which are sufficient for most students, given their capabilities. Some shidoshi and shihan have very little exposure to spiritual *shinken*, and there are even a few who refuse to teach it as a means of preserving their station, and a very few who use their incomplete knowledge as a means of keeping their students in the dark. As *shinken* is alien to our general culture, and confusing to many who would pursue Ninpo, Hatsumi-soke has asked me to share my experience.

In this chapter I discuss the healing, psychic, and fighting applications of chi in very general terms, so that you can allow your own experience to fill in between the lines. If you are following a meditative practice that emphasizes the control and following of the breath, much of what I discuss will be familiar. For those of you who are learning ninjutsu or some other fighting art only for the efficient destruction of your created enemies, much of what I now say will be imponderable. To paraphrase Gautama Siddhartha (the first universally recognized Buddha) on the nature of man: "All people are difficult to understand, those that desire are easiest to predict, but the one who has attained the Void can neither be understood as other men, nor predicted."

Healing

In the colloquial, the art of healing is sometimes described as "The Gift," and those who make you feel good are considered gifted. The gift of healing is most often discussed as a human characteristic that is accidental or even genetic, but it does not seem to be determined by sex, age, race, or social status. It can be studied and learned by the intelligent and sensitive. In the East, medicine and the martial arts have a long history of being entwined. Poison is the shadow of herbology, dim mak the shadow of acupressure, and butchery the shadow of surgery. The great healers often claim that self-love is the first step to becoming. Loving one's self, or even knowing one's self, requires acceptance of the shadow self. Acceptance of the rejected weaknesses we perceive in ourselves, or "ways that I would never be," or dislikes, is only a mild skirmish with personality or the social self. The intensity of battle increases as we awaken the inner demons that abide as survival mechanisms in our animal nature. The principles and disciplines of Budo, which I recently overheard some street kids discuss as "the ninja religion," are necessary safeguards for containing and guiding the beast within, particularly for those who were not raised in a loving environment. The masters of healing opine that you have to clean up your own act or at least be working on it before you will have any consistent success in healing others, particularly on the spiritual level. The Tibetan spiritual healers recommend transmuting one's own darker emotions and even the client's darkness into positive lighter emotions for the greatest healing power. This can be high-risk, as the stronger spirit wins.

True creativity resides in the survival mechanisms of the so-called primitive brain, as the cortex developed later and is the seat of analytical thought. Hanuman, the monkey general and hero of Hindu mythology, is a representation of our unconscious, or animal nature. The emotions and intuition can be greatly supported by analytical power, but feeling is the key to healing (probably why most medical doctors in the former USSR were women, and grossly under-paid for their expertise). Psychotherapy can help you accept your shadow, but chi kung breathing, energy circling, or some aspects of Kriya yoga will allow the total integration of mind, body, and spirit, resulting in the ability to focus one's attention and direction. I haven't mastered really damping down my energy, as I trust my self-healing mechanisms to keep me healthy. Modern microbes are becoming a severe challenge to the average immune system. The short-lived little bugs are careening through the survival course of evolution at an accelerated rate due to the misguided overuse of disinfectants, pesticides, antibiotics, and other pharmaceuticals. The resulting antibiotic-resistant bugs are very scary, as they are hard to kill. As chi kung meditation strengthens the immune system, among other things, that may be reason enough for the perceptive to value it as self-protection.

There is a growing body of empirical research describing emotional states that benefit the healing process (Elmer Green, Ph.D., "Mind Over Matter: Volition and the Cosmic Connection in Yogic Theory," *Subtle Energies,* Vol. 4, No. 2, 1993). Emotional states can be thought of as postures or attitudes that the healer brings to his or her work, similar to the affirmations or kamae used by the ninja in conflict situations. They are sometimes states of drug consciousness when they can't be achieved otherwise. Native American shamans developed a pharmacopoeia to drop-kick themselves into various states of mindfulness, but drug-dependency can be avoided through meditation on the following three very effective affirmations for you to add to your healing repertoire.

1. Assume a posture of genuine love for the injured party. Penetrate his or her body fields with these feelings and thoughts. Think only loving thoughts and desire their injuries to heal. Place your hands so that your energy can flow along the patient's meridians in the proper direction, and then breathe your own body energy into him or her while visualizing a growing green light. If you are religious you may ask that the relevant aspect of healing associated with your deity guide you in this healing and benevolent task. This is a technique used by many massage therapists and some chiropractors. The mood created is often enhanced with a soft musical background and dim lighting, which increases alpha brain waves (associated with creativity) and decreases beta brain waves (associated with reactivity).

2. Assume the posture of the teacher. Study up and know your subject matter. If you can't work up real affection, treat the subject like a well-liked pet known for its intelligence and obedience, such as a horse or dog. Some people who have been poorly trained to accept and use intuitive information find this emotional state easier than genuinely loving the patient, though in the long run it is far more difficult, as it requires learning how the energy affects anatomy. It is particularly useful if you work with animals, who can't explain their pain. A good vet is much harder to find than a good physician.

Carefully and gently rest your hands on the *koshi* (energy points) or pressure points that lead to and through the injury, and ask the subject in a soft and soothing voice to relax. Breathe into the circuit you have created with the thought: "Here's some healthy energy, learn from it what you have to know to get better." With the same attitude, brush your hands throughout the subject's spirit body in a circular movement from the head to the feet and do a few extra swirls over the injured area. This is called "The way of the teacher." You might teach the subject how to breathe properly and rub the air over the injury. Musashi recommended a variation of this technique, and the brushing of the aura is common shamanistic practice across cultures. The shadow side of the brushing is the ability to cut the energy with your own chi in what are called "secret sword techniques" that slow an opponent and cut-to-cut momentarily steal his strength.

3. One of Stephen Hayes' poems has the line "Let The Cosmos decide," which became a war cry for some of the fiercer hoshin students over the years (*Wisdom from the Ninja Village of the Cold Moon,* Contemporary, 1984). Assume a feeling of awe and gratitude for being present to participate in whatever happens. You just do what you do, to the best of your ability, and maybe the cosmos will decide in favor of the patient. You simply lay your hands on the meridians that feed the injured area with the attitude of "letting be" or offering a gift that the patient may use for whatever is necessary. After all, who knows how this stuff works? In Christianity we say, "Thy will be done."

This attitude favored by Zen warriors was a recognition of the process of evolution in the operation of the universe. Ideally one ensnared in conflict was prepared, but the way of nature (survival of the fittest) eliminates self-serving bias, as the better adapted human survives. This attitude requires the absence of desire. It is a recognition that everyone dies; maybe you shouldn't be meddling in what is a natural process. The shadow of this viewpoint can develop into Social Darwinism, where one believes everything about his or her culture is the fittest or best. As there have been no major adaptations of the human animal in the last 50,000 years this view is specious. The reality is now and has been for a very long time that the culture with the best technology wins if its intelligence gathering is effective.

While my partner Aree was pregnant with Sara Glenn Mariko, I poured a lot of energy into the womb. When the sonograph revealed the infant had settled backwards in the womb, guaranteeing a tricky delivery, I got out the medical books and memorized how she was supposed to be resting. Then I sent her the picture. She swam around until she was properly oriented for delivery. Now little Mariko is a year old, walks, talks, sometimes does rolls when she falls, has recognized herself in the mirror for six months, and exhibits a lot of other precocious traits. When I work late, she'll get agitated and wait at the door, starting about the time I leave the office. Jeff Pool, one of Kevin Millis' deshi, told me that a friend of his had miscarried twice and was attempting to have a third baby. He was being vegetarian and studying pranic healing at the time. He gave the baby some healing energy, and she came to term with no problems. The fun part was that years later he talked to his friend (the mother) and she asked him what he had done to her baby. To this day the daughter refuses to eat any meat. He thinks it is a "cool" story. So do I.

The International Society for the Study of Subtle Energy and Energy Medicine could claim the Amazing Randi's $10,000 reward for presenting a "psychic event" without fraud on the basis of their published double blind study on the effect of noncontact therapeutic touch speeding healing of dermal wounds by a very significant factor (*Subtle Energy*, Vol. 1, No. 1, 1990). If the study is replicated with similar findings, I'd start placing some of those people. The statistics and models look good to me, and I suspect the famous smiling physician Bernie Siegel wouldn't laugh at them. More and more professional medical people are becoming interested in energy techniques as an enhancement to speed healing. The techniques of what used to be called alternative medicine are becoming more mainstream with every passing year. The books *Zen Shiatsu* by Shizuto Masanaga and Wataru Ohashi (Japan Publications, 1977) and *The Complete Book of Shiatsu Therapy* by Toru Namikoshi (Japan Publications, 1981) will provide good information concerning both energy use and points on the body that have healing potential.

Psychic Applications of Chi

There are many tricks of *genjutsu* (professional magic associated with ninjutsu to make you seem powerful to the naive) that are merely sleight of hand or misdirection of your opponent. Fire-walking only requires a belief in the laws of physics and a quick step, as do the rules of angling and taking advantage of your opponent's ignorance or blind spots to disappear. Chi can be used to hide your spirit, as well as project it. Hiding your spirit can be fun if you assume enough humility to engage insect or animal spirits, or to totally negate yourself. Study on this.

Projection of energy, or casting a spell, requires control of the breath as well as an ability to channel intention. Projecting a thought requires visualizing fundamental principles in such a way that they are easily grasped by the receiver. If you want the person to like you, project feelings of love and respect. Feelings are much easier to send than words or pictures. There is a growing body of studies that support "far seeing" and telepathy and I'll cite some later in this section, but the scientized protocols preclude playful replication. This is much more fun to develop through repetition and feedback with a friend, and then simple pass/fail experimentation on the unwary and innocent. If you have access to animals, most respond if you can get on their wavelength with a request that uses their natural proclivities. It takes some practice. Dogs, monkeys, and cats are easy for me. My son Shawn gentles horses with ease. Some people have a gift for birds. The Native American shaman often specialized in a particular animal (see *Animal Speak* in Bibliography), and the snake- and rat-removing families in India have been well documented (J. H. Hutton, *Caste in India: Its Nature, Functions, and Origins*, Oxford University Press, 1963). Wild animals are more difficult than domesticated ones.

The eyes guide the thought and the breath pushes it out through the third eye at the target. A little testing of neurolinguistic programming theories may be necessary to get the best response. (NLP is the kindergarten Western area of psychology that provides a theoretical basis for shaping a message so it will be received by the listener in his or her most easily accessed learning pattern.) Some concepts are best expressed visually, others via auditory channels by allowing your feeling to shape the vibration of your voice, but the most fundamental drives respond to the rub of sensory expression of the actual feeling. Use your imagination. What do they want, and can you give it to them? Projection of a symbol sometimes arouses the appropriate response. A skilled observer will quickly learn what seems to work and what doesn't, but keep your notes in your head. People do not like to be manipulated. If your intent is strong and the recipient is unwilling, he or she will often develop a migraine. Subtle influence should be subtle.

Knowledgeable Ninpo masters will picture in their mind the perfected technique that students are trying to learn and then project it with their chi into the students to help them get the feeling of the technique. The learning curve goes up enormously, and the clumsy suddenly acquire grace. Shihan Kevin Millis and I spent years playing around with this teaching method. The results are difficult to quantify but seemed positive. Some of my hoshin students were able to get remarkable results.

D. J. Bem and Charles Honorton's recently published *ganzfeld* (in German, "whole field") studies of telepathy show significant statistical success. The most effective group studied included twenty-nine students of drama, dance, and music who consistently hit one out of two in their telepathic efforts (*Science News*, Jan. 29, 1994). Two out of four ain't bad. Random luck would be one out of four. The ganzfeld studies don't show that we read each other's mind but do indicate a transfer of visual phenomena that requires explanation. The significantly higher success rate by the burgeoning artists suggests strongly that intuition, sensitivity, and discipline are contributing factors beyond intelligence.

When I taught hoshinjutsu as a college course, it was immediately evident to me that the smarter students with an arts background or interest had a considerable advantage over the chemists, engineers, accountants, and other linear thinkers. Football players, particularly those in defense positions, wrestlers, basketball, and soccer players tended to advance quickly, as they got to apply their new skills on the playing field. Women were able to learn how to use the skills of "feeling intent" more easily than men. The young women at Hillsdale College were much more skilled than the young men at projecting and reading feelings. I suspect this is a result of a subtle form of natural selection, possibly accounting for the consistent fear conservatives seem to hold for women with power. It's called wicked witchcraft. Some "primitive" tribes, such as the Rjonga of Mozambique, believe that to predict behavior is a form of witchcraft because one cannot know another's thoughts any other way (Martha Binford, personal conversation, 1978, about her fieldwork with the Rjonga). They are very concrete thinkers. It's no wonder they've been the equivalent of slaves to their Zulu cousins for centuries.

Studies by William Ickes of the University of Texas, Arlington, showed that dating couples often infer each other's thoughts and feelings with significant accuracy. The studies also found that people with higher levels of mental health and realistic self-concepts were easier to read, and that people with low levels of dependency and little insecurity could read them (*Science News*, Vol. 146, No. 18, Oct. 94). Spock's "mind-meld" as seen on *Star Trek* is a fictional version of a reality occasionally reported by married couples. It is easier to merge with someone you know and like. It is easier to work with feelings and pictures than it is with words and numbers. At least this is true for me—you might be different. My mind is very primitive and quiet. Many students over the years have reported spontaneous "bursts" of telepathy, but found the skill difficult to sustain or control over periods of time.

Some people have better access to the unconscious while dreaming. Freud and Jung did a lot of work in dream interpretation. I've noticed that my dreaming usually relates to what I've been reading or watching on television—mostly entertainment and seldom worth remembering. Dreaming will tend to fade away once you get your head together, making sleep more restful, but visions may get interesting during the "half-asleep" period before and after slumber. The spirit traveling or astral projection techniques seem to work best early in the morning just before sunrise, in the evening as the sun sets, and of course the witching hour of midnight. "Lucid Dreaming" techniques can improve your skills in this arena, but taking control of your fantasy life has little to do with achieving harmony in your day-to-day existence. It is more valuable to meditate, though lucid dreaming can be used as a therapeutic tool.

Fighting with Chi

Fighting with chi is very risky business for three main reasons. (1) If you have not learned to relax when you fight, and you run hot, angry, male sexual energy through muscles and bone, it will not take you too long to burn some tissue and organs, as well as to fry your fascia. At least the genitals don't burn out first. I have had Korean acupuncturists reproach me for practicing chi kung, and tell me a story of a man who broke his collarbone when buttoning a collar button. (I did rip out a car door handle once with no effort one frozen morning and broke quite a few keys off in locks before I toned the energy down with gentler intention.) (2) When the spirit drives, you become focused and fast, and it is very easy to seriously injure your students. If you carry your shoulders down and really practice the breathing with the meditational orbits, you become wonderfully strong, and the mental aspects—which resemble paranoia if you are not a positive person—foster creativity. It is much more fun and practical to use chi to fuel doing what you love than staying in a constant state of combat arousal. (3) If you only use chi for combat, it is very difficult to control in other situations that cause a stress or fear reaction. One tends to over-react, which is difficult for our friends and acquaintances and does little to alleviate stress.

For these reasons it is imperative that you learn to calm and empty your mind through meditation. You may find that when your personal heat is doing you injury, you will want to back off a bit to keep from burning the internal wiring. (I describe what that can feel like in *Path Notes*.) A cooler head prevails. Cooler energy seems to work better for healing, while the warmer yang energy is more effective in battle. If you are right-handed you can draw cool energy by breathing through the left nostril and drawing more energy from your left side. If you are left-handed the whole process is easier, but I suspect reversing the nostril and skin-breathing probably will result in cooler energy. I received a number of letters from people using my first book requesting that I put stronger emphasis on the interior burning that happens when your body isn't ready to handle the higher voltage. My friend Shifu and C.M.D. Chengde Wu, a world-renowned expert concerning chi kung and internal Chinese medicine, says it is very important to be as relaxed as possible, and any disturbing side-effects are an indicator that you are trying too hard or going too fast. He says what feels natural works best.

The postures and movements in tai chi and Ninpo sanshin, and some in kung fu, are designed to stretch your capacity for movement of energy, if you move through them in a relaxed manner. Often the traditional Chinese master will hold in perfect balance for hours just to strengthen the running of the chi through his or her meridians. It's called standing meditation and the most powerful is called "hugging the tree." Mantak Chia does an excellent job of describing this powerful Taoist meditation in his book *Chi Nei Tsang* (Healing Tao Books, 1990). Many of these benign postures and movements thought of primarily as stabilizing and breathing exercises are part of a sword drill or combat technique that can only be used by a flexible master. The rolling in taijutsu as well as the stretching and some of the kamae specifically enhance energy flow. Flowing through a chain of kamae with a *bo*, or sword, will often provide many abrupt surprises for your opponent.

Now back to the spiritual side, or fighting with chi, or the art of war. First, hit the position "fudosa" or Sage Seat. When you are deeply relaxed in full meditation, roll your stomach muscles vertically from left to right like a thrice coiled snake or ice cream cake set on its end so you can see the swirl. This spins the chi up the spine and down into the pelvic girdle, resulting in orgasmic chi surges or *kriya*. Musashi recommends "wedging in," as the really deep breathing pushes down to the genitals from the hips, forming a triangle with its point down, pushing energy into the base of the spine. If the hands are laid open on the knees to broadcast or draw energy, they will naturally cup into a bear's paw. Your chi, with a lot of work, becomes your claws. How well you wield your secret sword will be adjudicated by your imagination and energetic study of anatomy. You learn to generate while sitting, but you have to learn how to move it while walking, and then add energy to your taijutsu. Eventually it will become a natural part of your practice, requiring no thought. You can project your chi in front of your hands or feet to provide a healing cover when you strike, kick, or grab. The movement of chi can soften a more rigid stance into an approximation of universality that is often leveling to an opponent. It does require a certain grace and tenacity to learn, but it is a learned skill that can greatly benefit both the neophyte and the trained athlete. Study on this.

Those are some of the yang projective techniques for subtle influence. The yin techniques are a mite scarier. If you've achieved neutrality in your own mind, you can draw energy into the vacuum. As the dark side has no fear for you, you can project entities, warning vibes, uneasy feelings, or terror at your opponent. Love may make him even more uncomfortable. The neutrality is important because you can affect yourself as well as the other. Some beginners like to throw their chi around as an attack, but a skilled vampire loves for you to do that. Nothing like a little free soul-suck-snack to fire up the big guns.

A knowledge of pressure points *(tuite)* and severe damage points *(kyusho)* enhances one's ability in fighting as well as in healing. Hard strikes to some points on the body can have rather destructive effects. I wrote a manual on dim mak *(koshijutsu)* with a Chinese kenpo practitioner and student of chiropractic, Steve Bernola (sixth dan), and medical doctor and ninja shidoshi-ho Mike Fenster (fourth dan), showing the points common to kenpo, kempo, jujutsu, karate, hwarang-do and ninjutsu, and what is effected when they are struck (*Butokuden Dim Mak*, 1994, in Bibliography). It ought to save some lives, as we include the reversing points. Dim mak exists on three levels: creating hematomas, disrupting and destroying energy flow along meridians, and the directional breaking of bones so that they pierce organs. This manual focuses on the hematoma. Hatsumi-soke once remarked that learning koshijutsu *(dim mak)* too early was bad for one's taijutsu, as one came to rely more on hitting the points than developing good avoidance skills. I can verify that from my own experience.

Some of the Chinese masters have backed off from teaching fighting applications of chi kung, recognizing that all a gunfighter has to do is keep squeezing till empty. A teacher of strategy, however, realizes that the health, creativity, and spiritual benefits of chi kung far exceed those of physical confrontation. Once you have learned to pay attention to messages coming in through the fields surrounding your body (blindfolds and feeling energy), you may want to experiment with sending your own messages of subtle influence. I do not recommend using the "exploding organ" approach to whacking other people's meridians and points of weakness, as I firmly believe, from close observation, that you can hit harder with no intention to harm. Musashi recommends achieving the Void before going into battle, and ninja let the cosmos decide. If your spirit moves you, you can perform incredible feats of agility and strength without harming your opponent beyond creating abject awe or terror.

The ninja way of using chi kung in combat is primarily as an escape mechanism that comes into play when they are discovered. Togakure Ryu ninja seldom sought open combat, as they functioned primarily as gatherers of intelligence, or military advisors. The ninja hides his "wa" until such power is needed and relies more upon his excellent taijutsu. The higher-level ninja, being aware of how devastating most of their techniques are when applied with full-bodied inspired movement, tone down their expression of the art when practicing. It is considered very rude to injure a friend or student.

Most people become so entranced with the extreme effectiveness of Budo Taijutsu fighting and finishing techniques they tend to forget that they come out of a flowing process of first avoiding the attack (which can involve myriad levels of subtlety) then unbalancing the opponent (which can be physical, mental, spiritual, or a combination depending on the skill of the ninja. It is the second process that makes the finishing techniques so frightening for the uke. The more their confidence is disrupted by moving them out of their comfort zone into new experience where they lose all semblance of control, the greater their appreciation of ninja skills.

I've heard ninja drop-outs claim that The Boss can't hit hard. They obviously were never hit by The Boss. I saw him send Nagato-sensei flying on more than one occasion. The gentle Nagato, a former All-Japan heavyweight judo and kickboxing champion, is the size of a medium sumo wrestler. It is actually a privilege to be chosen to serve as The Boss's *uke*. Up until recently he only beat on the higher-level Americans. This is for two reasons: (1) a normal human being usually cannot take more than one or two chi kung blasts without shorting out or breaking, and (2) The Boss is sharing energy with the person he is thumping, and that can have many interesting effects, as he passes on his feelings. At the Baltimore Tai Kai, The Boss picked a young Italian student of Jack Hoban's from the Bronx who was quite studly in appearance. The Boss repeatedly slammed him to the mat and had this young stallion flinching and dancing in pain all over the stage for nearly an hour. That night the young man came into the restaurant where Kevin Millis and I were enjoying some fine wine and pasta. We stopped to talk with him on our way out. There was not a bruise on his body. He was radiant and actually glowed in the dim lighting. He said he had never felt so good in his whole life. Excellent taijutsu forms a remarkable vehicle for higher aspiration. Study this well!

Seven

The Way

Poetry has been a traditional study of the warrior throughout history in many cultures, both East and West. Samurai composed haiku to exhibit their composure at performing seppuku. After I went through the experience of the kundalini, I tried to describe it in the following poem. In a way it was a death poem. If this were an age where the Inquisition ruled, it could definitely be a death poem. I'm too long-winded and blank for haiku, so this is my attempt at describing the feelings and mental changes that are part and parcel to the process. I wrote this in 1986 and was amused to find that some of my students had put it on their dojo walls as a guide when I visited them to do seminars.

The Way
by Glenn Morris

Jesus did it
Buddha did it
Bodhisattvas do it
Yogis do it, Sages do it
Warriors do it
Fools do it
I did it
You can do it too, If you do it!

Sitting is not enough
Turning yourself into a pretzel is not enough
Breaking bricks with your body is not enough
Harmonizing and healing others is not enough
Ecstasy is certainly not enough
Facing your death is not enough

Rules are not the way
Feelings cannot illuminate the way
Intellect cannot explain nor measure the way
Service will not open the gates to the Golden Paths
Being is the conscious part of being immortal
The way encompasses all
Yet the way is . . . enough

Enough to kill the ego
Enough to transport the spirit
Enough to be
Being born again
Being energy
Prana, breath, chi fire the blood
Meridians, channels carry the energy
Bones, fascia support the being
(Why human BEING???)

Holding still with the tongue up opens the ears to the flow of
    thought
Stilling the flow, not attaching, so it diminishes to humble
    silence
Closing the eyes allows internal/eternal vision
Using the darkness of the eyelids to SEE into the Void
Stilling the mind allows the secret self to steal forth. The Way
    of Stealth!

Building energy, becoming real with energy fed by the breath
Opening the blood, bone, and channels until the meridians
    burn with hidden FIRE.
(Fire In The Belly—Fire Down Below—Fire Away)

And the vision within, inflamed like a burning bush, or trunk
opening to the branches, veins, capillaries, bones inside out,
upside down, tree of living energy. Life.

Living you, part of you. Really YOU.

Drawn to the base of the spine
Driving up a serpent, burning to STRIKE into the brain
Amygdala, hypothalamus, third eye looks back at you
Altering perception
Shattering social reality
Killing the old you who (Who started—Who finished—Still
    you?)

Kundalini, Feathered Serpent, Enlightenment or
teched/touched by ..? God?

Assume everyone's birthright (godhead) with care.
When we speak as the ancients, of being liverish, acting from
the heart, going with the guts, having belly, voting with our
feet, being ballsy ... green with jealousy, red with rage, true
blue, fired up, cooled down, translucently sincere, cowardly
yellow... What are we talking about?

These are real descriptions—faint maps of reality, of knowing
    forgotten,
in our consensus material world.
Socrates said, "Know Your Self." Not your personality, nor
    self-image, but your self.
Your nature, natural, animal, self. The face before you had
    one.

Patanjali mapped the way
Huang Lao described the results
It's real, it requires more than est. You can do it, 'cause I did.
Getting IT requires:

FORTY (?) COUNT THEM DAYS IN THE WILD(?)ERNESS
Of your natural animal SELF. Hope you have taken good care
   of IT.

Through meditation
You must face those dragons of intention
Living within
Real as your social self
Powerful as your intellect

Rendered mute by your toilet training
Sometimes wounded unto death by the separation from the
   goddess womb
Frightened by parenting anger
Usually hiding silent in the seven major candelabra/chakra/
   caverns of the sacred/sacrum temple body
(Except when a mother lifts a car to save her child,
Or a genius eurekas strange new ground. . . .
Cleaned your temple lately?)

Earth red dragon of the rules, that which ought to be and is,
powerful knowing lover rapist teacher barrier/bearer of
convention. THE BASE protective erotic gripping thighs and
genitals

Watery orange dragon of the emotions, reacting, wanting,
drawing, never satisfied, seeking always stimulation,
sensuous needing love approval competition change
challenge flowing water from the hips kidneys liver retreating
from desire

Fiery yellow dragon of the intellect, dominating, seeking
perfection fearing failure, willing success, driven, cynical,
hostile, arrogant, or aesthetic, artistic JOY, harmonizing,
humorous, analytical, shining from the solar plexus. Solar
yellow star attacking

Windy green dragon lodged with heart under the sternum.
Correcting, protective, jealous, generous, caring, loving by
criteria, nurturing servant and link to the angels/demons/
gods.

There is more to IT once you pass these guardians
You must learn to use and relinquish the demonic power of
   the Void

Angel sky blue, clear, creating consensus, convincing,
building an image of self, communicating with others,
creating reality and ILLUSION

Angel night sky, lapis blue of indigo, third eye shadow above
the eyes, female dancer, temple whore, vagina of the forehead
taking it all. Empathic knower of the truth through reading
and playing in the fields. The sages' white eyebrows put light
wings on a dark flame.

Angel of nobility, amethyst/purple pink rotating in the fields
of polarity, confident relaxed peaceful, complacent, opening
into the universal, consciousness without an object,
intelligent energy unleashed or directed to pure WHITE, out
of BLACK, which holds all together.

Hormonal intelligence (as within/without—above/below)
   split off, rejected or merged with the self, id, subconscious
   shadow wanting to be all of you,
bearing at least three gifts of mystical knowledge....

Thwarted: a daemon, dragon, tiger, channel, psychotic
   schizophrenia, paranoia

Accepted: an angel, goddess/god, higher self, sage, seer,
   enlightenment

The dragons must merge with the social self to create the
energy for a socially conscious and fully aware subtle and
beneficial use of the Void to harness higher levels of energy

Cutting a deal with your dragons/devils/angels/tigers allows
   you to achieve
Immortality in the Void.

The refined spirit can merge with universal reality by
   escaping the body.
The personality and gross spirit die with the body.
Rejuvenating the body and integrating the spirit are the
   alchemical challenges of a mature human being.
You must tame and educate your inner deities.
The process requires a month to years, depending on both
   your physical and psychological readiness
The process is sometimes called creating gold from lead
The process is sometimes called creating a baby spirit or
   virgin birth
Or pulling the sword from the stone. (Stones would be truer)

Sometimes born again. Sometimes madness.

Sometimes the id/dragon is too strong for a negative social
   self
Lacking in character or positive self-image—the id wins (IT
   got you; not you got IT)

Temporarily: a channel, probably harmless and interesting for
   you as a fun way to raise money while amusing the id. A
   powerful entity is quickly bored with trivial projects. Stuff
   of legends.
If you play to change the game with pure intention, beloved
   of the gods and Bujin.

For the truly shallow: possession by your desires. Dante,
   Orpheus, and others described Hell.
Some claim it is an allegory for this strange place in bad
   times. Here, heaven and hell co-exist.

Because the middle path leads into great danger, even death,
   for the social self,
it is sometimes called the way of the warrior (great risk in the
   wilderness)
due to the discipline inherent in refining the spirit while
   living in the material world.

Not many are called, fewer are chosen. Most seem born to it.
   A pretty select group. Small club. Friendly.

Go for it, but study first. Fools get to be epileptics or worse.

Manners become very important to those who share your
   fierce travels on the Golden Web.

Bridging two, or more, worlds opens to more treasure than
   the grounded mind can comprehend.

Once you're there, here, now. Who are you?

You are still you.

Eight

Mastery of Intelligence and Power

Through simple attrition, politics, self-promotion, creativity, actual inheritance, and in some rare cases deception and corruption—more Americans are ending up as heads of martial art families. Those whose only real skills were fighting ability, tournament production, and longevity are quickly recognized as being somewhat shallow as fonts of knowledge. The stress of their positions often results in a barrage of psychosomatic illnesses if they have not developed their self-awareness through meditative practice. Hard physical training is a buffer to stress, but suppressed rage, hostility, need for approval, and competitive drive is a better predictor of ulcers and cardiac arrest than mere physical conditioning (Emrika Padus, *The Complete Guide to Your Emotions & Your Health: New Dimensions in Mind/Body Healing,* Rodale Press, 1986). Hatsumi-soke recommends finding balance in one's life to avoid martial art sickness—the tiger/pussycat analogy used by Takamatsu-sensei. One should remember that Jim Fixx, medical doctor who supported the "jogging" and running fad of the late seventies, died of a heart attack while running a marathon. There is a Tibetan saying, "It is better to be a tiger for one day than a sheep for a thousand years."

One of the major reasons the combat arts avoid competition is the fact that the rules of play are often subjugated by the need to win. This aggressive spirit often asserts itself in the desire to harm, as I well know from playing football, wrestling, and boxing. If your metanormal capacities include "knowing," the spirit may respond to the over-aggressive opponent by delivering a shot of adrenaline, which fires chi and performance. Moving meditation allows you to move with tremendous force. Bricks smash with ease, and flesh rips apart, reinforcing the Taoist admonition that the spirit is often better ignored. Meditation also teaches you to quiet the mind and soften the body so you can develop appropriate choices in your responses to others. The soft fighter takes his or her cues from the aggressiveness of the attacker. *Ninpo Ikkan* can be translated as "integrity, downward flow, enjoy learning the spirit skills the easiest way" or "keep going." *Bufu Ikkan* (taking pleasure in the integrity of the warrior spirit) suggests an even higher order concerning the spirit of martial ways. *Buyu Ikkan* (enjoying the integrity of warrior friends) is a guide for dealing with others in the martial arts—you treat them as friends. These are all important ninja mottoes designed to reinforce the concept that you are pursuing this art to enjoy personal growth while you are learning to improve your skills at self-protection. Budo Taijutsu may be the focus of the teaching, but personal growth is the result of learning.

Lao Tzu said, "Those who deliberately practice etiquette polish human nature and straighten out their feelings. . . ." Manners provide the grease for interaction. I explained the traditional rules concerning *giri* (obligations) in *Path Notes*. Hatsumi-soke describes Takamatsu-soke as being exceptionally kind and seldom scolding him when he made mistakes, taking full responsibility for his teaching. Becoming a real martial artist takes a great deal of time regardless of the talent with which one begins.

In Ninpo simply mastering the variations of *Ichimonji no kamae* can take years. The fundamentals of posture, movement, and balance must be relearned and made natural before the student begins to stretch into the advanced techniques. In Ninpo, the attainment of the master's rank by passing under the sword is similar to achieving the black belt, in that it is a benchmark, not an end in itself. The actual process is similar to the study of a complex mandala, but few seem to realize the charge is to become the path, as well as to walk it, or see it. A master is expected to develop his or her way while preserving the teachings, spirit, and artistic accomplishments of "the elders" (Masaaki Hatsumi, *The Essence of Ninjutsu*, p. 128, Contemporary, 1989). The elders in Ninpo become Bujin and are preserved in the absorption of the Soke in a lineage. This is accomplished through an energy exchange before the death of the grandmaster, and in Zen is referred to as "The Transmission from Mind to Mind." The Sanskrit term for this exchange is *shaktipat*.

Spiritual leadership requires transcending one's more base desires. Authoritarian leadership is concerned with maintaining power and preserving a particular status quo that rewards the leader. Democratic leadership is concerned with developing a group consensus where all involved can contribute to the organization's goals through being empowered to use their particular skills to the best of their ability. The military-like discipline seen in most martial art dojo preserves tradition in an authoritarian manner. The laid-back democratic leadership espoused in the Togakure Ryu Bujinkan is of a higher order and preserves a tradition similar to the Japanese family and village ryuha. Hatsumi-soke is not interested in creating robots and cannon fodder, but develops artists. He extends a great deal of freedom to his followers and hopes that by modeling what he considers the appropriate behavior and feelings they will find their own way while practicing and teaching. He expects us to learn how to work together, and to give up the petty fiefdoms for a more universal presentation of his art. The members of the shidoshi-Kai are being asked to assume greater responsibility for working together, and to put on joint seminars for teaching experience. Phil Legare did one in 1995 with thirteen shidoshi at *Daikomyosai* (The Boss's birthday party held annually in Japan and around the world as a training get-together similar to Tai Kai). They came from all over the States and each presented a different workshop for the attendees. I was supposed to teach a bloc but had a business conflict; if I'm a good boy he might invite me again. Kevin Millis told me it was a first-rate party.

The Togakure Ryu rewards members on three levels: what kind of person you are, how good your taijutsu is, and how long have you endured The Boss's attention. From what I've observed, ten years or so after one enters, unless one has very special skills, he or she begins to get more specialized information from the *shihan* (senior master teachers). It takes about five years for the Japanese to begin to really accept you as a serious player, someone who is likely to stick around. As Ninpo tends to bring out both the best and worst in people as the spirit emerges, they like to see what it is you really want, like, and bring to the party. If they don't like what they see, your training will be mostly of a physical nature and quite intense. Hatsumi-soke will rank people to see what they do when they have power, or test their loyalty to the Ryu by putting them in very interesting situations. Sometimes he does it to teach those who should know better that rank must be spiritually supported to be truly respected. Quite a few have fallen from grace when dragged down by ego needs, greed, or the desire to be feared. Many are drawn to this art but find it difficult to maintain the dual perspective with a happy and accepting spirit. The only thing that is actually expected of you is to be yourself, and be willing to share your expertise with the next generation. One must be careful not to fall into the trap of becoming what one hates. The shihan will eventually repair your ignorance, if you keep showing up.

Hatsumi-soke says of the training he is sharing with the senior American practitioners of his art, "I'm not training just fighters, I am making leaders, generals, and shogun. These people are strategists and gentle. They are like stars in the night sky." The Boss is concerned with developing the next generation of leadership for Bujinkan as well as damage control. Bujinkan has large organized groups of practitioners in Australia, Canada, Germany, Spain, England, the United States, Japan, Sweden, Brazil, Argentina, Venezuela, Israel, South Africa, and smaller groups in other countries. More than five hundred ninja wannabes showed up for the England Tai Kai in 1994 from thirty-two different countries. An exotic resort setting is becoming a typical scenario for these annual training sessions held all over the world. Hatsumi-soke is relying more and more on his senior practitioners to carry on the Bujinkan legacy. Where the traditional ninja operated in secrecy and stealth, the modern ninja is usually a well-to-do hobbyist having a great deal of fun learning the ancient skills of the shinobi warriors. The professional teachers of Ninpo and Budo Taijutsu are still a relatively small group of "real" ninja but the ranks are growing.

Gathering Intelligence

Seirigaku (a pun of Hatsumi's equating the study of physiology with strategy and intelligence gathering to give the ninja advantage in any life situation) posits that the training of the able spy should include getting to know competent and powerful people. When I was still a college professor, I had my Japanese students translate all of Hatsumi-sensei's published works from the Japanese. (The power of the withheld A.) The Japanese students were funny, because they kept telling me that ninja didn't exist anymore. It wouldn't be too long before their parents were sending them books to translate for me. Japanese mothers will do just about anything to ensure the academic success of their children. I had translations of many of his books years before they were generally distributed through the English-speaking Bujinkan. It put me ahead of the mob. When I was in Japan, I would pay some of the younger guys who spoke Japanese to translate for me. Not to speak for me, but to tell me what The Boss and others were saying. They were grateful for the money and I for the information. I would pay Kevin Millis' way to Japan so I could have an experienced guide with me. It made the training better for both of us. We would get together after a session and analyze everything that was taught as well as how it was taught, and conjectured as to why it was taught in that particular manner. We were two American spies digging into the masters.

Assumption of identities is one of the skills of the ninja. Often when ninja get together they share identifying factors concerning their jobs and local cultures, so that if the person being shown these factors has to assume an identity, he or she will appear to be authentic. Often these attempts at intelligence gathering are treated rather casually. Following are examples of how this can be accomplished among friends.

One time when I was out in California with Kevin-san, while he was still president of a fashion design house, he took me around the local industry pretending I was a buyer. He would give me little insights into how Californians typically reacted to various situations, and then I'd try it out. We'd do the bars, beaches, and then go rock climbing.

When Kevin-san and I are visiting with Fenster-san, he fills us in on the medical scene, letting us know snippets of useful medical lore. Mike's wife, Amy, and her father show us how a back-hills Virginia cattle farmer runs his herds, and we work on our Southern accents and idioms. We discuss how professionalism is recognized in our various fields of endeavor. I'll usually share some meditation techniques, esoteric energy lore, or my outdated military techniques for establishing and defending the perimeter. Kevin-san cleans up our taijutsu. Mike tells us the medical consequences of the techniques. After it gets dark, we stalk each other with paint guns.

When I'm visiting with my theater friends, they show me how to use disguise and make-up to radically alter my appearance, or share subtle techniques that create confused descriptions. With very little work and a wig, I find I can appear believable from thirty to eighty years of age. If people don't look too closely, I can pass from common laborer to financial don. It only requires curiosity, mimicry, and willingness to try out some new roles and principles. Being able to disguise oneself often allows one to observe the natural behavior of one's target. Call it camouflage for the urban adventurer or stalker.

Our Japanese counterparts are as curious about us as we are about them. The term "sensei" means "gone before," which does not connote "nice." I found it interesting to meet certain shihan at the Daikomyosai held at Ishizuka-shihan's dojo in Kashiwa, Japan, who I had met on the street, or in business earlier when being a tourist. They were just checking me out, and practicing their disguises. Often a high-level master will try out his favorite role on you when you are out playing tourist. Years later you might discover something familiar about one of your colleagues in the dojo. It's polite not to recognize them in the different situation, but it is a good idea to start building a catalog of who can pass themselves off as what. I have to admit they fooled me. Seno-san was particularly clever, and we spent quite a bit of time together while he showed me the sights around Ueno. It took me nearly a year to recognize his dual role. The ninja doing security works at fitting in invisibly.

Visiting Japan is a little like going to Mars if you don't speak or read the language. It is easy to make cultural mistakes, when what has little significance to you might be fraught with meaning to them. It is a very good idea to study up on some key phrases. (Please. Thank you. I don't understand. Don't hurt me!) A book like Schwarz and Ezawa's *Everyday Japanese*

(Passport Books, 1990) can be a big help in sorting out the maze of expectations. It is expected that a visitor to someone's home bring a gift. The type of gift is a reflection of the giver. The Japanese particularly like to receive examples of your local handicrafts, art, and music. Something that is unique to a particular region, has historical content, or status consciousness is considered of greater value. A gift you have made is more valuable than something bought. The Boss likes opera; the Big Band sound, especially the music of Hoagy Carmichael; works of art; but usually gets weapons from his minions. If there are children in the household, one should consider their welfare. When I trained with Ishizuka-shihan, I sent his kids T-shirts from Key West, something that none of their friends were likely to have. When I taught at Hillsdale, I would present college sweats. When Aree and I named my latest daughter Sara Glenn Mariko, Hatsumi-san and Mariko-sensei presented "Little Mariko" with an antique kimono fit for a Japanese queen. When I worked for General Motors Engine Division, I gave out a bunch of "Have You Hugged Your Engine Builder Today?" buttons for their children that must have had them scratching their heads.

Observations from a Safe Distance

In October of 1992, shidoshi-ho Mike Fenster invited me to Virginia to be part of a seminar with Kevin Millis. Shibu East under Dr. Fenster's tutelage is primarily medical personnel, which means that they're all smart as hell, as well as interested in refining their taijutsu. Kevin used Mike for his uke, which made me happy, as I'm getting a little old to be bounced around that way. My *ukemi* (falling, rolling, and escaping skills) isn't anywhere close to Dr. Fenster's. My specialty is shadow shinken, not classical taijutsu. After two days of bump and thud we went to camp in the mountains of Virginia where Mike intends to build his dojo.

Mike was twenty-eight, Kevin was thirty-eight, and I was forty-eight. We'd trained together pretty consistently for over five years, having become friends in Japan. Kevin is the professional ninja. Mike is our medical doctor. I get to play shrink-wrap to our little group of professionals. We usually go West to play on Kevin's turf, as it is so exotic and different from our sheltering mountain ways. We spent a long day of walking, sighting in a Chinese assault rifle, and building our shelter in a high mountain meadow over-looked by Purgatory Mountain. Even the mountains of Virginia get a little chilly in October. Being from Michigan, I was shirtless enjoying the sun, while Mike wore a T-shirt. Kevin was bundled up in a heavy sweater, long underwear, and a roll-down hat. It's hard to get him away from the sunny, warm coast of Southern California. (Like fine wine, he is best near his own vineyard.) It was fun to work on our balancing skills while avoiding cow pies. Kevin and I had a chance to talk deep into the night about how we thought the Bujinkan might be evolving.

Kevin feels that the doorway to Bujinkan may soon be closed again, as the next Grandmaster may not be as open to change, nor be as Universal a man as Hatsumi-soke. (Kevin occasionally lapses into paranoia, as he is a natural competitor.) If you are interested in learning taijutsu from the source, you should take advantage of the opportunities that exist during his reign, as his successor will require years of seasoning, and may also prefer the shadows of anonymity. Hatsumi-san has taken grave risks in opening the door to foreigners. Our names look very strange and out of place on the scrolls. Masaaki Hatsumi is in his mid-sixties. His successor is now in his twenties. It takes about forty years to learn all the stuff that is in the ryus, particularly if your skills at synthesis aren't high. The transition skips a generation so that the heir apparent can be trained by the best of his father's generation—one of the reasons that grandfather *(Si Gung)* is synonymous with grandmaster in many of the Taoist-based martial arts. The identity of the heir is usually kept secret. You can rest assured that Hatsumi-soke's successor will be Japanese. If he is who I think he is, he's a very polite, extremely intelligent and gifted young man whose nose I smashed in a training accident, but I could be wrong. This art has so many layers it is truly like peeling an onion.

Take this as a warning to get busy if you want to learn from the best rather than the shallower imitations. Hatsumi-soke only takes personal students now and has reduced his teaching in Noda City considerably to work more with his *gaijin* (foreign devil, or more kindly, "outside person") instructors around the world at Tai Kai. The Juyushi do much of the actual teaching of advanced taijutsu. It is expected that you will eventually make the pilgrimage to Noda and study with the shihan. Some of the Japanese shihan have been practicing for over thirty years and have amazing skills to share. I picked up many subtle little moves from Kevin's primary teachers that I'm still trying to master years later. Many practitioners of the martial arts would like the sobriquet "ninja" attached to their skills, but few have the heart for the actual journey. Some who have the heart, still lack the brains or character, but bad ninja go away from Bujinkan.

Portraits of Some Modern Masters Worthy of Study

All of the older masters and real Grandmasters that I have met in the last few years in traditional Japanese and Chinese systems have been very well educated and talented men in other professions aside from their martial studies. Most were the equivalent of medical physicians. Rarely do I see the term "master" reflecting only a knowledge of martial significance. Hatsumi-soke is a respected artist, TV actor, has a medical degree, has earned a Ph.D. through his writing, as well as an honorary doctorate through his teaching and videos.

Y. C. Chiang, teaching master of White Crane Kung Fu and tai chi, has a degree in both Chinese and Western medicine, and his paintings in both Northern- and Southern-style brush work are museum quality. It was a great honor to meet his family and a pleasure visiting his well kept house and gardens in El Cerrito, California. He sculpted my personal chops for me. The man who taught Shi Chiang herbology was also the teacher of the last Chinese emperor, knew Takamatsu-sensei, and was a master of Spider Kung Fu—in his old photograph the spider master had a foot-wide, white aura around his head.

Chengde Wu, a chi kung and tai chi practitioner who has an international reputation in the internal arts, headed up the trauma training at a Shanghai hospital. Dr. Wu is certified in Eastern and Western medicine, shiatsu, herbology, and acupuncture. I take advantage of his acupuncture practice down the street from my office in Houston. He remarked that my "wisdom breath" was "very good." His wife, Wang Jurong, performed with the Chinese wu shu troupe at the 1936 Olympic Games and went on to win championships in her craft and taught at the Shanghai Institute of Physical Fitness before they came to the United States. She does seminars all over the U.S. Dr. Wu is very mellow and quiet, doesn't trust his English, and writes an occasional article on chi kung. Once when we were discussing the heart attack of the head of a Chinese system of chin-na we both knew, he said, "He is so angry. He has never learned to let it go. That is why his heart is troubled." Aree went to Dr. Wu at my recommendation, and migraines that have bothered her for years were eliminated in one session. After an acupuncture session, she asked me how he could know certain things about her that Western-trained doctors never had addressed. Chinese medicine is so subtle.

I have never met a "traditionally" trained American martial artist, with the exception of my friend Grandmaster John Pendergrass, who studied shotokan karate for eighteen years in Osaka, who had a clue concerning energy flow and strike points at the level common in Ninpo and some of the Chinese derivatives of Shaolin. John always complains about how gentle my techniques appear and how much they hurt, but don't seriously injure. When we compare techniques it is as if I were using a rubber mallet, and he a sledgehammer. The results are often the same, but the approach defines the difference between "soft" and "hard." His American Karate Federation Academies in the Fort Wayne area are a definite step above what is typically presented as martial arts in this country. He specializes in training kickboxers, and he excels in teaching children's classes as well as street techniques.

We do seminars together and have a great deal of fun, as he trained long years in shotokan as well as achieved mastery in win chun and tae kwon do. Being highly ranked in both Japanese and Korean systems, as well as studying in a Chinese system, created interesting political experiences for him. John was a welterweight professional kickboxer back in the seventies. He has an MBA and a successful RV repair business to run in addition to his dojo. He knows all the old fighters and movie stars and is working on an introduction to the martial arts for people who want to know the facts from someone famous for his bluntness.

Robert Trias, the founder of American Karate, wrote a self-published book for his top hundred karate teachers. Pendergrass loaned it to me. Trias' discussion of chi and especially the importance of attacking the wrists, elbows, and shoulders to disrupt the flow of chi to the whole body and incapacitate one's opponents without killing them was very similar to what I had been taught in Ninpo.

George Leonard is the closest to enlightenment I've ever seen in a practitioner of aikido. He exhibits transfer of training, but his skills and viewpoint are more a product of the Association of Humanistic Psychologists, of which he is a past president, than dharma transmission. He is well worth studying, and studying with. He's a self-made human being and a good natural scientist. Aikido footwork and fundamentals are similar to beginning Ninpo, but the bugei applications of aikido have been considerably toned down from the aikijutsu applications of the Daito Ryu. The Daito Ryu's spiritual teachings have been subsumed by over-emphasis of technique, like many other famous and ancient ryu preserved for the modern practitioner. Aside from Dr. Leonard, I've never met anyone in aikido who had much juice beyond self-serving bias.

Korean master Jhoon Rhee has the advantage of teaching tae kwon do in the U.S. Senate's gym. He is laboring to establish a National Policy Board for the martial arts. This idea will have to be carefully watched. At least fifty percent of martial arts instructors are as iffy as their arts. The Korean martial arts lead this iffy category. The danger lies not so much with the quality of the good, but with the quantity of the bad. I have no problem accepting government standards when they measure reality. No one has time to research all the things that might better their loves and lives in a complex society like ours. I would like to see a long-term meta-analysis of both transfer of training and combat outcomes before putting the seal of the United States on a martial art. A National Policy Board could eliminate a lot of frauds who hurt the martial arts with their shoddy practice, and self-promotion. We require school teachers to be licensed under government regulations, and martial artists with legitimate rank and training would not fear such scrutiny. The impact of a rotten martial art instructor on the behavior of children can be very destructive. Mr. Rhee has the reputation for honesty, and no one seriously questions his skill as a teacher and martial artist. My friends who know him say he is on the right track with this. You might write your congressman if better controls over teaching licenses appeals to you. I would be very disturbed if any particular school of martial art were placed in a position of primacy based on popular acceptance.

I'm not talking about common men here. Martial artists spend long years developing their skills. The rigors of their disciplines require more realistic testing than most academic achievement. Relaxed attention as well as open acceptance or appreciation of the other as a human being *(amae)* is the key to building a relationship with the powerful. Good manners show respect. What is considered good manners can vary from culture to culture as well as creature to creature. Study intently on this.

Commentary

My friend and business partner, Dr. Robert Simpson, has demonstrated in his unpublished dissertation a positive correlation between education and accurate self-perception. When I think about realistic self-perception, which is often when one's experience is so different from the mainstream, I am forced to recognize that it is a rare and valuable personality trait that is nurtured in Budo Taijutsu.

The continuous drive to improve and the willingness to serve as *sempai* (senior) or *kohai* (junior) result in new integration of mind, body, and spirit. Most of the young men and women I trained years ago are now running their own companies or have created their own unique jobs in the arts or business. The discipline of studying an art that requires both physical and mental flexibility transfers into bettering one's relationships with other human beings as well as achieving higher levels of productivity. Good manners and listening skills generate friendship. If you are willing to let go of competition needs and study other martial arts, you often learn interesting things and meet exciting people. The concepts surrounding *Nin* or "emotions/patience/endurance" are every bit as important to martial arts as they are to any of the material arts. We feel before we think. The body has awareness that the analytical mind has never learned to identify and use. Michael Murphy's book *The Future of the Body* (Tarcher, 1992) catalogs much of what can be gained by carefully exploring the inner dimensions of experience. His exposition of human possibilities is brilliant.

After godan, the master level in ninjutsu, the dangers are to your mind more than your body. The players' record for care is shabby, if not irresponsible in Ninpo, but that is *Sen no Sen* (see Chapter Fourteen), which can also be translated as disarming your opponent through subtle influence. As the adrenals kick in to flood the bloodstream with ACTH and glucocorticoids, the negative thinker is forced to face insanity, or learn to develop a more loving heart. "Bad ninja go away." The real master martial artists strip you of the techniques in which you had faith and force you to begin your journey anew. At the Tucson Tai Kai, Hatsumi showed how to "destroy" some of the fundamental techniques used by practically everyone who has studied Budo Taijutsu. The consternation of many was easy to observe, as their faith was shaken. It was not a new experience for me. Just as Hatsumi-soke blew away all my favorite jujutsu techniques years ago, senior instructors Doron Navon, Kevin Millis, Greg Kowalski, and in Houston, Richard Cearly and Dave Bolin, two of Ed Sones' shidoshi, continue to strip away any pretensions I might develop toward great physical mastery today. It keeps one honest. Reexamine all that you have learned, right down to subtle adjustments of posture, breath, and thought. This cruel but ultimately benevolent process will force you to question your fundamentals and perhaps even to relinquish your past and start a new life. Whining about what used to be will not solve today's problem. This is a form of transcendence on the material plane. Most don't want to study on this, as it means going back to white belt.

Semantics Generalized

by Glenn Morris

Some say you can only understand the mind of a people
   through learning their language
Some say the soul is non-verbal
rendering ineffable
that which is difficult, if one doesn't know the old meanings.

In the beginning was the word.
In the beginning it was light.
In the beginning to understand the word was to have power.

In the beginning knowing the name
granted the knower of meaning and intention
power.

"What the Hell is that?"

Oh tah, nothing important, keep playing. It will ignore us,
flee and hide, or try to sneak up on us. It thinks we're
stealing its food. This will challenge you. I'll watch your
back. They move in packs—some large females and whatever
young are still alive. They're omnivorous, mostly vegetarian,
and quite intelligent. Their claws are short, flat, hard, and
sharp. Their tusks are their primary weapon. The big males
leave the pack and hunt alone. We hunt them. The big sows
will try to knock you over so the little ones can rip on you as
you fall. They hunt us. The little ones are fast. We call them
warthogs. They attack when they outnumber their prey, or
you enter their territory, and here we are. They are a lot like
us. They value their life.

Word.

Nine

Characteristics of Shugyosha Across Cultures

The Japanese term *shugyosha* (The searcher for truth, or one who knows the skills of spirit, or heart—*kokoro* in the Japanese martial arts.) encompasses many traits similar to the charismatic phenomena required for canonization (sainthood) by the Roman Catholic Church. The "seeker of truth" is also known as a scientist in *kensho* (esoteric martial traditions, or realization of one's fundamental nature). A comparison of the Roman Catholic Church's standards concerning canonical charismatic phenomena with my observations supplies some interesting insights. I would like to discuss them from the perspective of a chi kung practitioner and martial artist. I have witnessed or experienced eleven, and perhaps twelve, of these "saintly" characteristics or charisms as a result of my own practice, and the observation of friends. As Musashi wrote in his Void chapter in *The Book of Five Rings*, "By knowing things that exist, you can know that which does not exist. That is the Void." The charismatic phenomena differ little from the *siddhi* (natural magics) associated with a number of Indian yogic disciplines, the arts of Ninpo concerned with *chonokyu* (the state of unity with the divine), some of the characteristics of Zen practitioners while still in *Goseki* (stinking of enlightenment), the Western traditions of human alchemy, and some Wiccan manifestations. Cross-cultural existence indicates biologically based survival mechanisms.

In the Buddhist esoteric or mystical traditions, one does not emphasize these saintly manifestations, as they are only natural phenomena and tools to help you get to the next stage. Paying too much attention to these natural consequences of developing higher energy results in getting stuck at the level where they manifest. You are supposed to get past them—that is why the Zen practitioners use the pejorative "stinking." Fascination with charismatic phenomena is a barrier to achieving *fugyo-ni-gyo* (spontaneous right action). Spontaneous right action as a survival mechanism is particularly valuable when someone comes leaping out of the bushes brandishing a weapon.

In Asia, the warrior path has a long history of producing saints. In the West, Christianity and particularly the Catholic Church are not too kind to warrior saints like the Templars, whose property was seized by the Inquisition, who were tortured and then murdered like their leader, wealthy Jacques DeMolay. Jean d'Arc, inspired by an angel, led the troops of the king of France to victory, and when she wouldn't recant her divine guidance was very publicly burned at the stake.

The church finds it difficult to deal with living saints. Most are canonized long after they are safely dead, and their histories are rewritten by the living. The Vatican's Congregation of Rites has the job of identification and classification of saints and uses the following criteria. The terms listed in bold below are some of the Church's criteria and qualities necessary for canonization, as presented in *The New Catholic Encyclopedia*. After the definition I will comment on the martial practice that is similar or give secular examples.

Visions, defined as "the perception of normally invisible objects" or beings, operate on three different levels. (1) Some people, like Tesla the inventor, are able to see in their mind's eye a finished product or organization, and by taking the necessary steps they can bring their vision to reality. Mozart got complete symphonic works in visionary states. (2) The ancient Greeks referred to the ability to visualize as guidance from the Muses and often enhanced the process by imbibing hallucinogens, as do some Native American shamans. On a biological level, the functions of the eye can be enhanced by an ability to see deeper into the ultraviolet spectrum. This is a result of meditation, as well as spending a lot of time in the dark, which allows the dilation of pupils to detect subtle differences in light and energy. If the meditation results in *prana* or rejuvenation of the endocrine system, some of the body's natural chemicals are potent hallucinogens. We tend to see what we desire. What we see is also colored by our feelings concerning the vision. (3) People with deep religious convictions usually get what would be called religious visions, which are associated with prophecy across cultures. The more exclusive and fear-based the religion, the more likely the vision will be paranoid. On a more mundane level, as the chakra in the forehead above and between the eyes, associated with pituitary gland, is stimulated through meditative energy techniques, the meditator begins to "see" energy, both within and without. This is usually referred to as "opening the third eye." The enlightened vision requires a third eye, so that one may see the past, present, and future as well as heaven, hell, and the middle ground with practice or biogenetic proclivity and luck. Time and space are dimensional rather than concrete. Intelligence manifests as spirit. The spirit appears to you as a holograph in meditation and represents itself in many forms. This vision has a life of its own, but it is colored by one's expectations, so *mushin* (the state of no mind, divine emptiness, or innocence) is important to penetrating the illusion.

Mystical Aureoles and Illuminations are defined as "radiant light around the head or body of a sacred personage, especially during ecstasy or contemplation, which is considered to be an expectation of the Glorified Body" or "the heavenly crown worn by saints." Radiance from the body, and particularly around the head, is simply the manifestation of higher levels of energy, which is a by-product of meditating properly to bring the energy to the head. It usually washes out enough under modern lighting conditions that you won't disturb your friends. Practically everyone has a visible corona around the body, and most martial artists who meditate have the equivalent of halos. The difference is in degree, color, and intensity, not presence or absence. Anyone in a state of arousal of any type will glow more intensely to someone who can see into the infrared; that is one of the reasons the Zen practitioners point out that the Self is always with you. Read Bassui, the 14th-century Zen monk associated with Koga ninjutsu. Seeing into the infrared becomes much easier if you are able to relax and use your night-vision in the daytime. I've taught many people how to "see auras" and describe the process in *Path Notes*. A psychotic will look no different from a saint in intensity, but the colors tend to be darker and the body more agitated.

Compenetration (you won't find this word in the dictionary, as it is archaic) **of bodies** is defined as "when one material body appears to pass through another" or "being receptive to being entered by the Holy Spirit or a departed saint." This seems remarkably similar to what is called channeling today. The religious term for this is transfiguration. Spirits or energy beings exist on certain wavelengths and can manifest in a receptive person's body through sustained intention, meditation, or "channeling." Jesus was said to transfigure Moses and Elias when he was meditating on a mountain (Roman Catholic Bible, Matthew 17:1–9). They were Old Testament prophets and became holy spirits. The Bible says Jesus's "face changed" (Roman Catholic Bible, Gospel of St. Luke 9:29–36). This is similar to the Native American shamanistic practice of "face dancing," where the faces and bodies of spirits appear in the aura of the meditating shaman. Mohammed was lectured to by an angel during meditation. Each culture has guides that are worthy of study, and some may draw you to worship. Worship that is not internalized through behavior is hypocrisy and serves no purpose beyond duping the naive. With practice one can send one's own spirit into the Void and "see" into the spirit world, or energy fields that surround the material world. A skilled healer exchanges energy with his or her patient. In many different esoteric traditions, the master/teacher shares his or her spirit with the *deshi* (disciple). Often when looking into the aura of a deshi, you will see "the teacher" looking out. The interaction of the spirit with the material body can be effected in *mushin* (divine emptiness). The spirit flows in to the empty vessel. The high-level practitioner of Ninpo opens to and interacts with the *Bujin*—our immortal warrior spirits who do not always appreciate being called. When this transcendent interchange happens to a child or innocent person, it can be quite frightening and is often regarded as demonic possession when the stronger spirit wins. Locutions (another archaic and esoteric term missing from *Webster's Collegiate* except as rhetorical peculiarity) are similar but inanimate, as energy is identified with an object rather than a person. Locutions sometimes appear as a word, usually in Latin or Sanskrit, sometimes accompanied by a vision and seeming to proceed from the object.

Locutions or "interior illuminations," or glowing light surrounding an object, relate to the energy that can be associated with favored weapons or articles frequently used by a master. In *Path Notes* I describe the bitch sword Lydia, which was actually made in the Muromachi period, judging from her robust durability and *hamon* (blade grain markings) by a Seki smith. She faintly glows in the dark. The bones of saints are often made into rosaries by the Hindus, Tibetans, and other sects of Buddhism and are said to hold the characteristics of the spirit that imbued them. Just as American Indians would wear a medicine pouch with bear claws or eagle talons to remind them of the characteristics of the totem, a monk or martial artist might treasure the feeling of a realized human being. Such items are usually worn over the heart or thymus in hope of affecting the endocrine system. My student and friend Bill Kesterson told me that horses shy away from the bones of a long-dead deer, which suggests something. We've done some pretty strange things with the bones of our elders—for a group that is supposed to be resting in peace. The ancestral power is in all of us. Deep in the bones lurk the patterns of evolution and intelligence. The dancing skeletons in Zen and Voodoo are icons to remind us, if we fear no evil, that death holds no dominion. When people meditate properly the body's energy changes, and if one is able to "see" auras the meditator will appear to glow brighter. This brighter, glowing field around the body can be moved by the meditator through intention. The oft-handled practice weapon, particularly when made of wood, absorbs some of this energy. The sensitive person can identify the owner of a bokken or hanbo. Often the stick will glow after being handled by those with higher energy. I let Doron Navon-sensei use my octagonal oak bo staff at a seminar, and it glowed yellow for over three years. I almost retired it. In Budo Taijutsu and other martial arts, it is considered an insult to handle someone else's weapons without permission.

Reading of Hearts is "receiving" telepathic knowledge of secret thoughts or moods without sensory cues or being "able to perceive the inner motives of others." *Kokoro* is the term used in Japanese martial traditions. Telepathic knowledge can be easily understood by someone who has worked to acquire the sensitivity necessary to read information from the fields of chi. Reading of hearts could relate to the skill of aura viewing as well as intuition. So-called female intuition is a learned skill that requires opening to elemental knowledge. It seems to be a characteristic of a number of alternative healing systems in many cultures, Reiki and non-contact therapeutic touch being the best known in contemporary U.S. Reading of intention and the avoidance of lethal threat is a ninja specialty that George Leonard seems to have replicated for his aikido students. Tantric lovemaking often results in peak experiences and telepathic exchanges. (Bonding with electric screws. What a concept!) Fugyo-ni-gyo is driven by *kokoro* (knowledge from the heart), which functions continually in the enlightened.

Incendium Amoris is defined as "burning sensations in the body without apparent cause." These include interior heat, usually a sensation around the heart which gradually extends to other parts of the body; intense ardors (when the heat becomes unbearable and cold applications must be used); and material burning that scorches clothing or blisters the skin. What a great name for the arousal of the kundalini and "burning with love"! The Church's descriptions of material burning are probably a result of not drinking enough water. Wine-drinking Europeans in Medieval times put themselves at great risk due to the dehydration effects of alcohol and disgusting eating habits like enjoying decaying meat. It is probably very important to keep a supply of good water handy, or you get the Gopi Krishna effect. Almost all religions in some way sanctify water, both materially and metaphorically. Itzhak Bentov's research identified one of the dangers of improper spiritual practice as charring toes and fingers (*Stalking the wild pendulum*, Bantam, 1977). Spontaneous combustion of gin drinkers in Victorian England probably correlates with this phenomenon, and the exploding chickens reported by CNN in the Midwest during the 1995 heat wave clearly indicate that intestinal gasses can ignite. One of my students actually burned his handprint onto a hanbo when we were playing with energy. When I was running hot, back in the mid-1980s, students would receive burn marks and raise blisters when I slapped them. There is a school of internal kung fu called "burning hands." When chi is developed through deep intestinal breathing, the hara feels like it is on fire. The Chinese call this effect "steaming the kettle." The Hindu recommend breathing through the right nostril to increase body heat. The Tibetan breathing and meditative practice of *tumo* is measured by how many wet sheets a monk can dry with his body heat in sub-freezing temperatures. Inuit shamans had to dive through and swim seven spaced holes in the Arctic ice to prove their breath control and ability to generate healing inner heat and energy. If you didn't make it, you obviously didn't have the gift. Frauds got to be fish food.

As the energy opens the second and third chakras, the body's energy fields glow orange and then yellow. As the base chakra opens into red, the individual appears to be surrounded by flames. If you can handle the heat of spiritual passion, you get to feel *rut* (Anglo-Saxon for horny), or what a cat or spider in heat feels like. It is why the experienced in human folly recommend celibacy, particularly for the novice. The tantric viewpoint recommends the study of sex magic.

Bilocation is "the simultaneous presence of a material body in two distinct places at once" or the ability to be seen in more than one place at the same time. Spirits seem to appear to a number of different people across great distances during dream states. I've had students who could cast multiple reflections on a mirror. Yogic saints are said to appear in more than one place at the same time. I think it has more to do with telepathic projection than actual physical presentation. (But what do I know?) I've had a number of ninja friends visit me in visions over the years in different locations, so I was the target, not the site. I've had students claim to see me in visions: walking toward them in Buddhist robes with flames around my legs; sitting in meditation surrounded by saffron flames; or more bizarre behavior, like running through a dream in a crouch wearing a black dogi with a big joker grin on my face. It's a wonder I have any friends left at all. Greg Kowalski turned up once in meditation and we exchanged some funny postcards, so I know it is not just a trick The Boss does to amuse us. Some esoteric systems claim the spirit exists in different bodies across dimensions and the mathematical models from quantum physics suggest this is a real possibility (Franklin Merrel-Wolff, *The Philosophy of Consciousness Without an Object,* Julian Press, 1973).

Aree, the woman who shares my life and teaches me fear, informs me that she sees me looking back at her whenever she closes her eyes, but then she adores me. I have no idea how any of this works. Baba Faqir Chand, the yoga master who wrote *The Unknowing Sage,* reported that his students often saw him in visions, but from his perspective he had done nothing. I've had similar experiences reported to me by students (and people who followed the directions given in *Path Notes* who wrote me letters), as well as seen others in meditation. Faqir Chand stated that he felt the yogis who faked knowing what their spirit bodies were doing were punished in the spirit world. He also suggests strongly that the appearance of the master in meditation has more to do with the students' desires than the skill of the master. Bilocation may just be another way of describing astral projection. When I asked The Boss to tell me what he had seen when he turned up in my meditations, his rather cryptic answers were markedly accurate. According to his writings, one of the ninja esoteric skills is being able to project illusionary multiple images to distract hunters as one form of *kyojitsu* (weird airs). This is a night trick and may cause the observer to think there is more than one body present.

Agility is defined rather strangely by the Congregation of Rites as "the instantaneous movement of a material body from one place to another without passing through intervening space" or "passing through another" and is associated with escapes from dangerous situations. We just seem agile to the people who don't stretch. Real good avoidance and disappearing techniques could easily be mistaken for passing through someone. Stealth techniques as well as bilocation might apply. Adrenaline surges can make time seem to slow down and are associated with remarkable feats. I've met martial artists who had trained their bodies to release adrenaline by cracking their necks. When you are really relaxed you move much faster and with many more options than a person who is stiff. The angling footwork in ninjutsu usually moves one to the side or rear of an attacker. If they flinch when striking, or being struck, we do seem to go through them to reappear in a better position for retaliation. I've had students tell me I disappeared when they were trying to hit me. I was usually taking advantage of their blink rate.

Levitation is defined as "elevation of the human body above the ground without visible cause and its suspension in the air without natural support." It may also appear in the form of ecstatic flight or ecstatic walk. Flying or defiance of gravity by floating in the air is rare even among saints and invariably reported as hearsay. When one gets out of his body, the sensation is like floating or flying, and this phenomenon is usually called astral projection. I'd substitute astral projection for the legendary levitation reported in Roman Catholic, Hindu, Taoist, and Buddhist literature. Actual levitation might be accomplished by reversing your polarity vertically to achieve a magnet effect. I suspect levitation is a tale used as a teaching device or metaphor to keep students working. I've heard stories about levitation for years but have never witnessed it, nor met anyone credible who had. Reports could also stem from the use of hypnosis by the guru. The glutal frog hops in lotus position presented in the late 1970s and early 1980s by some enthusiastic transcendental meditators are hardly acceptable. There are techniques in Ninpo, judo, and aikido for making the body heavier for fighting, and lighter for climbing and moving swiftly. People are able to make some astounding leaps with hang times that put them in a class with Michael Jordan, but no levitation that I'm familiar with. It might be a "Keep Going" kind of thing. Probably a weird primate genetic twist, as some like to fornicate while falling (spider monkeys, gibbons, and orangutans). It gives them fish dreams. You'll have to study on this!

Body incombustibility is defined as "the ability of bodies to withstand the natural laws of combustibility" and the examples are usually drawn from the Old Testament. Jewish prophets in the Old Testament walked into fiery situations with great regularity. You might recall Daniel, Shadrach, Meshach, and Abednego. There is even a warning concerning hanging out with firewalkers somewhere in the Book of Exodus. Putting your hand on an electric burner without crisping might be a more conclusive test of holiness. The seeming impossibility of firewalking has more to do with the viewer than the firewalker. The observers confuse temperature with conductivity. I've walked fire so many times with my white and gold belt students that I am certain this one is simple physics. Stepping across hot coals in one's bare feet is no big thing. Powerful chi does seem to lower the incidence of blistering. Walking across a bed of glowing coals serves to focus the mind and certainly can be used as an aid to restructuring self-image.

If you want to test your ability to brave the hot coals, make a big bonfire of wood. When it has burned down, use a metal leaf rake to spread a bed of coals about eight feet long and half an inch or less deep. Do this in the evening so the smoldering wood and glowing coals and ashes really look scary. (It's fun to roast a few wieners and have a drink or two to lower the inhibitions before risking your own dogs.) John Porter, a ninja friend, used to come to Hillsdale to run the firewalks for me. The first time I did it, I followed him into the bed of coals, walked across, and then walked back through it again because I did not believe how easy it was. The hoshin class lined up and walked with no problems, and some of their friends who had come to watch tried it, too. It became a once-a-semester event in which I would hand students their new belt ranks as they completed their walk. It made for a memorable ceremony. In Shinto, there are temples that specialize in firewalking, and people do it all the time. Shidoshi Greg Cooper (based in Orlando, Florida) told me he walked the coals at a temple in Japan after watching a really old lady do it while carrying her cat and a bag of groceries. When you live in houses made from wood and paper, like most people in Japan, freezing when confronted by fire is not a survival trait.

One of my students stood barefoot in front of the coals for a long time. I asked him what he was thinking, and he replied, "I can't get my legs to move." I took his hand and we walked together. Then he did it by himself. Fire is one of the first things we are taught to fear as children. Another student meditated on the question of how one should firewalk, and received a vision of a man running with his hair on fire. Just do it. There are no points for grace or dignity. Most people who firewalk find the experience to be confidence-building. I have never had a student volunteer to go first, though I always make the offer. They want to see it before doing it. I can't blame them, though it creates a strong urge to walk halfway and then start screaming and dancing. It helps if you are scared. A little adrenaline increases chi. The benefits of the experience also include increasing the sensitivity of the feet.

Bodily elongation or shrinking is defined as "the body of the saint changes shape during states of ecstasy." This shift in size and posture probably relates to the stretching of the spinal column and may simply refer to the release from curvature of the spine and bone deterioration during ecstasy. Most of the examples given are old women. (We try to prevent that with calcium, yoga, exercise, and chiropractic these days.) The shrinking would occur when the ecstatic state abates and one returns to one's normal state of being. A supple spine and neck are necessary to the easy spiritual movement of energy. A stiff neck in folklore ties to the saying, "Pride goeth before a fall" from grace. Posture can reflect personality, and subtle adjustments can have major effects. According to Suresh Goswamy at the 1994 convention of the Kundalini Research Network, when *shakti* (the holy female energy) or chi enters into the throat chakra and brain, the body is straightened and lifted as the spine begins to adjust to the higher energy. People naturally get taller as they hold themselves more erect. Shape-shifting is a shamanistic practice. People with presence seem larger to those without, though they may seem to shrink with greater familiarity.

Inedia is defined as "abstinence from all nourishment for great lengths of time." (It's another archaic term you won't find in your Webster's.) Going without food for long periods of time is amply recorded throughout history, including Gandhi's famous fasts and those of others. Yogis (showing off) will even feign death and cut air use down to minimal. The Taoists warn against becoming "breatharians" by reducing your food intake too much when you are learning how to control and generate chi. Some Tibetan practices are said to eliminate the need for food. The metabolism does seem to slow down to the point where you can live comfortably on seven hundred calories per day without losing weight. From the kensho viewpoint, it is very handy to be able to slip through your enemies' territories without stopping for nourishment or leaving traces of your cooking fire. Takamatsu-soke recommended only eating raw food. Hatsumi-soke is a vegetarian. I still like meat, but I'm a short-path survivor and preservation of the body is not always a high priority. If you continue to eat like a normal person, or drink alcohol, it is very easy to get fat. Lower-protein, no-fat diet is associated with longevity and cancer reduction. I have been called an "eater of souls and virtue."

The Odor of Sanctity refers to the saintly personage who "exudes an extraordinary fragrance." Alexander the Great was said to have it. It must be understood that he bathed regularly at the direction of Aristotle when it was hardly the fashion, and his mother was a priestess. Europeans haven't always prized cleanliness. Some of our pioneers who settled the Western frontiers recommended washing only when you changed your long underwear, which was an annual event. I've seen references to the concept that washing weakens in more than one holy order (usually associated with vows of poverty), and daily all-over bathing was something that only the wealthy or someone who lived by a body of water experienced until recent history. Diet has a lot to do with body odor, as the sweet-smelling Chinese and frequently hot-tubbing Japanese might inform you if you ever question how milk, red meat, and cheese affect one's odor. When you go through the purging fires and sweats of chi kung meditation ("rising from putrescence. . ." in Corinthians does not refer to copulation, as interpreted by some Christian fundamentalists), many toxins are eliminated. In fact, there is usually a period in which if you don't experiment with your diet, a little zephyr from your nether eye will cause others to fear and tear. (Very sulfurous.) Once the body has purified itself so that the spirit can move freely, bacteria that do not contribute to health seem to be much more difficult to sustain, which may account for a number of saintly characteristics. Body odor is reduced, the saliva sweetens, and perhaps one smells better, but in this age of aftershave and personality-enhancing perfumes, it would take a wise nose to know. Vegetarians have very little body odor. People identified as saintly usually have little interest in killing and eating animals. There is probably a link.

I have yet to see religious stigmata (where the body of the saint is marked by bleeding wounds similar to those suffered by Jesus during the crucifixion), or bodily incorruptibility (where the dead person's body does not rot), which are two among other characteristics sought by the Church of Rome. The Egyptian pharaohs and wealthy members of their courts went to a lot of effort to preserve their bodies through embalming. I don't think artificial means are considered fair play in the bodily incorruptibility category and have no idea how long modern embalming techniques work after the body is interred. There is a documentary concerning autopsies that is shown occasionally on HBO. Reverend Medger Evers, a Black activist who often walked with Martin Luther King, Jr., was shot down outside a motel in Memphis during the 1960s Freedom Rides. Medger Evers' body was without corruption when he was disinterred for an autopsy some twenty years after his assassination, according to the doctor who performed it and the witness of his son who had never met his father. The doctor was impressed enough by the results to discuss it in the HBO documentary which dealt with forensic applications.

Charisms in Eastern and Primordial Traditions

The human species has survived in many econiches, and there does seem to be a wide variance in talents and abilities as well as common features available to most people with practice. The description of the Abhijna (Sanskrit, meaning the attributes of a Buddha, arhat, or bodhisattva) includes six supernatural powers resulting from meditative practice, the first five being mundane and the sixth, being the goal to be obtained. These six are universally recognized in both the Mahayana and Hinayana traditions.

1. *Riddhi* (Sanskrit, meaning well-being through wealth of powers), referring primarily to the ability to project multiple forms of oneself, as well as to change shape, to become invisible, to penetrate solid objects, to leave the body and travel in the astral plane, to emanate a mind-body from one's own body, to receive pervasive knowledge that allows one to remain unharmed in times of peril, and the power of complete concentration. These descriptions are similar to what I've described above from Christianity.

2. "Divine hearing" or increased perception of human and spiritual voices.

3. Perception of the thoughts of other beings.

4. Recollection of previous existences.

5. "Divine vision" or knowledge of others, and the cycles of birth and death.

6. Knowledge concerning the extinction of one's own impurities and passions, which should be humbling and is said to signify the certainty of having attained liberation. Bodhisattvas are distinguished from arhats by the characteristics of compassion and altruism. Bodhisattvas pursue the welfare of other beings to the point of choosing to reincarnate in order to help others attain enlightenment, a fate far worse than death to the arhat who does not look back.

The *arhat* (Sanskrit for worthy one), *lohan*, or *rakan* (Chinese and Japanese terms for sages or saints) attain the terminal or highest degree in enlightenment, meaning they are fully free of the ten fetters to the cycle of existence on the material plane *(samyojana)*—to wit, freedom from belief in individuality; freedom from skepticism; freedom from rites and rules; freedom from cravings and desires; freedom from hatred; freedom from attachment to or craving for a more beautiful body; freedom from craving for incorporeality; freedom from conceit; freedom from excitability, or equanimity; and *avidya* (recognition of the illusory nature of material existence as the only reality), or freedom from ignorance.

The Buddha man or woman (completed practitioner of Vajrayana yoga) develops the nine siddhi ("perfect abilities" or mastery of the body and nature), which I described in *Path Notes* but will repeat here since they are a crucial part of the path. The first eight are more ordinary, or mundane, and number nine requires them all but uniquely manifests spontaneously. They are: (1) the sword that renders one unconquerable, which is sheathed in the spine; (2) the elixir for the eyes (energized water, quintessential embodiment, a code for chi) that makes gods visible, penetrating the illusion; (3) fleetness in running, agility; (4) invisibility; (5) the life essence that preserves youth (chi again); (6) the ability to fly, astral projection, lightness of being; (7) the ability to make certain pills, healing and giving of energy; (8) power over the world of spirits and demons (get a good dictionary when you look up demons and don't stop at the first and most commonly accepted definition); and (9) enlightenment, which contains all of the above. These abilities are side effects (powers) and outcomes (skills) of various meditative practices concerning concentration, shaping intention, and developing will power and mindfulness, as well as inquisitiveness and daring.

The shaman (medicine man/woman, or indigenous folk healer, often mislabeled as sorcerer by the ignorant) acts as a bridge to the spirit world to bring healing to his tribe. The shaman's work differs from the yogi model of relinquishing desire to remove suffering by instead following the emotions (like the ninja) to mine emotive powers. Shamans are as rare as anti-matter and view this world as the "mad shadow" of the reality, which is the spirit world. The shadow is where they operate through the practice of intense concentration.

Shamanistic practice is a means to enter the Void, and is similar to the way of paradox, or holy madness. Shamans learn through pain, treating suffering as way to knowledge. They undergo spiritual dismemberment, and wound themselves to capture healing, spiritual rebirth, and development. They die in order to live. They enter the darkness inside the mountain in order to experience light. Darkness as light. They possess two bodies, and can see with the eyes of the soul body. They do not perfect the physical body, but leave it to travel in the spirit worlds. Their friends are spiritual, invisible to normal eyes, vibration forms from another dimension. Self-healing comes before healing others. They act as the channels through which natural, primal powers can flow. They draw upon the natural energies of the universe to perform real magic. Real magic is the total coherence of life, when all facets of life are felt with intensity. Shamans have been mostly ignored until recently. We tend to treat our enemy's wise as fools. It is one of the darker manifestations of cultural competitiveness. Many American ninja have ventured into the practice of Native American shamanism in their pursuit of enlightenment. Interestingly enough, some traditional American Indian shamans feel that "white-eyes" are incapable of assuming their art. As some shamans inhabit the land of the living dead, a wise person might want to know a little about their cultural perspective.

While Ben Franklin was impressed by the Huron and Algonquin, Thomas Jefferson, and later Sam Houston, were friends to the war chiefs of the Cherokee. Many Indian tribes had the tradition of creating warrior-shaman-chiefs whose only responsibility was the conduct of warfare. They were too crazy to ever be left in charge of any other government function, but were always consulted about the effects of change. The young men who studied under these paragons of hostile thinking were referred to as Braves, a term similar in meaning to knight, except little armor was worn, as the Indian prized speed and mobility.

The recent movie *Last of the Mohicans* fairly represents the American ideals of romantic love, family values, and appropriate view of the government. Our founders modeled our democracy on the concept that the government must always be controlled by the people, and those in power must be carefully watched, as "absolute power corrupts absolutely." Government is a servant, not a master. When we forget that, we have lost the American Way. The Iroquois, Huron, Choctaw, Chickasaw, Creek, Seminole, and Cherokee functioned as independent republics, understood separation of powers, and were liquidated when white settlers moved into their territories to exploit their resources. They were referred to as "The Civilized Tribes."

Counting coup was acceptable behavior for those who wanted a better relationship with their traditional enemy. This was usually done with a stick the length of your forearm decorated with feathers so your opponent could not be sure you didn't have a tomahawk. You were allowed to frighten. Touching was considered a kill and very humiliating. How would you like to be known as somebody the enemy counts coup on in a warrior society? Yichh. You'd never get laid that way. I never heard of a "Chief Many Times Swatted" in my boyhood reading of Indian legends and practices. Shamans would often carry a "spirit-chaser or demon-chaser" stick that was used to frighten off evil spirits. The Native Americans never understood the European concepts of total war, or that human beings could so demonize their enemies that they would be thought of as vermin to be exterminated.

Read some histories of guerrilla warfare and unconventional warfare. The best guerrillas use natural laws to defeat their mechanistic opponents. The high-plains Sioux were considered the finest guerrilla cavalry that ever existed in the West. They could be compared to the Mongols and Huns, who easily whipped the flower of Western knighthood whenever they came off the Russian Steppes. The Russians were famous for using distance and winter to protect their cities from hostile invasion. The Apaches used the desert and mountains of the Southwest to great advantage. The winners get to rewrite history eventually to pretty up their story if they outlast their opponent through many lifetimes. The Indian war bonnet of dark feathers with white tips looks like the spread halo of the ancestral spirits when it comes howling at you out of the night, hatchet in hand. Subliminal persuasion of the fiercest sort. It's no wonder the Puritans sold them blankets infected with smallpox. Our founding fathers are usually pictured writing, as the pen is mightier than the sword. Their quill is tall and white for upright purity, with a fluffy fringe denoting eloquence and creativity.

Opening to the Chakras
(Go Dai, Mythology, and Symbolism)

Practically every esoteric energy system that has made it into the literature has some form of chakra system. Ninpo emphasizes the four body chakras and associates them with particular attitudes. The chakras of the neck and head are grouped together as one, the Void. The best descriptions of the chakra system exist in the Hindu and Taoist literature. "Chakra" is the Hindu term for wheel or circle and identifies centers of energy that have correspondences on the physical body that connect to the soul and interpenetrate each other. Each chakra has *nadi* or meridians radiating from it. The meridians are best described in acupuncture literature. In kundalini yoga the aroused energy is brought up the spine, activating each chakra which is associated with particular psychophysical properties or a center of consciousness. The opening encourages particular gifts in the practitioner, which are expressed through various symbols (colors, *mantra* [sounds] and *yantra* [designs], animal symbols or totems, divinities, etc.). Some Native American systems include the hands and feet as separate chakras. Ninpo includes the feet and knees with Earth and the hands with the heart or Wind. Some systems differentiate eleven to thirteen main chakras. Most Hindu systems discuss seven principal chakras. I will describe what I have seen and experienced, which differs in some ways from the classical literature.

In most mystical systems the openings of the first two chakras, Earth and Water in Ninpo, are considered mundane. The opening of Fire (the solar plexus chakra) is considered the first benchmark of a "real human being" in ancient Taoist nomenclature as it is associated with achievement. When the heart chakra, or Wind, manifests, the seeker may find that benevolence, compassion, and altruism take on new meanings. As the throat chakra (first level of Void) opens, the personality shifts to more creative pursuits, and as the major chakras in the brain energize, one experiences realities that are only associated with mythology and esoteric religion. As the greatest danger is in succumbing to the negative aspects of the first two major chakras, it is important to understand how spiritual awakening can be perverted by the need for power, approval, and material gain into a trap for the naive seeker. The greatest danger to the mind of the practitioner, particularly the power seeker, is in thinking the journey has ended with the opening of the water chakra.

Following the breath with your mind's eye is a very subtle process that is easily shaped by suggestion. Learning to just "let it be" and relax into what is there will give you more than enough to do before you have the power to storm the mysterious pass or portal. Learning to appreciate one's ancestors, in depth, requires acceptance of all nature as a never-ending process of sentient expression. Shiva rides the white bull into battle, but out of respect for its bravery does not eat its meat, just as we seldom eat horses except in hard times, unless we're French. We tend to recognize the intelligence of the animals we know well, or consider wild. Shamans sometimes wear the skins of creatures lesser men fear most, the rulers of the night and fierce oppressors of the ancestors. The super consciousness, Void— or if you like Greek philosophy, Noumas—contains animal spirits that link up with chakras in ways that I have only seen described in Native American shamanism and esoteric writings of some martial artists. This animal and insect consciousness can be extended to plants. From the conservative perspective of Chinese medicine nearly all of these experiences are considered the hallucinatory result of linking up various organs to the endocrine system. It is interesting that in the last year Western medicine has reported that organs like the stomach have much greater nerve density than expected and actually function like autonomous brains within the body. (I read it in *Science News* and *Discover* but don't remember the issues.) It's all very strange, and you will have to study on your own, as the bullshit published concerning the mystical experience is deep and wide.

Earth/Stability/Muladhara (Bear)

The lowest major chakra—which is associated with the color red, primal sexuality, muscular power, conventional stability, and the shadow rule-bound or anal retentive—seems to be associated as well with a carnivorous nature or carnality. The genitals, perineum, stomach, intestines, and eyes are supported by the power in the legs and feet. As the base chakra opens, the resulting consciousness flogs desire into the most astonishing passions. Obsession becomes a mild perfume under the driving power unleashed by the opening of sexuality to the spirit.

A firm foundation in basic manners and societal conventions distinguishing right from wrong will keep you from doing too much damage while you're wiping drool from your garments. Stealth in the material world can preserve your sanity as well as your reputation. Hide your red light under a veneer of civility while you are learning how to use your tools. You ain't a licensed carpenter by a long shot just because you can feel energy or have opened a chakra. The base chakra can create a real dick in one's mind. This is a mental variation of the mountain that erects by sexual intention. It is not necessary to act out one's sexual intent to open the chakra, but creating the image in one's mind to love with all one's heart and soul makes me grateful that baggy pants are back in fashion. You get more work done if you wear loose cotton or silk clothing of mostly natural fiber when you meditate. There are some techniques that will actually cause the cloth to crisp as if it were burnt. The breathing while you are opening and building your foundation is called "The Buddha Breath" or "baby technique." Opening this base chakra through affirmations, body shifts, and stillness is the second task at which most meditators fail. The first is silencing the social mind. It is at this beginner's stage that the primary Zen admonition comes into play with great difficulty: "Do not do anything evil; do good, and purify the mind yourself—this is the teaching of all the enlightened." As Dogen Zenji opined, "A three year old may be able to say it, but an eighty year old man cannot practice it." (Thomas Cleary, *Rational Zen: The Mind of Dogen Zenji,* Shambhala, 1992.)

Every chakra has its positive and negative alignment, and you must tame both before moving on to the next, or you will pay a heavy price when entering a later realm. Wherever you enter you still have to complete the wheel, or join and integrate all the body chakras, if you want to master freedom in the Void. Once you have built a foundation for advancement, you begin to melt the energy blocks around the hips and kidneys to open your movement to flow. Mother bear defends her cubs. The one-punch martial arts could be associated with this chakra.

Water/Adaptivity/Svadhishthana (Dragon)

We all change, and opening the second chakra is sometimes referred to in Chinese alchemy as steaming the cauldron. Cauldrons offer visions of witches as well as interesting stews. The kidneys, liver, and ears tie together for the water chakra in Chinese medicine. The triangle as well as angular movement, "wedging in," learning to use the hips, and walking are fundamental to the second chakra. The shadow is waking up the adrenal glands that sit upon the kidney—paranoia. Paranoia is channeled into creativity by positive thinking. Paranoids can be very clever. Fear can be a powerful motivation for the materialist. Strong emotions are contained by relaxation, the Secret Smile, and positive thinking.

The orange light of awakening fun and laughter is fueled by terror and disapproval. Negative thinking and depression lead to darkest paranoia when there is little hope or light. The materialist seldom can get this stage lit, and so wanders screaming warnings as he or she flounders through a horrific landscape in perpetual darkness. After a little more experience in this realm of terror and burning orange landscapes you may find its inhabitants fun and challenging, rather like your cranky veteran uncle Charles, who still carries Vietnam around in a constantly playing microchip on his shoulder. It does take some effort at calmness to channel this excitable viewpoint into legitimate creativity, passion, and love for your enemies as well as friends. Trust is a hard-won commodity. Trust me. You see? Even the phrase sets off warning bells. Trust is based on behavior, not words.

Endurance is part of the waterway to personal growth. The reptile stirs as we warm the furthest base of the brain, bearing a resemblance to some beasts with bigger brain to body size ratio. The dragon was a wolfish cow on land and returned to the sea as a whale. Orcus rules the deep, but seeks the light, and will align with fire as well as water. The martial arts that emphasize dodging, ducking, multiple attacks, and surprise are good for training in this chakra.

Paranoia and Mysticism

Jim Jones (Christian), the wackos from Waco (eclectic religio-magic), and Shoko Asahara (Buddhist, Hindu, Yogic), founder of *Aum Shinrikyo* (a new Japanese religion that seems to hold murder, kidnapping, and poisoning innocent train riders as part of its rites), are all examples of the paranoia resulting from charismatic pursuit of enlightenment. The "Moonies" provide a Korean example. Osho, a tantric fraud who used to be called the Rajneesh, set up a heavily armed commune in the United States and published ancient translations as his own work, but never completed the journey himself, given the descriptions he published and his needs for exploiting his followers. When a *guru* (spiritual teacher) starts speaking of his admiration for Hitler, or attacking the legal prosecution for financial fraud of some religious types like the Bakkers (empathy reveals the true colors of the beast), demanding worship, harassing his followers sexually and separating them from their social milieu for indoctrination, selling his body fluids, and is purported to levitate, it probably is wise of his observers to move on up the road. Messiahs and madmen can suddenly seem very similar when the mental controls are not in place and the adrenals begin to release organic "speed" into the bloodstream. Evil is usually easy to recognize in hindsight once the veil is lifted. Spiritual hunger allows minor gifts to appear grail-like to the innocent lambkins who want to be shown the way rather than travel it through their own effort. Usually the martial art masters who have obtained enlightenment avoid this kind of silliness because of the rigors associated with the various *ryuha.*

If the reward does not correlate with the effort, your attempts at magick will only cost you friends in the long run. "Big Talk, no payoff, another madman, and we fell for IT again. This spiritual stuff sucks!" Freud was probably right about a Christ complex being the first sign of madness. See the Peter O'Toole movie/video *The Ruling Class.* A less delusionary presentation of paranoia is Michael Douglas' recent movie, *Falling Down.*

The negative and positive polarities of the Earth and Water realms of experience are described primarily by psychotics, takers of LSD, or psychologists who have begun to follow Stanislav Grof's Holotropic Breath, Guided Imagery and Music techniques (Stanislav Grof, M.D., *The Holotropic Mind: The Three Levels of Human Consciousness and How They Shape Our Lives,* Harper Collins, 1993). Unless you are a very happy camper, in love passionately with someone or something, paranoia becomes a real risk if you are sane enough not to act out your insights. Defense, not offense, is the name of the game from this point, if you want to finish your task in peace. The sage keeps his observations locked within; the fool thinks they are now complete. Positive affirmations combined with the Secret Smile technique make the transition through Earth and Water relatively easy, depending on the practice and the practitioner. Some recommend solitude during this stage. Jumping at shadows, screaming inappropriately, and vivid dreams limit its appeal, but it is a necessary staging area for the leap into the Void, or over the abyss.

Stan Grof tells a story that is often repeated in Kundalini research circles. "An old wise man was sitting nude in a tree meditating. A young man that the community called crazy came stumbling by. He saw the old sage meditating and decided to join him. He removed his clothing and climbed up into the tree, positioning himself for meditation next to the old man. After a little time had passed, he asked the old man, 'Why do they call me crazy when I do things like this, yet you are called wise?' The old man opened his eyes and said, 'I know who to tell my stories to.'"

The major difference between the madman and the mystic is that the soul of the mystic can go in and out of the unconscious, integrate what the experience has revealed, and live in the community as a helpful guide. The madman's experiences seldom have lasting impact and are accompanied by a desire to forget. For example, people suffering from a psychotic disorder rarely fear they are going crazy, even though they are. A true visionary experience usually has the presence of a positive exploratory attitude and has lasting significant impact over time, where the hallucination characteristically has no lasting value or impact. In altered states induced by drugs, alcohol, or meditation, we readily see images in natural formations, like clouds, landscapes, tea leaves, and leg hair. If the vision is accepted and concentrated on, we see complex patterns, phantasmagoria, and mirage-like moving pictures—we hallucinate. When the brain is isolated by closing off the senses, it can produce its own worlds on the basis of stored excitation patterns. Dogen Zenji *(Rational Zen)* suggests that after climbing to the tip of a hundred-foot pole we must go farther. Beyond the level of phantasmagoria awaits the spirit world, the goal of esoteric and occult philosophies and practice. Entering here we are able to communicate with the dead, spirits, animal entities, amorphous beings, and the creative superself. Plunging deeper into the Void, one's efforts may result in psychic, or divine emptiness sometimes referred to as the absolute. Socrates remarked in Plato's *Phaedrus,* "The greatest blessings come to us on the way to madness."

The differences between the saint and the paranoid can be seen in their action, not their words as the paranoid or psychopath imitates the speech of the saint. The saint or shugyosha adheres to moral standards, pays debts, keeps promises, tells the truth, and insists associates do the same. The psychopath breaks the rules of morality, writes bad checks and has many unpaid debts, lies to close associates and expects them to lie for him. Where the the saint is usually healthy, the psychopath displays variable exotic health problems. The saint enjoys stillness and silence, but typically psychopaths can sit still only when the center of attention. The saint encourages others to be self-reliant, where the psychopath manipulates others into dependence. Where there are long-term benefits in associating with a shugyosha, association with the fraudulent psychopath is invariably damaging. The saint can face mistakes, apologize, learn from them and move on. The fraud apologizes only when trapped, and their organizations tend to degenerate over time. When confronted with wrong-doing the shugyosha respond by making amends and avoid making the same error in the future. The psychopath ignores, denies, or attacks the accuser as the one who is "really" guilty, and if that doesn't work threatens or attempts to harm. This description of differences simplifies situations that are often quite complex, but the pattern is one that is often repeated, and constants should not surprise.

Fire/Intensity/Manipura (Tiger)

The fire chakra comprises a network containing spleen, pancreas, and solar plexus. Opening this chakra is considered by some to be the center of the middle way and the heart of the intellect. Musashi recommends it above all others for the warrior. It is the sacred cross of the Christian, Buddhist, Sufi, Wiccan, Hopi, and Navaho. Opening it is the first step in becoming a real human being from the Taoist and Ninpo perspective. Only those who are awakened to their inner self are free to manipulate their own existence consciously. The rest are fertilizer from the religious mystic perspective. The American Indian map of the spiritual reality and the opening of the chakras with their associated archetypal spirit animals are revealed on many totem poles (particularly Tlingit). The shamanism associated with the American Indian that is now gaining respect by many non-Indians is a sophisticated transpersonal psychology described from a naturist and different cultural point of view. The ancient martial systems of China, Japan, and Korea also associate with animal spirit guides in a hierarchy for the practitioner.

Opening to fire is the Way of Strategy. The curved spine of Happy Kokopelli, spirit scout to the fourth world, is not a hunched back but the posture of intensity seen in the musician's exhale as well as in the raised foot of the dancer. Here the triangle is reversed. The mountain turns over. Male must begin to feel female. Orange burns into yellow gold. The cat seizes its prey and rips away at it until it is food, or plays with it until it is food. The mind of the firewalker seizes on a problem and works it, until the solution is squeezed into reality. "Fire gets more done; 'cause Fire has more fun." The dark side of Fire is anger, degrees of contempt, and individuation that create distance from the universal self. The light side of fire is inclusion, wild laughter, and joy. One must turn one's wounds into lessons that spell happiness to sustain the gold of fire. The warrior technique of reversing breath by tightening as you inhale, and relaxing as you exhale, can now be used as well as "Buddha Breath" to draw energy higher up the spine to strengthen the core of the body. Expanding and contracting the body as you breathe is called *tai no shinshuku* in karate. Taoists use the same principle in advanced Turtle Breathing, which uses the bones as energy pumps for just walking around. I describe fire in the following manner in *Meditation Mastery* (see bibliography):

> The physical response is to joyfully leap forward to embrace your destiny, as your attacker is the test for which you have been training. The shoulders are squared to your opponent, the trunk is angled forward, and the legs drive your punches in rhythm with your steps. You drive through any resistance. You see beyond deception.
>
> The mental attitude is assertive intensity. It might be called exuberance. You are concerned with the attainment of excellence. You are warm, dynamic and expansive, using your powers of reason to control and manipulate your environment. You are not aggressive in the hostile sense of needing to dominate, but enjoy the challenge of solving problems and using power. You are emotionally stable and relaxed physically, developing harmony of mind and body. You have little concern for status and control, as you are trusting of others. You see yourself as a truth teller and tend to be strongly forthright in your speech which others sometimes perceive as blunt and tactless.
>
> Your enthusiasm draws others to you like moths to the flame so you must be careful of your impact as your energy increases. Fire is associated with charisma or star quality. You find empirical and precise study interesting and may develop into an eloquent and expressive communicator of new and creative ideas. You have to be careful to frame your thoughts in ways to make them acceptable to others, as you tend to forget that others do not have your perception of reality as an integrated human being. You must be careful not to fall into paranoia or cynicism, as you are not alone only rare, as most never learn how to open themselves.
>
> The point of concentration is the center of the spine behind the solar plexus. You can bring up the inner fire by touching

the index finger to the thumb, or leaning forward as you step. The color of the aura and phosphenes behind the eyelids are bright yellow.

Fire is the way of the teacher and the teacher is a thrasher. When you thrash your opponent, you do not kill but instruct. You take the soul and heart out of him or her, so they begin again in humility. Show them kindly that their skills are not up to higher standards. Time to get busy again. It's a knack that few can master without slipping into danger. Only love makes it possible with grace. Serious pain control and the ability to remain calm when all about you are losing it is what others see. Your internal landscape is lit bright yellow and bug-eyed with joy at the chance to ply your skills in the real world. Iron body skills are augmented here. God help your opponent if you have lost your kindness. The negative side of opening this chakra is the intensity can turn into obsession. The paranoid expression is need for distance from other and a belief that one is the "master of the universe." Bruce Lee might be considered an avatar of Fire.

Wind/Developmental/Anahata (Eagle and Lion)

The heart chakra connects the thymus (considered a separate chakra in some systems), heart, and tongue with a lime-green energy. As the meditator works his or her attention farther up the spine and energy wheel, or penetrates more deeply into the reversed triangle of the light expanding from the mountain top, spirits of the air begin to make their presence felt. One may find oneself face to face, or eye to eye, with fluttering doves and gape-mouthed bats.

The birds associated with the gods of wisdom in the West are the owl, vulture, and raven. The eagle and hawk connect to war and sometimes healing. The crow is generally regarded as a wise trickster and the Greeks considered sparrows to be psychopomps. The crane is a creative war spirit that only associates with the intelligent in China, and happiness and longevity in Japan. The giant vulture flies high with powerful magic and great vision drawn from Egypt. The bats are associated with the female spirits of mammalian antiquity, while the birds are snakes with wings. The birds take wing as the heart chakra is opened by the warm light-green fires of love. Women often enter the cycle here, as chi is stored in the breasts. All winged spirits represent courage and higher spirituality, as one is risking all to travel where support is tenuous. The ninja consider the red dragonfly a harbinger of luck. It is the symbol of winning and wealth. Mastery of the creatures of the air is part of the mythology that surrounds the Wind chakra. In *Meditation Mastery* I describe it this way:

> The Wind attitude is associated with the opening of the heart chakra. It is the last cauldron of Chi Kung and for most people who actually do this it is the last body chakra to be opened. This chakra acts as a buffer to the brain and can cool energy before it enters the skull. It is better not to force energy through this chakra as I did but wait for it to melt, thus reducing the risk of damage to the base of the brain and hypothalamus. As higher energy enters the heart chakra irregular beating may occur until the mechanism stabilizes. This can be scary if unexpected.
>
> The postures associated with the wind are very erect with the neck raised and head tilted. The arms are lifted with the elbows dropped slightly forward and parallel to the shoulders with the hands forward of the face; the palms showing as if you were surrendering. The legs are loose and the weight is off the heels so you can twirl and leap like a dancer. The chest is lifted and expanded so you've full lung capacity. Response is to turn sideways as you twirl into your opponent like the wind. Here you develop your skills of working close to your attacker, merging with his movement, and using him or her to shield you from other attackers. The

wind draws on righteous anger and the fear of the mother for its fighting power.

Wind reflects the potential to develop others with wisdom, humor and love. Wind in a martial sense can be defined as the orientation toward instruction, repair or control of another human being without doing irreparable damage. This is the hardest personality configuration to learn if you did not have good models and usually only develops with age and extensive experience. The wind is associated with compassion, forgiveness and healing. It is the manifestation of mature love needs based on the need to be generative rather than as a reaction to external factors. Many religious systems focus on developing this chakra alone, as it is considered the most predictably beneficial.

You do your part to make the world a better place. You are generous with your time and material goods to help others who've had less opportunities than you. You are openhearted or benevolent in the purest sense of those terms. You have to be careful not to waste your energy on the hopeless and helpless as the mean and poor of spirit will be with us always.

The point of concentration is the heart or thymus. You can increase the energy of the Wind by pressing the forefinger to the thumb, or simply turning the hands outward with the thumb extended and up. The colors of the aura and phosphenes behind the eyelids are bright lime green.

It takes great imagination to get a human being into the air, whether wave or particle. Angels and muses will appear to the meditator who has purified his or her desire. The breathing here can be different. If you want to enliven your vision, try hyperventilating as you meditate. Pant after your own. When the heart chakra opens, healing power flows easily through the body and down to the hands. Green energy can easily be seen around the upper body and there is a strong tendency to become more vegetarian with the realization that you are part of nature, as well as a spiritual being. An olive-drab green is associated with lying, and darker shades of green and brown with greed, and jealousy. Exercise some care as you build your catalog.

The Void/Self-Actualizing/Vishuddha-throat/ Ajna-brow/Sahasrara-crown and above (Elephant, Crane, and Spider)

Once you have opened all the body chakras, the last task is to open the head chakras. In Ninpo these are considered as one, though there are three levels which inter-relate, and together this process is called entering the Void. The endocrine glands that are rejuvenated are the pineal and pituitary. The first level is associated with the base of the brain (medulla and cerebellum) and the Jade Pillow or Jade Gates. It is referred to as the throat chakra in the Hindu systems as it seems to be an aid to eloquence when one feels more emotion and the location at the base of the brain and back of the head is parallel to the larynx when viewed from the front. The color of the phosphenes are blue, which is activated or affirmed by passing the sword test. The parts of the brain affected are the lower brain (limbic) that is the seat of the emotions—elephant or Vishuddha chakra. The second level results in indigo phosphenes activating the brow or Ajna chakra, comprising pituitary, throat, thyroid, nasal passages, and hypothalamus (often referred to in Western mysticism as opening the third eye). The third and highest level associated with meditative practice activates the Sahasrara chakra, referred to as the lotus by Buddhists. The pineal gland and higher brain functions connect to produce violet phosphenes, which over time saturate the whole body, then evolve into the white associated in almost all mystical and religious mythology with perfection of the *siddhi*.

Relax and enjoy the adventure. Feel the beat. Get connected. Launch yourself into the Void. The Void on the positive side is

201

sky blue unless you're a night flyer, which is the way associated with wisdom—and the good-looking goddesses, if you can handle some serious PMS. When the chakras in the head rejuvenate, the tree or flower metaphor becomes more meaningful as the energy which was flowing up now begins to overflow the brain like a fountain, soaks back down through the body to the earth, and spreads out through the fields of air surrounding you. The aura color indicates the driving chakra and reveals the associated behavioral and personality traits to the wise. There is no reason to fear death when you have personalized your spirit through this ancient process. Everything that exists in the material world is part of the Great Spirit.

Spirits are attracted to you, as you are a bridge for them to enjoy the material world, and if they find you worthwhile will guide you to enjoy the spirit world or adjacent realm. The throat chakra is associated with eloquence and song. Muses and angels will tempt you with their work, if you will play it or write it for them. The music of the spheres is light stuff in comparison to the vibrations of the material world where word and voice can be immortalized. Apollo awaits a twelve-string guitar player. There are too many sitars in the string section. Ry Cooder will be challenged. Channeling can get pretty strange when you depart the arts. The Tibetan Yeti spirit is a high country beast that resembles a gorilla, as well as a sea lion, and moves easily from wind to Void as a manifestation of the death god Yama. I'd stick with the dancers and protective spirits until you work out some gender understandings around turf, power, and truth. If offered a beautiful foot, kiss it, decorate it, and climb it. If it helps bring you across... Love it to death. For even then you may not part.

The Hindu Brahmin paint the ajna red to indicate both caste and the connection of the genitals to the brain. Earthy. The meek or stealthy shall inherit it. Medieval alchemists used a rose as their symbol. Earth is associated with hell by the sky gods. Its supposed to be peaceful, dreadfully dull, and conservative of life. All life is considered sacred by the earth lovers right down to insects, as all intelligence is seen as an interaction between fields of energy and influence, as well as being particle material that has animated at the will of higher powers. Insect intelligence is a hive mentality that is multi-faceted like the eyes of Artemis. If you are interested in telepathy, insects will gain totemic consideration. Even the gods bear watching from the mind and eyes of the ninja master who gathers and occasionally reports intelligence. The winners in this contest get to have great influence in shaping the direction of the game as they increase in power. Shelley and Yeats may have been the last Europeans to make it as visitors. Jung backed off, but got a lot of good information. The American Transcendentalists, like Emerson and Longfellow, were a terribly positive lot. I don't know if they got to the phase of shapeshifting and bilocation as normal reality. It makes a conversation fraught with visible symbols a telepathic experience that is shared by many. Very strange, but doesn't hold a candle to some of the weirdness of television as a predictive measure of reality, fashion, or even reflection. In the *Meditation Mastery* course I describe the indescribable as follows:

> The Void for the Japanese is inexplicable, as it is reflected in spontaneity and intuition. From a human alchemy and mystical yoga viewpoint, it is the opening of the fifth, sixth, and seventh chakras. For the Chinese, it is the final collecting points for energy that are in the throat and brain.
>
> The fifth chakra is associated with verbal skill, sky blue, and social creativity. You enjoy expressing yourself and are able to empathize with others. Ideas are your playground. You enjoy the company of writers, speakers, and artists, and have some interesting projects you call your own. The point of concentration is from the joining of the collarbones up through the tongue and the base of the skull.

The sixth chakra is often referred to as the "brow chakra" or "third eye," is associated with the pituitary gland, and is considered to be the psychic center. The color is dark blue, shades of indigo, or purple as it mixes with the other chakras. It is associated with nobility. You trust your perceptions and make appropriate responses to external conditions with calm. The point of concentration is made by slightly crossing your eyes and looking up.

The seventh chakra, often called the "crown chakra" or "thousand-pointed lotus," is at the top of the brain and is associated with the pineal gland. As the base chakra is associated with the Earth, the crown chakra is associated with Heaven. For the Chinese, Heaven and Earth must combine. It is considered the gateway to the spirit world and guidance by the higher Self. The color begins as violet and eventually becomes a silvery white. It just develops as your brain becomes more accustomed to receiving more chi. To increase Void ability, surround the thumb with the tips of all your fingers when you meditate.

"Balance is the key to truly powerful body dynamics. Breath provides the life force with energy and chi kung ignites the archetypes, hormonal intelligence or "gods within." I've heard it said that Budo Taijutsu alone is a Way to enlightenment. If so, my observations lead me to the conjecture that it takes a hell of a long time and many, many beatings at the hands of the Master to get you there. Being as American as fast food, I recommend the 30- to 90-day method described under Chi Kung Meditation. I recommend meditating more at night, as the cooler Yin energies are easier on your spinal column and skull. If Chi Kung meditation isn't dangerous enough to get your adrenals pumping, try rock climbing, open ocean scuba diving, or sky diving, as they force you to do something dangerous in a very controlled and disciplined manner. You should fear god but most people today don't know what a marvelous stimulus to spiritual growth fear can be. Primal fear brings out what you are, good or bad, so think positively. Traditionally, it was the Grandmaster's job to hunt down and terminate his or her students who went over to the dark side.

Having no ego is a consequence of the lesser enlightenment. It sweetens one's nature. It can only be achieved, in my opinion, by being raised by remarkably loving and developmental parents, spending a few years with extremely skilled therapists, surviving 25,000 "mics" of acid, being in love, or combining Zen with chi kung. (Actually the Zen priests receive chi kung training, but only after proving their sincerity and vocation, about four years into it after you've received your degree in Buddhist theology. I'm told it's a big secret. My informant stretches the truth some.) Anyway, if you want samadhi, get cracking! Your body is probably never going to be any better than it is right now. Do it now while you have guides and help.

In this blue realm (heaven or the Void) which begins with the opening of the throat chakra, one can always hear the blues, but the rhythm is seldom sad if fired from below. It is driven by the heart as well as the intellect, which leads to understanding emotion as a tool that can be used to make truth more attractive. When truth attracts the scientifically trained eye, which often has all the imagination whipped out of it by the educational process, she has a hard time establishing empathy. However, creativity in the natural scientist is traditionally called inventiveness. It fuels business like an elephant's natural gas. It can be destructive, but in America following Columbia's admonitions, the war axes are supposed to be used only in defense. Exhibiting and exploiting these skills or powers is usually considered a violation of monastic discipline, and pretending to possess such skills is grounds for dismissal from the training group *(sangha)*. The practitioner of Ninpo, coming from a warrior tradition that emphasizes living in both worlds, as a necessity of Bugei, regards all this as simply tools of subtle influence.

Commentary

My own experience and conversations with others have reinforced my awareness that in males the greatest powers are rooted in the rejected feminine aspects of the subconscious. Murphy's concept of pantheism (*Future of the Body* see bibliography) corresponds to my experience, even to the types of visions that students report: visitation by angels, archetypal demigods, foreign and animal archetypal spirits, and what other religions consider their gods. Doorways to other realities appear with a simple shift of mindset, and one is suddenly confronted with mythical beings. These visions, given attention, grow stronger and less vaporous with every contact. Some of these entities seem to be quite helpful and delighted to make your acquaintance; others seem a bit annoyed that you are in their space. Some regard you as a new toy, others as a source of food, others a threat, and some attack. If your chi is strong you do seem to have dominion. *Noumas* (Greek for allness or suchness) is within you. The human sensorium contains some wildly mythopoetic structures that can be perceived as having a life of their own.

There is no absolute Way, as human variability and uniqueness preclude that what works for me will have the exact effect on you. The ancient Taoists as represented by Lao Tzu and Sun Tzu have been remarkably honest in their presentation of a universal esoteric path. They based it more on biological and neurological process than behavior or personality traits. They seem to have concocted an alchemical winner. I will say that paucity of accurate translation and distribution of these extremely worthwhile ideas and exercises is a great loss to many in the West. I find it interesting that many spiritually inclined individuals seem to develop religious systems remarkably similar to Native American shamanism crossed with Yoga, Zen, and Shintoism: Carlos Castenada as Tibetan lama from Hell's Kitchen, or Lydia White Eagle, moose woman out of Giorgio's of Hollywood. It's often New Age masturbation from an urban hell peopled with practitioners of limited but fantastic experience of heaven. The Romans started with Zeus and Hera, as the Void was beyond comprehension. They squabbled a lot; they represented the male and female essence or attributes of all living nature, showing that opposites attract, and a little friendly warfare is part of a long-term relationship. Some of the godlike disasters described in Roman mythology are similar to the *Challenger* explosion. Your family represents your skill at keeping all the godlike factors straight and operating properly.

The Vikings and Romans were ultimately subdued by the Goths, a long time after the giants took over the child's mind of Wodin. Death Angels—those Valkyries on horseback humping their way home to heaven, were not just the love objects of bloodlusting Norse berserks. The Hindu, Native American, Polynesian, Chinese, Japanese, and African indigenous folk religions all have warrior traditions that reward the protector with love and a place in the permanent war games. (Lots of adrenaline in that way of life. Heaven must be awash with the blood of heroes.) Winner takes all is part of much religious thought. "Are you saved, Brother? Brother, can you spare a dime?" Understand the concept of *jihad* (holy war), or better yet, *Islam ab harb* (similar to *Deutschland Uber Alles*). In this game the Sufi dances above the warring mob. "See only bones covered with rotting skin." (Buddhist exercise for eliminating sexual desire). "Crush your desires. Sex is the Great Satan." (The Ayatollah Khomeini before discovering the United States was the Great Satan.) People are willing to die for this kind of nonsense. Lords of Life and Death Queens. Queens of Light and Death Gods. "As above, so below" is a warning that evolution still operates in the spirit realm.

Grof's attempts to scientize consciousness using holotropic modeling strike a familiar resonance (see bibliography). On the lighter side, the Eastern Maxim "that one can only teach to the level of one's realization" shows great compassion for the ethno and egocentric. Michael Murphy has done us all a great service by cataloging many available human repertoires (see bibliography). The emerging field in Anthropology of biogenetic structuralism will have tremendous impact as it enters into the colloquia and brings deeper understanding in respect to contemplative practice. Drs. Laughlin, McManus, and d'Aquili have synthesized a neurological map for transcendence, as well as a living model of human consciousness (see bibliography). In their effort to be academically impeccable they are almost as esoteric in their description as what they are describing. Homeomorphogenesis indicates a rich neurophenomenology of human consciousness and the value of structuring epistemic process (welcome to the language of biogenetic structuralism).

Child Mind
by Glenn Morris

What is it like to perceive all information as truth?
What did you learn at your mother's knee before the shields went up?
What is the knowledge sleeping in your bones
Learned through osmosis without translation at the feet of others?
Did it make you scream in rage, or terror?
Or were you a child of Love, raised in an open and disciplined manner?
Who do you serve?
What do you owe your teachers?
How can you fix your problem?
Giri.

Mushin, Empty spirit or potential, is often translated by speakers of Japanese as innocence.
To be free of the negative is not embraced sarcastically.

When one is raised in a fearful environment, unskilled,
    where a wrong move is rewarded by a slap or smile,
Who defines the wrong
shapes the excuses for failure;
creates more fear.

Wa, harmony of spirit is more mundanely translated as
    getting along with other people.

"We have nothing to fear but fear itself" (Winston of the well-
    turned word during the Siege of Britain).

The return to hell as an adult restores insight to the
    intelligent
removing blinders.

The child knows ignorance as innocence.
The child sees life and death close-up as mystery.

Ten

Learning Theory

Mastery of strategy *(heiho)* on the higher planes is augmented by intellectual skill, verbal, and motor, cognitive strategy, acceptance of the unknown, and the ability to visualize information. These elements can all be tested and measured. To quote Musashi (a critic at heart), you must "Distinguish between gain and loss in worldly matters." The ability to evaluate is one of his more important qualities for warriorship and mastery. The other eight are in the Earth or Ground chapter in *Go Rin No Sho*. The external skills of movement can even be graphed and charted, if you are inclined toward that sort of thing. There are recognizable benchmarks for both external and internal skills. Some of the more esoteric skills may require years or a clever experimental model to verify, but are worth the attempt to achieve. In Bujinkan Ninpo the *kyu* ranks are concerned with learning the fundamentals. The dan ranks from one to ten focus on mastering taijutsu and tools, and the last five, (eleven and up) extending the usual tenth dan to fifteen, return us to the elementals or archetypes of spirit.

Sport, life, and combat differ in their fundamental rules. Life and combat have no rules beyond natural constants. Winning all through your life requires continuous reform that can be regarded over time as improvement. Freedom to experiment is a greater mother of invention than war. War often does speed things up, but the collapse after the charge is usually the death of the good. "Only the good die young" is supposed to encourage the brave, not lead to wanton ease as a life-preserver. Knowing the meaning of words is important to the burgeoning spirit turned loose in a world that changes with the speed of a thought brought into productivity by the spread of good information and the rejection of the old way as archaic rather than classic. True learning must involve the senses, as learning is learned behavior, and instinctual in the aroused or excited.

Intellectual skills can be tested as a learning category simply through observing the organism's ability to apply problem-solving, recognize principles, and use concepts. Cognitive strategies can be revealed through observing behavior as well as discussion of internal methods of critical thinking, organizing information, and learning. Verbal skill can be measured as verbatim retention, or at higher level, in continuous improvement of descriptive information. Motor skills or physical prowess can be observed through accuracy, rapidity, smoothness, and force of muscular movements. Esoteric skills concerning intention and energy can be observed through outcome. Hatsumi-soke wants a scientist to examine Ninpo from a biological perspective. As a route to physiological longevity it seems effective, as there are quite a few practitioners that are in their sixties, seventies, and eighties who seem to sock and roll with vigor.

There are many methods for testing empiricism, but few are as reliable as the scientific method. You can work out your own experimental designs if you are prepared to reject a lot of background noise. Applying the bleak methods of objectivity to your own teaching only verifies your faith in the endurance of truth. Teachers are best recognized by the characteristics, abilities, and skills of their students. Transfer of training is important to "The Way of the Carpenter." An outstanding teacher develops the ability to apply principles and generalizations already learned to new problems and situations. He or she has, and nurtures in others, the capacity to think for oneself, to develop new solutions appropriate to their experience, and to move with internalized confidence. In the martial arts it is often recommended that a prospective enthusiast take a hard look at a master's senior students with the expectation that they will be able to perform a reasonable percentage of the master's technique and have a professional perspective toward the knowledge they've acquired.

I always expected my students to better my performance in what they chose as their areas of expertise, and most very quickly could. When accepting challenges from other schools, I would run their champions against my senior students first. I seldom had to lift a finger. The knights defend the source of their power. Having high expectations applies to the home as well as the training field. My son Richard Binford used to get embarrassed, and even accused me of not giving him a serious game, when he started beating me consistently at chess in the tenth grade. He would complain to his mother in Spanish that I wasn't trying. In actuality the two years of casual instruction that I had given him, plus directing him to read Tal, Morphy, and Fischer (great chess masters), had put me at a pretty hopeless disadvantage. He was a better chess player than I. When my son Shawn Phillips was thirteen he chastised me for trying to teach him ways to injure other wrestlers. When Shawn was sixteen, I asked him about his meditative practice, most of which he had learned from Taffesse-sensei. He told me, "I sit very still until a large eye appears in front of me. When I'm ready, I leap through it. It opens into a whole new world." I never asked him again, and just said, "Keep going." He is twenty-five now, and is so much nicer than I was at that age. He carried a Chemistry load at Hope College, working nights as a bouncer, and went on to grad school at

University of California, Irvine, California. He's smarter than I am, too. When he talks shop, I'm lost. His colleagues claim he is more Japanese than the Japanese, which amuses me.

The learning of physical skills increases one's feelings of competence and control, which results in greater self-confidence. A teacher who understands the importance of spiritual development will prize the attributes of self-confidence, tolerance of diversity, and motivation. Secondarily one develops analytic skills and learns the terms and facts relative to any subject matter as cognitive skills. In the modern consumer-oriented educational process, American cognitive skills are shaped toward economic expansion rather than greater awareness.

Hatsumi-soke, in a 1981 letter that Stephen Hayes published in a 1993 *Musubi* article, wrote:

> In teaching others you will learn much. To fully mature as a warrior in all aspects of life requires forty years of study. The first twenty years of learning are spent on the *omote* [yang, or right-handed, public] aspects of life. These are the years of training in the concepts of honor, respect for seniors and parents, guidance of those who would learn and serve, endurance in developing a warrior spirit, and the strengths one gathers by being just, honest, and forthright. The vast majority of martial arts systems stop at this level. [From my observation the vast majority of martial arts are not arts and are simply a glorified way of doing push-ups between cold showers. Hatsumi-soke is an exceedingly generous man.] The ninja, however, must keep going.
>
> The second twenty years of your life are spent exploring the *ura* [yin, or left-handed, private] realm, better known as the feminine, interior, hidden, or dark side of life. These are years in training yourself to recognize the ways in which the good and beloved can be twisted, and in learning realities in which loving hearts have appearances that are frightening and confusing to the masses who lack the discipline to achieve the perspective of enlightenment. Weaker souls

are quick to label 'evil' that which they don't understand. [Particularly when they are running and screaming as they look over their shoulders.] The ninja does not fear strength.

My translation is a little less formal than Stephen's, as my relationship with Hatsumi-san is more casual. Japanese is such a tricky language.

The viewpoint of an enlightened ninja master is greatly refined in the training that begins after fifth dan and again after tenth dan. Those who have achieved the tenth dan are expected to master the traditional techniques of the *Shinden Happo Biken* (the eight true spirit ways of the beautiful sword). To quote Hatsumi-soke's *Kuden* (Creator's Guiding Principles for Practitioners of Ninpo), "People of the tenth dan are avatars of Bujin, learning virtue through the treachery of the world destroying life. They are charged to develop the heart of the gods and the eyes of the heart through self-control and perseverance, and possess natural justice" (*Sanmyaku*, Vol. 1, No. 3. 1994). The tenth dan and above patch, which is rarely seen, has a light blue border, with green kanji on an orange/yellow field. The white stars above the badge represent the *Sankhya* sect (Buddhist School of Three Stages popular in China during the Sui and Tang dynasties) concept of *Go Dai* from a martial art perspective. An understanding of religion and philosophy from an inner experiential martial viewpoint is expected, rather than an intellectual or ritualized external worship interpretation. The three stages are quite complex and in Ninpo require transmission from a natural consciousness *(mushinka)*. The resulting consciousness is mystically called *kami-musubi* (tied to the gods). Some have a little difficulty living up to this description, but rank hath its privilege, and *kohai* are forgiven a lot. The darker side of *shinken-gata* is that habits and faults which should be eradicated in the achievement of full human potential are, of course, associated with death.

In the last fifty years, particularly after World War II, there

215

has been a gradual accumulation in the West of authoritative Eastern philosophy, translations, and commentaries. Modern transportation allows one to make journeys in days that in my youth were considered adventures taking months and years. It is possible to train with the masters. If you are couth enough you might get to have dinner with one, and bullshit about the quality of the others.

People live in paradigms. I think of myself as a social scientist deeply involved in human effectiveness and/or development. I have been trained as a communication theorist, spent a little rewarding time as a graduate student in anthropology, and have spent most of my life working and teaching as an industrial psychologist. I was a tenured associate professor before leaving academia for consulting. The paradigm that makes me most comfortable is called western phenomenology. It differs from the Taoist, Ninpo, shamanistic, Native American, and Hindu perspectives in being skeptical and reductionist. It is an analytical approach to ordering information, and commonly entails stripping away the perceived extraneous elements to isolate what is considered effective, whether behavior, compound, chemical, or movement. Eastern and/or indigenous phenomenology tends to emphasize process as an approach to achieving balance, wholeness, and integration with spirits, and community. When emotion is integrated into the Western perspective the differences between Eastern and Western paradigms are not so great, though the new vocabulary may create some problems in understanding the other. For the closed mind, the distance between the mindsets is more than a thousand miles, and the conversation more like a battle. In the nineteenth century the popular position was "never the twain shall meet." In the martial arts we find "masters" who accuse chi workers of fraud, and even in Ninpo I have friends who haven't a clue concerning the "mystical side" of the art after years of being exposed to it. (In hoshin I could usually drive the "bricks" out of the system, as it was a waste of our time to try to wake them up. Hatsumi-soke seems to tolerate a wide variety of skill and expectations.)

In transpersonal psychology the "feeling" function is distinguished from the "thinking" function. Thinking involves ideation and conceptual connection, while feeling involves acceptance and rejection, or valuing. Although the two work together, they are fundamentally different psychic functions, rather like smell and taste are different sensory functions. Valuing relates to emotion. There are many terms in the English language concerning the thinking function: logic, analysis, induction, deduction, strategy, conceptualizing, calculation, planning, synthesizing, and so forth. Nouns that represent aspects of the "feeling" function include empathy, avoidance, trust, grace, enthusiasm, hatred, fear, and love.

Mastery is a key word in the martial arts, and in Ninpo mastery includes the struggle to evolve consciousness through realizing internal subjective response. Just as mastering thinking requires intense, demanding patience and discipline, so too does taking our feeling functions to higher levels which include love and psi (telepathy, visions, telempathy, etc.). Russell Targ, physicist and one of the foremost pioneers in scientific psi research, described some of his experiences of psi in the *Journal of Scientific Exploration* (Spring 1994). Dr. Targ posits that harmony *(wa)*, and acceptance *(amae)* are necessary for experience. The emotions are centered in the limbic and spinal functions of the brain and spine and encompass what are thought of as instinctual powers—including intuition, keen sensing, far vision, acute hearing, insight, healing, tenacious loving, and endurance. More than two thousand years ago Patanjali described the processes by which the higher feeling functions are accessed and mastered by becoming (Georg Feuerstein. *The Yoga-Sutra of Patanjali: A New Translation and Commentary*, Inner Traditions International, 1989).

The attitude of *mushin* (Child's Mind or divine emptiness) contains tremendous analytical power when directed by experienced intelligence. Being able to know you don't know allows you to begin to ask realistic questions and get to the basics. If the basics work well and give you pleasure, you may miss the exaltation of total mastery of mystery farther along because you stopped when you were full. The "empty cup" stuff. Remember for a moment the curiosity that drove you to finally experience the pleasure in your sexuality. What did you have to go through? Was the quest worthy of the journey? If you were to apply your child's mind to the end activity with your more recent experience driving your curiosity, do you not think you could improve the experience for all concerned? A mature perspective when observing behavior from an attitude of awe renders pleasure and joy from creating a new sensation. Age and depth may enhance experience. Deliberate creation is powerful manifesting magick to the receiver of the gift. Hiding your light under a bushel basket only applies to those who have little to offer, for charity begins at home. A bearer of light can function in many environments and makes strange friends. The higher your standards, the more interesting the journey. If you want to be a fireman, examine the role and responsibilities of the Fire Chief and learn the routes to attainment. Having *taigan* (large eyes, great desires, or great body skills) is the foundation for growth and learning in Budo or Ninpo, using the self as the tool of your humble resolve. There comes a point when you have to outgrow desire. Or as my Texas friends say, "Git over it!" It is a puff of smoke, or attachment to illusion.

Social Learning

The assumption of our consumer culture is *not* that an individual is a vessel for spiritual power that exists in multiple levels of being, but the individual is a cog in the economic wheel of production or consumption. Our schools prepare us for taking a place in the economic machine, and our education is so lacking in humanity that the phrase "Get a life" is no longer synonymous with "Get a job." Universities and religion have generally failed as the custodians of the spirit to become joyless trade schools of indoctrination greedily collecting tithe and tuition to support their own bureaucratic machinery of socialization. The trappings of social status often become more important than learning, or the realization of our intrinsic humanity.

Learning is process, and the rules of intellectual development are the same for physical skills and spiritual growth. We move from the fundamentals toward ever-higher levels of sophistication until we reach our limits. It is like learning to drive. Many of us can remember the struggle to master the shifting of gears. We had to deal with a clutch we could not look at, and a gear shift that pulled our eyes from the speedily approaching horizon. Automatic transmissions are not the same. Safer, smoother, but the feel and knowledge are not the same challenge. Those of us who are gray and gnarly can remember jerking across fields and parking lots in winter and summer, working on mastering the clutch and wheels. Sometimes an older relative or friend would risk their lives to give us a lesson. The driver training instructor had to have nerves of steel to climb into a motorized iron box with four or five hormonal sixteen year olds joyfully risking death to get their certificate. I almost plowed into the back of a dynamite truck on one of our winding two-lane Allegheny mountain roads, on a steep downhill curve. All the instructor did was bite through the pencil that he chewed constantly. I tend to be a screamer when teaching driving. I totaled a few vehicles in my youth and remember the consequences of crawling from the wreckage. My daughter Teri Dawn almost drove through the filling pumps while showing off to some tight-jeaned boy. I did not handle that too well. Screaming and pointing is not how skills are transferred. Grandpa Thomas did a far better job than I when it came to teaching driving. He was a retired trucker. The above is an allegory concerning learning and teaching in general.

The ninja is first and foremost a seeker of enlightenment and harmony. A student who seeks truth is worthy of respect at whatever age. Such a search requires creativity. The psychological components of creativity are: (1) a well-developed base of knowledge; (2) imaginative thinking skills; (3) a venturesome personality that can tolerate ambiguity; (4) moderate risk-taking to overcome obstacles and seek new experiences; and (5) intrinsic motivation, or sensing value in the work itself (Sternberg and Lubart, "An investment theory of creativity and its development," *Human Development,* 34, 1–31, 1991). Countless studies have shown that the human being learns best through play and experimentation. Relying only on imitation can lead to dead ends. The teacher who cannot compensate for variation in ability and environment is setting up his or her student for failure in the tests of life and death. Play is different from work, as play implies pleasure and enjoyment. We learn most quickly when we play. We do best what we love, and we improve what we love by exceeding our own standards. Just as the learning to drive a car requires mastery of basic skills, so do other activities in our lives, and all are open to criticism as well as continuous improvement. Discipline requires that one keep going regardless of the obstacles that normal living throws out. As the goal of enlightenment is achievement of the Child's Mind, how do we return to a natural state, or avoid acquiring a false sense of self?

Infants

The human being, when born, is neonate. What that means is the size of the brain prevents complete development while in the womb. A human newborn is not wired up completely. We're not totally blank slates, but lots of functions are incomplete — for example, the rectum doesn't come under mental control until the nerves hook into the brain, which usually takes about two years. Until that happens, toilet training is a waste of time. Mental process at birth is probably the equivalent of a very slow puppy. Even the eyes and hands have serious problems in discerning shapes, but the learning process begins with entrance into the new environment. For the next seven years the child is basically a learning machine. Monkey see. Monkey do! Monkey feel and think about.

According to David S. Sobel, M.D., M.P.H., who performed a meta-analysis of pediatric studies using random samples for intervention with gentle touch and passive movement, preterm infants had fifty percent weight gain, were more active and responsive to their environment, were discharged six days earlier from the hospital for a $3000 cost saving, and showed improved growth and mental and physical abilities eight to twelve months later when compared to the control groups in the study—preterm infants who did not receive the gentle touch intervention. The intervention consisted of a nurse trained in the methodology taking each preterm child in the experimental group three times a day for ten days, and gently massaging the child and moving its limbs through a cycle of stretches for fifteen minutes.

One of my black belts, Kevin Brown, teaches in Colorado. His first daughter was preterm. He gave her daily meridian massage (a chi kung massage technique in hoshin) and she is now above average in size and intelligence for her age. The value of gentle touch for therapeutic intervention cannot be overestimated for children or adults. I have made certain my daughters know the importance of playing with their children and breast feeding. Breast feeding transfers the benefits of the mother's immune system to the child. In some cultures breast feeding continues until the child is five. In cultures where breast feeding is longer than two years, the survival rate of infants is higher and neurosis lower (William Goode, *The Family*, Prentice Hall,

1982). America no longer leads the world in infant survival, and bottle feeding is probably a factor in that fall from grace.

If children are not damaged or discouraged, the learning processes of the child's mind continue into adulthood and beyond. If the learning skills are not encouraged and rewarded, the child learns to focus on content as opposed to process, and fails to internalize, becoming primarily motivated by external factors, lost in and to the illusion. I suspect I was indeed fortunate in having a mother who was an elementary school teacher. Even if I wasn't interested, I was exposed to a lot of useful information, music, and travel as a child, and was always allowed to read whatever I could lay my hands on. My parents and instructors didn't teach me any foreign languages as a child, which is a great disadvantage to an adventurer, but my non-verbal skills have filled that weakness. My father went to the elementary school a number of times to request I be given more challenging things to learn. My mother made certain I stayed ahead of the pack. I was no prodigy, but I wasn't having a real good time, either.

In my opinion, only the very smartest and gentlest should be allowed to teach at the elementary level. Classes should be small. Personal attention and time for questions and answers are essential to learning. The optimal number of students in a classroom is fifteen. When the classes become larger, personal attention is often replaced by peer distraction. The young human being learns quickly when the desire for food is not present. The human being is attracted by warmth and a well-lit environment. The climb out from the cold and darkness is a lifetime task in which the best skills that drive a cheerful spirit are learned young. It would solve so many problems downstream. Talk about a head start. The United States is one of the few industrialized nations that does not have a policy of universal child care (Ian Robertson, *Sociology*, Worth, 1987).

The ninja concepts concerning child-raising involve

providing children with positive experiences that allow them to test themselves against their reality in ways that they can master with practice and effort, building confidence and skills at the same time. The Japanese child seldom hears the word "No" and often appears unruly and undisciplined to our eyes. *Amae* indulges the young. The Japanese take to heart the admonition to "Spare the rod and spoil the child!" as a command rather than a warning. A good friend tells me my interpretation of Japanese child-raising should include the scold terms *dame yo* and *ikenai yo* which imply socially incorrect or adroit behavior rather than wrong or right. The regimented Japanese school system and its challenges, along with tremendous peer pressure to succeed, keep the average kid well-behaved. In fact, Japanese students often commit suicide if they do not win entrance to a "good" school or college. The dark side of socialized high levels of achievement motivation is the awful stigma associated with failure to perform.

Child Abuse

In the area of child abuse and neglect, many counties in America report statistics of children raised in poverty increasing by fifty percent during the "kinder, gentler" eighties. In rural counties the figure increased by up to eighty-five percent. This is a severe threat to the quality of life for the next generation, and a recognition of what happens under the rule of the complacent elite. The poor we have with us always, but the children are being abused at the rate of 45 per 1000. Child abuse correlates with spouse abuse, depression, inability to learn, psychosomatic disease, multiple personality, psychosis, child abuse, and criminality (Wenner and Goodson, "Poverty and Child Abuse," *Abstracts in Sociology,* Nov. 1992). One per thousand is enough to keep most police departments in business. Prosecution for sexual abuse of children has become so common that children now use it as a threat to control their parents. The Department of Social Services tries to handle a job so vast that they've turned to the tactics of guilty until proven innocent, rather like the IRS or the Napoleonic system of law favored by France and Mexico. Research on violent criminals reveals that over ninety percent of murderers grew up in abusive situations. Over sixty percent of welfare mothers were physically and sexually abused as children ("Delinquent Development," *Science News,* May, 1993).

Ignorant people bearing children, and raising them in horrific circumstances, places an increasing burden on the public schools system. Kids raising kids tend not to do very well as strategists in a competitive, ever-changing world market, and often fall into the overloaded welfare system. Family income predicts the IQs of five year olds far more accurately than measures of social status like mother's educational background, ethnicity, and number of parents in the household. Children raised in poverty display more fearfulness, anxiety, and unhappiness when compared with children from affluent households. Depression is common among unemployed women, and depressed mothers report greater reliance on harsh forms of child punishment such as hitting, yelling, and threats of violence. Unrelenting poverty, whether urban or rural, is significantly associated with harsh parental discipline, divorce rate, fighting at home, criminality, disruptive and hostile students as identified by their teachers, violent death, and the catch-all low self-esteem. (*Science News,* Vol. 144, No. 6. 1993) In my lifetime I never thought that the medieval philosopher Thomas Hobbes' timely observation "The life of man, solitary, poor, nasty, brutish, and short" would apply to a major percentage of Americans. Even worse are those who don't want to recognize that ignorant people need very little motivation to do the most awful things to their offspring. The average newborn cries for two and a half hours a day, as a reflex to strengthen its lungs. When they are teething, they whine and cry constantly along with diarrhea. They aren't like Barbie.

If you have a short fuse, that alone can drive you to attack, particularly if your self-esteem is low, you have lousy parenting skills, or think of beating children as natural from your own experience.

Conservatives like unquestioning consumers, and ignorant voters, and paint the educational system as an arm of government propaganda. Wake Up! School is where you learn to be what you are. If you are failing, pay attention. There is no class for parenting because you were supposed to learn that at home before you hit the streets. Sex education, too. You can't fix a kid, or a marriage, by kicking it like a malfunctioning Coke machine. Wake Up. Its a huge problem. The government hasn't a clue. Clean up your neighborhood, change your behavior. Cool out. Child abuse in any form must not be tolerated. WORD! The results of poor parenting, child abuse and the relation to violent crime are quite clear.

The Impact of Reading When Properly Taught

One of life's greatest pleasures is reading and learning through this wondrous tool to develop your own imagination. Reading is to the mind, as exercise is to the body. Illiteracy is a criminal waste of human potential and cannot be tolerated whether as an offshoot of prejudice or laziness. A good writer creates a picture in the mind using the symbolic knowledge of words. Prose and poetry can have a life of their own, as you discover when a movie does not live up to your visualization of a favorite book. Reading without visualizing the events portrayed is like watching television with the sound turned off—one misses a lot. Good writing paints a picture for your child's mind. I've seen quite a few good young minds put to risk by boring reading material that did not challenge them, so they turned from school in disgust. If you have a child that is falling behind in reading, may I suggest reading with them, and giving them Marvel or Classic Comic books, as reading is reading. Reading comics is easier for children with dyslexia and certain other learning dysfunctions. It is also an aid to visualization through association for the beginner.

The classic myths and legends of all cultures tell not only great gripping stories of love, war, and hatred but also transcendence. The Gods and Goddesses are described in both their strengths and weaknesses, and how they interact with humans. Children love this stuff, and just like prime time television and movies, it may take some adult interpretation to put what they hear and see into useful perspective. When I taught my dyslexic son Richard how to read at fifteen I used Classic and Marvel Comics. He was supposed to be retarded. The way he was being treated by his blood relations was criminal. He loved the game of chess, and when he won his relatives said he cheated. It is not just a crime but a sin to waste a mind. The local junior high wanted to put him into special education classes because he flunked two grades. I talked the principal into putting him forward two grades so he could be with his peers. It only took two months of summer coaching for him to catch up. Dyslexia often fades away in adolescence. As he read aloud to me he would describe how words would disappear or move around—it was fascinating. The comics were easier for him to handle. I took him from comics to Edgar Rice Burroughs, then to Louis L'Amour, and then to Tolkien's *Lord of the Rings.* After that he was hooked. He made the National Honor Society his senior year.

Children who have no models, have no heroes. The heroes and heroines of all cultures provide lessons for children so they can make more sense of their experience. It must not be forgotten that Little Red Riding Hood and Grandma were eaten by the wolf, slain too late by the government-appointed protector. I once tried to write a children's book based on *Aesop's Fables* but found I couldn't improve on the originals. The Mutant Ninja Turtle mythology teaches teamwork, ethics, social change, respect for the master, and a positive view of the martial arts. The Power

Rangers do not have the same benefits. This is a far cry from the entertainment myths like The Lone Ranger, The Shadow, and Crimebusters that fascinated me as a child covertly listening to a crystal radio with the bed springs for an antenna, or reading with a flashlight under the covers when I was supposed to be sleeping.

Children learn to read by being read to. If the adults around them do not read, then they will not accept reading as desirable behavior. Read to your children and make certain they see you reading often. Reading for pleasure, as well as information, is one of the universal characteristics of modern leadership. A household without books is a sure sign of blighted spirit as well as economic problems. Passive learning from television, music, and radio is not as effective as reading, but it is still important. The correlation of violent behavior and watching violence on TV is well documented. The sexual awareness of youngsters today far exceeds the relative ignorance of my youth, and TV and the movies seem to be major contributors to their overheated viewpoint. Rapes in elementary schools are not that rare. I have noticed that the people I know who take most of their information concerning the world from the boob box snippets have major problems grasping complex social issues. Not even "All Things Considered" can fill in the gaps. The TV and music industries are finally beginning to realize the message is a massage, and the masseuse lacks social graces.

Teaching of Children in the Martial Arts

My friend, Master Harold Wheeler of Tennessee Isshinryu Karate, has been described to me as a deeply religious man and Christian gentleman as if that were a handicap. I disagree. He is extremely good with children and even has tutors for his karate students having difficulty with their homework and studies in general. He requires as part of their white belt training that each student find a person to sincerely compliment for what they perceive as a good act. Those are discussed in class each week. I have not been able to think of a better exercise to focus the mind toward the positive. Children hate to fail a master if the relationship is loving, and the standards high, and that is understood in the community. Jhoon Rhee revolutionized the tae kwon do world by requiring his students to hold a B average, or no training.

Thomas LaPuppet, one of my martial art heroes, has taught karate in the Bronx for as long as I can remember. I was finally blessed to shake his brown hand when I met him a few years ago. LaPuppet used to hold free clinics for children in the New York City parks. He was nationally known as a fighter and one of the early elected members of the *Black Belt* Magazine Hall of Fame. His videos indicate great patience. (Kids do the strangest things.) I was surprised to see how mellow he is in person. He's much more gentle than I am. (There are some fierceness problems in the short path. It's for war.)

I only like to teach kids in pairs or triads. I prefer that they learn with their parents, but it is a lot more fun for them to have a peer to pound on and throw around. Adults quickly lose patience with a sixty-pounder trying to toss them; the kid learns a lot about failure, as well as leverage. The little people should play in their own league. Monkey See. Monkey Do. Monkey doesn't think a lot once he thinks he knows. A kid killed his friend while playing Bruce Lee in Detroit in 1991. The temple does not respond well to crescent heel slaps. It takes more skill to shake them off than to deliver. The struck boy went to bed with a migraine and never awakened. Accidental dim mak. It was play. The signature of a child is not binding until eighteen.

I've had parents insist on training with their children as a bonding exercise. It is a good one, if they are learning something that might save or improve their lives. Recently a twelve-year-old who had trained in karate and tae kwon do as a knee-high came to me with his father. His legs were very flexible, extremely strong for his size, he was friendly and playful, but he couldn't get the hang of rolling to save his life. He was stiff as a board from the hips up and moved like he was made of steel without ball bearings. He loved breaking boards and working out with weapons. He enjoyed jumping on me with practice weapons from ambush while I was talking to someone else. I began to feel like I was in a Pink Panther movie, teaching the reincarnation of Kato. It's hard to keep them interested when there is no one of approximate size in the class, and I have no dwarfs. Often the ancient royal courts used dwarfs as teachers for the children so they would learn an adult perspective as well as gymnastics. There are many myths across cultures concerning dwarven teachers to the gods. Discussing this young boy's meditation practice was very interesting, as he had to deal with witches. Listening to children explain their experience often gives a teacher clues on how to better present what you want them to learn. Study on this.

Camper Walker, my first hoshinjutsu black belt, was so thrilled as a teenager by his yellow belt in tae kwon do that he dragged it behind his car to age it like the frayed black belt of some masters in their seventies. I've yet to lose a thread on any of my black belts. Some of those tattered belts I've seen in Japan must be lineage belts. By the time Camper was a high red belt in tae kwon do, it took one lesson in combatic jujutsu to show him how he had been wasting his time. One-shot learning is a characteristic of octopi, as they are very intelligent, but many humans who have to conquer ego needs, past experience, inflated self-esteem, and social pressure require more lessons and repetition to problem-solve efficiently. Camper was smart and crazy as a bugbear. He told me with humor his mother used to beat him before they went to parties as a preview for what would come if he lost his manners while in public. His mother must have been terrified he'd escape with the family reputation. He taught me a lot. He's still going.

When my son Shawn began to think the pain in this art was applied with malice, I gave him to Taffesse Alemu to train. (Toff was my best student.) I took Shawn to seminars given by martial artists I admired so he would avoid picking up my mistakes. I learned the seminar trick from the young men on football scholarships. They'd say things like, "Hey, if my father hadn't sent me to football camp I'd never be here. Learning from the pros and coaches is so important." I made certain he saw Masaaki Hatsumi when he was quite young. Shawn at twenty-one and nidan found he knew far more than most so-called professionals, and was often asked to teach and demonstrate in their dojos and train for free if he'd lead meditations and show some soft technique. He liked that; it gave him confidence when he could set up and take out a tae kwon do master without hurting him. Achievement, optimism, hard work, and ethics pay off eventually.

Turning out a successful kid takes about eighteen years. Self-directed study of great examples and the understanding of principles and social values are necessary for a student to surpass his teacher. It is the Way of Stealth and the mark of a true master of strategy. Your children are hostages of your fortune and in most cases your only hope of survival. Age, disease, and death, as well as love, conquer all. I have been fortunate with the children in all three of my families. They taught, and are teaching me, a lot about fathering. I cannot even imagine the fate of the unwanted child, raised by the ignorant, and thrown into the maelstrom of American life. I do see the wrecked lives around me in Michigan, Florida, and now, Texas.

The martial arts master from the Zen or Chan disciplines has an awesome reputation for shaping behavior, and a fearsome responsibility when given the minds of children to shape for defense of the beloved. The child's mind is open to probability and their imaginations raise the normal to mythic levels as a natural process of admiration (the John Wayne syndrome).

One hardly has to advertise if one is willing to truly teach children that which is worthwhile and its application to reality. When I gave a seminar in Trinidad, I had mothers beg me to return and teach their children. It blew my mind. I'd never had that experience in Jonesville. Of course, in Jonesville and Hillsdale, I was "a high-level member of that evil ninja death cult" as far as the general population was concerned. To quote The Boss, "There are all too few people **stupid** enough to keep going to the end, following their intentions through and not caring what is said about them or to them" (*Sanmyaku*, Vol. 1, No. 5, 1995). Finding a great teacher is as difficult as finding a great student. It is similar to the concept in esoteric religion of being a holy fool. Hatsumi-san occasionally describes himself as Takamatsu-soke's fool.

Teaching and Learning in a Ninja Dojo

Unlike militaristic ryu, Budo Taijutsu is taught from a relaxed, family-oriented perspective. Since much of the training is full-contact and the training groups are small, the participants through shared experience develop a sense of collegiality which usually deepens over the years into genuine friendship. When you enter a ninja dojo you won't see long lines standing at attention, or be disturbed by demented robotic yelling in unison. Ninja climb all over each other to form a circle so they can see what the shidoshi just demonstrated from all angles. They aren't into meaningless ceremony, empty protocol, or repetitive kata. They regard life as process, and self-learning and discovery as the way it is best enjoyed. It is not only superior but more fun. It is also the way that most ancient *ryuha* operated in Japan.

The bows in Bujinkan are treated casually, except at the opening ceremony to summon the Bujin and the closing ceremony to thank the Bujin for their protection while training. While one may choose not to politely revere the dojo by bowing upon each and every exit and entrance, the opening ceremony, where the senior instructor calls for the Bujin to protect all present during training, is quite different. The class forms a single line facing the senior instructor, with the highest ranks usually to the right. Everyone kneels to receive the instructor's blessing and claps to invoke the Bujin. The instructor says a brief prayer for the students' safety, and the students beseech the spirits to grant them enlightenment, "May this be the time!" in Japanese. Once the bow in has been accomplished, the shidoshi begins to demonstrate and everyone else tries to figure out what they have just seen.

If a senior belt is familiar with the technique being taught, he or she will wander around and help the beginners discover the finer points. When the training period is over, the group lines up again and the shidoshi or shidoshi-ho thanks the class, and the class bows out thanking the shidoshi. Its simple. Ninja don't put much weight on ceremony, rank, or bows, as they are essentially seeking the source together, learning Budo Taijutsu as a process. The process can take a life.

Ninja are concerned with building relationships with people they can trust during hard times. Beating someone into submission does not make sense when you are forming alliances to protect your friends and family. Sport competition encourages different attitudes which are extremely limited off the playing field. The need to dominate, or to win, has no place in a temple of learning. That only leads to cheating. The way is in practice. The way of the heart is best sought through love (Wind) and joy (Fire). Athletic prowess has its place in sport, but not in Budo/Bugei, where false confidence can lead to death. Strength is defeated by speed. Speed is defeated by surprise. Surprise is defeated by strategy.

Commentary

It is difficult for the linear thinker to make the intuitive jumps necessary for long-term strategy. Desire causes a continual focus on reward rather than process—one of the reasons that behavior modification fails to move the spirit in the more intelligent. Traditional American values can easily be set aside when the need to achieve material goals overwhelms the growth process, as when grades become more important than learning. It is easy to understand an A. It is difficult to understand algebra, or if you're more right-brained, iambic pentameter. When learning is not based on skill accomplishment, cheating becomes rampant. The more students in a class, the easier to cheat. A class over fifteen is at risk. Grades can be a metaphor for belt ranks. In a martial arts class you have to learn how to get along with a wide variety of people, or you may suffer accidental harm when techniques speed up. Shit happens. The climate that the teacher constructs keeps that sort of belligerence at a minimum.

Massage therapy, acupuncture, and shiatsu are the adult equivalents of gentle touch and passive movement, and in the hands of a skilled practitioner have the same effect. If you are ever fortunate enough to experience a masseuse trained in shiatsu or deep massage, you may become so relaxed that you can transform your body at will. Treesa Weaver, my massage therapist in Hillsdale, in just five sessions restructured some damaged fascia and muscles I had been trying to heal for years. After one session, I was so relaxed I had to retrain my eyes how to focus. The ninja practice of *junan taiso* (stretches and massage) before and after training is a beneficial boost to achieving a more flexible body similar to massage therapy and Hatha yoga. The techniques of Feldenkrais (a modern form of healing yoga) are highly regarded by students of ninjutsu from the exposure of Shihan Doron Navon. Allow me to suggest that there is utility in the Alexander Method (which focuses on subtle adjustments in posture and voice production developed for actors).

Joan Ryan has written an important book, *Little Girls in Pretty Boxes: The Making and Breaking of Elite Gymnasts and Figure Skaters* (Doubleday, 1995), which may be an eye-opener for those in pursuit of their fifteen minutes of fame. What goes on in elite sport could often be regarded by the outsider as child abuse. When a coach or parent begins to see the career of a child as their own, the kid is usually in big trouble. Ryan asks questions most fans and parents don't ask, like what happens to those who spend their lives pursuing the dream and fail? How can we have high-level competition and still keep it fun and healthy for the kids involved—because they will not all win medals?

My father always told me to watch how children and animals acted around another human being, paying attention to how close they came and how long they stayed. It was very good advice. I do not take the teaching of children lightly. I did not teach any of my children until they asked me, and I sent them to better teachers when I could afford it. Only my third son, Shawn Phillips, could absorb my lessons and now he laughs at me. Its so much fun. I wish I had been better friends with my father before Alzheimer's, but then I'd probably be a cop in Pittsburgh with six unhappy kids, or a Methodist minister with a very irate congregation. (What did he say about Mercury and Shiva, Martha? God has a wife named Devi who changes faces! How do we get rid of this guy?) When I was sixteen my father told me he would, "pay for everything" if I went to Muskingum (his alma mater) and became a Methodist minister. When I replied that I really was considering a career in theatre, he told me, "Then you are on your own." He was true to his word. It took the Vietnam GI Bill and twenty-five years of part-time jobs to complete the education I wanted.

Life can be seen as a book or a movie but you are the star, and director, and everyone else is cast as characters; the story goes on, and on, and on. If our children are our future and our future audience, would you, in their place, bother to read the words set before you? The child's eyes do not have to be pulled to the attractive, as the id seeks the pleasant. The child's mind

is drawn to adventure. Imitation is the easiest and most fundamental way of learning. Children begin to exhibit imitation memory during their first year (*Science News,* Vol. 148, No. 6, 1995.).
The creation of robots is frankensteinian, and golem are washed
away by water, as their feet are clay. Denying our children a scientific education as well as access to the arts is very poor long-
term strategy. Meditate on this.

Doggerel
(Some Haiku by me, Aree, and a Quatrain by Campbell Walker)

Poor Basho Richly Loved Wisteria
Pain in the butt
Is the first mastery
For the sitting child's mind

Water Which Is Too Pure Has No Fish
In emptiness
Directions melt
Spiders silently *katsu* wonders

Who Tires of Children Feels Not Flowers
Smiling into pain
Shows compassion
Practicing the wishful

Mirrors
by Aree Marquis, without her the world lacks pleasure

All that was
or will be
Lies in the reflections of our mind

The Ken Master

by Campbell Walker, my first black belt

Along the shining shaft of steel
With supple wrists and strong appeal
He thrusts his force that nurtures weal
And still insists that he must kneel

Eleven

Mud and Water, Purity and Power

The fourteenth-century Zen master Bassui Tokusho Zenji spent many years in reclusive practice, moving from one Japanese hermitage to another. He meditated in trees, and was expert with animals. When he was finally ready to devote the rest of his life to teaching, he came down from his mountain hideout to become the abbot of Kogakuji temple in the ancient city of Enzan. His talks were in the colloquial, as his followers included lay people among the nuns and monks. The central theme of his life and teachings was that the act of seeing or comprehending one's original nature defines Buddhahood. The name of his temple (*Koga*, ninja stronghold, and *kuji*, intentional magic techniques) might give a clue to his emphasis on sticking to the fundamentals, and being very clear in order to ensure transfer of meaning. Perhaps Bassui, Suzuki Shosan, Dogen Zenji, and Takuan are the most transparent teachers of the fundamentals of Zen, as they achieved mastery before accepting the role of the teacher. It is much easier to describe something when you have actually experienced it. Those who can only report what the elders have said have translation problems around the ineffable. They tend to rely on mimicking behavior like the dispensation of Zen teaching koans. (I'll give you a couple of years to figure out "What is the sound of one hand clapping?" ... or ... "When the Bodhidharma Da Mo broke Chen Tsu's leg, Chen Tsu finally attained enlightenment." ... or ... "The nature of the dragon is a fish that evolved into a bird on the way to finding monkeys while studying spiders!") "Tell me what it means, master" is not a way of self-discovery, but of slavery.

Bassui's Mud and Water metaphor is sometimes interpreted to mean that the person who has achieved clarity dislikes descending back into the mire. However, Jesus enjoyed the company of prostitutes and thugs as well as some of the better minds of his community. Most of his disciples were fishermen. His selection system merely involved noting who showed up. Life was simpler then.

Mud and Water. The ancient Taoist tome for guerrilla warfare, Sun Tzu's *Art of War*, recommended becoming invisible as a fish in the sea. The big ones are quite old and feed near the bottom. The ones that don't need much light stay there. The *Wen-Tzu* (179) posits that unless the water is dirty "no fish, turtles, or water snakes will take to it." The yin/yang symbol for Taoism used throughout the martial arts can be viewed as two tears enclosed in a circle. One dark, one light; with a bit of light in the dark, as well as a bit of darkness in the light.

Mud and Water is a warning that in the search for clarity, one will see and hear many dark and cloudy things. You must learn to separate the discardable from the useful. Often when martial artists attain master-level ranking they get caught up in politics, ego needs, greed, or apathy. "I have worked half my life to get here, and I am confused, or I don't know what to do with the rest of my life, or I can relax and quit training so hard, or now everyone will truly respect and listen to me, or now I can make some real money." Image and expectations create real problems. This dynamic is apparent in many of the Westerners Hatsumi-soke has promoted or put into a particular position so he can observe what they will be like if given real power. (The

Boss is the only source of real power in the Togakure Ryu Bujinkan, regardless of what others may say or do. This is a feudal organization that exists in two realms of reality.)

The Boss has changed little over the years in his open sharing of what he considers the important elements of Ninpo and Budo. His lifestyle is commendable. Some of the shidoshi have learned to fear their driving demons. Many will fail to hold up under the pressure of public scrutiny, which always reveals the false to the astute. Quite a few have disappeared as the years go by. Some lose interest; some can't cut it; some become frightened; some realize their particular dream is martial art sickness; some lie about their experience, lineage, and length of actual training. Some exult in the quest for self-improvement as adventure. The Boss accepts the prodigal and the professional.

Mud

As a martial artist who serves on the World Head of Family and Sokeship Council, I interact with senior martial artists from other schools and ways. Frank Sanchez-soke, head of the Council, regulates the credentials necessary for acceptance into this group of high-level martial artists. (Stephen Hayes, Richard Van Donk, and I all belong, indicating that Steve and Richard consider the Kasumi-An system and American Bujinkan as a separate ryu, or are using their high dan ranks for entrance. When I asked The Boss if he would be interested in joining, he didn't think it was appropriate for him.) I noted with interest Sanchez-soke's statement, that the only two martial artists he had to remove for fraudulent documentation were advertising themselves as purveyors of Christian martial arts. The church is not the only last refuge for scoundrels.

It must be remembered that students like to embellish their stories concerning the power and powers of their martial art instructors. Tall tales are not just a product of Texas. A knowing listener will keep his or her cuffs ready to be rolled up. The

239

stories that keep me rolling on the floor, or moving quickly toward the door, usually concern Ninja or Kung Fu Death Duels, particularly to achieve the rank of master. (I've always wanted to have a psychopathic killer train my children, particularly one who is certified as expert. The killer *kumite* myth and shoot-fighting garbage are the sort of fictive exhibitionism that only occurs in B movies!) Frank Ducs and, before him, Count Dante were exponents of this sort of ego-enforcing trash for the gangster at heart. Dante even managed to get a couple of his students killed in a dojo/kwoon brawl in Chicago. When I mentioned I'd trained with some black belts by Dante back in the sixties, Steve Noonkesser told me that was like admitting you used to be a 99 percenter (a special achievement in the Hell's Angels). Dante thought breaking bricks was a big deal and called his expression of karate The Black Dragon Society, not realizing the implications of that name. Ashida Kim claims Dante was his teacher.

The only American master martial artist I have ever met who really experienced an adventure that faintly resembles these "blood sport" death duel tales is Dragon Wind Grandmaster Jim Hopkins of Venice, Florida. The Chinese love to gamble. Hopkins repeatedly won a gambler-sponsored tournament in China conducted on no-rules beyond "don't try to seriously maim your opponent or we'll hurt you big-time." This admonition was enforced by thirteen nasty old men holding eight-pound sandbag clubs who surrounded the arena. Hopkins is an incredible athlete and emerged the victor three times. He used the money from his winnings to start his business. He has gone to the ancient Taoist center hidden in caves above the clouds in the mountains near Beijing to train, and is well known to the Dragon societies of China through his teacher Master Lum.

I've heard some great brawl stories over the years, and have even participated in a few when I was a lot younger. Getting in fights over face is infantile behavior. Eventually, if your foundation studies are correct, becoming invisible will be much more important than being invincible. Some people tell stories and some people get stories told about them. I have often been surprised by how I might be described by students, particularly when they say something like "and then he taught me this by doing this to me." Often the event meant nothing to me beyond doing what seemed natural at the time. Such is the stuff of legend and infamy.

A story line that quickly indicates psychological pathology in the martial artist is the secret training relation with the CIA. The unarmed self-defense training that the CIA, SEALs, or Special Forces people get seems like good stuff to high-school kid civilians, but the real shooters do just that. (Read Marchinko's *Red Cell*; his somewhat fictionalized descriptions are close to the reality.) Most modern soldiers aren't very good at unarmed or primitive-weapon martial arts, unless it was their specialty, and even then may have some real wasted movement in their favorite techniques, as close-combat with skilled opponents is not emphasized nor taught well. Nowadays professional soldiers radio in the zoomie-zoomies to lay down napalm or explosives and snipe at the surviving crispy critters. I taught O'Neill Quick-Kill when I was in the Army, and am familiar with SCARS training, which are considered the ultimate collection of military close-encounter fighting skills. They are effective against the run-of-the-mill fighter or black belt. For twenty years, combining those skills with jujutsu and karate, I was able to chew up most people willing to take me on, until I ran up against the real ninja. Budo Taijutsu practitioners ate my lunch, as they say in Texas, and continue to fatten on my training fees.

It should be a warning to the student when his or her sensei makes noises like, "I have found the True Way. Follow Me. Don't pay attention to those older guys who have trained for years and have gone to Japan for intensive help. I've seen the video tapes. I can do back flips and jump out of splits." They've usually got something that is flashily attractive, but their avoidance moves and footwork stink, as they haven't figured out the real thing isn't going to be a fist fight. This "Follow Me" behavior is an introduction to nightmare to the burgeoning shugyosha, as well as the youthful military who respond to the whistles and pipes to charge into the shredding weapons and entrapments of no man's land. It is also a fundamental betrayal of *giri* and *Budo*. They were not taught their skills without the risk and sacrifice of their teachers. Ninja try to keep it light for the first twenty years, regardless of when you start, but hold onto your hat when you begin to extend the envelope of readiness, particularly after the godan test. You might not recognize the portents of your totems in a New Age. Arrogance is punished by ignoring the offender, as behaviorists (and Taoists) will first use that as an extinguishing strategy attempt. It is a way to laughter that can be harsh indeed to the egocentric. If ignoring doesn't work, then there is pain.

The Japanese concepts concerning politeness require an attitude of "speaking no evil" or "not saying anything if you can't say good." Ninja lore recommends *fu-mu-go* (avoiding dishonest words). Sometimes I have to work hard to keep from tittering when training with certain people, or attending some tournaments. Musashi warned against becoming enamored of "indoor" training. There are quite a few people in various martial arts and ninjutsu whose political pomposity far exceeds their natural abilities. They are the ones who are always trying to correct other people's stances or behavior, while trying to enlist them under their own school, as it is the best. They always seem to be putting together large conglomerates that appear to the outsider as means to ensure greater attendance at their events, so they can make more money. They usually have the fanciest belts with their name displayed prominently on their uniforms. They seem pretty funny to people who have worked with more self-effacing artists. They certainly stress my skills at compassion.

The legal repercussions for injury have reduced most combatic arts to sport, even when the practitioners do not recognize that fact. Ninja usually have very little to do with competitions, or other martial arts, but I have learned to enjoy such events for what they are. I'm usually classed as a "visiting dignitary" or hired to put on a seminar. The first time I refereed a point karate match, I cracked up Grandmaster Pendergrass, as I was giving points for fouls. (They looked like they would work to me.)

Though the Japanese norm is to speak no evil, I'm not Japanese. There are some ninja frauds who are having such great success in the marketplace, it is beginning to legitimize the snake oil they are passing off to the naive for a goodly price.

Master Higuchi, who teaches martial arts near Cleveland, Ohio is a former policeman considered a champion of *taiho-jutsu* (police jujutsu). Higuchi's Bujinkan International Brotherhood is regarded by purists as a fraudulent ninja organization that has nothing to do with the Togakure Ryu Bujinkan Ninpo. I know The Boss doesn't get a dime. Hatsumi-soke told me that Higuchi was not one of his deshi, and he only attended one of his camps to help a fellow Japanese get started in America (as well as see for himself what passes for ninjutsu in America). I've had Higuchi's students show up at seminars I was giving when I lived in the Midwest, and there were major holes in their knowledge of the art. A lot of what they were doing looked like an eclectic hodgepodge of isshinryu and judo, with some legitimate ninjutsu tricks thrown in without the body dynamic.

Ronald Duncan, "the father of American ninjutsu," has created his own ryu out of jujutsu and deserves some recognition for that. He does some very interesting things with his students, but it is not taijutsu, nor ninjutsu from the observation of a knowledgeable critic. Hatsumi-soke actually praised Duncan's student Loriega as "bright and intelligent" and told him to "keep going." Duncan's art looks more like aiki-jujutsu than ninpo.

Shoto Tannemura, another ex-cop, who teaches and sells videos of "samurai jujutsu," learned it from Hatsumi, not Takamatsu. He is Hatsumi's cousin. (Ben Franklin reminds us, "He that has neither fools, whores or beggars among his kindred, is the son of a thunder gust." *Selections* ... in Bibliography.) He contests the ownership of the Gikan Ryu and the Hontai Takagi Yoshin Ryu with the Boss, claiming ownership of the scrolls, which he may have "borrowed." As he used to claim he was head of the Togakure Ryu I feel this claim should be investigated by the girls from Missouri. The grandmaster of a system designates his successor. The grandmaster of schools Tannemura claims was Takamatsu-soke and Takamatsu-sensei chose The Boss. There is something about former policemen that the old saw about becoming like your enemy is too often true. The negative thinking that makes for good police work resulted in severe ego problems when Tannemura's chi began to manifest, and criminals are notorious liars.

I've watched some of his robotic videos, read articles by, and talked with a few of his students. When people put major emphasis on testing and ranking they are not following the ancient traditions of the Japanese combat ryuha, but are imitating the money-machine ranking systems of the Koreans. Quite a few American "ninja" who failed in their obligations to their Bujinkan teachers are "hiding out" under *Genbukan* (school for those who fight for money). From a rhetorician's perspective their motivation and communication indicate severe defensiveness. I had a couple of Tannemura's students call me to facilitate their return to Bujinkan. When I asked a shidoshi friend to accept them into his dojo he said, "It is too difficult. They are like working with abused children."

The Harunaka Hoshino ninja, out of San Francisco, don't have a clue as to proper footwork, or body dynamic. Their sensei may have a great sword collection, and he publishes some interesting research as well as goofy opinion—like ninja cutting their own faces off to prevent being identified. (You might cut off somebody's face after changing clothes with them so the authorities would stop hunting you.) Mr. Hoshino really shouldn't show pictures of his elemental interpretation of tai-jutsu. He claims to be nineteenth linear soke of the Fuma Ryu. I've had some great laughs looking at his weapon techniques. His students do seem to be having a good time. I remember that before the ninja boom he was calling himself Yuan-sensei, claiming Chinese rather than Japanese ancestry.

Robert Bussey, "The King of Combat" (snicker, ralph), studied a couple of months with Bujinkan under Toshiro Nagato-sensei. He's smart enough to pick up a lot in a short period of time. The sword test and Bujin scared him and sent him off to become another Christian self-promoting martial arts business man. His Warrior International is a money maker, but hardly represents Ninpo, or advanced ninjutsu. Scott Morris (no relation to me, thank you for your letters of condolence anyway!), Bussey's best fighter, was easily nuked at the Gracies' slug and grapple fest, as he didn't have a clue concerning angling or setting up a take-down. Caveat Emptor. Gracie Jujutsu is solid, conventional jujutsu applied by a technician of many years of professional experience to relatively inexperienced fighters, from my watching of the Ultimate Fighting Challenge (UFC). The fact that most of the competitors had to opt out due to injuries says a lot about their avoidance skills. For a highly touted brawl, most of these fights are incredibly boring.

General Choi Hong Hi, the founder of tae kwon do, is outranked by many of his self-promoting followers. His only traditional ranking was shodan in shotokan karate, according to my Japanese sources. (One of the reasons he always wears a suit, rather than a dogi at public demonstrations.) Choi says nidan. In 1951, during the Korean War, martial law allowed him to unify the Korean martial arts under the tae kwon do banner. The *hyung* (forms) of tae kwon do look like very poorly presented shotokan karate kata, with high kicks thrown in to their detriment. When a Korean instructor hops on a plane for the States, he is automatically bumped three belt ranks. (I don't know if they are demoted three when returning to the homeland.) The average tae kwon do practitioner chooses to ignore the shoddy record of arthritis, aggressiveness, injuries, inappropriate appointments, break-off renegades, Korean politics and lobbying scandals, and the contempt of older and more traditional systems. It is hoped that this old boys network falls apart under its own weight. The tae kwon do practice of awarding a fourth-degree black belt the title of Master is a sales gimmick that attempts to transform the ignorant. The proliferation of grandmasters in tae kwon do is even sillier. Any seventh dan can use that title and many do. Soke, Si Gung, and Grandmaster translate as founder of a lineage, or "teacher of the teachers." I cannot even count the number of tae kwon do black belts who have come dancing into my outdoor dojo to be eaten like Christmas cookies.

When Hatsumi-soke stated that the way Americans had been taught the martial arts was a grave insult, he did not include the slap to Koreans that was financed by the USA and delivered by shotokan to General Choi during the Korean Conflict. Asians like their revenge served cold.

The Koreans have come to believe their own propaganda, have forgotten their actual roots, and are earning the contempt of more rigorous and less financially rewarding systems. The teachers who can actually use tae kwon do have to study something else to make it work. Good salesmanship; poor performance. If you enjoy Korean arts, hapkido and hwarang-do will serve you well. For anyone facing skilled fighters with tae kwon do, I recommend learning another martial art that teaches useful hand techniques in order to be more balanced.

Wen-Tzu (174) offers, ". . . if you have the unworthy rule over the good, then even strict penalties cannot prevent their treachery. The small cannot regulate the great, the weak cannot employ the strong. This is the nature of the universe. So sages promote the wise to get things done, while unworthy rulers promote their own associates: observe who they promote and it will be clear whether there is going to be disorder; examine their associations, and you can tell who is wise and who is unworthy."

Water

Hatsumi-soke's natural behavior can be pretty interesting. I've seen him do what I perceived to be rather amazing healing of wounds, burns, and broken bones. I've seen him freeze animals in place, and perform weather magic. I've seen him break weapons to show how dangerous it is to use poorly constructed practice tools. His art work is always intriguing, and I've heard stories that if they were about any other man, I would check out the teller's aura for liar's green. I call these "Tales of the Grandmaster." Some are terribly funny. One at least is terribly sad. It must be remembered that we are first and only human beings.

The Boss was attending a celebration dinner. The man being feted had been a high-school classmate of Hatsumi-soke's wife. In the passing years he had risen to the title of *yoribun* (I think that is the title for leader) in the local yakuza family. A rival gang hearing of his birthday celebration at a famous restaurant sent an assassin armed with a sword. (The smaller-town Yaks like to maintain the traditions—rather like shooting a gangster in a barber shop, giving a wrapped fish, or after an Italian dinner a kiss and bullet in Brooklyn.) The assassin drew his sword, and howling his war cry rushed past The Boss' table to get to the head table where the yakuza was sitting with his underlings. The ultimate shock came when he completed his murderous cut with empty hands. Hatsumi-san had used a *muto dori* technique to remove the sword as the killer tore by his table. I'll let your imagination fill in what then transpired.

247

Mrs. Hatsumi, exposed to the open sharing of emotional and romantic love common to life in America, and moved by the example of Bud and Bonnie Malmstrom's obvious caring for each other, broke down in tears when she tried to express what had impressed her the most about her visit to the States. Hatsumi-san said in amazement that it was only the second time he had seen her cry in all their years of marriage. The first had been when her cat was driven over by a car. He remarked, "As a dancer, she is so disciplined... There were times when I thought I was married to a man." When he said this, I turned to my table companion, Dr. Mike Fenster, and remarked that The Boss may have some weakness in wife-jutsu. Wife-jutsu very important. It must be remembered that the Japanese regard marriage less romantically than we. Hatsumi-soke has remarked on more than one occasion that a wife is an excellent tool for learning to lose gracefully. So is a daughter, son, or anyone you love. After he had finally constructed his own dojo in Noda after paying back his father's gambling losses, she took it over for her dance studio. No invincibility where the Kunoichi are concerned in Bujinkan.

An outdoor wedding was being held in a city park. The groom was a Togakure Ryu member, and martial artists had flown in from all over the country to see the happy couple tie the knot. It had rained hard all morning. The wedding was at 3 PM. The city was under a huge low-pressure storm front that covered the whole coastline. The rain suddenly stopped at 2 PM. The leaves had turned over on the trees in expectation of more rain. The Grandmaster said it would not rain again until 5 PM. During the wedding the sun punched a small hole through the cloud cover to brighten the park. The crowd went to covered pavilions to eat under a storm-dark sky. At exactly 4:59 the cloudburst returned, but by then the wedding was over and most of the families and guests were on their way. The Grandmaster, being driven to the airport, looked at his watch and laughed, saying, "You can't trust elementals to be punctual." Good weather at outdoor training events is part of the legend that surrounds Hatsumi-soke. At the 1995 Tucson Tai Kai, Hatsumi-san stopped morning training for a moment to allow us to observe the beautiful rainbow that encircled the noon-time sun on a nearly cloudless eighty degree day. Those of us from the East had never seen this uncommon phenomenon.

The Boss always recommends practice with wooden or soft weapons for safety reasons. Boys will be boys and play with dangerous toys. Kevin Millis had managed to slice his finger rather deeply with a K-Bar. The Boss noticed the blood spraying about, walked over, and ran his finger up the cut. It stopped bleeding, closed, and healed in about the same amount of time it takes me to write this. Once when I had managed to cut my thumb knuckle to the bone grooming the bitch-sword Lydia, Taffesse used healing cold energy to close the wound to the point of my needing only a butterfly bandage rather than stitches.

Kan-sensei didn't believe a particular arm lock was dangerous enough to hold him, so Ishizuka-sensei, at Hatsumi's command, put on a little more pressure and snapped his arm. Hatsumi-soke pulled the bone straight from its interesting angle, held it in place for about a minute, and went back to teaching. Kan-sensei went to the emergency room at the local hospital. The X-ray revealed the break was already healed with no need for a cast. Kan apologized to his teachers.

Shiraishi-sensei was severely burned and blinded by an explosion at the soy sauce factory where he worked as an engineer. When I studied with him a few years later, he was driving a car with glasses, and had only two small burn scars the size of my little finger on his chest. I was told Hatsumi-soke visited him daily at the burn hospital, set up a shrine in his room, and prayed over him for months.

At the New Jersey Tai Kai, one of the American instructors was using a real weighted chain *kusari fundo* instead of the rope and cotton balls usually used while practicing chain techniques. The Boss borrowed it. He popped it once, and the chain broke, sending the weight flying to the ground. He looked surprised, and said, "It is very dangerous to practice with hard weapons, and poorly constructed tools." I was glad he hadn't borrowed mine.

At the Los Angeles Tai Kai, held at the Polo Grounds, The Boss was receiving punches and demonstrating various avoidance techniques when the crowd gasped with astonishment, then laughter. As he was being hit in the shoulder, Hatsumi-soke had bent his body in a strange way and his opponent's fist bounced off in an arc so that it ricocheted into his own face. We all yelled to see that one again. The Boss seldom repeats a technique, but this time he did it again. It's on the video, but I've never seen anyone else pull it off. It was definitely a Three Stooges move. Dick Severance reminded me of it, when I was discussing this chapter with him.

At the Madrid Tai Kai in 1993, Sveneric-shihan reported that during a *bo* demonstration with The Boss, his role was to attack, but when he did he lost all energy, will, and physical strength, with a lapse of consciousness in which Hatsumi-soke removed his staff. When he asked The Boss what had happened, The Boss replied, "It is *Shingen*... It depends on *hara*... If I had chosen to do that to someone with less experience than you, maybe that person would have gone crazy." *Shinken-gata* is part of all nine of the schools under the Bujinkan umbrella. The Boss wrote in his *Kuden*, "It is possible to cultivate a sixth sense of stillness and movement, for living through both real combat and ordinary society, it is a survival mechanism. In the Kuki Shinden-ryu (dragon, not the school) this is called *Kuki Shinnen-jutsu* (nine demons' divine intention techniques) and is regarded as a secret transmission." The earth-bound human being is capable of moving in the water of the spirit.

I was teaching a meditation seminar in Houston for some

jujutsu and taichi practitioners in May of '95. I was showing them how to integrate the chakras using Taoist orbiting techniques. I felt something enter my mind. When I felt the mental knock, I checked inside and saw Hatsumi-soke. One of the high-ranked jujutsu enthusiasts, Robin Martin, a former police lieutenant who told me he was very cynical about learning anything from a "ninja," found he had a real talent for seeing into the aura, to his surprise. I asked this martial art *buyu* if he saw anything interesting happening in my aura. Robin exclaimed, "I see a baby and an Asian gentleman." Later that evening Wayne Oliver pulled out a drawing of The Boss he was planning on presenting to him at the Tucson Tai Kai. Robin said, "That's the guy who was looking out of your aura." I laughed and said, "You'll have to meet my daughter Sara Glenn Mariko sometime."

I've had a number of people write me about following my methodology and getting into the Void and finding The Boss there to greet them. It must be interesting for him to have these "auslanders" suddenly pop into the Bujin's turf. They told me he told them, "Don't be afraid. Everything will work out OK."

Some rather amazing things happen at the Tai Kai. If you belong to the Togakure Ryu Bujinkan and are not attending, you are missing a great opportunity. These events are open to all, and rank is mostly ignored, so it gives you a chance to rub on some of the "legends." The annual Tai Kai provides opportunities for the local shidoshi to exhibit their skills, and invariably some of the shihan and practitioners who have been studying in Japan will act as *uke* for The Boss, or demonstrate when asked. The shidoshi who have spent years in Japan training daily walk around and help us figure out what we are supposed to know. It always surprises me when people do not take advantage of their much deeper expertise. Tai Kai performances show us the standards toward which we are supposed to be reaching. They also provide a challenging and fun way to get together with friends. When the "legends" aren't attending, it usually means they have done something to give The Boss a "case of the grunts" and are hiding out until he forgives them, or have broken off relations with the Ryu. Some pretend they still belong for the prestige, but if they are not showing up with a bunch of their students when The Boss is in their country, it reveals a failure to recognize some serious *giri*.

Mud and Water Equals Earth to Void

The Mud and Water theme can be represented by the water lily, or lotus, whose roots are buried in the mud for nurturing from the earth, and whose petals are spread to receive from the sky. The stem bends like the spine. This is a favorite symbol of the first recorded Buddha for its leaf placement and shape. The purple thistle flower was a similar mystic symbol for the prickly and warlike Scot, and the acorn for the faerie and Druid. Takamatsu-soke said, "Your heart must be like a wildflower." Earth to Void. "Beam me up, Scotty!" The Zen meditator by following the deep currents within his or her body becomes aware of these connections through the awakening of the intuition and may even see this flower representation on the phosphenes of the eyelids.

Mud and Water. "And the lion shall lie down with the lamb." Woody Allen in one of his books closed with the lamb sleeping lightly. "When at war, prepare for peace. When at peace, prepare for war." Yin and Yang. "The lion like great warrior is gentle, has a heart like a woman, breathes with his feet, and is beloved of the gods." The old Ethiopians knew this stuff (Toff discussing things his grandfather had said to him). When the shadow is encouraged to share in the light—or as Will Rogers, our Cherokee Cowboy comic, used to opine, "I never met a man I didn't like,"—we see both the good and evil in any situation or person. It is a fabulous aid to seeing clearly. Better than niacin.

Mud and Water. In strategy the concept of looking at both sides is usually taught through having the student role play, or construct worst- and best-case scenarios. What are all the things that might go wrong? What can we do about them? What will happen if everything goes right? What can we do that will make it go better? In the *Wen-Tzu*, the scholars say, "When the deal which is supposed to be good goes bad, one has not paid enough attention to strategy at the beginning of the process."

Commentary

Following the light, Budo Taijutsu is a martial art that fosters creativity. Where most other martial arts prize conformity and claim you can tell who someone's teacher was by how she or he moves, Ninpo adjusts the *Kihon Happo* (eight basic kamae and movements) to the body of the practitioner, rather like the *bunkai* (finding the combat applications in one's kata) of karate, assuring the practitioner of a solid base, yet allowing individualism to flower in the application. No Ninpo master's body of knowledge and movement is identical to any other's. The more you study with different instructors, the more you will learn.

If your primary desire is to learn the *shinken*, your search and journey will be long and arduous. You have to start somewhere. There are now many legitimate teachers of Bujinkan Budo Taijutsu all over the world who can teach you the physical fundamentals of the art. But, if your spiritual foundation is not correctly secure, you will never achieve survival in the Void, whoever you start your training with. As Joseph Campbell said in his video series on religion, "It is terrible to spend your life climbing the ladder to find you are on the wrong wall." When I was a consultant to General Motors Engine Division, I would often wonder who was smoothing the path for some incredibly inept asshole in the GM hierarchy who seemed to float like a rat turd in the cream at the top. In Bujinkan bad ninja go away, and the nice thing is that their disappearance is usually by self-selection and has nothing to do with rank.

Hatsumi-soke in his *densho* writes, "Rumors of supernatural powers are prone to arise, but stories of human 'natural powers' do exist for certain. I occasionally saw hard-to-explain phenomena with Takamatsu-sensei, which later happened to me personally. I make a personal point of regarding such reality as something important, with sincerity... Let me explain with an example from cat adjudication (at a contest/show for domestic cats). Imagine that five splendid cats, who have been selected from local contests, are there on the table. The judges proceed to eliminate those cats which have any faults, i.e. quirks. In other words, the one with the fewest faults and no quirks gets to be Grand Champion. Whether in life or Budo, you should treat this view as important, and use it as sustenance for your training... Takamatsu-sensei left this for me in writing, in the phrase *Kajo Chikusei* (literally Flower heart, bamboo spirit). It means the practitioner of Budo should have a heart as kind and pure as a flower, and cross straight over all obstacles by being flexible [such as the joints on bamboo which represents the spine]. So what is the endpoint of all this? I can answer that immediately. It is the paradise where the flower blooms."

This statement can be interpreted esoterically by recognizing a flower heart as being open—the chakra opening is often represented like the open petals of a flower. The bamboo, like the willow, is a common Asian symbol for flexibility. Spirit is essence. The endpoint is the brain, or heaven (paradise) where the flower blooms, another metaphor for the opening of the lotus chakra. The five cats represent the feminine side of the five elements, and the judges [the Bujin] eliminate those with faults [Bad ninja go away. Some faster than others.]. The cats are domesticated, indicating a tempering of their wild nature, as cats are not as pliable as dogs. Cats can be trained as guardians, but we don't think of "cats of war." There are obstacles and traps to achieving one's goals and you only get through them by being flexible enough to go with the flow that lifts them above their local accomplishments.

Bujinkan is a world class organization. This shaggy cat story is a metaphor describing both the selection system and experience of promotion in Bujinkan Ninpo. The Boss takes you around a corner and you are supposed to be bright enough to light up the rest of the alley way. Takamatsu-sensei recommended being known as a pussycat was more useful than being a tiger. Meow.

Gargoyles
by Glenn Morris

Dante, like Orpheus, traveled through Hell,
Love, friendship, and wisdom were his guides.

Dante saw Christ as a Griffin,
Half lion, half eagle!
Was the medieval mind so different?
Grotesque faces contorted with demonic power
Peer from the roof bosses of Canterbury Cathedral.
Saint Mark's Basilica bears a creature of two bodies.
The weight-bearing corbels at Schaffhausen, Switzerland,
are Mermen . . .
Strange waters for mountaineers.

Notre Dame and Chartres,
Constructed on ground the Druids deemed holy.
Our Virgin Lady's higher planes are surrounded by
Chimera, sphinxes, gorgons, harpies, sirens,
Dragons and unicorns.
Through their spines and from their mouths flow water.
What hidden meaning
Can be drawn from monsters guarding sanctuaries of gentle
   purity?

Twelve

Entering the Void

Religions across cultures claim the right to guide behavior based on sets of rules that have proven beneficial for those who follow the precepts of the religion. All religions reflect the social structure and culture in which they exist. The feudalism of Roman Catholicism is readily apparent to the more democratic, capitalistic Protestant. I use Christianity as an example, as most Westerners are familiar with various aspects of that belief system, in which I was fortunately raised. According to Hatsumi-soke, the ninja master must not only understand the spiritual path subsumed under his or her own religion, but all religious experience and feeling. This is a very ecumenical position, but in this day of power-mongering Christian and Islamic fundamentalism and cults in general, it makes a great deal of sense to me. Silenced by Pope John Paul II and then expelled from his order on charges of being a feminine (sic) theologist among other sins, former Dominican priest, Matthew Fox, has annoyed a lot of conventional people with his essentially correct position that "where the church has failed to address and teach mysticism it has failed" (Keynote address at Common Boundary's 15th Annual Convention). I take that one step further. It is only through meditative practice directed toward integrating mind, body, and spirit through loving intent that we achieve a relationship with God. And she is not jealous.

Becoming one with gods and God has very little to do with religion. Mindless worship only preserves the past in all its horrific imperfections and exclusivity. Wrong-headedness is easily taught from the perspective of God's Word (as it is from the perspective of "this is how Master Dung Flo passed on his irreparably bad techniques to me, and now I will teach them to you, as I have never had an original thought in my life"). Religion is what you do when you have failed in your own attempts to achieve virtue and need some supporters. We need only to observe the Serbs' murderous treatment of their lifelong Muslim neighbors to see how history repeats itself when the people are without decent and forbearing leadership. We are to find ourselves and become the best we can, which is godlike. The phrase used in Ninpo is "seeing with the mind and eyes of the divine." The divine to a traditional Japanese are the *kami* (spirit Gods). To see in this manner requires a spiritual viewpoint derived from developing the characteristics of the shugyosha (see Chapter Nine).

What follows is a brief description from various world-wide religions of the core fundamentals of spiritual development as espoused by their founders. Understanding "religious feeling" requires rising above ethnocentrism. Rising above ethnocentrism requires understanding and accepting one's culture while rising above its shadow. To accomplish this, one must gain a somewhat objective perception of consensus reality, which in Zen is referred to as "the common mind" and for most of us is the ordinary way we see our world. Gurdjieff pointed out that from the Sufi perspective "everyone seems asleep" (P. D. Ouspensky, *Tertium Organum: A Key to the Enigmas of the World*, Vintage Books, 1970). Understanding one's self immersed in a stream of consciousness that is shaped by one's environment is the first step in waking up. Waking up can be accomplished at nearly any time in one's life. The traditional ways favor introducing the process to those in middle life, after forty for most. This book is not addressed to children, but to adults who have decided to become as children, in the sense of being born again through learning to regard themselves and reality in new ways. In this chapter I will describe the process for entering the Void, and in the next, getting to know some of its inhabitants.

Underlying Secular Theory

In his autobiography Albert Einstein came to the conclusion, "A human being is part of the whole called by us 'Universe' . . . a part limited by time and space. He experiences himself, his thoughts and feelings, as separate from the rest—a kind of optical delusion of his own consciousness. This delusion is a kind of prison for us restricting us to our personal desires and to affection for a few persons nearest us. Our task must be to free ourselves from this prison by widening our circle of compassion to embrace all living creatures and the whole of nature and beauty."

This was from the greatest hard scientist of this era. His theory of relativity was the foundation of much of contemporary physics. He provided the insights that led to the development of atomic weaponry. (Einstein was less flamboyant than the famous contemporary American theoretical physicist Richard Feynman, and with much less information to work from than Steven Hawking, today's media darling physicist who can fill a football stadium when lecturing on the living nature of the universe.) As a Jew, Einstein had to flee religious and racial persecution in Nazi Germany. He is sometimes made a figure of fun because of his humble presentation of self (baggy, comfortable clothes and a wild shock of up-sticking hair), but he was neither shallow nor arrogant. He often helped the children with their math homework in the trailer park where he lived for a while after coming to the States, taking payment in jellybeans.

Einstein well understood his role as a teacher and where effort was best rewarded; like Christ, he suffered little children. The prison to which Einstein alludes is reminiscent of Gurdjieff's comment that "everyone seems asleep." Cultural expectations as well as learned socialization can explode or strengthen the prison shell of mental slumber. Creative thinking is hard work; reacting to pattern with habitual response is easy.

Abraham Maslow, a great American theoretical psychologist, felt that one's metaneeds (spiritual needs) could only be met when one's basic needs for survival and security were met. He proposed a four-tiered hierarchy of needs starting at survival. Next came security, then self-esteem, and at the peak was the rarely seen self-actualization. In business his model is used to develop motivational strategies and reward systems. He ignored the scriptures, tales of the aesthetes and ascetics who sometimes achieved enlightenment (self-actualization) through eliminating and shaping desire to higher needs. His emphasis on understanding peak experience was a major step in developing a psychology of the self-actualizing, mentally healthy human being in the West, where the psychological focus had been primarily on the clinically neurotic. He missed the tools of relaxation but easily saw the benefit of natural flow, interaction, and appreciation of nature (Abraham Maslow, *Religions, Values, and Peak Experiences,* Penguin Books, 1978). He was wrong only in ignoring the importance of compassion. Not surprisingly, Maslow also missed the stage of generativity and development of others (which I and psychologist Milton Erickson place above self-esteem) in his hierarchy of being, since he came from an academic environment where the laws of publish or perish often preclude a more interactive exchange with others. Magic is pretty much degenerated to a folk art in the West, so he also missed a lot of very valuable focusing techniques. Furthermore, he was handicapped by not having a circle of friends who exhibited the characteristics he was studying. Maslow had to rely upon reports concerning historical figures, a technique usually relegated to religion. Alan Watts probably wasn't the best source of depth experience, as Watts missed the importance of chi kung breathing techniques in his exposure to Zen. When a psychologist or rhetorician looks at religion he sees a very different world than the person immersed in the system of thought. The same is true of the higher-level martial arts and artists. Religions, transpersonal psychology, and philosophy may provide the basis for meaningful examination of life as well as provide clues for entry into other states of consciousness. Let us now take a brief look at the history and underlying esoteric principles associated with some of the major religions.

Buddhism

This is an eight-fold path that results in nine, or the principle that allows the one to become the ten thousand things by adding zeroes until all desire has ceased. Elements of the path were first formulated by a man named Siddhartha Gautama, an Indian prince of the Sakyamuni clan who left his wealth and family out of fear of death and sought for twenty years to find an answer to suffering. Gautama Buddha was a *Khsatreya* (Sanskrit for member of the noble warrior caste trained from infancy in the martial and esoteric arts), which gave him a considerable mental and physical advantage in his researches. The Hindu Khsatreya were considered holy warriors, followed concepts *(Dharmavijaya)* we would consider chivalrous, and according to the surviving *Sutras* (holy writings), were warrior monks from noble families, the "sons" of deities, who embodied principles symbolized by the deities. Their training, which was referred to as "following the light," consisted of literature, history, religion, esoterica, philosophy, and the weaponry of the time, with particular emphasis on the bow and arrow. They were expected to fight in the forefront of any battle where the righting of injustice was the prime motivation, regardless of who had committed the wrong. Their form of physical development was called *nata* and later *Vajramukti* and greatly emphasized self-control, calm, moral development, and a whole slew of combat-derived fighting techniques. The most famous of their forms was named "Lion's Play" *(Simhavikridita)* and is believed by Buddhist scholars to be the basis of esoteric *Chuan Fa* (the Chinese boxing art made famous by the Shaolin) and "The Lion Dance" of Chinese New Year festivals. The Muslim invasion (circa 800 AD) extinguished the Khsatreya light in Northern India and forced a flight of Buddhists and Hindus out along the Silk Trail. These noble warriors were considered to be the precursors of the *Bodhisattva Warriors* (Shifu Nagaboshi Tomio, under Strategy in the Bibliography). Much of what is preserved in the records concerning the Hindu Khsatreya caste resembles Mikkyo and some aspects of the practice of Ninpo.

In the West many people tend to think of Buddhism as a Chinese and Japanese phenomenon. In reality the Dharma is a product of India, coming out of the 8000-or-more-year-old civilizations of the Hindu, or people of the Indus and Ganges river valleys. These people were truly the oldest and most sophisticated of the ancient cultures, arguably as far advanced of their Chinese contemporaries as the Chinese were to the Europeans at the time of Marco Polo. The Buddha of the Sakya clan, Siddhartha, who we think of as the first and last Buddha (imposing our Christian or Middle Eastern model of prophetic achievement), claimed knowledge of forebears and taught techniques for enlightenment through achieving experiential knowledge of one's true self.

The result of Siddhartha's study is known as Theravada Buddhism, a philosophical religion that is primarily, but not exclusively, exercised in the training of monks and nuns, but also has an extremely popular lay version that is particularly enjoyed by artists who would be drawn to Zen. Like Jesus, the Buddha's words were not recorded until about four hundred years after his death. His most important points are recorded in the *Path of Nature*. It's a book about self-discipline and morality. In the East, the Buddha's teachings are usually referred to as the *Dharma*. He argued that morality, meditation, and wisdom should all be pursued simultaneously.

Morality consisted of choosing to avoid, or refraining from, five things:

1. Causing injury to living things (Thou shalt not murder.)
2. Taking that which is not given (Thou shalt not steal.)
3. Sexual immorality (Thou shalt not covet thy neighbor's wife, nor his ass.)
4. Falsehood (Thou shalt not lie.)
5. The use of alcohol and drugs since they tend to cloud the mind. (Islam forbids the use of alcohol, and so do some Christian sects.)

Meditation for beginners just requires sitting around and being still. (Like some aspects of going to school. Dead easy.) For the experts, however, the constructive concepts are liberation and all that entails in freeing one's mind from Einstein's Prison. Liberation requires mind control to the point of controlling all sense experience, enabling one to examine data without social filters or expectations. An extremely scientific viewpoint regarding the value of both objective and subjective truth.

Meditation is associated with right effort, right concentration, and right contemplation of ecstasy. This translates in Hoch 'Merikan vernacular as "If you want to find peace and end suffering, learn to use your mind well without expectations. If you don't want to blow all your circuits, ruin your sex life, and become an epileptic by choice not chance, then put your sexual energy where the least does the most good—in your head. Really pay attention so you don't get hurt, and nobody else does either, because of you. REALLY have a great time finding out who you are."

Wisdom, for Sid, was a little easier, as that only consisted of grasping and living up to the truth about the relationship between suffering and desire—then resolving to do something about it, like observing rather than participating. Take a survey of the environment and decide what it is you really want to do, and how much you are willing to sacrifice. You might recall John Lennon's song about "watching the wheels go round"— a little ditty about waking up. Personal strategy.

Wisdom is associated with right view and right resolve, which can be translated as "If you do not want to suffer, look at the big picture and have the guts to do the right thing." Morality is expressed by right speech, right action, and right livelihood. This translates into Lower 'Merican vernacular as "If you do not want to suffer, learn how to use your language well, act in a way that is pleasing to others, and find a job you really love doing in which you can grow that does not harm others or the environment."

This is nothing to declare a holy war over. I only wish that most of my acquaintances, and all of my friends, were so enlightened and benign enough of spirit to behave in this way. This is pretty simple, human, basic stuff. In fact, Buddhism is considered by many of its proponents to be not a religion but a Way of living. Martial artists tend to like the bleakness of the Buddhist viewpoint, as it emphasizes truth. (Good principles of depth psychology, fully usable as considering lilies in the field and loving one's neighbor regardless of what a pretentious ass he can become.)

Taoism

"The Teacher of the Way does not know the Way" means it cannot be taught, but must be learned. You are on your own as far as your experience. Because the process is tricky and dangerous, it's helpful to have some directions that sages were kind enough to keep out of code. Dr. Thomas Cleary and Robert L. Wing are probably the best translators of Taoist concepts into English. The *Tao te Ching* (The Way of Creative Energy) which is ascribed to Lao Tzu, and the *Art of War* to Sun Tzu, are the two most translated if not best-selling books in the world, after the Bible. Taoist esoteric yoga as taught by Mantak Chia is one of the safer methods of developing chi. What I consider to be the best introductory texts are listed in the Bibliography of *Path Notes* and this book.

Islam

Mohammed, another great spiritual leader born into a less-than-affluent noble family, received the standard desert training in horsemanship, weaponry, and survival associated with his rank. Legend has it he was not taught to read and write, as that cost extra. He traveled with his grandfather as a young man, learned the caravan trade through practice and observation, and became a respected businessman. When he was twenty-five he was proposed to by and married, a wealthy and sophisticated older widow of forty who provided a jump-start to his career of introspection. He took over her already established trading business, and spent a great deal of time contemplating in the hills around Mecca and Medina, observing the behavior of the local flora and fauna. As he had opportunity to interact with other cultures and traders, his channeled philosophy granted through meditative interaction with an angel (recorded by the third generation of his followers) poetically stresses equality between the sexes, respect for Judaism and Christianity, elimination of vices, denunciation of idol worship, democratic process, generosity, and an ethical mercantilism balanced by strict usury laws.

Mohammed's word, the Koran, is a powerful statement, even in translation, and is often better than a mere drink of water. The language and wisdom are best conveyed in Arabic, and the book itself is considered Mohammed's greatest miracle. My favorite chapter is entitled "The Spider." Mohammed did not establish a clergy, nor require any form of ritualized worship beyond prayer and self-study.

Sufism, which preserves the esoteric core of Islam, has many parallels to Zen. Islam, like many nature religions, proscribes the picturing of God, partly because it posits that God (Allah) cannot be represented by picture or statue. God is everywhere, in everything. God is nature and thus is part of all you see and hear and touch, and is within you as well. Repression of graven images in Islam has resulted in wonderful mathematics and design work, especially in ceramics. Like Christ to Christians, Mohammed is perceived to be the last prophet by traditional followers of Islam. During the period of Arabic cultural expansion, parallel to Europe's Dark Ages, Islam became one of the dominant world religions, spreading from Mecca across Africa into Spain, to the Middle East, the Balkans, and into India and other parts of Asia. Wherever Arab traders and military went, the words of Mohammed went with them. The followers of Islam tended to treat the followers of other religions in about the same way as Christians of the same period—a threat to be removed. They burned the Buddhists out of Northern India, resulting in a flight of knowledge to Tibet and China, which eventually extended all the way to Japan.

There is a movie called *The Message* about the life of Mohammed that is very well done, but very hard to find, starring a slew of Hollywood actors like Michael Ansara and Anthony Quin. The movie is interesting in that Mohammed, like Allah, is never seen. I saw it in Amman, Jordan, when visiting Karim Abu Shakra, one of my black belts, to do a leadership development seminar for Aramex. When I was finished performing for the managers, Karim took me into the same desert Lawrence of Arabia crossed to silence the guns of Aq'aba. We were off to see the sights in Jordan. The incredible frying pan barrens and heat had me wishing for a canteen and desert boots before climbing the 821 steps to the ancient Nabataean-built monastery for the worshippers of Artemis in the ancient, "rose-red," hidden, mountain city of Petra. The desert-dwelling Tauregs who run the tea and souvenir shop across from the ruin identified me to Karim as a Holy Man, which I found rather amusing. They said I should call the people to prayer, as if there were any people interested in that forsaken pinnacle of forgotten real estate. (It made me wish I spoke their language. They allowed us to rest in their cave and recover from the three-mile climb and 100-degree-plus heat. We were grateful for their hospitality.) Petra is the desert city nestled in the cliffs where Indiana Jones' "Last Crusade" finds The Holy Grail (another interesting movie). The followers of Islam can be kind to the infidel who respects their ways.

Hinduism

Hinduism (*Sanatana Dharma* or Universal Truth) is usually, and wrongly, regarded as polytheistic. It's just very syncretic, combining many useful paths. In Hinduism, the One is achieved by three vehicles: good works, resulting in caste systems, dependence, and trickle-down economics, called Brahma; forgiveness and mercy, whose preservative shadow is dependency and laziness, called Vishnu; and spiritual development through psychology, whose shadow is a very small (but powerfully magical) success rate named Shiva, or Shaivanism, and sometimes simply Yoga. Within these three ways, which correspond to god-like archetypes, are both male and female elements, which are sometimes worshipped separately, as well as locally, in tuning the worshipper for transcendence. Within each of the archetypes are four female pairs representing the polarity of the chakras as well as the essential female nature of human beings. Patanjali, the first psychologist and a Yoga sage, wrote down his research in yogic *sutra* approximately three thousand years ago.

Mythology, Folk Tales, Once Popular Religions, and History

"Mud and water" is a common metaphor describing the relation of light and shadow in the human being, as does the yin/yang symbol of the Taoist, or the Tibetan Buddhist Yab/Yum graphic of the gods making love. These symbols also represent male and female aspects that must be merged within to achieve androgyny, which is a characteristic of the enlightened. On another level, these same symbols represent the merging of the material (particles) with the spiritual (waves). In Mikkyo Buddhism, the focus is on understanding the opposites that exist in one's nature. In Budo Taijutsu, the practitioner is presented with the physical problem of learning the *omote* while discovering the *ura*. Over the centuries, people called mystics by the pragmatic materialists have developed techniques for accomplishing this merger. Mystics often refer to these techniques as pathways, as they relate to nature and not many people risk exploring them. The paths are often hidden in the symbolism of mythology, folk wisdom, and religion resulting in people accepting the symbol but forgetting what it represents.

The short path (tantrism) is usually presented as very fierce and dangerous; the gods wear the dismembered limbs of those who failed to conquer their discipline. It's not a pretty sight but does represent the truth. The object of the worship, however is to submit if you want success in your endeavors. That's pretty easy. Short-path gods are pretty scary. The bear-like Yama, when holding up the mirror of the universe, has frightened eyes. The fierce-path survivor and gods are sometimes portrayed riding totem animals or standing on dead spouses, dead cows, and ignorant dwarfs.

Yab/Yum is usually shown as a dual mandala. One is fierce and one is gentle. The gentle way is primarily accomplished through meditation and removal of karmic debt in order to win

268

a higher place in the next round of reincarnation. It takes a long, long, long, long, long time and people usually forget their problem and keep going through it over and over, taking no responsibility for their actions, as they haven't a clue to their frustration. People following the gentle path are usually very nice, as they may faintly recall being lambs for the slaughter. The gentle path places great emphasis on forgiveness, as we all benefit by it. Gentle or fierce version of Yab/Yum, both figures of both paths are wreathed in smiles and the flames of their passion for each other. The symbols represent the two faces of god and the bliss of reaching the one. Truly understanding the path requires great bravery in either case. When one unites the dual mandala he or she is one.

Mud can represent the material world and water represents the spirit—just as Gaia represents the earth and feminine creative spirit, and the many sky gods represent the male creative aspect, the mind, or illusionary material. In the West, particularly in the Greek and Roman pantheon, yin and yang as energy concepts were personalized into the characteristics of the various male and female gods or archetypes.

Zeus and Hera were the male and female archetypes and squabbled constantly. The Greeks treated their war god Ares with great ambiguity and embraced Zeus' daughter, Athena, for wisdom. She had a considerable reputation as a warrior for cause, but was more popular for her blessings on education and commerce. Athens, named after her, was the hub of the known world at that time. Some Athenians, like Pericles, are well worth studying. Athena has more talents than you can shake a finger at, and like Nepthys and Isis of Egypt, espouses those who serve freedom. The Kali archetype, often encountered on the short path, seems similar to Hecate, who scared even Zeus. Kali also has an Egyptian face that is more beautiful than Cleopatra. Aphrodite, the goddess of love, stepped out on her husband Hephraestos quite often to bear Ares' children. On the positive side, she was also consort to Hermes, messenger to the gods. A reading of Homer indicates that interaction with the spirit world was much more common in ancient Greece than today. Here in America, our founding fathers seemed quite fond of Athena. Columbia and/or Liberty are/were our Athenian archetypes. Statues of Columbia were everywhere until about World War I, and her head or figure embellished the silver dollar. It is a global tradition to put the heads of your gods or rulers on your coinage. That must explain Hermes/Mercury on the old dimes.

Folk tales abound with esoteric clues concerning the process of enlightenment. For the prince to awaken Snow White with a kiss, he has to get through the seven dwarfs. Jack's beanstalk to the land of giants grows from three magic seeds for which he trades his mother's cow. The princess that will marry the prince has to be so sensitive she can feel a pea through seven mattresses. The pot of gold is at the end of the rainbow. The beauty must tame the beast.

Theological Positions Considered Heretical by the Christian Establishment

Religion for most people is a set of concepts which we are taught to believe. We are usually taught our beliefs by those we love, at an age where we do not question the wisdom of our elders. Bishop Wicke once said according to my father, "Give me a child until he is seven and I will show you a Roman Catholic, forever." What we learn first, we tend to like best.

There are new translations of the Bible based on Aramaic which give a different flavor to the teachings of Christ. For instance, "Be you perfect" becomes "be you all-embracing." "Heaven" in Aramaic translates as "the universe." "Lead us not into temptation, but deliver us from evil" becomes, "Do not let us be deluded by surface appearance, but free us from the bondage of attachment." These translations are considerably different from the King James Version that I was raised reading.

Much of the writings are attributed to followers of James the Just, Jesus' brother, rather than the accidental Christian, Saint Paul. The Paulines are referred to as "liars" by the followers of James which has interesting implications concerning modern dogma (Robert Eisenman and Michael Wise, *The Dead Sea Scrolls Uncovered*, Element Books, 1992).

Origen, a third-century Christian and church founder, speculated about reincarnation. His writings were condemned in the sixth century by the Emperor Justinian, but religious scholars report that St. Augustine, St. Gregory, and St. Francis of Assisi had similar ideas. Reincarnation and karma are the bedrock of Hinduism, Buddhism, Jainism, Sikhism, Tibetan Vajrayana, and Zoroastrianism. In the West, Pythagoreans, Orphics, Platonists, Druids, and Gauls shared a belief in reincarnation. This doctrine was also prevalent in the Middle East—held by the Essenes, the Pharisees, and the Karaites and became an important concept in medieval Judaism relating to the Kabalah. The universality of this common human concept, which was largely rejected by Roman Catholicism and the industrialized Protestant West, can be seen in the belief systems of Native Americans, Rastafarians, Zulu, some South American tribes, Polynesian kahunas, modern Theosophists, and your local neighborhood New Ager. Where the cross-cultural smoke is this thick, there is usually fire. Various therapeutic interventions in the transpersonal literature strongly support the concept of life after death, or the survival of individual consciousness. Some of the California transpersonal schools are claiming outrageous success rates using past-life therapics. They're publishing papers with protocols that seem to work. (Dr. Edith Fiore, *You Have Been Here Before*, Ballantine, 1978.) It's scientific method, even if it is a bit strange.

Those who are interested in reincarnation tell me that having an enlightened master guide you can easily shave three or four lifetimes of experience and intelligence-gathering off your karmic debt. (Being a knight of the four ways has some surprising legendary duties and obligations toward serving the impeccable truth, and may include helping one's attacker to achieve his next level of karmic responsibility. If he has a death wish you might choose to help him realize his desire.)

Spiritual development, which is the esoteric side of religion, is rather like peeling the proverbial onion. Gopi Krishna's autobiography *Living the Kundalini* describes spiritual development or enlightenment as both a mental and physical process (Shambhala, 1993). He tries to make it clear that you should be in marvelously good shape and mentally disciplined, or you will be in for a very bad time. The journey is heroic. He often refers to the Shakti or Goddess as intelligent energy, and I share that opinion from my own experience. He is also correct in that insanity, paranoia, religiosity, and kundalini survival (*samadi* or enlightenment) are points on a continuum that is mediated by the body and the environment. His descriptions of events from the terrible burning of the unprepared nervous system to the linking with cosmic consciousness reverberate with a truth I have personally experienced. (Some of the Kundalini Research Network researchers, who actually knew him, told me Gopi Krishna was a bit of a hypochondriac, which exaggerated his symptoms.) Where we differ is approach, but there is enough commonality for me to join with Hatsumi-soke and those other spiritual adventurers who say, "All the ways are one. The differences are only outgrowths of the local perspective."

In the more masculine-oriented religions of light or yang, (most European-based religions that were eventually subsumed by Roman Catholicism) there is often a prejudice against women, nature, sexuality, and the intuitive that refers to them as "demonic." This left-brained prejudice can extend to snakes and spiders as symbols of promiscuity, with marital sex associated with swans, doves, or honey bees. The eternal, esoteric, internal secrets of all major religions have been mystically hidden in the open, but the hordes of ignorant worshippers seem more in tune to political than spiritual reality, as they have bred themselves into continual poverty to feed the armies of an expansion that no one but they can desire. Methodists often remark that those who most proclaim their Christianity least exemplify Christlike behavior. That seems to be true of most religions. Mohammed, Yeshwah (Jesus) ben Nazareth, and Patanjali would be surprised at the behavior of modern-day proclaimers of the "true" faith. The Ayatollahs keep their worshippers ignorant, so they can be easily manipulated politically. The Ayatollahs proclaim the Prophet as the only source, but the Sufi are practicing something. The smarter, wealthy Arabs send their children to the West to be educated, for good reason. I have learned to respect them through teaching their children, as a child is a reflection of the parent.

Religion and Sociology

All the major religions have an esoteric mystic tradition that is the true base of their authority, and the ones that grow develop organizations that produce social welfare for their members. Religion shapes the minds of the young to feed the spirits of the ancestors; in return the political establishment favors the priests who train the largest or loudest herds. Karl Marx saw organized religion as a soporific for the masses, allowing the ruling classes of Europe to keep their stranglehold on the peasants. His concepts of large organizations and private enterprise only exploiting the working class have resulted in much folly, but he does provide an interesting perspective from which to examine foreign terrain. A dreary place to visit, and you really wouldn't want to live there. Private enterprise is hardly squeezing the life blood out of the lower classes. Marx regarded religion as a bit like getting hooked on tobacco, or for a real tour of hell, crack cocaine. Narrowed opportunities to express creativity and have a good time. Working for somebody else, always. The idea that an organization can help you to develop yourself by acting as a filter and translator of your wishes to the employer. Think about it.

Sigmund Freud put it this way, "Religion then would be the obsessional neurosis of humanity: like the obsessional neurosis of children. . . . If this view is right, it is to be supposed that a turning away from religion is bound to occur with the fatal inevitability of a process of growth. . . ." Rudolph Otto liked the idea that "Religion has its own independent roots in the hidden depths of the spirit itself." St. Augustine of Hippo may have glimpsed religion's nature when he psalmed, "You have created us for Yourself, and our heart is restless until it comes to rest in You." Does the saint foretell Marx's "sigh of the oppressed" living on illusory opium until they are dead? Emile Durkheim, one of the founders of modern sociology, pontificates, "If religion has given birth to all that is essential to society, it is because society is the soul of religion." The social structure of religions definitely reflects the culture of their establishment just as the above quotes reflect their author's interests concerning religion (Peter Bishop & Michael Darton, *The Encyclopedia of World Faiths: An illustrated Survey of the World's Living Religions*, Macdonald Orbis, Great Britain, 1987).

Heresy is a very useful tool for confronting reality. Too often in the martial arts, like religion, a particular school advertises itself as the only true and supreme system. Putting on a white belt and agreeing to serve in humility is the first step in achieving higher knowledge. It is when we think we know that we lose our childlike perspective and begin the fall from grace. Process and growth, or becoming, is far more important than imitation. Imitators are only that. Process is the way of the world-class engineer. Process is the whole ball of whacks to the flowing spirit that creates positive and useful change.

Responses to the Outland

As you can probably imagine, my first book resulted in my receiving some rather strange mail forwarded from my publisher. I get a letter or two a week, which amazes me as I read a lot and have never written an author. Must be something about martial artists. Accusations of betrayal by some, and New Age lunacy by others which will probably be put to rest by Hatsumi-soke's introduction of the second edition. Old friends reconnecting; pissed-off Koga ninja informing me of their Osensei's planned visit to "The Boss"—or, God forbid, to *me;* and thank-you notes for improved meditational and sexual experiences, or just a more together life. I thank you all for letting me know my word has effect.

The letters that were most poignant, however, were those saying, "Emphasize the chi sickness! Warn people that they can burn themselves when they do energy stunts." One must acclimate one's nervous system to higher energy, which always seems to feel extremely hot or cold to the neophyte. Use your internal rheostat with care. Pain is a message that you are making a mistake, so slow down and solve the problem.

This process takes from thirty days to numerous years depending on your path, skills, and intent. Its not necessary to take damage, though you can really learn a lot through self-healing, as you will be personally involved. Is that a good enough warning? Get to know some competent healers, as they can speed your development through acupuncture, shiatsu, massage, therapeutic touch, Reiki, and other healing modalities that make a vampire's life more acceptable than just having expert skills in bump, slice, and slug. There are herbal remedies for restoring the kidneys and adrenals if you burn too brightly. You will have to experiment to find what works best for you. Many people in energy work have done no or little research beyond what they have been told by their teachers, and the psychic claptrap that is passed down as "the truth" becomes a clear warning to the circumspect to wander on up the road, or do their own work.

Androgyny, represented by Kuan Yin, the Chinese female healing deity who manifests as a man riding on a lion in her "Kimera" form, is worshipped as a lucky monster who could dampen fires because she or he is one of those esoteric warnings indicating the hot male energy must be tempered by the cooler female energy. You have to balance the yang with the yin, so learn to play with the girls. Awaken your inner princess. I wanted to say something about letters describing women's physiological/spiritual complaints, but they mostly report on the rectal behavior and hircosity of their male counterparts and teachers. They report no symptoms more dangerous than an awakened viewpoint.

Because your cards and letters keep coming in (mostly thank you notes for being so frank) with questions concerning meditation and practice that I thought were well answered in *Path Notes of an American Ninja Master,* I'm going to give a quick rehash here of the basics of building your own path. It is useful to have a teacher, but only one who has gone through, or is ahead of you. It's a given, that finding a genuine sage will be difficult. If you pay attention to what I wrote concerning characteristics of a kundalini survivor in *Path Notes* and those of the *shugyosha* in this book, your search may be accelerated. Otherwise you'll just have to sort through the smoke, mirrors, and rituals for years. There are many frauds—also sincere ignoramuses—in the spiritual-psychological-warriorship-martial arts game. A little learning puts one ahead of the pack, and is still dangerous.

The Actual Practice that Results in Entering the Void

(1) It helps to be in shape, with a relaxed musculature and upright posture. (2) You have to be able to quiet your mind so

that you can observe internal functions as energy and external situations without expectations. (3) You should practice chi kung breathing techniques until they are natural to everything you do. The Secret Smile is the most important exercise. The microcosmic orbit is the most important technical skill for moving energy. Keeping your tongue up on the roof of your mouth is as important as deep breathing through your nose. (4) You should spend some time discovering what you want, and who you are, and incorporate that into your affirmation or Secret Smile. Some consider this a form of true prayer. (5) You should meditate every day and experiment with what seems to have the most beneficial effect for you. (6) If you begin to develop higher energy and experience radical changes in your consciousness without taking serious damage to your nervous system, then you are probably not going to end up in a rubber room somewhere. If your head starts feeling too hot, drop your tongue below and behind the lower teeth on the exhale.

I talked to a group of people at the Kundalini Research Network's annual convention, all of whom had experienced rather mild kundalini awakenings. Five of the six had panic attacks and had been hospitalized as schizophrenics with paranoid delusions. Be careful in your sharing until you have achieved mastery of self-generation, or endurance. (Lucky 7) After you've played with your energy long enough that you can project and maneuver it (sexual play is the easiest way to learn energy work), see what kind of spirits you can attract. (8) Observe carefully whatever or whoever shows up in your meditations. A picture is worth a thousand words. Explore and gather intelligence. Healing chi is more useful than war chi, but power is a transcendent process. (9) Project your energy persona into the Void, but return to the beloved with your new friends. The essence of leadership is the transformation of expectations into behavior that supports the completion of a particular task.

The steps in meditation necessary to entering the Void on

a sustainable basis, not a one-shot accident like a near-death experience, are: (1) integrate the mind, body, and spirit (energy) through chi kung meditation and physical exercise that trains the intention (such as Budo Taijutsu); (2) empty the mind of chatter through silencing the social self, which reduces ego-centrism and desire; (3) once the mind is able to operate smoothly and silently without expectations, begin contemplating the positive and beautiful with feeling until you have a full understanding of passion, or integratively focused intention, taking the time for developing Self-Awareness; (4) open each chakra and bring its energy up your very erect spine until all the energy is circling upward to the brain—this process is guided through following the breath and then guiding it; (5) be certain to complete and seal the microcosmic orbit with the tongue pressing onto the roof of the mouth, as you patiently focus your total attention on the area between and above your closed eyes, taking the time to let it be; if you don't enjoy being fried, remember to reverse the orbit and send the excess energy down to the *hara* for storage; (6) with no socialized expectation, allow yourself to experience whatever begins to happen, but be stealthy as you approach the darkness recommended by Bishop and Meister Eckhart, Lao Tzu, and St. John of the Cross (in *The Dark Night of the Soul)*, remembering the ninja does not fear power or evil (if you do not understand power and evil, be prepared to take some damage); (7) with joy and reverence in your heart, enter the unknown terrain like a polite guest who does not intend to overstay his or her welcome in the spirit world, which is the home of the powerful dead.

As Gopi Krishna makes perfectly clear, as do shamanistic texts preserved by anthropologists studying various cultures, you are who and what you are, in this space and time, with whatever challenges you may have. The messages or visions you receive as you focus all your attention on the point between and above your eyebrows in meditation are simply taps on the telephone line that let you know you are becoming wired into a different reality. As you build your internal energy through developing a potent macrocosmic orbit through chi kung breathing, you can heal and strengthen yourself, and make your energy positive by running the Secret Smile to power your affirmations. This positive field attracts energy.

When you first begin to meditate, you should pay attention to the movement of energy on the back of the eyelids called phosphenes. As your skills increase, the phosphenes will change color as your internal energy increases. Carefully observe what happens to them when you are relaxed. They may begin to offer you mini-hallucinations. Observe these patterns and figures. Give them attention, feed them more energy by concentrating your energy around the eyes. This is called "developing the third eye." After a while you will be able to "see" into your body. It's like looking down into an empty barrel. The legs and arms are like tunnels going out from the barrel. As your chi level increases the blood, bones, and organs will begin to light up, until it is like looking at a tree that is on fire (the burning bush or tree of life in esoteric legend). The more you run your orbits, the brighter the barrel or vessel becomes.

This is the first stage and often results in the healing of many physiological problems, as the body re-energizes and strengthens as your chi develops. The second stage is learning how to move the energy around when you are walking, healing, or practicing your taijutsu. While you are working on developing the ability to move chi around your body, your sensitivity will increase, allowing you to feel other objects and beings with the energy. Continue to pay attention to the phosphenes as you work on extending your ability to feel. Once you have reached the point of being comfortable with accepting energy, attempt to push it out of your third eye through the practice of concentration and breath regulation. The third stage is following the breath or energy wherever it may go.

With enough third-stage practice, you can enter the spirit world with your spirit in meditation. (This is easier to accomplish if you have mastered the Da Mo's cave exercise in *Path Notes*.) Create an image of yourself on the back of your eyelids. Give yourself permission to see with its eyes and feel with its senses. Push it forward into the Void using your life force or chi. Be cool, the natives are restless. See who you can make friends with, or merge with, as you are now a creature of energy. Make sure your trade goods are above standard, and fit your customer's concept of quality.

Commentary

The spiritual process continues and deepens with experience. It is not a one-shot inoculation, conversion, or instantaneous accumulation of insight. I liken it to the step functions in mathematics or intelligence. One step up makes a major difference in the perceptual quality in one's life journey. The *siddhis* manifest differently in different people and may come and go where there is not conscious effort to catch the wave. There are many surprises, and careful attention is necessary to avoid harm or capture.

As one develops a functioning third eye and begins to manipulate and observe the layers of reality that can be visited with that hard-won skill, many religious teachings become both acceptable and questionable. I now know that reincarnation is a reality, that survival after death as an energy being can be accomplished, that there are dimensions of reality that are near to ours, and they are inhabited. Certain types of consciousness seem to be universal as archetypes and can be readily tapped through chi kung and other methods. The Taoist concepts concerning yin and yang have both positive and negative forces imbedded in each side of the equation. If we want to live in peace, with love in our hearts, the positive aspects of the yin (female) have been too long ignored in the West, which has been severely injured by negative yang (male) in the last five thousand years.

When there was no mass education and most of us were peasants tending our flocks and fields by night, it was easy for the rich, well-trained, or clever to appear godlike in our eyes. I often hear stars of music discussed as such. Eric Clapton is a god of rock and roll; Janis Joplin, Whitney Houston, or Mariah Carey might be goddesses. Caesars and the Egyptian ruling class were treated as such, with temples established in their names. The greater the distance from the worshipper, the more powerful and mysterious the god becomes. I personally find Anne Rice's "God of Cell Division" very real. A Polish wise man once told me when we were walking together in a stableyard, "If you read good literature, develop friendships with intelligent, competent people, and learn to work with and for the benefit of others, you will seldom have to worry about your own survival." It strikes me as good general advice.

The Western science of neurophenomenology will soon penetrate into these realms in ways that will demystify much of mysticism, but the guiding spirits will still exist in the universal knowledge that is buried in our ancestors. East and West are coming together, and the results are exciting for those who have a positive vision. There is much in democratic materialism worthy of preservation, just as there is little to fear in coming to understand Eastern mysticism, which is more feminine in nature than Western alchemical techniques. The ways to power that are beneficial to the seeker all have a core of love rather than domination. Those who truly seek shall find grace. Those who seek for more mundane reasons shall find that the gods have the means to punish the trivial with some very scary weapons. Like attracts like.

As an agnostic failed Methodist, I find my own spiritual experience rather incongruous, but as a scientist feel it is worthy of reporting, since I've managed to replicate it to the benefit of my students who are interested in arcane matters. For the last five years or more I've been synthesizing and scientizing a process for integrating mind, body, and spirit that results in the development of chi in the average person in less than a year, if they are willing to exercise to a reasonable extent, put up with some physical abuse from their friends in a pleasant environment, and learn some things about their bodies that are easily learned if they practice. I've trained over four thousand supervisors, managers, and executives in the fundamentals of chi kung breathing and relaxation techniques as superior stress management. I've taken over a hundred people through the lesser *Kan* and *Li,* and of those probably thirty have managed to work out the kundalini with minimal direction from me. How you want to wire into the universal is your own business. *Shingitai* (mind skills body) can be developed faster in a group, as feedback opportunities are developed through interaction. You still have to do the internal work yourself.

In the condensed language of science attempting to rationalize the index of order or information in energy we face intriguing problems in the apparently radical distinction between objective and subjective information, involving as it does cultural, aesthetic, emotional, and intuitive stimuli, as well as perspective, context, and value. Having no desire or expectations allows you to see the truth. That is just part of your side of the equation. The ineffable other will truly tax your ability to describe if you are the typical New Age boob saddled with the vaguest of cultural blinders as well as inadequate tools and terminology. Like Wow, man.

Lots of Lao Tzu

Selections from Lao-Tzu Te-Tao Ching
translated by Robert Henricks.

Ruling a large state is like cooking a small fish.
When you use the Way to govern the world, evil spirits won't
    have godlike power,
Actually, it's not that evil spirits won't have godlike power,
It's that their power will not hurt men.
But it is not just that their power won't harm [real human
    beings] men,
The Sage, also [in return], will not harm them.
Since these two do not harm others,
Therefore their Virtues intermingle and return to them.
—Chapter 13

Therefore the good man is the teacher of the good
And the bad man is the raw material for the good.
To not value one's teacher and not cherish the raw goods—
Though one had great knowledge, he would still be greatly
    confused.
This is called the essential of the sublime.
—Chapter 27

Weapons are instruments of ill omen.
When you have no choice but to use them, it's best to remain
    tranquil and calm.
You should never look upon them as things of beauty. [They
    are only tools.]
If you see them as beautiful things—this is to delight in the
    killing of men.
And when you delight in the killing of men, you will not
    realize your goal in the land.
—Chapter 31

The valley spirit never dies;
We call it the mysterious female.
The gates of the mysterious female—
These we call the roots of Heaven and Earth.
Subtle yet everlasting! It seems to exist.
In being used, it is not exhausted.
—Chapter 6

Thirteen

Denizens of the Deep,
or Here Lie Monsters:
A Fool's Map
of the Promised, Purer Land

The *arhat* (sanskrit for sage who subdues) concept of compassion is much less generalized than that of the *Bodhisattva*
who takes an oath to keep returning to the world of *maya* to
teach until all sentient beings are enlightened, and may be manifested in the warrior by the occasional thought: "The world
would probably be a better place if more people knew how to
enter higher realities, but realistically, most shouldn't try. I'm
certainly not going to proselytize, considering the consequences
of screwing up the process. Let it be. They have to figure it out
for themselves, anyway." As much as I admire that viewpoint
my essentially democratic and Christian upbringing abhors a
vacuum. And the vacuum is significant in terms of actual working religious and martial practice that results in enlightenment
in both the West and the East. As a social scientist and designated *Busato* (a title Hatsumi-san gave me, which probably has
the double meaning of "real flamer" in Japanese) I'll try to share
my shadow.

Theory

The vision I have received seems more like William Blake's than
any other, but that may just be the gift of Scottish *maucht*.

(Raymond Buckland, *Scottish Witchcraft: The History & Magick of the Picts,* Llewellyn, 1993). My friends say I do have some dour tendencies. The ancient Picts or Scots used the word *maucht* (energy underlying all forms of magick) for inner power fueled by a state of ecstasy which was induced by dance, usually deep in the woods, around midnight, on a high point so you didn't get turned in by the neighbors. Having a piper and someone swinging a sword at your legs could be used to increase the excitement. (Bagpipes release a primal vibration, and in more civilized times the clans would actually walk into battle to the tune of "Amazing Grace.") The dance is not necessary if you know how to use your breath and bones as an energy pump to raise the energy or chi from the genitals to the brain.

Skrying (seeing with the mind's eye) or second sight was considered a rare genetic trait common to the people of the Hebrides in Medieval times, associated with the gift of prophecy. There were even some research papers about it done by the Rev. John McPherson of Skye in the eighteenth century. The Pict, Welsh, Gaelic, and Norse/Saxon magical traditions emphasizing merger with the gods through meditation—somewhat preserved in modern Wiccan practice—are similar to the ninja practice and relationship with the *Bujin.* In any case, the ninja concept of *shin-shin shin-gan* (the eyes and minds of divine spirits), offers a perspective that I was never taught, but being a genetic descendent of Welsh, Scot, and Irish immigrants, I may have some propensity for it.

The training of the self to become aware of its original face is lonely, hard, and can break the will of the most powerful seeker when the instruction book is misinterpreted to the advantage of the reader. Take nothing. Take nothing for granted. You will spend most of the journey alone regardless of who you try to take with you. You will doubt your own sanity, and you will be forced to change your mind if you wish to break the wheel and rise to higher experience, particularly if you are not ready.

Athena, the Goddess of Wisdom, wears a helmet and carries a shield because she is smart. Step carefully with me into the valley of darkness. The Buddha (Gautama), according to Da Mo, said concerning his position as *Tathagata* (one who can go beyond, one who lives in both worlds), "One who shows reverence for the bodies of spirits knows nothing" (*Ta Mo Hsieh Mai Lun,* part II. See *Bodhisattva Warriors* in Bibliography). This is both a pun on *mushin,* and a tip on how to regard the boogies. If you don't like my map you can try Swami Muktananda Paramahansa's written down in *The Play of Consciousness* (Shree Gurudev Siddha Yoga Ashram, CA, 1974). The swami is one of those navel-contemplating tree-huggers from India afflicted with visions and visitations.

Topography of the Holograph (Map of the Void)

Jesus said, "In my Father's house there are many mansions." There exist different realms within the Void—wheels within wheels, and layers and layers of various types of spirits. As each chakra opens one gets another wavelength of experience to explore. Entering the holographic realm of the energy gods of essence requires an effort of will that is wholehearted and sustained. It seems, for most people I have witnessed, a process that takes approximately ninety days if your body is young and far enough past puberty to be stabilized in growth and sexuality. The energy rushes *(kriya)* are benchmark that foretells more work. Most of the old texts recommend the kundalini for those in their late forties, so the mind's content will reflect actual experience as well as knowledge to feed the gods. That does not mean that younger people can't do it. They just have to work harder. A sacrifice that is less than perfect is a waste of a mind. A communal offering of mere blood and sweat will not suffice a god that eats its children and wears their skins for camouflage. Primal gods take things so personally. But fear not evil— that is only a surface tool to scare away the faint of heart. It gets worse before it gets better, like most things, but there is great power in aligning yourself with nature.

When you take the tantric short route, the war route, what the Tibetans call "Short Path" or "Fierce Path," you get to enter through the back door. This means you must reacquaint yourself with all the ancestors who are sentient enough to preserve essence in the Void, if not in the illusion, material, or particle world. You have broken through the matrix, slipped out of the mold, and thus because you are still lodged in the body, but exploring and moving in the spirit reality with the use of the third eye, you have opportunity to observe and make some decisions on your own. This does not mean you are home free. One of the easier ways into the Void is through using the exits from "Da Mo's Cave" to enter the noumas. The problem with this is working through your own imagination, which will color the experience. William Blake was disgruntled with Emmanual Swedenborg because that great Swedish mystic described the Void, or heaven, as being a bit like a nice suburban neighborhood. Blake saw the poison in that apple; he was a graphic artist, mystic poet, and no diplomat. He produced his best work in the late eighteenth century. His vision included evolutionary force and his description of the spirit life resembled a cross between mythology and a war zone, portraying the shadow dualistic unconscious as the opponent Urizen (William Blake, *The Book of Urizen,* Shambhala/Random House, 1978).

The old alchemists always showed the adventurer's head stuck through the veil of illusion that separates the realms. Day here with the body, night there with the head (yang and yin). The wise man could serve as a conduit or bridge from the realm of the gods of death to the realm of the illusion, and in so doing acquired a compatible relation with those who had gone before. Entering from the shadow side is not recommended for the living, nor the faint of heart. Entering the Void from the dark side or yin reveals to the shaded eyes of the stealthy shamanistic adventurer a reality best described in fairy tales, or the teaching myths of the ancients, or perhaps among contemporary nonindustrial cultures. Since the person who excels at one field can excel in all fields if his or her fundamental application of principles is good, the person who trains for life to go all the way can gain the ninja ability called *chonorokyu* (the state of unity with the divine). Close and subtle observation of the divine may cause you to expand your definitions to include some surprising beings. According to Hatsumi-san, the ancient ninja Tozawa Hakuunsai described the spirit life as *"banpen fukei"* (Endless variation, never surprised).

Once you poke your head through to the other side, it's a good idea to be able to identify who you meet quickly, as most can change shape at will. This is a side corridor of Dreamtime that is deeply imbedded in the neck, limbic lobes, and upper spine that is commonly called imagination. "Oh, that. That's nothing. That's just your imagination. A little voice. Nothing but your conscious. Something your mother tried to trick you with. You know. The voice that screams 'Run! Run!' or 'Don't you ever touch that dirty thing again.'" It can be a severe handicap when you are trying to be calm in the face of the unknown. You had better be able to identify your curious new friend quickly in terms of greater, lesser, carnivorous, herbivore, intelligence, weaponry, talents, works, feel, and feeling. If you wish to be known as a friend—name. You may have to present your pass or solve a riddle, which indicates you're ready for the next level of play, dead or alive. Playing in the spirit world usually means that you are dead, or can bilocate. Bilocation is similar to having a split personality on some levels.

Tests continue all through your life as peek-a-boo, and hide-and-seek riddles similar to *koan*. The bigger the opponent, the more grand the conflict, unless you are invited in for personal attention, as the way of stealth results in friendship. Some of those you meet have fierce, as well as gentle aspects, so you will be required to deal with the whole package with respect and love, if you hope to learn from the interaction. The whole package may include relatives. It's a bit like a marriage if your attachment is cross-sexual. Often in mystical ritual practice that rite is performed. (Nuns as the brides of Christ.) Storing up treasures in heaven can begin to seem like living in a dream if one is not careful. Traditional relationships include adoption, marriage, ownership, scourging from the temple, and giri. The way of the spirit resembles the fox-headed gods of Egypt and Japan. The fox will gnaw off a leg to escape the trap. You are to regard the trap of your body and culture in the same light. Very few human beings intentionally follow the way of the spirit.

The esoteric foundation of religion provides values and behavior that are recognized as desirable spiritual practice in both realms (esoterically they are referred to as "Virtue" or "Values of Children"). The Buddha's command was to create sentience not organization. The average good student in a liberal arts program has an enormous amount of information packed into an organ that approximates one hundred billion neurons or nerve cells, creating a web of possible interconnections that is greater than the number of stars in this universe. Think with that. These days one is expected to direct some of the brain's biomegabyte power outward and thus connect a little more deeply to one's total environment. This neuronic web forms and connects to a holographic universe that seems to exist in some ways as a school, and in others as a holding tank. Parts of the holographic university are inhabited. The reigning faculty of former sages was beloved of the gods because they chose to reincarnate. The bad news about reincarnation is you start out as a baby. The twice-born have to find the means for attaining enlightenment again, and if they don't make it, they return to the cycle of living and dying. It's a high-risk choice that the *arhat* can reject by electing to remain in the spirit world. When you're dead you're a spirit. An energy field. Energy travels at certain frequencies and your frequency is attained by what you do in your life (or how you breathe and focus your intention).

There are some researchers in this area who think it is more worthwhile to discuss energy as consciousness, rather like Heisenberg talking of fields and matter being interchangeable depending on the viewpoint of the observer. Anyway, the esoteric teachings of many cultures resemble to some degree the direction that modern physics is taking through the insights of such scientists as Stephen W. Hawking and David Bohm (Stephen W. Hawking, *A Brief History of Time*, Bantam Books, 1988, and Bohm and Hiley, *The Undivided Universe: An Ontological Interpretation of Quantum Theory*, Routledge, London, 1993).

Application

The ninja phrase "with the mind and eyes of divine spirits" *(shin-shin shin-gan)* has shifted to "seeing with the minds and eyes of gods and spirits" as I've explored the "mansions" inherent to one whose third eye functions. Telepathy, which is much more difficult than telempathy, is primarily a visual skill and is historically recorded as such by visionaries. The woodcuts of Blake resemble the dark holographic hollowness of the shape-changing energy beings that assume the postures and forms of ritual presentation of the gods that ruled in the distant past. As like attracts like, the denizens of the rejected shadow are a tidge rough-hewn in their humor as well as their appearance. They will never be accused of being politically correct. The gods can be treacherous and were forged in very different times. Technically they haven't a clue; artistically they can be very beneficial, as the function of a muse is to gracefully amaze. If your fundamentals are not in order, they will show you to a glorious death. Some people have strong needs to be crushed into oblivion. The ladies of yin are exceptionally well versed in crushing. Survival is the law of endurance, which is reflected by the cosmos. Evolving or learning to exploit the environment is their highest skill. Love is their answer. Death feeds their compassion. They have caught and held the wave for centuries. They surf the Void on the force of their wills and like pioneers in the material world, the first in or oldest have accumulated the most power.

Using the third-eye methodology is more difficult than mere dying (which also releases the spirit from the body), as you have to learn how to project energy outward and construct a spirit body to animate with your personality. Often while you are learning these skills, you will attract the attention of the local fauna as you penetrate their econiche. Trailing a silver cord behind so you can return to your body is not recommended. Hansel and Gretel's strategy can leave a trail back to your body. Not very stealthy. If an energy being is curious about you, and you're lucky, you may find that you've captured a spirit guide. As like attracts like, you may find the relationship resembles the "stalking of an ally" described by Carlos Castaneda. If you haven't yet achieved impeccable intent, your interaction with energy beings can become a learning experience. People who followed my methodology have told me they often have to confront and accept the rejected shadow entities of their self before they can project into the farther-out dimensions of the Void.

Looking through the porthole or window of the third eye can be like looking at a dim blue cliff face or television screen that you have to begin to move into to see with holographic depth. Sometimes the very stones and trees are covered with eyes. If you are peering at a night terrain, you will have to develop stronger vision to feed the light. If you want your vision to clear, you must feed energy through concentration, exercise, and relaxed attention. Relaxed attention can carry you to the mythic white room as well as the Medicine Wheel's Moon Lodge. Aladdin's genie lights his lamp in a cave of wonders, and the dragonfly's back he rides is a prayer carpet energized by five prayers a day and an admonition concerning the importance of water to a dry people. The eye of the artist helps to collect intention from the overwhelming kaleidoscope of images available within the holotropic reality. As the Zen answer goes, "Attention. Attention. Attention!" The Christian cathedral's spire, the head of the pagan's unicorn, and the Buddhist stupa represent projecting with the third eye. Looking up into the interior of the stupa, one is presented with an architectural icon of an energy tunnel.

Picture yourself pedalling a bicycle up a yellow brick road in that pearl of the morning that greets the rising sun. You may want to face West, the direction of death, as you do this. Just keep filling in the detail as you observe yourself going deeper into this environment. You may want to picture something worth pursuing in front of you, as you use your orbiting chi breath to add power to the third eye and enhance the image. Be aware of anything that forms unexpectedly. Make sure you have a good time, so fire up your strongest Secret Smile. Whether your projected spiritual scout is a bicyclist, swimmer, mountain climber of the Iron Man variety, or uses the gossamer wings of the dragonfly or bird to lift his spirit lightly to the next level is related to both luck and skill. Spiders know their way around the Web of Life.

There is something like a spiritual food chain to climb, and a less biological model might suggest a hierarchy. Some of those who have gone before have set traps along the trail to preserve their real estate. Sphinxes and other hungry ghosts will take up lodging in the innocent. "Well, lookee here! Some free brain space, and the poor dear doesn't have it sealed. Yummy." Stuff of legends, and exorcisms.

As you approach a mountainous cliff, there will be a path that winds up it like Jack's beanstalk, or a golden curved stairwell, resembling the stretched spiral ribbon of DNA, or the spine entwined by those twin serpents, Ida and Pingalla. Keep pedalling for the light. The Way is more important than the destination while the vessel still lives. Chaos is cousin to the Void. Each realm has its own archetypes and all can be used in Dreamtime as a vehicle.

I have no idea which is the greater vehicle. The Void seems large, and mostly empty to me. Some realms are war zones, and the inhabitants have mythic appetites and habits. I never expected following the breath to lead to a superconsciousness that seems to include all living things and can personalize them on command as well as hold them in a whirlwind of changing time. (A boogie for consenting adults is the study of meditative Bugei.) The boogies are shape-changers, but are often winged. They often appear as Greek, Egyptian, Chinese, and Hindu Goddesses, with males being a rarity. Shape-changers prefer the most powerful aspects of shaping to appeal to the eye of the beholder. Often one's first experience will be with the scariest aspect, and if you are not scared, a less frightening presence will develop.

Layers of the Onion or Cracks in the Cosmic Egg

The ghosts of the past may haunt you with the fever dreams of the present, but ghosts are to be ignored as they are simply the dead—dead waiting in a holding pattern called purgatory by Roman Catholics, a concept I found ludicrous as a Protestant child but which now holds more validity for me. Ghosts of relatives always seem to be warning you about something they forgot to tell you when you were too young to doubt them, but now you're going to find out anyway. The others laugh and call, "You'll be sorry!" and make little spinning motions around their ears indicating the fate of your poor scrambled mind. Some of the myths concerning the spirit worlds have remarkable sticking power across cultures, epochs, and geographical arenas. Some fairy tales are more real than the religion or belief system that replaced them.

Ghosts of relatives seem to be fairly close to this slice of vibrational reality. Ghosts often seem to be waiting to deliver a message, and then they fade away. Some seem attached to a place, or something they really liked, or the site where they died unexpectedly. They tend to be pretty one-tracked and not too bright. Some seem able to possess the unwary, such as alcoholics. The Chinese call these Hungry Ghosts. You can eat them, or exorcise them by sending them home to their moms.

Spirits and Demons are a little farther into the web. They get to eat what they can catch. They're hungrier and tougher than the ghosts. The cannibals among them seem to be most successful, so if you leave a little of what they eat (life force) to distract them, you can often slip by onto the next level while they fight over the tasty snack. It's like giving a guard dog a drugged hamburger ball. Ground glass is so noisy. Induced sleep is a better choice when you are slipping by what you don't understand. If you whip a few, you might want to put some of the lazy dullards back to work at challenging the self-righteous. Historically many mythological figures enjoy this activity. The master/slave, noble/peasant relationship was well established in the lands of our forefathers, and we well know the sucking tendencies of a tax-free upper class. The land of the dead's social structure was established in antiquity. Hierarchy is relevant. A demon gives a wild ride. If it serves the good, it will provide a lesson you will never forget. If it serves evil, it will provide a lesson you will never survive. The most dangerous predators are shape-changers or use extensive camouflage. The chameleon, a small lizard, is able to slip up on creatures that fly by appearing beneath their notice until the moment of attack and consumption. The honey trap and the badger game are more human examples of spiritual folly. The predator/protector balance fades quickly when the prey has fallen and the beast seeks to feed. "Devil or Angel? Which oonnne are yoouu?" Either way, it is Yippee Yo Ki Yay! Ride that bull, cowboy!

Above the predators is the level of the protectors. Working angels seem to be like the Pony Express. They are messengers and have a job to do elsewhere. They are working for somebody or something. They are busy and will ignore you. Guardian angels are like genderless soldiers and may support you in your efforts to conquer demons, but often a hanged man's perspective is necessary to sort out who is helping who or what. The appearance of a savior is seldom mellow if you've been following wilding ways, and your angel has to fight his/her way to reach you. If you've ignored your angels and not fed them properly with prayer and attention, as creatures of spirit and former ancestors with power, they may ignore your pleas. The best servants can be rendered fearful from constant pain, terror, and lack of nourishment. There is no guarantee that it is strong enough to respond to your call. The planes quit flying when the fuel is gone. A bird's metabolism requires high energy. The troops we leave behind usually do not survive the new regime's tender mercies. Angel territory appears to be a war zone. According to a 1994 *New York Times* survey, more than sixty percent of Americans actually believe in angels and quite a few claim interaction with them.

The metaphorical world of the holograph is fraught with symbols and the symbols have a life of their own. From an ego-centric position, all this is either nuttiness or the result of multiple fragmentation of the personal identity.

Higher Realities

If you get through the predator/protector screens you hit the realms of the lesser gods which are also archetypes, and often present themselves as cultural symbols of power and possession. Of course, if you don't know about spiritual culture or the codes of symbolic behavior, as well as the symbols that are most frequently meaningful, you can be captured and spend some low-quality time in onion-skin econiches that don't hold much profit for a person seeking liberation. "What's the secret password? Don't know? Well, welcome to my world, Pilgrim."

The lesser gods serve as a screen to protect the big thinkers from intrusion, but they haven't had much work lately. The old riddles that stumped Theseus for about the length of a breath still are used. It's easy to slip by the complacency of mid-level managers if you really have something of interest for the top dogs. Wearing the right uniform helps when you've crossed lines of demarcation and you're not sure your intelligence is good. Looking like family or being mistaken for a distant relative helps you get closer to the sources of power. Energy control allows you to shape appearance in the Void.

Major gods have many aspects. The Law of Attraction becomes an educational process as your complete package without direction or instruction arrives via meditation and prayer or just meditation if you want to be brave. If you get a demon, it is God's will that human beings hold dominion. Blood lust aside, you're in for the fight of your life. What does it mean in deep meditation when your right side shows you a pair of triangles coming together at the base to form a parallelogram and your left side presents a giant vulture flying at you with a naked goddess hanging in its mouth? What am I to make of this offering? She looks tasty to me. I suggest a positive interpretation will save you worry. When a war goddess takes your pubic scalp in mutilation, she is claiming you for her own. It's a scary way to show her love. The gods feed on strong emotions—fear as well as ecstasy. Some are jealous of their privileges. Some gods have known no other food than fear. Their worship is a death trap for the unwary. Those who love domination must also enjoy creating dependence. Those who confuse respect with fear need to study their language. Words have magical implications in the spirit world, but sticks and stones chew you up over here in the material world. Reincarnation might be preferable to staking out a claim in the Void, given the competition.

Gods shaped in the cauldron of fear and destruction are two-faced—some I've come across have more than five. The fierce way to power requires holding onto your faith that there is a better way than corrupt, smash, and grab. If you can survive the temptation to unleash your rage against that which you fear, you may find that calm acceptance of the fierce results in a change to beauty.

There seem to be major transcultural archetypal deities that intermix to create all sorts of interesting combinations depending on your needs and their mood. They are shaped by their culture, and manifest according to your intent. The Chinese medical sages associated these energy deities with the meridians of movement, the endocrine system, and particular organs, which corresponded to the Hindu chakra system. Personality traits were assigned to the balancing of energy within the body and big changes to injury or abuse to a particular organ or meridian. Western medicine's symptomology is moving more in that direction from the influence of psychiatry and chemical reaction. It also seems the emerging acceptance of the Chinese descriptions of bioelectric therapy are gaining credence (See Chang, Chia, and Padus in the Bibliography). "As the interior, so goes the exterior."

When you enter strange territory you examine the lives of the inhabitants and ask questions to get their view of their econiche. "You guys ever hear of a guy named Jesus?" "Oh, uh, Hebrew enlightened peasant that does the horah with his wives over on level three." "How about Nepthys?" "Yeah, the drop-dead beautiful and smart one with the snakes and laser eyes. Heard of her, huh?" "Who else is a name around here?" "Uh, uhm. Kali? One of the consorts of Siva?" "Killed thirty thousand demons herself? Uhmm." "What about him?" "Adventures in the maya and leaves her to run the show. Interesting!"

Ancient goddesses seem to particularly enjoy the company of martial artists, for powerful women love revenge. You can't pay attention to everything they might want you to do, as the crime detection technology today far exceeds their grim imaginations. According to Homer, some of these girls went in for eating each other's children in tasty little hors d'oeuvres as a warm-up for the main course, which might involve the guest. A tableau of terror orchestrated by a scorned goddess might be the final payback for picking the wrong one as winner in some sort of beauty contest. Favoring a spirit for appearance, rather than beauty of soul can be very risky, as paybacks are hell. One of my students was forced to make a choice between Aphrodite and Athena. Being a horny devil, he almost made the same mistake as Paris, which led to the fall of Troy. He wasn't very well read, and didn't have the advantage of a liberal arts education.

Once you've been accepted as a player—depending on your skills in generating energy, and your intelligence as gauged by your responses to a series of attacks, mazes, and opportunities for dalliance—you will be afforded tests in both the spirit and material world to define your fitness to play in the realm of the dead or spirits. Both heaven and hell are possible extremes for the pleasure seeker. Intelligent and not so bright become better guide words than good or bad when you don't know the local customs or practice.

One might do well to examine the record left by artists in stone. What the statues of gods and goddesses are doing, wearing, or carrying tell you important characteristics about them. Athena carrying Zeus' shield represents a fighter concerned with defense. Kali holding up the head of a long-haired man indicates the conquering of masculine vanity or ego. A stone picture outlasts a thousand words. The statues of the Gorgons, those early Greek sisters and primitive goddesses with snakes in their hair, are built like linebackers. (Strength of the body contributes to strength of the spirit.) Snakes in the hair or around the body indicate the kundalini. Hercules had his snakes in hand as a baby. When the most ancient ancestors are shown with

animal bodies—like centaurs, who are prized for their wisdom—
it is artistic license praising the barbarism of the times that
required animal skills for survival. Let the phrase "She or he
was strong as an ox or lion" slip through your child's mind and
see what gets pictured. Women of virtue are often shown with
horses or unicorns to show their mastery over animal nature.

If this seems confusing to you, rest assured an agricultur-
ist feels similar panic when dodging uptown traffic. A few years
ago I watched a video on the news of a cross between a kan-
garoo and a wallaby that escaped its Chicago Zoo compound
and made it into the city. It was panicked. It was going like hell,
through and over the cars. It was risking it all to escape what
it perceived as a bum deal, but had no idea that something far
worse lurked over the wall. Confusion and terror were its only
response to the horror of the city, which any slum-raised dog
handles with calm acceptance. We keep our beasts inside the
wall. Streets paved with gold seem to be a picture painted to
appeal to a beast so avaricious that it will make war on its neighbor when it can't find a more distant enemy to sack and plun-
der. Wealth to the best of my knowledge has never soothed the
savage breast.

Wen-Tzu (130) states, "Therefore it is said to know harmony is called the constant, and to know the constant is called
illumination. To enhance life is called auspicious; the mind mastering the energy is called strength. This is referred to as the
mysterious sameness, using the radiance and then returning to
the light." The true sage has no need to act out, or build an edi-
fice. Finding the true self is something like peeling an onion;
something like looking in a mirror. That which is feared, prefers
worship to warfare, and the one that is all is the highest, thus
knows no jealousy. Sacrifice indicates desire, and desire warps
creativity into a particular form. Submission is different from
sacrifice. The unicorn and the wizard's pointed hat are both
representations of the power one discovers by piercing through

to the eye of the whirlwind and staying around long enough to get acquainted. Read your mythology and look inward. The Chinese unicorn symbolizes truth. The Tibetans recommend developing a lung horse, meaning breath control can carry you into the realm of the *yidam* ("firm mind" or personal deity reflecting one's attributes that acts as a connection to a traditional lineage and supreme reality). There are snakes and spiders feeding in the holographic onion, and Gaia communicates on an evolutionary scale.

Visions Peeled from the Onion

A light-blue smiling Buddha sitting contemplatively in the Pure Land is often shown with four pairs of women representing the spectrum of the chakras—four on the left, and four on the right, alternating in dark and light complexion. The young women rest on lotuses in various stages of dishabille, and each bears gifts to her lover who lazes above. Often the Buddha sits upon an animal skin, or wears silk brocade, or rides upon a white totem archetype like a white toad (luck and drugs) or elephant (strength of breath, work, brains, and balance). The route up the mountain spine to where he rests is a pleasing contoured trail, up through streams and blossoming gardens. Climbing the mountain to the gods reminds us of Olympus, Meru, Fuji, or the Big Sky Mountains. The Taoists speak of the hidden mountain, and all those pyramids with religious significance on three continents certainly are more than one finger pointing. The royal gardens in Koyasan and Kyoto are exquisite, but worshippers stare at the *kongokai* mandala in hope they can replicate the picture in their memory of the sweet-faced healing Buddha, not realizing it is a map of the terrain they will have to travel to reach their goal.

When I enter by this route, the trail is well lit and nothing can be seen in shadow. Cherry blossoms shed a pink luminosity, and all the tree branches are covered with flowers. The vampire lurks hidden in the skull, if at all. Nature appears tame and well-groomed here. Dau Hsing serves up bean sprouts and arrays his guests in purple silk. No sound in the vacuum, but you can see into the hearts of those you meet. Everything is presented visually through the third eye and is seen with no expectation. What you see is not always a mirror of your expectations if you have learned to distance yourself from desire.

When I close my eyes in contemplation, I fear no evil as I walk through the valley that shadows death. The dry and rotting bones crunch between my toes, and the air is filled with the unforgettable smell of burning corpses. A sharp reminder of the sweetness of life when adventuring in an opponent's territory. . . . We all like what we learn first, and may be forced to let it go quickly. The dead-end cliff face that will have to be scaled to leave this place has a broad road of skulls and mutilated corpses piled from the valley floor to a center cave which bulls-eyes the spread-legged, stone-like image of a giant naked woman in half-squat facing you with eyes for tits. Her legs, thrust open, seek balance like a spider, and her pubic hair is burning. She holds the head of a long-haired man in one hand, and an ax in the other above her head. She moves her many arms and legs in silent triumph. She changes shape with the burden. Her lips blow kisses and mime yodeling with the joy of recognition. It appears you've been gone a long time. The natives have been restless.

Kali's skin is black as coal or red where the blood and energy show. All three of the eyes in her head are opened and the pupils are dilated with delight. She thinks you are cute. She's hungry—no fresh meat for some time in these realms. Spread out in concentric circles from her is a web of smaller caves that contain a smaller, more human counterpart. There are corpses hanging in the webs. They have come at her from all directions and still she dances. Outdoor training. No easy climb to glory here. Great dojo. I wonder when and what she charges? A little slice of heaven nestled here in hell.

302

The Goddess of Creativity and Death who likes shining light in dark places close to the abyss whispers at my back, "She who is closest to the Great Mother is showing you that the way of worshipping your own is a dead end. The living improve on their lives and get out of the cave. Many are willing to fight and die for even the touch of a dark goddess who crushes all to feed her offspring. The dying bemoan their situation, not recognizing that life is part of death. Even religion and gods must overcome their egos if they are to escape the endless repetitive circle of death. A dead queen is chaste. My existence is so dry that I burn just for the sight of you. Watch my behavior, as there is no sound where silence is golden." For a goddess, maintaining the home hearth is no small project when the suitors are powerful. Remember Ulysses did more than conquer the one-eyed Cyclops in a cave; he had to return and reclaim his wise and prudent Penelope with a powerful bow and arrows.

Kali, with her circle of skulls, is considered the hardest way to God, as she forces you to face and eradicate all your fears through loving your opponent to death. A somewhat neutral position regarding the educational value of life, as held by most Buddhists. But what mature male has not bruised his ego against unrequited love, or feared being bested by a female in this land of freedom? Kali is often shown hovering over a reclining masturbating male. This tantric scene is not the vengeful mother chastising her son for wasting his seed, but is meant to show the relation of sexual energy, relaxation, and powerful creativity and symbolizes an acceptance of birth control at the source of the problem. The ancients were no fools.

Like a tourist, you must slip through Lucifer's huge, dark, empty throne room buried deeper than a bomb shelter—a shattered bunker at the end of a desolate and blasted path through the legions of the damned—before you appreciate the kindness of the war angels of the Great Mother to whom everything is personal. Her eyes see every sparrow, yet you doubt that you are not already categorized within the web? Dream on. Angels who get uppity also learn to fear Mother Nature. When the old mystics opined, "As above; so below" they may have been referring to the power struggles that exist in both light and shadow.

Living the Dual Mandela

If you are more individualistic, like most properly socialized Democrats running loose and free in America, you probably would rather do this yourself. Study your mythology. See which gods had reputations for what. Pick one with a reputation for granting success to its worshippers or appellants. Study its interests and hobbies. Study means practice. You don't become a god of rock and roll by doing lip sync. Like is attracted to like. When you meditate you should include what the god recommended as part of your goals and aphorisms. When you enter new situations, ask yourself how your guide would handle this situation and then engage in a little theater. When you are doing things you think might be interesting to your guide, invite him or her to see through your eyes and ride along. When a level of trust has been established, let it have the reins when you are engaged in pleasant activities that you can do in your sleep. Depending on the strength of the relationship, you may want to substitute her name or join it with yours as you howl into battle. It's a family thing. You don't have to do it, but it adds a little color to what otherwise can be very lonely and frightening.

If you make friends in the Void, you may find that they occasionally enjoy having the use of a body to play again in the material world. They find it easiest to enter your realm when you are meditating. Invite them in when you are doing things they used to do when they were alive. You do have to invite them, as most spirits cannot cross water. The folk tales about the dangers of invitation concerning vampires, or the warnings about carefully wording your wishes, may test your impeccability when the truth manifests. This is called living the dual mandala, or being in both worlds. Warriors like martial arts. One of my black belts was watching a possessed wrestler in Turkey who easily defeated opponent after opponent, and then to the shocked horror of the spectators, snapped the neck of the opposing finalist for the championship with a scream of triumph. Horsemen think automobiles are great fun, but don't concern themselves with speed limits or understand that the flying box can crumble. Lovers seldom want to miss an orgasm. Actors get into the new part. You get the picture. It's not necessary to construct elaborate rituals, or forms of worship, if your relationship is one of casual acceptance among equals of different type. One builds trust by sharing the pleasant and easy as a form of preparation for the difficult and hazardous. On one level this body is only a vessel for the spirit; on another it is more like an apartment house. You are the landlord unless the stronger spirit wins. You've probably seen how funny and stupid some channels act. The way of subtle influence is smoother. At the third national convention of the Kundalini Research Network in 1994, one of the presenters said you should never take for granted that a spiritual entity is any smarter than you are. It's good advice.

Some of the good spiritual entities love a fight if they are defending the meek from the greedy. Neutral spirits get into the excitement. They're full of surprises. Tricksters ... the name spells out the consequence of acceptance. Tricksters do seem to have a problem finding lengthy employment, so are often available to launch the neophyte in unexpected directions. I was asked to warn you about trickster spirits. Well, they are part of the shadow side of enlightenment. Smart and tricky seem to go together when we're adventuring or gathering intelligence. Coyote fills that role in American Indian mythology, which also has a spider goddess similar to Kali. Loki, the dark and clever warrior of Norse mythology, was always tricking his slower companions until one-eyed Odin, who meditated on a giant tree and rode the gray eight-footed horse Sliepnir, got tired of his spite and collaborated with Thor to imprison him. Odin's sense of humor ran to cruelty as well, but he served a deeper power. Legbo in African mythology seems to enjoy times of chaos. The Saynday tales of the Kiowa often take a trickster twist.

All the higher-levels gods use camouflage, or they are shape-changers. Gods always expect you to tell the truth, punishing you horribly if you lie, but are not bound by such laws of behavior themselves, being creatures of the Void, or waves rather than particles. How dead do you have to be? The spider is the trickster, the darker side of Gaia. She can lead you to fertilizer if you don't understand creativity has a dark side. You can think it without doing it. Knowing how to do something is not an indication that you intend to do it. Dishonesty, like charity, begins at home. People often accuse you of what they would do themselves, given the opportunity. A little fun... A sense of humor is one of the marks of the mature great.

Theory and Application

The third eye acts as a projective screen that allows you to use and share the hormonal viewpoint as well as whatever else attunes to the natural circumstances you face. It's not that big a mystery. It just takes work if you want to control the phenomena in a pragmatic manner. I see through my glass darkly, yet I've friends who receive their visions as if they were in a dream or movie. The spirits pantomime their vision through feelings and acting out, and for me it is like watching poorly projected holographic cartoons. When I borrow the eyes of Hatsumi-soke or Takamatsu-soke—both great artists—details become more apparent, but they like to throw in lots of jokes to make me laugh. Here's one from Takamatsu-soke:

Picture a mushroom, the mushroom turns into a penis. The penis turns into a mountain. The mountain turns into a volcano. The volcano erupts into a large golden Buddha. The

Buddha's head erupts, and out of it pour thousands of little bud-dhas that come running down the mountain at you, burning, raping, and killing as they come. What do you do? (I think the message is clear. It appears a universal riddle. I won't tell you my response, as he may use this *koan* again.)

Meditation in a skilled group can be very valuable. In the interactive growth and development of a group that come together through meditation, you learn from your companions through a feedback loop until you are indeed a demon god, and a good friend to that which needs no controls. You can play jokes and send messages to people who share your passion for the esoteric. You can send your gods within to meet with them, or set up schools so their spirits can come and train with your guiding spirits. You can dress your spirit friends up in funny clothes and send them to visit. Then check on their appearance to make certain they arrived as you sent them. It only takes a phone call. You have to play with them to figure out how to use them. The Buddha reminds us that "whatever manifests as a whole is delusory" (*Tamo Hsieh Mai Lun,* Part II, see *Bodhisattva Warriors* in Bibliography). The Zen perspective is to regard all apparitions as delusionary parts of the mind that can capture your attention to divert you from development into Buddha-hood. The pragmatic Western perspective is revealed in the old saw, "The gods help those who help themselves."

What you "see" in the Void when you look up is from the perspective of the seeker. When you see eye to eye, holding your head level, you accept spirits as they are, no matter how intri-cate the intertwining of the multiplex reality. When you look across vast vistas, first look down to be certain your foundation is good and the important details are in place. The messages that are sent up from the dark animus have dour consequences when ignored. When you ride the gossamer wings of the light spacecraft, avoid the turbulence created by heat. When you ride the dark bull elephant with the light girl, remember the

Rockefeller Syndrome if you want to be a sage with good breath and a hearty breakfast. Soixante-neuf is the breakfast of champions, and is often represented as the sign of the Cancer water spirit, which resembles yin and yang, or reverses the Yab Yum. This paragraph is cryptic to protect the innocent. Those of you of a slyer perspective may brighten up your incubus.

The spirits may talk to you by showing you pictures in your third—eye screen. It's an intelligence test. "Are you quick enough to get this one?" "This action leads to disintegration. Watch how it changes me." "This is fun, how are you feeling? Look how it has us all whirling in dance. Thank you." Learning something new, even if by visual riddling, is such fun—particularly when its a new sensation to be praised when accomplished by the fearful.

When you use the external mountain or pyramid as a symbol of your rising sun, you may want to practice tilting and focusing it from both a megaphone and diamond-tip perspective. This exercise is similar to the hypnotic feeding patterns of snakes and spiders. The funny blocked cone hat of Nefertiti, the beautiful wife of Akhenaton, represents this use of third-eye projection, just as the cobra crowns of the pharaoh and striped spread-hood hats represent the kundalini's halo glow to the eyes of worshipping subjects. The crystal crowns of European nobility served the dual purpose of appearing like a halo while keeping energy sources near the brain. The Jewish rabbi's phylactery is a similar focus point for prayer when tied to the forehead. It is an external means of focusing sentience or intention. As the exterior, so the interior, with a little artistic license to reinforce the image for the psychically blind. Directing the mountain cannon, or focusing your intent, can be fun as well as a means of feeding your guests and receiving manna.

Do not mess with Mother Nature to your horror. The pursuit of perfection eventually renders chaos, from which the beauty of the natural process of selection hides. It does not take much awareness to see dangers to our econiche. The quest for perfection and beauty can quickly result in toy French poodles everywhere. Armies of Madonnas indicate a lack of attractive alternative models as well as poor understanding of the goddess market. Democracy as a media event is as fickle as putting trust in your representatives by paying them first. Study the real thing, not the imitation.

Plato's *Republic* lacks a variety of roles necessary for a valued, meaningful, fun life in a complex modern society like the U.S. His model, however, is popular with the dragons from whose cave he stole it. The city of mythological proportion is not an abstract in the minds and eyes of the former great builders. The garden exists in harmony, the city of light is walled, the baths are shared, and the views are planned for their magnificence. It's breathtaking. The path to reaching it requires a deep knowledge of endurance. There seems to be more than one approach to the Pure Land, Isle of the Immortals, Avalon, Heaven, and Hell. The modern conscience has been too dumbed-down to be your guide.

The Chinese sages fed the deer and collected "their horns of many directions." The unicorn horn was used to fascinate the innocent, which does not connote stupid, but sometimes is associated with ignorant. What you don't know about, you don't understand, and what you have never seen accomplished is difficult to personalize. Even female lions will support a philosopher king, as was demonstrated by the pride at Florida's Budweiser Gardens in the late 1960s when they kept killing the males introduced by their keepers to replace "Old Charlie" who eventually died in the saddle. The goddesses are waiting in their pure gardens starved for affection, and bored after waiting a few thousand years for a prince to show up with a kiss and an encyclopedia. The real estate is only limited by your information and your vision.

For the imaginative, language is a painting. The Chinese

and Japanese have maintained a graphic quality in their written language that is an aid to visualization similar to Egyptian hieroglyphics, if the context is understood. It only takes plane geometry to build a pyramid. The pharaoh has the third eye. The king is a sorcerer who heals the land. Moses was trained as a prince in Egypt. Noble intention, intelligence, and a relationship with the spirit world were thought to be characteristics of bloodlines in those times, not secret training from your Mommy and Daddy you never ever told anyone but your successor about. The Hassidic symbols reek of tantric mysticism. The Kabalah is very straightforward. A lot of information gets lost to bad translations, concretizing failures to understand codes, or oral transmission as hearsay. How good is your teacher of experience? "I have looked down upon the stars" is an actual experience you can have on the astral plane.

Dreamwork

Dreamtime provides an arena for meditators to exchange symbols and knowledge of the various ways. Dreamtime shares residence with the oversoul and leaks into this reality as well. You can visit people in their dreams, which is fun if you can tolerate some surprises. Others' internal stories may not fit your expectations, and when you are part of their dream, the stronger spirit wins. I once had an Arab student who became quite skilled at slipping into dreams. It's a "sub-conscious" process. He tended to project his desires on others, and didn't listen too well, a common cultural characteristic nurtured by the constant feuds of the Middle East. Not realizing my interests often function as a bully trap, his expectations concerning my expectations were far from the mark and he embarrassed himself mightily when he visited me. When he awoke, instead of coming to train he fled home to his parents for no reason he understood beyond his terror. I found his attempted escape somewhat schizophrenic.

After that incident I thought I would make my turf a little

more challenging for the intruder. I told Kali to make it a better test, as my openness was getting too well known. Three days later another student was teaching a friend of his how to construct Da Mo's Cave. He had told his friend what my cave was like. (You can actually visit each other in Dreamtime, or if you have the proclivity, in meditation.) The student said he thought he would go visit the master's cave. He was exploring a sandstone cave with straw on the floor and had just lit a candle to look around when a voice shook him to his bones saying, "Get out of my cave!" and a giant hand seized him and threw him out. I cracked up when I heard this story. (It would seem D&D is more useful than an easy way to teach kids achievement motivation, strategy, role-playing, and how to use their imaginations. Playing magic users and clerics can be more useful than thieves and fighters for developing survival skills for the Void. Study on that.) I haven't been back to that drab entrance to the realm of the undead for years. I hope the boogies put up signs like "All Ye Who Would Enter Here Must Relinquish Desire." A sphinx or two guarding the entrance would be nice. There seem to be a lot of unemployed monsters with little to occupy their time in the higher realms. We're happy to give them some amusement as well as challenging work. "Hey, Carrion-breath! Think you can get into being a temple guard for Glenn? Go for it. Figure out your own job description and have some fun. Don't eat anybody worthwhile. Remember what the owner likes. Soften them up. Tender. Focused higher energy." None of this "Glenn slept here" crap. I'm curious to hear from the outlands. Some of my ninja friends have told me they left messages for me in my cave. Come on guys, use the telephone or e-mail, if you know me that well (spider1@firstnethou.com).

NDEs and Alien Encounters

NDEs, or near death experiences, are sometimes extolled as being similar to the kundalini experience. Though profoundly meaningful to the person who nearly died, such experiences are not nor equivalent to the kundalini. They are an opening into the spirit world, and some people report entrance to heaven, but quite a few find the experience to be hellish. NDEs might be regarded as a wake-up call for the lucky, a second chance at getting their values straight before passing on to their earned reward. I consider this realm a holding tank or form of purgatory, a spiritual recycling center where the incoming are either put in a holding pattern to be retooled for their next spate of schooling, or if raw enough, sent to feed the hungry ghosts like cattle to the slaughterhouse. One may find one's relatives hanging out in or near this realm. If they cared about you, they might pass on some message they feel is important, or give you a tour. To get beyond this level you must enter a tunnel that resembles a worm hole, the pit of a trapdoor spider, or the nether eye. It is a darker route to a different light. Sometimes the entrance hangs in space before you like a giant eye.

Gods, spirits, angels, demons, noumenal animals, ghosts, fairies, shamans, warriors, sages, and sprites are not the only inhabitants of the spirit world. I've been seeing a lot about alien kidnapping therapy lately, popularized by psychiatrist John Mack. If you are interested in UFOs, folk tales, and Vedic cosmologies, Richard L. Thompson's *Alien Identities: Ancient Insights into Modern UFO Phenomena* (Govardhan Hill Publishing, 1993) will hold you spell-bound. I found alien kidnappings pretty amusing at first, until I started seeing some fairly credible studies of comparative descriptions from people who had little to gain by lying or publicity. Now, given the dimensionality of Dreamtime and the psychic gift of farseeing, I'll dance out on this limb and someone else can try for a good science fiction novel. I haven't read *Communion* (a Jordanian friend said its aliens were similar) but this is what I saw meditating under a waterfall:

I was scanning outward through the third eye when

suddenly looking back at me was a pair of huge nonhuman eyes. The eyes were set in a very high forehead above a small mouth; extremely white skin, thin neck, narrow shoulders, no wings, didn't see the manipulators. Nocturnal or cave dweller, no natural enemies. The physiology could also result from generations of urban living where the sun's rays are considered very dangerous, and hard labor is a thing of the past. Might be from the future. . . . The brain-to-body ratio indicated propensity for high intelligence. It immediately attacked me with energy and hypnosis. Tricky, sexy little devil, used to having its own way. Definite vampire tendencies. Being a nightrunner the telepathic power was probably an adaptation of echolocation similar to dolphins or bats. The feeling was of love powered by strong sexuality, which would make an excellent offensive weapon, if Americans weren't so numbed by the florid ploys of Gorgian rhetoric and modern advertising.

I let him think he had me fascinated, took him in, and then ripped right into his energy and grabbed his mind. Being a mirror has its advantages. I don't know what he got from me, but this is what I got from it. They're nocturnal. They may have evolved from a more reptilian base, and like king cobras hypnotize their prey. They mine energy and have been star-faring for a long time. They like our energy. They're very smart and high-tech and come in one flavor. Their planet did not have the variety of speciation that blessed Earth. Winning continuously over lesser competition creates a great weakness. In psychology, it is called unrealistic confidence; in the vernacular, it is known as folly. In anthropology, it could mean adaptation to too limited an econiche. For whatever reason, this being had no psychic defenses that come up with any speed, so he was not like a human being. He broadcasted with power, but he was an open, wide open, receiver.

They canceled out their competition so long ago that physical warfare isn't part of their repertoire. That does not mean they frown on domination. Sun miners could probably screw up a planet pretty badly if that became a necessity. (That scenario is my own projection. I didn't get that from the Space Critter.) I couldn't tell if they have to travel through dimensions as well as across space-time to observe us. I got the impression that our Earth is a long way from normal hunting grounds, but is considered interesting as hell due to its terrifying dominant species. They really aren't supposed to mess with us, but idle manipulators are the Devil's playground. If we were to finally chew our own legs off and destroy ourselves through screwing up the environment, or engaging in total war, they would be happy to invest in some terraforming and real estate. There is some population pressure at home, wherever that may be.

The protocols of the alien kidnappings indicate a stealthy random sampling of those who won't usually be missed for short periods of time. The hypnotic talent would explain the amnesia. (As human beings are not just cortex, it takes a while for the victim's subconscious to cough up this violation of privacy in coherent form. Maybe some of the schizos aren't so whacked out after all.) They've decoded our language, follow the soaps, and monitor our politics. Our technology of mayhem is frightening to them. We're regarded as potentially mad dogs, and quarantine is not quite official policy, but there is an unspoken consensus that the meat-eating, environment-manipulating primates are going to have to find their own way to the stars. These beings are not particularly creative, just smart. There is not much variety in their lives, and their ships do not even have windows to gaze upon the vistas of distance. They are truly engineers. They make their observations through technology. They have plenty of curiosity.

He didn't enjoy my laugh when I ripped into him, and I was being pretty careful. I don't get to do much mental surgery on aliens. Tit for tat, hope I didn't damage anything. I hope he was the boss. I'm beginning to understand the functions of a yidam. I know I scared and surprised the little prick of misery. He didn't respond well to mental rape at all. He had no defenses for chi kung other than to slam the door and run. He was an easy mark for a spirited attack. I hope he likes his new nightmares. We're awake. We can find you if you're in our space. Trick or Treat. Negotiate or die. Make the future worthwhile. We play rough with those who hurt our women and children. Hell, we'll level a country over oil. We nuke and don't apologize. "Don't Tread on Me."

That was the first encounter. About a week later when I was meditating with Hatsumi-soke and his teacher Takamatsu-soke in the Void (which I used to find very strange, as he is dead), Big Eyes' big brother shows up—a more muscular and fangier version that comes in on the attack. We easily avoided his first charge. I deferred to Takamatsu, who tore him/her to shreds. We watched the light in his/her pieces go out. I'm not certain what effect soul death has on one of these suckers, but humans find it very unpleasant. They usually sicken and die. I wouldn't plan on setting up a resort where that could happen with any degree of regularity. I have not been bothered since by these little cuties.

These aliens are being very careful, but their sense of ethics doesn't run nearly as far toward individual freedom and sanctity as ours. A rather Argentinean or Brazilian viewpoint on human rights. . . . The reported rapes may be sample-taking, lack of respect, boredom, or even fantasy reaction of the victim to their attack methodology. The stories concerning surgical implants certainly remind me of how we keep track of animals when we're trying to get a handle on their migratory behavior. The aliens would probably make interesting friends or allies. The aliens have amplified their natural biological skills with stealth technology. The two that came after me were both wearing plain cover-alls with a large belt buckle. It shouldn't be too hard to burn out a belt buckle unit. Those who work it out get

315

a space ship and a slave crew. Most governments would pay well to advance their status. On the other hand it may be a rare form of schizophrenia shared by science fiction readers and *X-Files* fanatics. The retired Air Force general and psychologists I spoke with who were doing actual research in this area were sincere.

Anyway, that's my alien sighting in Dreamtime. Check out your neighborhood and give one a swat. Their little love wave is a pale imitation of true human passion for someone who has experienced the real thing. Invite them in, close the door, and have yourself a ball. Its not a crime. Its a lesson in respect, like handing them a wrapped fish as an invitation to dance. They aren't human beings, nor friends, yet. They've never had to deal with giants or negotiate. Forewarned is forearmed. Communion, my ass!

Animal Archetypes Can Serve as Guides to the Higher Realities

Native Americans have the belief—which is not universal to all tribes—that there are archetypal animal spirits similar to Plato's concepts of noumenosity. They also have beliefs concerning the spirits of place similar to Japanese kami, Middle Eastern Jinn, and Chinese land spirits. The Black Hills of South Dakota are sacred to the Sioux. The Hopi and Navaho (still tied to their land and gods) greatly valued establishing relationships with the animal spirits. The red buffalo and the eagle are used as earth and air equivalencies for healing in Native American shamanistic lore. The groundhog and mole were highly valued as totems by those who wanted clearer night vision or who worked with energy. Recently published studies of the hunting habits of star-nosed moles reveal a propensity for electroreception (*Discover*, August, 1993). Our Iroquois brothers admired the telepathic ability of the groundhog, its hermetic lifestyle, vile temper, and great digging ability. Because it hibernates, like the bear, it was associated with "death without dying." The mole was even more mysterious to Navaho cave dwellers as it was blind, yet created complicated tunnels and was a voracious eater.

When I taught meditation in the arboretum there was a young groundhog who would sit with us. Back in the eighties, its father used to dislike us intensely enough to be felt when we trained in its territory. We eventually won it over. Once when hoshin shodan and ninja Leo Langwith was training with us, he kept remarking that someone was watching us from the brush. I laughed and introduced him to our groundhogs. My shidoshi friend Kevin Harrington, from near White Plains, New York., who teaches in the beautiful Hudson River Valley has a small wolf pack that plays in his back yard, and owls visit his children. A huge flock of birds surrounds my office building every evening in Houston. When I lived in Michigan, I had a raven and an owl that would visit my back yard.

If you want to catch an animal's spirit to take a totem, rather than just eat its body, you have to enter its field. You have to slip up on it and hold it transfixed with your eyes while you get face to face. It must perceive your interest as beneficial. Its body may attack you, but its spirit will remember your offer of friendship. If it remembers you when it dies, the spirit archetype will suddenly wax large in your practice. You have to figure out how to take advantage of what it offers the relationship. Ted Andrews' book *Animal-Speak* (see the bibliography) might help you. An apprentice shaman friend traded it to me for a signed copy of my first book.

Studying the animal from the viewpoint of an expert can be helpful. The Jack Nicholson movie, *Wolf*, has an interesting discussion of animal spirit possession when Jack's character goes to talk with an old Russian scholar after being bitten. Someone did a little research. So-called primitive people established totem relationships with various animals for sound reasons. If you are a woodsy type, establishing a friendly totem relationship can be quite a challenge. Many of the ninja who enjoy this sort of stalking study with the famous tracker Tom Brown, Jr.

You might start with the spirit of the rabbit. It's a survivor, hides well, hops prodigiously, and its sexual prowess is part of colloquial expression in the jokes of all English-speaking peoples, as well as the Native Americans. This might be a fun animal spirit for beginners if they've a strong control on the libido. God knows what a wild lion would do to a beginner. I really tried to find a wild elephant when I was in Africa, but only tracks and smashed trees were granted. Elephants are a bit shy. The relationship with humans has proven tenuous. Elephants are said to be very smart and have incredible balance. In Hindu mythology, the Lord Ganesha has an elephant's head, loves businessmen, and supports literature. I did find a couple of leopards, a pack of wild dogs, lots of giraffes, a troop of baboons, and a zillion antelopes on camera safari in South Africa at Notten's Game Farm.

Insect totems are regarded as fierce and primitive by Native Americans, but are respected and sought after in Asian mythology. The mantis was associated with stillness and prophecy. The dragonfly was important to the ninja and samurai as a totem for luck and winning, and the spider to the Scots, Norse, Hindu, and Japanese for creativity, feminine power, understanding the past and future, and achieving one's goals. As the spider creeps into shadow consciousness, like a whale slipping over a scuba diver, you find yourself in the divine web. Where albino is an accident, the darkness dweller's white skin reflects its evolution. Spiders provide wonderful lessons on how to move with stealth, speed, balance, and power. Their webs are traps for the unwary high flyer. They lay about and wait for the right vibration on the line. Some spiders, like kings of yore, do not kill other similar spiders when they fall into their web. In American Indian mythology the spider is referred to as Grandmother and is associated with creativity, feminine power, story telling, and some darker talents. Old Inky Dinky is probably the first connection the baby mind makes with fantasy and fear. Its shapes both attract and repel. The Goddess Kali can manifest on a continuum from a spider to a beautiful woman. I once asked the *I Ching* what her function was, and it replied "Cutting Through the Crap."

Personal Commentary

People get pretty angry with me sometimes when I suggest they have forgotten their ancestry, but it seems to me that in spiritual matters, many scientists have flung out the baby with the bath water. *Keiko* (to meditate upon the old) is the Japanese term for following the process of training for the *Bugeisha* (one who studies Budo deeply). Phenomenological experience of a spiritual nature can be empirically examined; even passed around if you know how to play on that level. If you have a good teacher you can make quantum leaps in subtle influence. If you've paid attention, I've presented a cross-cultural map of shamanistic practices that actually result in attaining your heart's desire. If your heart's desire is entering and surviving the Void. The process is at least eight-tracked and I've described some of them with emphasis on avoiding religious madness, so common in the Third World, where church and state are frequently the same. I prefer the agnostic route of chi kung, following energy routes with the breath of life. I describe the foundation-building practices necessary for that route in *Path Notes* from a master's perspective in esoteric martial arts. Your own body will teach you when it is time to transcend the foundation. There are no shortcuts, unless you are willing to pay the toll. In the material world we search for a teacher of true knowledge; in the spiritual world the teacher of true knowledge searches for you. When one looks down from the astral plane, normal people look like goose bumps on a gray skin, but the person who has gone through the kundalini looks like a volcano rising from the ocean.

I wouldn't wait too long to enter the Void. It appears pretty unlimited right now, but who knows how crowded things get during warfare. (The dead don't seem to be on the higher levels. They seem to be more like beggars hanging about the gloomy gates leading to the city of bright lights, or waiting for their moms to come and get them.) If you intend storming Heaven's Gate *(tenshingakure)*, I suggest the way of stealth, as the inhabitants won't look familiar, certainly don't inspire contempt, and will test you to see if you can handle life holding the high ground. It's a mind game played with powerful spirit in a gentle, loving manner. Wimps and frauds are scourged from the temple by wrathful deities.

As I grow older, I become convinced that a Masaaki Hatsumi is rarer than dragon's teeth. I still have no idea how much he chooses to show each particular student or how much help he offers. His lessons to me in Dreamtime, or in person, have primarily consisted of "Can you handle this, or figure out how I'm doing this one?" A lot of show, but little tell. It gives me something to work on until he comes up with the next little giri gift. So far we have conquered cross-cultural telepathy across short distances (fifth dan); acceptance of foreign guiding spirits in one's body and reception of telepathic messages over thousands of miles (sixth dan); and subjection of foreign devils and projection of messages over thousands of miles (seventh dan). I'm still sorting out the spiritual or *ura* aspects of eighth dan, as I tend to stumble through the physical techniques with a great deal of guidance from my professional taijutsu teachers.

These are psychic accomplishments that are mostly apocryphal (or anecdotal concerning one's mad aunt Tilly, before she died) types of stories in Western experience. I'm not certain of the utility of these little experiments, but it certainly is more interesting than breaking bricks with my forehead. My concept of martial science at this level is closer to rolling in a hand grenade than looking for a sparring partner. To test whether this reality was shared across cultures, I asked my spirits to present themselves to Hatsumi in meditation and taught them how to find him. Then I wrote him a note asking what was new. He sent back a picture of himself with his darkened reflection looking out of a store window that displayed video components set off by porcelain sculptures of Chinese guardian spirits. His commentary was, "I find it interesting that you would teach archery *(kyujutsu)* and modern science to angels." It seemed a pretty close hit.

We'd exchanged demons earlier in the year, but the Japanese variety are pretty wimpy in comparison to their rejected and starving Western cousins. The tree sprite I sent him to heal loved his dogs. When the sprite finally got back to its pine tree in the arboretum, he could say *domo* (thanks) and *genki desu* (I feel good). It's nuts in the holograph. As the crown chakra unfolds like a water lily, it broadcasts your location into the Void. The feeling is like wearing an upside down hat. The visual Zen koan to solve might be a man or monk walking with sandals balanced on his head, meaning "I can travel with my mind and see things thoroughly from humbly walking up to observe." Seekers of the purer land may be presented with a landscape that has appeal for their type. If the landscape does not reflect reality as you know it, approach cautiously with your foundation in place. Removal of predators that unbalance the ecology is rewarded with bounty in both worlds.

Commentary by Experts in the Field

Bicameral brain theory indicates that this type of phenomena may only be a form of biologically based schizophrenia. Philosopher Carl Becker, who has published considerable research concerning NDEs or near death experiences and their relationship to paranormal events, comes to the conclusion that there must exist a subtle vehicle capable of housing consciousness separate from the human body—temporarily during life, more permanently after death. He believes that the research strongly indicates survival of consciousness after death, and may well support the concepts concerning other dimensions and worlds of existence. Becker also discusses the reasons why most of the scientific community continues to reject the evidence appraised by various researchers including his own (Carl B. Becker, *Paranormal Experience and Survival of Death*, SUNY Press, 1993). Susan Blackmore, a more conservative member of the parapsychology community, reexamines the idea that certain facets of NDE and paranormal visions, such as tunnels and the appearance of deities, relate to cerebral anoxia disinhibiting the temporal lobe and causing cortical excitation resulting in visions, suspension of the experience of time and space, and panoramic life reviews. She considers the research concerning out of body experiences, ESP, and NDEs to be unconvincing—preferring the dying brain hypothesis and concluding there is no survival after the body's demise (Susan Blackmore, *Dying to Live: Near-Death Experiences*, Prometheus Books, 1993). Where Becker may overstate his case, Blackmore ignores research that does not support her position, but does produce a compelling argument for the relationship of brain states to ecstatic visions.

Excitation of the cortical nerves and irregulations in the temporal lobe caused by meditative practice may remove filters to perceiving ecstatic experiences. Having experienced much of what they describe in altered states of meditation, I reject death of the brain, or anoxia (lack of oxygen in the brain) as necessary. The reports of mystics and meditators over the centuries aren't given much credence by the scientific community, as they are so often accompanied by a religious baggage that eludes common sense. A dimensional or layered description of the Void or inner world that has connections to other realities has been written about in slightly different ways by mystics from different cultures to indicate a common if rare human experience.

Dante, Swedenborg, Blake, and the Russian Daniil Andreev (see bibliography), described spiritual cosmologies derived from their meditative practice, not as a result of a near death experience. If you find that your out-of-body adventuring begins to feel like a religious journey or quest, don't worry too much about it, but you might want to take notes.

Meaningful Quotes

"The idea of God can become the final obstacle to God."
—Meister Eckhart

"There is no excellent beauty that hath not some strangeness in the proportion."

—Francis Bacon

"A stitch in time, saves nine."

—Benjamin Franklin

"If a man wishes to be sure of the road he treads on, he must close his eyes and walk in the dark."
—St. John of the Cross

"We may be compared to owls trying to look at the sun, but since the natural desire in us for knowledge is not without a purpose, its immediate object is our own ignorance."
—Nicholas of Cusa

"My spirit, like love, cannot be contained within the horizons of my mind. It soars above reason and swoops down into the chaos beneath rationality. It travels with its own passport and freely crosses the frontiers of the known and explainable world."

—Sam Keen

"And now, my friends, all that is true, all that is just and pure, all that is lovable and gracious, whatever is excellent and admirable—fill your thoughts with these things."
—Philippians 4:8

"To laugh often and much; to win the respect of intelligent people and the affection of children; to earn the appreciation of honest critics and endure the betrayal of false friends; to appreciate beauty; to find the best in others; to leave the world a bit better, whether by a healthy child, a garden patch or a redeemed social condition; to know even one life has breathed easier because you have lived. This is to have succeeded."
—Ralph Waldo Emerson

Fourteen

Exercises for Those
Who Would Rather Kick Butt

Lao Tzu according to the *Wen-Tzu* (128) said, "To master themselves, the highest adepts nurture the spirit, while those of lesser rank nurture the body." Ten years ago Hatsumi-sensei said, "As I say all the time, martial arts are all power and guts. Too much emphasis on power and guts put you at a disadvantage. It is the same as atomic power's power. You created it, but it may destroy you. Do you understand? Feelings of relaxation and happiness are also part of the martial arts. I want you to practice them. I wish for you to become better martial artists in your way than artists like Picasso and Machis were in theirs. Leave the hard physical practice to manual laborers" (*Knife and Pistol Fighting With Complete English Text*, Yougen Publishing, Tokyo, 1985).

Training in the higher-level martial arts, if you have developed the beneficial habit of endurance or "keep going," results in greater flexibility, greater sensitivity, and willingness to accept discipline. It often leads to relationships with very interesting people who understand the value of pain as a teacher. As the body ages, and if one fails to stretch oneself, that simple process of contraction associated with withdrawal and death begins to limit one's ability to move and extend. The body reaches its peak of strength to weight at approximately eleven years of age. Everything is downhill from that point, physically. The body replaces all its cellular structure every seven years. The more sedentary one's lifestyle, the greater the tendency for fascia and muscle to atrophy, setting up the individual for arthritis, diverticulitis, high blood pressure, and hardening of the arteries, as well as drooping breasts and "dunlop disease." If we recognize natural process we tend to slow the aging process by staying active. Studies at UCI Brain Institute reveal boosted intelligence in those who followed complex exercise routines, and that the elderly showed slower deterioration of mental dexterity. Beware the killer couch, TV, and rocking chair.

The body's function is to move. Its fundamental practice is atrophy and change. There is no body-brain separation. The body, however, is the crucible that refines the spirit from desire to perception. The "sow's ear" base must become as "spun silk" or "white gold," from the viewpoint of the ancient alchemists, if one is to achieve nobility in this lifetime. In Japanese esotericism, this evolutionary process is referred to as *shinka* (becoming divine). Under the direction of Hatsumi-soke in Ninpo, the emphasis is to treat religious experience as a category of rational philosophy necessary for some personality types to develop goodness and kindness. Religion has little to offer the art. Hatsumi-san writes about esotericism in *Sanmyaku* in the manner of a martial arts historian.

All functions of the body feed the emotions, which come before thought. Emotion is guided by thought if the human being rouses from the reactive sleeping state and begins to learn how to manipulate the controls. One may discover with curiosity and feedback that there are many interesting tools available to the self-absorbed. Discovering all that you can do may take the rest of your life, if you keep going. To paraphrase an ancient Taoist warning, "When one is young there is no time for the Way, when one survives to the middle years he hears much talk of the Way, and when one is old, one has the will to listen but has lost the strength to follow the Way."

Practice as Metaphor

There are some interesting medical consequences to studying the physical side of Ninpo, which is taijutsu. Each of the *kamae* or fighting postures which are normally treated as end products of exemplary movement when applying a technique—or avoiding one—are also *asanas* (Sanskrit for yogic postures) that if held and used for affirmative meditation will greatly strengthen the body and develop one's sense of balance far beyond normal limits. The physical postures strengthen the spine and encourage the body's electrical systems, and the rolling techniques add to one's flexibility, while massaging the shiatsu points along the spine. When the physical posture *(kamae)* is enlivened by a righteous attitude or affirmation appropriate to that way of standing or being, we refer to it as flow or integration, which is often the compelling effect of being completely natural. Athletes call this state "being in the zone." Proper Budo Taijutsu is based on natural relaxed body movement flowing from the subconscious mind without intellectual intervention. In that sense, it is closely related to tai chi or nei shen kung fu, as one flows from kamae, to kamae in battle. Many modern ninja use the Feldenkrais Method as an aid to body softening and better movement. A righteous man is relaxed, as he fears no evil. A relaxed man finds righteousness intelligent as well as natural. A teacher who does not emphasize gentility in practice does not understand Budo Taijutsu and probably should be avoided by a beginner, as this art is incredibly dangerous, as well as effective and challenging.

Those of us who move the body around a lot tend to take injury, and the injuries normally associated with the martial arts (such as broken noses, cracked ribs, vertebrae, and shins, broken hands or fingers, sprained and torn ankles, as well as blown-out knees) are common in sport practitioners, but greatly reduced in the combatic martial arts by the realistic teaching of falling, rolling, and walking. Chi kung is also a great help in reducing injury. But the greatest buffers to injury are sensitivity, stretching, and mobility.

There is a metaphorical lesson in learning the art of falling and recovering to be on your feet again that is enhanced by grace and the avoidance of crashing as you go down, because you know you'll be coming back up. It's one of those little hidden things that are supposed to be obvious. Anyone who has never fallen has never risked, or is playing in an illusory arena. The concept of going with the flow is particularly important to the art of falling. If you are falling, relax into it and get to the ground fast with the most padding. If falling backwards, sit down. It's that simple. Watch the babies. They will show you how. Start slowly on soft, smooth surfaces and work your way to speedy comfort on hard, irregular surfaces. It is the reverse of "study hard to learn the soft." Once you learn how to fall safely, the next step is learning how to turn the fall into a roll in any direction. One of the important lessons in rolling is to get as close to the ground as possible when you roll. It greatly reduces the probability of injury to move the point of impact off the shoulders onto the muscles that protect the scapula by looking up as you tuck into the roll. It also helps to quiet your roll. The roll is done most safely by allowing the spine to touch the ground only once. This is accomplished by angling the body so the down shoulder is followed to the ground by your opposite hip. The legs are kept apart so that you can place the feet or knees in a wide stance as you come up ready to fight. Low rolls offer a harder target. You are a spy, not a gymnast.

I have often noticed in observing and practicing both tai chi and taijutsu that through stretching and slowing down particular kata and movements, one increases the range of movement as well as power and muscle memory. Atrophy is better avoided by increasing flexibility than strength. (Some martial artists disagree with me concerning this, but I have noticed that I am older than they are, move better, and am generally more creative in my violence.) It is very important to stretch the ligaments of the ankles, knees, feet, wrists, and fingers. I have had more than one Togakure Ryu shihan point out that the toes should be exercised by gripping and releasing as one walks. (When a shihan suggests one "should," that means do it.) The spine should be worked by walking daily, and rolled at least once or twice a week. The ninja walk, discussed earlier, is simply using the tai chi foot stretches as part of your everyday walk. These are all extremely beneficial and seldom practiced outside the dojo. Most people walk as they learned from observation as a child, and thus lack grace, balance, silence, and skill. If you are going to be effective as a fighter, it is necessary to develop footwork that is as natural as walking. If you are working on chi development, walking teaches you how to pump and balance energy.

Research Findings That are Helpful to the Martial Artist

The most recent research strongly suggests that moderate exercise that contributes to endurance is associated with longevity, and brutal regimens are not. The research concerning raising your metabolism and burning off fat suggests strongly that one should take many little walks during the course of the day; that one should take a walk before long rest periods; and that one should build muscle mass through resistance exercises, particularly when dieting. Breakfast should be hearty, followed by a morning walk. Increasing your complex carbohydrates while reducing dietary fat is important for maintaining a healthy weight. If you are attracted to brutal regimens, then hill and mountain climbing, crossed with multiple workouts and interval training, will test your mettle. Dumbbells and nautilus are considered safer than free weights for strengthening bone and muscle. The study of yoga can be of great benefit, particularly the warrior postures, and we sometimes joke about the wonderfully painful positions one can find oneself in while doing taijutsu, calling it "ninja yoga." A lot of athletic sex can achieve the same results, particularly if you've developed the skills of sperm retention. Most people train emphasizing speed and power and thus develop sloppy fundamentals. As you age, speed is replaced by positioning, balance, and timing; brute power is replaced by precision and surprise. The mature mind returns to the child and can alter the past to change the future. Study hard on this.

Jutaijutsu (soft body skills) and Sensitivity

Sensitivity to using the least effort to have the greatest effect requires a great deal of self-study, as well as a useful supply of students to bend, fold, and spindle on a regular basis. If the students are of both sexes and a wide variety of body types, teaching through continual experimentation on what seems to work best keeps the learning process interesting. The more relaxed and softer you are able to do a technique, the greater will be your ability to react to your opponent's response, which allows you to adjust appropriately rather than "getting stuck" or attaching to the technique which may no longer be effective, depending on the response. Sensitivity results in effective adaptability. Transfer of training is almost guaranteed, as the greatest part of the process occurs subconsciously. Those skills acquired in life-threatening situations tend to remain with us. (Ask any combat veteran.) Remembering that your martial art skills are developed to save your life, not win a contest, will aid you in internalizing what is effective.

I received a letter from John Nibarger (a young training partner) on the same day I was given the rank of *shichidan* (seventh dan, also known as *nanadan*) by Masaaki Hatsumi-soke.

(He continues to embarrass me into working harder.) John's query concerned the meaning of "train hard to understand the soft." He's a very bright young man attempting to learn the art in the right way. The people he was training with enthusiastically beat the snot out of each other and believed it to be good training. I suggest that if your technique does not take your opponent into absolute helplessness from the initial movement into flow, you are studying sport—and something that is too hard for you to make work in a real emergency when you are fighting many opponents. If a physical fight with one person lasts longer than a second without you taking total control, you are doing something stupid.

Most techniques in ninjutsu are designed to cripple and disrupt the opponent's skeletal, nervous, and electrical system. If you attempt to go full bore on a friend with proper taijutsu, using these techniques, you won't have many opportunities to train with that person again. Most American practitioners don't realize that dim mak *(koshijutsu)* exists on three levels; (1) strikes and grappling techniques which break bones in such ways that they pierce organs or rip blood vessels to create internal bleeding; (2) striking and grappling techniques that create hematomas so that blood is blocked from reaching organs, or nerves are damaged to create interesting problems; and (3) multiple strikes along meridian lines that overload organs and send the receiver into shock. Budo Taijutsu done with respect for your training partner allows you to learn these techniques without serious harm. This is why the older or smarter practitioners are so gentle with each other, because they know how much damage can be caused. Some dim mak techniques take months to kill you if you don't have an acupuncturist rewire the circuits. Kindness is essential to learning and particularly to teaching this art, especially when weapons are involved. The major reason that Hatsumi-soke continually exhorts us to use soft weapons is not only metaphor, but concern for our lives.

Bruises from training indicate clumsiness, not competence. When I first started training in Ninpo I received some remarkable shiners of glorious hue—no broken bones, however. Many of the striking techniques create deep tissue bruises that won't begin to show until a day or two has passed. My wife at the time would often look with wonder at the side effects of my inability to avoid, saying things like "I can't believe you do this for fun." The fun was usually experienced when it was my turn to try the technique on my training partner—sometimes thought of as dummy. I have been accused of making "green belt sacrifices" as well as "great kindness" by people who should know better. I am but a mirror. Pain contributes to the understanding of compassion in the slow. Win or lose, no one has ever picked a fight with me twice. The softer you are, the faster you can move and the harder you can hit. The softer you are, the easier it is to feel the intention and predict the opponent's next move and act accordingly.

Training in the martial arts presents students with problems to solve, as they are forced to come to terms with the truth of what they can and cannot do. With a real master teacher, these lessons will penetrate mind, body, and spirit. A young martial artist who approaches his or her school's teaching from the perspective of how can I make this technique work for me, rather than mindlessly imitating their instructor, will often discover there are many opportunities concealed in the traditional teachings. If the student brings a knowledge of anatomy and nerve structure *(koshijutsu)* to what they are learning they will find that precision can replace power, and sensitivity to distance and timing will replace speed. "Soft skills" is sometimes used as a code term for subtle energy or mental control techniques.

Subtle Energy Skills

Higher-level martial arts are filled with interesting claims that require astute observation to verify. Few live up to their PR, even when the sincerity is evident. For example: being able to shift or stop the strike of the opponent and redirect it by force of will rather than knuckle and skull is discussed in Japanese martial arts as *sen no sen* at the level of *ainuke*. According to my *buyu* Richard Kim-hanshi, "It means that the martial artist stops the thought of the attack before it occurs in the opponent, and that the opponent thinks of something else. Therefore, there is no attack, just a mutual passing through." A very crude translation of *ainuke* would be "harmonious nooky" from the Noam Chomsky school of grunt phonetics (which I attend) or possibly "very harmonious, perceptive, and seductive," or very powerful and overwhelming electrical control of a human subject through intentional projection of will. "Don't do that. Do this." Hatsumi-san is the only martial artist I have ever seen, or felt, pull it off. Yagyu Munenori wrote in his family *densho* that it existed, but wasn't able to pull it off himself. *Seigan no kamae* (the correcting eye) is a variation of the avoiding stance used in the Warring States Period in hand-to-hand and sword applications and can be similar to *sen no sen*. The stance alone causes an opponent to reconsider his attack. *Sen no sen* is general knowledge in the Taoist School of Inner Elixir, as well as the Taoist Hygiene Classes for the Inner Deity. The mountain tilting method described in Chapter Thirteen is a tool for its direction.

Grandmaster of Bujinkan Budo Taijutsu, Masaaki Hatsumi can bring out a peaceful feeling in the fiercest, as well as show them their nightmare in the same heartbeat while preserving the value of their life. If this is a personal style, then it reflects and absorbs Bujin. "Voice of command" (controlling someone with your vocal tones) and vocalized *kiai* are not *sen no sen*. Nor is passing the sword test a manifestation of *sen no sen*. Passing the sword test is simply a demonstration of increased empathy, or the achievement of animal awareness. The human being who is able to pass it demonstrates an accomplishment that makes him or her equivalent to a white-tail deer or slap-dodging house fly. *Sen no sen* requires a higher grace and purpose and is generally a product of *giri*, endurance, and self-sacrifice beloved of the Bujin. With a lot of practice it can be part of your "secret swords." It is considered a "grandmother" skill. Projection of a specific action is more difficult than reception of a feeling. The effect is described in the late Terry Dobson's short story "A Soft Answer," published in *The Overlook Martial Arts Reader* (Overlook Press, 1989). Shidoshi Ed Sones removed an irate drunk (who couldn't let go of Pearl Harbor) from the Hawaiian Tai Kai by gently talking to him as he walked him away from the outdoor training. "A soft answer turneth away wrath." The mental training in Budo Taijutsu is far more important to master than the awesome fighting skills.

Exercises and Applications

Ninja often do the following as a blindfolded exercise. The group forms a circle facing out. The dirty back-stabbing assassin (geek) goes to the center of the circle, picks his target, and slips up to lightly bash his target with full intent; the weapon is well-padded in case he gets into his role or has a grudge. If the victim, blindfolded and facing out, feels the stealthy approach, he or she raises an arm, and the geek taps the arm to indicate the correctness of the feeling. Some bodies will twitch wildly as the killer/geek approaches, but the victim does not respond. When the victim raises his or her arm correctly, they are not struck. When the victim fails to lift in response to an attack, he or she is swatted. The swat serves as notice to leave the circle and observe your more sensitive training partners. It is a minor wound to one's ego that is well remembered if treated as life and death. The last person in the outer circle takes the center of the ring for the next round. This exercise deeply impresses the pragmatic thinker, registered by a quick conversion to ninja techniques. Everyone worth knowing has been blind-sided. The exercise can be made even more challenging by putting in ear plugs. I have seen blindfolded students in another form of this exercise bat rubber *shuriken* out of the air with *bokken*. It never fails to amaze me, as I'm not very effective at batting shuriken with my eyes open.

When engaged in *chi sau* (sticky hand) or *kumite* (controlled combatic sparring) with an opponent, attempt to feel and counter an attack by sensing with the body. This can be done blindfolded, or with the eyes shut. You should slow down the techniques for the beginner, but project the intention and maintain realistic body movement. You might think of this as sparring using the Stanislavski method. Slowing down movement allows you to feel what is actually happening in the body, and is necessary for developing "muscle memory," which results in amazing speed when you are relaxed. You will be pleasantly surprised by how paying attention to feelings can improve your skills in both avoidance and control. You can make this more exciting by putting a weapon in the hand of one of the players. You can find out if you can control a determined knifer by starting out gripping the knife hand. Magic markers make good practice knives for the pragmatic. A hard wooden knife makes for a more realistic exercise than a rubber one. A bruise or two is worth having to discover vulnerability. The knifer should concentrate on the chest and arms until avoidance skills are learned. This can be made even more interesting if the knifer calls his shots. You can count both hits for the knifer and misses for the attacked. The fight is always to the simulated death of the knifer or the attacked.

Dodging the sword stroke blindfolded requires similar skills. First do it slowly with the eyes open, using a *shinai* until the proper avoidance movements are mastered. Start with downward cuts at the front of the body, then cuts at the legs, then from the rear and sides. Proper footwork will be quickly learned by the dodger if he thinks of the shinai as a yard-long razor blade. Being missed by a hair-breadth provides more opportunities for reprisal than being missed by a mile. Karate people who take pride in breaking bats over their shins aren't getting the point, as they are forgetting the edge.

If you are the "chopper" rather than the "choppee," you can practice getting power into your cut as follows: Bundle sticks together, as recommended in the Bible story concerning Joseph and his brothers. The stick bundle can be wrapped with various types of cloth, cardboard, and leather to test their protective value; their resilience may surprise you. When you get so you can cut right through the bundle with one stroke, your body dynamic is supporting your sword. Ninja sword technology stresses using the last two inches of the blade and pushing your cut rather than pulling, knocking the opponent away from you. A ninja *to* (straight sword) goes through a suspended plastic milk jug filled with water like a laser through butter, if your body dynamic is correct. The water will splash away from you if you have the cut right. (No sense messing up one's clothes. It could be evidence.)

Hand Conditioning, Striking, and Gripping Skills

Strong hands are important to successful manipulation and grappling. The fingers and hands can be strengthened by doing "Greetings to the Sun" on your fingertips, then knuckles, then wrists with your palms up. You can make push-ups Japanese or American style more interesting by doing them on raised fingertips, and then taking away a finger on each hand as they become easy—or institutionalize this practice by associating it with achieving a particular belt rank. Black belts should be pressing up on their thumbs alone. You might also try pressing up with extended knuckles. It takes a while to build up to these stunts. Another effective finger-strengthening technique involves the Sunday newspaper from a major metropolis. Read the paper, and as you finish each sheet spread it out on a table. Once you've read, separated, and stacked the sheets in a pile, stretch your arm over the center of the paper stack. Lower your hand and begin to ball each sheet individually into the palm using only your fingertips. When you have finished the paper, your fingers will feel well exercised. Alternate hands by week, or buy two papers.

Finger fanning by stretching your hand as open as possible, until it hurts, then closing the fist finger by finger, little finger first, with the thumb stretched up, will bring chi into the hand, greatly extending the ability to grip as well as enhancing finger coordination. Pull and bend the fingers and wrists whenever you happen to think of it. Stretch the wrists by pushing against and with their natural direction. Be particularly careful to stretch in the positions that are typically used to control or break the wrist.

When you strike a hard surface, don't use your fist, as you can hit harder with the base of your palm with less danger to the bones of the wrist and hand. When you have to use your fist, be certain your wrist is held flat to your knuckles, as a bend in either direction can break it. Practice thinking of your knuckles as a cutting edge, not a bludgeon. Adjust your knuckles so you can hit up with the three bottom knuckles, and down with the larger top knuckles in the same way that a carpenter uses a hammer. When you strike with your palm, hold the hand as if a ball were in it. If you use your thumb to gouge with, learn to let it rest supported on the top of the fist. Attack the hard with the soft, and the soft with the cutting edge of the hard. If you have learned to pinch as you hit with the thumb, twist, shake, and exhale as you rip. Use a heavy bag or a canvas-wrapped rug to practice on, rather than your *buyu*. Board and brick breaking with palm techniques will help you develop proper focus if you forget muscle. When you get to the point of being able to rip canvas with your thumb pinch, you will find that most people respond with alarm when you apply your flesh-ripping skills.

Now, the following technique is another way to turn the nether cheek when you want to hit something really hard. The hip provides the power if you haven't mastered the ninja techniques for shifting from the ankles without cocking. When you move the head back out of the way of a blow, shift your weight to the leading knee and then rotate right back into your opponent's proffered rib cage with your thumb flattened on the top of your fist with the nail extending past the knuckles. After you have made the initial strike with your knuckles, dig the thumb in and push to complete your follow through. *Bushi* thumb applications can make the most stolid attacker leap to a distant drummer. Ribs aren't the best target, but can be thrilling.

Practice moving your whole body into a punch from any position, at any distance. Practice turning your spine with the hips into every punch using the opposite shoulder or arm like a counterweight. Step into the punch and as your leading foot hits the ground, your hand should hit the target. This is called "the sun punch" by the Chinese, as it lights up your opponent, and may cause him to fly. If you've stepped into your opponent, push, gouge, and pinch as well, after and with the strike.

A few years ago I was working out with Dave Friederick, a kickboxer and Canada's heavyweight kempo champion. We'd been hitting a heavy bag in his basement that registered pounds per square inch when struck. He could hit harder and faster than I. I remarked that I thought I hit harder than the measurement, as my opponents almost always flew through the air and landed on their duffs. He, of course, wanted to experience that, so I had him hold a blocking pad for a target on his chest so I wouldn't break any ribs, and belted him. He flew across the basement gym and crashed through his daughter's flute stand, a distance of eight feet, but he didn't go down. He's tough.

In a similar instance, when I got back from one of my trips

to Japan to train with the shihan, Rick Groves, a sandan in isshinryu, wanted to see if I could knock him out of his grounded stance. He flew backwards twelve feet and landed on his butt, absolutely astonished. No one had ever knocked him off his feet before. This is simply a result of good taijutsu and natural body movement. Often tai chi teachers of "push hands" will send a beginner sailing this way to show the "power" in their art. Because most American-trained practitioners have not learned how to sink their weight or receive a full-bodied blow—as Bruce Lee used to demonstrate regularly—they tend to fly regardless of their rank. Moving fully weighted into an arm bar or sweep has the same effect, except the bones tend to break.

If you add a blast of chi to a center line strike, the opponent will often black out for a second. A second is a very long period of time for a well-trained martial artist. Someone trained in speed hitting can whack you from eleven to twenty times in a second.

If you use "continuous and returning fist" techniques, which are common in upper-level ninja training, speed hitting is a superfluous skill. Try mastering these two: (1) Strike into the center of the chest over the base of the sternum—this can stop the heart, as well as injure the lungs as the ribs collapse. Allow the striking hand to slide up the body so the fist smashes into the chin with the large knuckles hitting the jaw and the small knuckles digging into the trachea; as the head snaps back, shift your weight forward as you drop your elbow onto the top of the sternum, or a clavicle. Three hits for one. If the opponent doesn't fall, sweep him. (2) Think of this one as a right cross. As your fist strikes his face, shift your weight behind the punch so your elbow also strikes the side of the head. Allow the elbow to pass through the opponent's range of motion, laying his or her head on her shoulder, as you shift your weight back, hitting him with the same elbow on the other side of the face, followed by a backfist knuckle cut as you knee, or sweep him. Four blows for one.

339

In twenty-five years, I have never seen anyone recover from the second technique and get back into the fight. It is a good little peacekeeper. If you prefer palm strikes, follow the first procedure by sliding up to push the chin back, then drop the fingers to grab the upper jaw beneath the nose, and locking the head back, throw the opponent by his lips. It is a ninja favorite.

When I was younger, I believed I could take just about any punch—which was true if you defined taking the punch as not going unconscious. This is silly behavior, particularly when many of the blows in combatic martial arts are directed to points on the body that can cripple or kill. It is much smarter to move your precious body completely out of the way. Completely means avoiding being hit, which exists on a continuum of feeling the fist with your body's energy field as it rushes by, to leaving the party early as you sense hostility. If your opponent wants to fight and you do not, by avoiding the fracas you have won. Sensitive use of the body's ability to move is necessary for either strategy.

Kicking

When you kick, use the same hit-and-push principle utilized in hand strikes. Use the heel as your primary point of contact. Practice stomping and pushing rather than snapping. When you kick someone, you should knock them down. If they don't go down, you haven't done it right. Here is a groin shot kick that won me the title of "totally amoral" from some isshinryu purists. Square off with your opponent, then step with your lead foot at about forty-five degrees. As your opponent shifts to stay with you, opening his legs, drill him with your dragging foot. Try to break his coccyx or prostrate with your toes; use your instep as a swatter to crush the testicles. The ninja uses the continual and returning principle by adding, as your opponent stiffens from shock, a push-off with your back foot as if you're leaping forward, allowing the swatting foot's shin to rip along the inside of the thigh, with luck injuring the penis, until your knee slams into his pelvic girdle. With careful practice you can direct the knee to slam into dim mak points. The opponent should fall backwards at great speed and is usually incapacitated.

In your training, you should spend an inordinate amount of time on one foot. You can practice walking and shifting all your weight from one foot to the other as you move. It is not done as a fifty-fifty or seventy-thirty distribution, but all or nothing. Do it going forward, backwards, and to the side. Practice until it is natural and easy. Fighting on one foot is every bit as challenging as fighting with one hand behind your back, which is how my father taught me to box. (You get hit in the head a lot when you learn that way. Avoidance techniques are a smarter way to learn.) Take your time playing with it until you find your balance and quickness are improving. See what you can get away with when you are knocking down your partner, so you can stomp on him more easily. Stomping on joints tends to prevent having to engage again. It always amazes me in movies when "the good guy" knocks down "the bad guy" and then lets him back up, or runs away so that he has to do it all over again later. Being good does not have to mean being stupid when it comes to fighting.

When you have an opponent down, it is safer to keep him or her on their belly rather than back, as it limits their striking ability. You can stomp on joints and hands or use knee drops to pressure points. If you are taking a prisoner, joint locks that are extremely painful can be used to hold the person down. You can use your shins to cut into muscle, or your knees to pinch down on muscle, or grind into pressure points. A little practice with a willing partner will let you learn how to apply the knee to pain and pressure points when holding someone down. If you get good at ground techniques using your legs only, you free up your hands to do nasty things. Hatsumi-san showed me how to use the knee, together with the back of the thumb knuckle, for striking dim mak points in a less damaging manner on the head and the body of Blackwood-san. It was not a fun time for shidoshi Ron, but I learned new stuff.

I never had any respect for practitioners of tae kwon do, supposedly a kicking art, until I met grandmaster and head of the American International Kickboxing Association John Pendergrass and spent some quality time with real professionals. Tae kwon do still falls into my "worthless" category for combat, but the kicking skills can be adapted into useful applications for a sport fighter. Being able to really weigh and balance one foot lets you use the other for speed techniques as well as shift to powerful stomping kicks that if applied below the waist usually knock your opponents ash over tin cups. Being able to sink your weight into your knees and ankles can open many opportunities for knocking an opponent down by using your legs as levers.

In India all the gods of war are dancers. They are shown on one foot regardless of their sex. In yoga many of the stances associated with enlightenment are also referred to as warrior stances and require great balance and control. One-pointedness is a posture connected with quality and excellence in ballet, meditation, concentration, tai chi, and chi kung. Study on this deeply. Practice daily in stealth, wherever you may find opportunity. The kamae serve as ultra safe positions for the fighter use as a basis for controlling his opponent while building power for the next move. With practice you can hide the kamae in fear reactions so your opponent still thinks he or she has a chance of winning. For the hobbyist it is only necessary to be able to pass through the kamae or stances as a way to stabilize a moment in the shifting reality of a fight. A professional yogi is a different matter altogether.

Pain Control

The use of pain as a teaching tool is somewhat controversial. Many of my methods have raised the eyebrows of my contemporaries, but I have always been able to create growth in my students. Pain is a fierce teacher, and conquering it without taking serious damage is one of the marks of the intelligent. Pain is the mother of fear. (My massage therapist jokingly refers to pain as an opinion.) Fear is the father of anger. Loss of fear is the doorway to real knowledge and growth. A student will never learn to extend his or her limits if they cannot relax or push through pain. The former is more effective in the long run, but both hold essential life-saving knowledge in emergency situations. There are many painful techniques that aren't particularly dangerous but can be used to illustrate how pain can be controlled by the mind, or better yet by the spirit. Slowing down the technique but holding on to the full intention and control allows you to experience and participate in all the nuances of a body unbalanced and in pain.

You may find it constructive to face a friend who places an extended knuckle on your sternum. You may then push against the knuckle while trying to control the pain, wish the pain away, thank the body for the pain and relax into it, or whatever else you might think of. If you like a contest, you can stick out a knuckle for your friend to practice on while they are pushing on you. This can be a challenge as well as fun. Once you have mastered the experience of manipulating pain in one part of your body, you might move on to other parts and see what lessons can be imparted through your tears. If you really do the work you also get the experience of practicing self-healing. Rick Groves told me after a pain-control session that I was "cruel and malicious." (I found it painful to have a *buyu* regard me in such light.) When Julia O'Brien threw him to the ground while he was in such pain that he couldn't figure out how she had done it, he decided that my methods might have some merit after all. He swallowed his black belt pride, after being defeated by a white belt girl, and studied with me for five years. Pain control is not usually taught until godan in many traditional martial arts. In some it is not taught at all, as the practitioner is supposed to learn from the experience of pain taken, that he is not to give it. As many take a sadistic pleasure in hurting others, I don't think this strategy is effective. It is important when serving as an uke to relax into the pain and pay attention to what the sensei is doing to you so that you can pass on what you have learned. The uke is often too concerned with surviving the technique to learn from the experience.

Good *ukime* (receiving, falling and hitting the ground techniques) is very important to learning the art. Since I entered the Ryu with an extensive background in jujutsu, I started teaching too soon. It is very important for one to be thrown around for a few years so that one becomes very flexible. I found it amusing that my black belts used to argue over who got to be my uke so they could learn all the little ways to make techniques hurt more. As soon as I was done showing a new technique they would gather around the uke and discuss what they had seen and compare to what she or he had felt. Tapping out before you were in serious trouble was regarded as wimpish.

Dulling pain by becoming calloused is a callow skill in the martial arts and is often taught as an insult to those being prepared for cannon fodder. It consists of beating the joints and striking areas until the nerve endings no longer function. It is not for artists or anyone who respects the gifts of gods. I'm not even going to describe it. It's so stupid. Boxers don't even do this kind of stuff, beyond toughening their skin, and a good boxer has to enjoy pain at some level. I've known a few who get erections when they're hit. I won't go into the psychological implications of that, but they loved to mix it up. You've probably seen what many blows to the head can do to its range of movement, particularly if there wasn't much to begin with. It's the same with the hands or the feet. Huge calluses on the knuckles of the hands are considered the mark of a real practitioner in some of the hard karate schools. Knuckle callus can be useful if you have to fight someone wearing armor and you don't have any, or on the off chance that you might run up against an enraged bear when you are naked, but don't plan on making music. I like everything to work at maximum efficiency: mind, body, and spirit.

Throwing

To build arm and shoulder strength for over-the-shoulder throws, use a weighted bar of about one hundred pounds placed parallel to your side. Reach across your body to grasp the bar, and then haul it over your head, one-armed, into an erect clean and jerk, full squat, or kneeling position. If you don't tear your head off or fall down, you are doing it right. As you gain greater sensitivity to balance, you will tend to prefer the use of sweeps, bars, and knockdowns to throws, as they take less brute strength. A reverse hip throw or arm-breaking shoulder throw is a rather spectacular attention-getter when applied to the surprised. It is important to remember that you can choose where, and how hard, to drop the person you are throwing.

Practice falling and rolling out of throws. Practice reversing throws while riding with them. Practice stopping throws with body shifts. When you are throwing someone, break the rhythm of the throw to disrupt his or her receiving techniques. Learn to throw in ways that the person being thrown cannot stop, attack your body, or shift control. When being thrown, practice cutting your opponent. Being disemboweled or having your throat slit can be a consequence of not understanding how a throw is properly undertaken in a real combat situation where weapons will be involved. Every joy has its danger. It is easy to disembowel, cripple, hamstring, or throw your opponent on his head if he throws you with a hip throw as is normally taught by American judo enthusiasts or the military. The use of arm bars, foot throws, locks, and timing will become very important parts of one's throwing skills after one has mastered the basic entering techniques which set up the throws. The thrower may learn to take more religious care of his body while moving into the opponent. The police in Japan study an art called *taihojutsu* (the real body skills), and those teachers study with Hatsumi-soke. I have learned techniques in Ninpo for tearing up most police come-alongs that are pretty funny. I've dropped a lot of my cop students to their horror, even when being held by two, and wearing handcuffs behind my back. The standard goose neck is a set-up for a really sweet taijutsu throw.

Kiai

The voice of command is based on tonal qualities that are best learned through song. The Six Healing Sounds or breaths of Chinese medical practice can be directed and shaped by intention to strengthen the effects of speech as a secret sword, amplified by practice with esoteric charging the fields or vibrations produced by speaking with emotion (Mantak & Maneewan Chia, *Chi Nei Tsang*, Healing Tao Books, 1990, for "Healing Sounds" techniques and Chinese medical breathing techniques are discussed in Wu and Ping, *Therapeutic Breathing Exercise*, Hei Feng Publishing, Hong Kong, 1985). Speech and theatre courses can enhance one's confidence in using the dreaded roar of *kiai*. Yelling as you strike something or someone is the kindergarten version usually taught in every self-defense class. The yell has two primary effects. It can freeze the attacker in surprised fright. It can give a jolt of adrenaline to the screamer. In hoshin, kiai practice is not usual, as we are similar in viewpoint to the ninja. If you practice with ninja, you will quickly notice the absence of sound when avoiding attacks. Breath control alone is enough when you are following the way of stealth and do not wish to attract the attention of the so-called authorities.

I hadn't taught my students at Hillsdale yelling as I didn't use it myself, being a growler. When my isshinryu comrade Rick Groves was helping Suzanne Carlson test for her green belt (part of the test was sparring black belts from other systems), he walked out on the mats, screamed at her, and hit her. She crawled over to me and said, "Is he allowed to do that?" Rick and I almost fell down, we were laughing so hard. He had scared her near to death. I had to do some explaining and gentling to get the test going again. Rick found that that trick only works once. Once may be all you need.

Take a good hard look at how you throw a kick or punch, and eliminate any movement that telegraphs what you are about to do. Once you have mastered striking without cueing your opponent, work on your acting skills to see if you can make your set-ups look like fear reactions. This encourages your opponent to enter your web of destruction. If you still use audible *kiai* (shouts), don't imitate Bruce Lee, but scream "No!" or "Don't hit me!" or "What's wrong with you?" as it confuses the opponent as well as the witness. Kiai like a martial artist and someone might shoot you, as you appear and sound dangerous to the ignorant. You should never give a clue to your opponent.

Commentary

It's very important to master the fundamentals of whatever it is you are studying before moving on to the so-called advanced techniques. In the rush to achieve the black belt, one almost always misses many of the little details that contribute to longevity—like breathing properly from the genitals, or leaning forward to kick so you have some real power, or pulling your toes back so that contact is made only with the heel, allowing the sciatic nerve to stretch without injury. Or learning to relax, so you have some real speed. Take the time to consider what would happen to your multiple-point attack if you were charging into someone with a sword or pistol. Most empty-handed arts come up on the short side when facing the sword, as the opponent is usually thought of as empty-handed. Combat arts that are based on combat reality take it for granted you will have to avoid the weapon as well as face multiple attackers with unknown capability. As Shiraishi-sensei would say, "First, make safe make! Then unbalanced make." Hatsumi-soke remarks that the most beautiful taijutsu comes out of the practitioner when facing the sword. Effectiveness and function are associated with beauty by the Japanese.

Since I moved to Houston, I've started offering seminars in chi kung meditation, combat applications of jutaijutsu, dim mak, weapons, finishing techniques, and other fun things that don't seem to get taught too often. As I usually work with martial arts other than Ninpo, teaching open seminars is a bit like being a missionary to warriors. In the martial arts everybody likes to think what they do is best and seldom enjoy being corrected, so you have to allow them to experience in a manner they can accept. I often get paid back for sharing by being shown nifty techniques from their particular arts, which add to my knowledge. Hatsumi-soke's openness has reduced the ninja as "bad guy" image put out by various sources, so I usually don't have to fight my way out of seminars. The nut fringe of "night-suited combat experts" bristling with nunchaku and claws, and ninja wannabes with swords strapped to their backs, still raises some police eyebrows but such people are pretty easy to deal with when they discover the real thing. These workshops have been well received, so I guess I'll keep doing it when my schedule allows. I did one in California in the spring of 1995 which was attended by some ninja black belts, healers, and participants from other martial arts. They were all grateful for what I shared, and what really surprised me was that it was new stuff for all concerned. I had to laugh when my friend shidoshi Greg Cooper called me to come do a seminar in Florida featuring my specialty—"ninja weirdness."

There is a tremendous advantage to be gained by studying with more than one high-level teacher (and possibly, if you are clever, more than one art), particularly in Ninpo. I've been training with some of shidoshi Ed Sones' black belts and they are excellent. Their dojo are friendly and their skills are extraordinary. I've been learning a lot, and was surprised to find *Path Notes* as required reading.

Many people become overly attached to their shidoshi as the font of all wisdom, forgetting that Hatsumi-soke is the true source. It can be lucrative for the shidoshi to encourage that sort of dependence. It can be lucrative to break away from the Bujinkan and start your own thing as Robert Bussey has shown in the martial arts world. It is a song oft repeated and the results should be heavily researched by the seeker.

There are a lot of self-promoting masters of many martial systems. Few actually deliver what they advertise. When you enter a strange dojo, be certain to look for certificates of training or teaching licenses. Better yet, check out the average age of the practitioner. If the instructor says he has trouble keeping older practitioners due to the injury rate, there is a high probability that he doesn't know how to teach the soft side. A lot of trophies indicate a sport orientation. Use all your senses. What do you feel? Look at their faces. Does their practice increase peace and happiness or result in arrogance? How do they treat each other? Is respect only given to belt levels?

Being a master in a stupidly stolen system, or even an eclectic system that is not properly layered, is like knowing how to jump off a cliff when there are others who know how to fly. Studying with a good athlete who is stupid is similar. Studying with a "master" who cannot teach can be a huge waste of time. Being a leader of lemmings is not my idea of a fun time, though it is Nature's way to cull the herd of the sick, lame, crazy, and stupid. The halt leading the blind through rough terrain had better be humble. This is hell; heaven is no different, judging from the rather antique but functional weaponry of the angels and gods. The Tyger doth know who made what.

Where to See the Real Thing

If you really need to see authentic Ninpo at the zenith, then the videos of the 1993 Washington/Baltimore Tai Kai are available from Philip Legare-shidoshi, P.O. Box 1321, Ft. Meade, Md. 20755, in a three-cassette set for $65. They include "slo-mo" of some of the more interesting techniques, and showcase many of the USA's instructors as well as the Indian, Canadian, and Israeli shidoshi. The opening ceremonies include performances by mistress of the traditional dances Mariko Hatsumi-sensei and Noguchi-sensei. Bud Malmstrom offers videos of the 1990 and 1994 Tai Kai held in Atlanta. Bud's dojo is in an Atlanta suburb: P.O. Box 923, Tucker, GA, 30085-0923. Jeff Prather's tape of the 1995 Tucson Tai Kai which featured naginata and sword stealing is available from P.O. Box 11801, Tucson, AZ 85734. For general training tapes, Dick Severance offers the best. Each of his tapes is masterfully documented with clear, precise explanations and multiple examples and views, and the price is ridiculously low for what you are getting. In the *kenjutsu* tape, there is a segment where the camera actually picks up the students' auras during the sword work—perhaps giving the astute observer a clue to why Bujinkan is the school of the divine warriors. shidoshi Severance can be reached at 119 Donna Rd. NE, Palm Bay, FL, 32907. Dick is also one of the best sources for customized and durable training tools.

More Meaningful Quotes

> "Darkness within darkness. The gateway to an understanding.
> ... The Tao that can be spoken of, is not the eternal Tao."
> —Lao Tzu

"Living is a form of not being sure, not knowing what next or how. The artist never entirely knows. We take leap after leap into the dark."

—Agnes De Mille

"Endurance is one of the most difficult disciplines, but it is to him who endures that the final victory comes."

—Gautama Buddha

"The best and most beautiful things in the world cannot be seen, nor touched . . . but are felt in the heart."

—Helen Keller

"Energy will create anything that can be done in this world; and no talents, no circumstances, no opportunities will make a two-legged animal [hu]man without it."

—Goethe

"He who sows sparingly will also reap sparingly, and he who sows bountifully will also reap bountifully."

—Second Corinthians 9:6

"Not enjoyment, and not sorrow,
Is our destined end or way;
But to act, that each tomorrow
Find us farther than today."

—Henry Wadsworth Longfellow

"Follow the light of truth—as far as the eyes can see."

—Alan Parsons

"When the five intelligences all occur together, and none know of the method, this is called the divine web. This is the treasure of the ruler."

—Sun Tzu

Fifteen

Living with the Shadow to Have More Light

There is a consensus reality that this corporeal life is the most real. (Contemplation may force you to search for a second opinion.) William Blake—foreseeing Einstein and Gurdjieff—in the eighteenth century named this consensus the "single vision and Newton's sleep." Emanuel Swedenborg stated that one's destination after death is determined by intention or "true affections." Daniil Andreev speculated that the "weight" and positive or negative charge of spiritual energy result in a particular destination and described a number of purgatories as possible destinations for the less than buoyant soul adrift in the afterlife. The journey within opens correspondences between natural and spiritual phenomena. The mystics of all ages, both East and West, have described experiences that correlate with what I've experienced through chi kung meditation and Budo Taijutsu. The deeper you go, the stranger it gets, if you hold onto a concept of how it is "spozed to be."

This year (1995) I am fifty-one. That is twenty-six more years than I expected. I was once told that the average reader of *Original Ninja Magazine* is fifteen. I hope my readers are considerably older but haven't a clue to the demographics. Most of the people who contact me seem to be in their twentysomethings. To them, I must seem older than death. They treat me with great respect over the phone. The awe in their voices seems like something I might reserve for the last living veteran of the Battle of the Marne, Jonas Salk, or Hakeem the Dream. Rest assured—barring accidents—I intend to keep playing for another fifty years. One of my ninja friends, Big Al, who operates a *shibu* (training club) at U of M, Dearborn Campus, remarked to me that he believes in Ninpo because I'm "older than dirt, dangerous as hell, and seem to be having an awfully good time." There is a retired dance instructor from Baltimore in the system who is in his eighties who has earned membership in the dan ranks. Life always chooses life.

For life to be spiritually felt, it may be worthwhile to assume the samurai posture of accepting oneself as dead, or about to die, so that one treats each event in one's life as if it were the last thing to be experienced. This has a similar focusing effect to emptying the mind and treating each event as new without expectations, but is more serious. This last chapter deals with strategies important for achieving what might be called "the good life." To accomplish this Joseph Campbell recommended following your bliss. Following your bliss is as important as helping others to find theirs. Pleasure will eventually have no more meaning than pain, but that is the price of endurance. Reducing one's expectations or desires has the effect of reducing one's disappointments. The following topics and strategic principles may be of use in constructing a life worth living.

Politics

I remember a quote by Ernest Hemingway that went something like, "We remember most fondly those services we did for our country, or for women, as we age." It was one of the reasons I enlisted as a medic back in the early sixties. Ernest had some problems around facing age, living with fame, women, adjusting to war, learning new things, and giving up the past, etc., but I often find myself sharing his viewpoint that seemed so worldly when I was in high school, and so adolescent when I was in graduate school. All things totaled, he was one hell of a writer. His comment concerning service can be expanded to include others in general. My children and students are still the most important people in my life. Vietnam and other blunders like the War on Drugs—embracing the Conservative religious agenda, trickle-down economics, and the incredible maneuvers of media spin doctors—have tainted my view of "government work." If you are having a tough time figuring out what is wrong with being an unthinking patriot swallowing the party line, it might be useful to follow in Newt Gingrich's shadowy footprints and read Alvin and Heidi Toffler's new opus, *Creating a New Civilization* (see bibliography, under Organizational Strategic Guides).

Being a public person, like a grandmaster, politician, or professor, incurs some expectations and obligations around association and behavior that can be uncomfortable for the natural democrat, but also reflect the natural hierarchy of accomplishment. Birds of a feather oft do stick together, and it is important to rationalize your associations if you want to be effective. In certain situations it is important who you are seen with. Sometimes it is the only way you can learn certain things. It is a political expedient that comes with becoming important to many. Some people who are negatively motivated by politics go out of their way to get in yours, or more harmlessly just want to be seen with you. If you are going to make good decisions, it is necessary to seek advice from a wide variety of experts.

Even sycophants can be useful, but most are not. Daidoji Yuzan (sixteenth-century Japanese strategist and military advisor) said it like this: "For if, out of weakness, for fear of offending or opposing people, he [a leader] exhibits a maladroit hesitancy, and turns aside from what is just and agrees with what is not reasonable, and, in order to avoid a rupture, allows unsuitable things to be said and burdens to be laid on others, then he will eventually be noted as a futile counselor and reviled and despised as well. Again if anyone is so stupid or arrogant as to think himself too much a personage to confer with others, arguing that there is no need for consultation but wishing to decide everything according to his own opinion, and so making a mess of things, he is likely to find himself not very popular among his fellows as a result" (A.L. Sadler, *The Code of the Samurai,* see bibliography). What can be said of the individual can often be extended to the group, and the words of a wise person often transcend race, place, history, and gender to continue in meaning. Daidoji Yuzan's commentary on borrowed and stolen authority is as useful today as it was four hundred years ago, and is particularly important for Bujinkan practitioners to understand. A samurai of the negative political persuasion who followed his lord's will against his own conscience was called *neishin* (sniveling, cringing, fawning parasite) or *choshin* (a favorite who steals his superior's affection by servile compliance). *Seppuku* (suicide) was the preferable alternative. (It appears to be a human universal that everybody hates a suck ass.)

With age and sophistication comes the realization that there are three kind of politics: positive, neutral, and negative. Positive politics may include making sure you get credit for what you do, making friends with people who have power, being of service to those who can benefit your causes, and championing change that benefits society. Neutral politics include belonging to groups, working for charities, supporting others, maintaining quid pro quo. Negative politics include taking credit for others' work, tearing down others to enhance one's own position, or blindly executing the will of one's superior regardless of the results—going with the majority or power, even when wrong.

Political relationships are part and parcel to living with power. If your political action is primarily neutral or positive, then you are creating a better life for many, which is usually regarded as serving the good. All human interaction is political to some extent, and to ignore that is not good strategy. It is like not paying attention to non-verbal communication. Dumb.

Getting A Life

From my observation, those whose primary motivation is enhancing their own image, or selfishness, or me-ness, don't seem to have much fun in long-term relationships, and have considerably more stress-related, psychosomatic disease symptoms than their more altruistic fellow human beings. They age faster and look older than their years. Negativity, assholishness, cardiovascular, and gastrointestinal problems correlate significantly. (There is research to back this.) Those who claim to have done everything they wanted to do in life and are still depressed and unhappy reflect the truth that being successful by other people's standards may not do much for your own feeling of self-esteem. The suicide and overdose rate of many astronomically well-rewarded, financially flush, public people should stand as a warning that money and power are not the only measure of a meaningful life. Be nice. Be helpful. It is not that tough, but sometimes it requires letting go of the past, which can be very difficult. You often get what you want by providing what they need. It is called service and is considered a characteristic of the professional.

One of the interesting things about aging is that time speeds up rather than slows down. This gives a feeling of urgency and importance to what one does and with whom one associates. Relationships become less casual, as one hates to waste time. This often creates a degree of discomfort with some of our more frivolous acquaintances and companions. Time-management techniques become a therapeutic means for balancing one's activities. One of my clinical psychologist friends even scheduled time with his wife and children, as he had strong workaholic tendencies, and once he started working would forget to go home. When I was a college professor I tended to be that way; my spouse interpreted it as being more interested in what I was doing at school than her and home. If you want to avoid divorce, it is important to remember that one's job, because of all the time spent at it, is almost like a second marriage or a mistress that your primary relationship will come to resent for good reason. You will fare better as a professional if your partner has a life of her own that is as time-consuming as your interests.

Although longevity was never high on my priority list, I remain convinced that the Chinese martial arts practices concerning chi are valuable in sustaining a powerful and healthy body, which allows you to have a great deal of fun learning the things necessary for wresting an enjoyable lifestyle. When you are immersed in the doing of your life, you seldom notice gradations of style and reward. It is only in the pauses or periods of recovery that we tend to compare our progress to others. Happiness is a by-product, not a goal. Joy is a mental state associated with productivity and longevity. If you are not experiencing joy in your life, you have probably made some poor choices and may wish to restructure your adventure from a more mature perspective.

The easiest way to salvation is through continuing education. That with which we feed the mind is with us always. It is not necessary to return to the drudgery of earning advanced degrees, but it shows wisdom to learn from experts. In this electronic age all sorts of courses and experiences are available to the seeker. I have heard some of my well-educated friends speak bitterly that they wasted years in low-paying jobs, or more often in bad marriages, forgetting that their experience is or can be a means to deeper understanding of self and others. It may not be too rewarding to have a Master's degree in theatre or dance and still be waiting tables because you can only find part-time work in your field. You do have to get over it. It is just part of the price one pays for doing what one wants.

Sweat correlates with achievement in most occupations. Most business executives and successful academics put in ridiculously long hours. The naive only see the success, and fail to realize there are no shortcuts in achieving quality. You can either do something well, or you cannot. Eighty percent of success is showing up; the other twenty is who do you know, and whether you are lucky enough to be in the right place at the right time to be noticed. The hardest lesson to learn in life is that no matter what you know, or how great your skill, you are always a white belt to someone. Fairness and justice are social constructs.

Life and Love In The Material World

It may be just a reflection of third world stats or city population, but to those of us who are college educated and economically mobile, the survey result that most people marry someone born within one mile of where they were born is hard to believe (Ian Robertson, *Sociology*, Worth, 1987). Maybe a whole bunch of people marry their high school sweethearts. Anyway, most marriages last five years. Fifty percent of marriages end in divorce. Most second marriages last no longer than the first. The reasons given for divorce most often are bad sex, and no money. As most marriages in this country still take place before the couples are in their mid-twenties, there is a certain logic, based on ignorance, to the pattern. Like marrying like seems to support Grandma invoking, "Marry your own kind." Like much good advice, it lacks excitement. Since I haven't been very good at maintaining long-term marriages, this will be a short topic.

Learn what it takes to make you comfortable economically, and carefully avoid judging or comparing yourself to others on financial accomplishment or other matters. You must learn to earn enough to live well, and if you want a family, better than that. Become part of a worthwhile community. If you are recognized as being the expert in what you do, you will never hunger. Seriously consider who you want to live and work with, and why. Don't settle for mere ease or respectability. Get as much education as you can, not just what you think you need. Education correlates with credibility, expert knowledge, and financial growth.

In 1994 I participated in the cesarean birth of a daughter to Aree Marquis. She had always wanted a child. She found me about the same time she found she was pregnant, and strangely believed both events to be blessings. She had been told by the medical community years back that it was impossible for her to have a child. The medical team had the infant out of the vessel before I could change into scrubs. (Watching a cesarean birth is a bit like watching a hog slaughtered, or gutting out a deer.) As the doctors washed Aree's intestines with saline and treated ancient adhesions, the nurses cooed over and cleaned the blood and mucus from the perfectly formed, six-pound, mildly complaining infant we'd already named Sara Glenn Mariko. Modern medical technology and skill are so amazing. The miracle of a birth; the risk of death for a loved one; the responsibility of another daughter. Raising step-children, I had never been present at the birth of a loved one. Now it's grandchildren that create concern.

Couvade (French for feeling the mother's pain) is one of the more interesting aspects of enhanced empathy. I had spent the night before throwing up and had little desire to faint in the birthing room; facing an emergency operating room required screwing courage "to the sticking point." I was wide-eyed. The birth was a new and glorious experience. A lot rougher on the mother than either of us expected. My first wife often told the story with anger and disgust about how the men in her first family would go deer hunting whenever a baby was expected. I was not about to miss something that meant so much to Aree.

Friendship

Friendship is extremely important to the martial artist. *Buyu* (martial art friend) relates to the pursuit of enlightenment, as friends exchange information they have found worthwhile. Ninpo gathers intelligence through friendship. I hate to put numbers on complex concepts, but it seems to me there are some basic reasons for friendship that help categorize relationships for strategic purposes.

1. We become friends with those who share our interests (or work). If there is genuine liking that leads to biochemical bonding, we may develop the proverbial friend for life, transcending the original interest. If you are male, and fortunate, you can count these relationships on one hand as opposed to one finger. Research indicates that making a new friend for an American male past thirty is very rare—a sad commentary on modern experience.

2. We make friends with those who have something we want or need. This desire can be subconscious. The initiation of friendship is often accomplished by studying the other person and supplying their needs. When the friendship provides a balance, or is synergistic—where expertise from differing arenas leads to new experiences for both   the friendship deepens. When the relationship is based on material gain, the friendship seldom moves beyond recognition of the parasite. People who claim or give friendship lightly should be watched carefully, particularly in the business environment, where competence is a major factor in completion.

3. We become friends with those we find attractive, or admirable. This is like "puppy love," which is proto-biochemical, and often lasts as long, for beauty is indeed skin deep. Beauty without depth is like owning the shell of a Ferrari but not the engine or transmission. I have known many beauties, male and female, who make the term "shallow" appear a bottomless

chasm. Admiration must be supported by competence, and action is a better measure than the words spoken. Beauty is an easier way to high self-esteem than accomplishment. Friendships based only on mutual attraction are usually short.

The visual aspect of sex is powerful, as it relates to biological proclivities. It is not like we didn't already know this, but it is important to remember when letting your body go that it is a matter of choice. In the March 1995 *Journal of Personality and Social Psychology,* researchers found women rated men as more attractive if they were dominant, but solicited their partner's opinions, showed sensitivity to their partner's perspective, and displayed warmth and agreeableness. Ratings declined swiftly if the men were critical or insensitive.

You can see that friendship is usually based on an exchange, and the exchange may have various components relating to mind, body, and spirit. A friend smooths the way for a friend, but friendship is not discarded when the friend does not accept the easier path. Women tend to be better at developing meaningful friends than men. I suspect it comes from willingness to work and serve, as well as greater intuitive skills being emphasized in the socialization process. We all learn from our own perspective. A warped perspective regards kindness as weakness. Keeping such a one close can provide more danger than war but can be a valuable learning experience in strategy. The Taoist admonition that one should treat both the good and the evil person with kindness often leads to dangerous friends. The way of stealth may protect you from the downside of such relationships.

It is easier to destroy a relationship than it is to build one. Destruction often results from simply ignoring what the other considers important in personal matters. Even in physical matters we often forget that the builder serves a more important social role than the maintainer and both serve a higher purpose than the person who can tear things down. Friendship is probably the most important emotional relationship you will experience. The *buyu,* both students and colleagues, continue to play, and that relationship seems to hold as deeply as the more ordinary ones mentioned above. Ninpo emphasizes the concept of being a good host as a tool for building friendship. If you want your relationships with others to last, study them as well as these ideas.

Learning Attitudes as Response to Other Arts

Hatsumi-soke will often quote from or recommend artists, movies, music, and books to his students as the work will reveal or emulate a feeling that he suggests will help them in refining their spirit of Budo. For what is the point of training, if not to discover happiness and become self-aware? As the object of Ninpo is to produce a fully-realized "real human being," and the object of our culture is to produce a "cog in the industrial/economic machine," we may find ourselves delving into history and anthropology to develop a deeper psychological understanding of living and dying well. In this day and age, the medium of film replaces the singing of the legend by the Skald.

Film brings interesting lessons for the martial artist, particularly the ones who don't read much. For urban dwellers, the attitudes valuable to Native Americans revealed in Kevin Cost ner's *Dances with Wolves* or Brad Pitt's *Legends of the Fall* are very similar to concepts prized in Ninpo. *Bunbu* (appreciation and participation in art) is every bit as important to mastery as proper taijutsu. As I watched the recent French production (with Gerard Depardieu) of Rostand's *Cyrano de Bergerac*—a play full of rich poetic language, wonderful romance, and one of my favorite plays since I was introduced to it in high school, I was amazed by the reference to cross-sex friendship in Cyrano's death scene. I had remembered Cyrano's words concerning his "enemies" all my life, but had forgotten the reference to a dress, or had a different translation. Jodie Foster and Richard Gere in

Somersby hold one's attention as well as present a tale of what makes a meaningful life and death. I have been delighted to see the return of "The Legendary Kung Fu" with David Carradine to the Turner Network. I missed most of it when I was a kid in the Army. The correspondences between the Shaolin and Ninpo are occasionally shown in the not-so-fictional training of the monks. I particularly like the episodes "One Step Into Darkness" and "The Thief of Chendo." There is a kung fu video, misnamed *Master Killer,* to attract the prurient, that shows actual Shaolin Monastery training. It has the usual goofy revenge plot, but the training sequences are excellent. Jeff Bridges' *Fearless* has many aspects that the practitioner of esoteric arts or Budo will recognize. Oliver Stone's *The Doors,* starring Val Kilmer, is a warning tale concerning mixing drugs, magic, music, and shamanism without internalizing the sacred. Mel Gibson's love story concerning William Wallace, *Braveheart,* gets very close to the reality and carnage of low-tech, close-quarter combat, attitudes, and strategy.

Nutrition

Takamatsu-sensei abhorred the cooking of meat. Hatsumi-soke functions mostly as a vegetarian. "We are what we eat!" Nutrition is important. The American Medical Association has finally recognized that vitamins are extremely beneficial, and there is a pile of research that indicates they are a buffer against many diseases, like cancer, that you would not like to develop as you age. Eating lots of varied veggies is the best way to get vitamins and fiber. Take a daily mega-multi-vitamin and mineral supplement even if you eat your broccoli. (I don't know anyone who really eats as they should.) The new food supplement *Juice Plus* is loaded with live enzymes, anti-oxidants, fiber and replaces the messiness of juicing with the ease of swallowing a couple of capsules. I can say from personal experience that it is a good source of "grain chi" which is what the Chinese call the energy we get from nutrition. Research in Germany and the USA indicates *Juice Plus +* significantly raised the levels of anti-oxidants in the blood of those who ate it as a whole food supplement. The taking of zinc actually increases the strength of the immune system beyond that of taking supplemental anti-oxidants such as C, E, and beta-carotene. Zinc, as well as garlic, seems to create a blood environment in which viruses and bacteria do not thrive. The vitamin niacin reduces delusions, according to herbalists. Eating oatmeal reduces bad cholesterol and will drop your triglycerides like a stone. The veggies provide roughage as well as fiber, but oatmeal is like being cleaned out with a sponge, so much nicer than being scrubbed with a handful of twigs (softage versus roughage). Quitting smoking is very beneficial in avoiding hardening of the arteries, wrinkly skin, emphysema, and a whole slew of nasty lung and bronchial problems, if fear of cancer is not motivation enough.

Turmeric and cumin, herbs popular in most curries, destroy bacteria including salmonella, the one most often associated with food poisoning. Turmeric also works as a topical to reduce inflammation in open wounds. Taking an aspirin every other day significantly reduces the chance of a heart attack. Herbals can be an interesting source of valuable home brews that treat many common disorders. Local honey is said to reduce allergies.

A large number of studies now link carcinogens to the nitrasamines and nitrosamides that are produced when meat is cured or cooked for a long time at high temperature. Carcinogens cause cancer. Mark Twain's "frying pan demon," smoking and charring are major culprits. Not just how the meat is cooked (fried, well-done, or charred) but the type of meat is important. Chicken and beef have five to eight times the risk of fish. The really big surprise is that the *failure* to take vitamins significantly increased the risk associated with eating meats. The Buddha said there is a special hell for those who are cruel to animals, and that eaters of meat would have great difficulty in achieving knowledge of the higher self. I won't bother to get into the effects of antibiotics and hormones given to animals we eat, and how that endangers our own immune system over the long term. There are lots of reasons to avoid regular consumption of red meat, or any meat that is commercially prepared. Takamatsu-soke recommended only eating raw food as cooking removes many of the natural enzymes' benefits. Freezing vegetables destroys glutathione, which prevents the spread of macular degeneration in the eyes.

Ginseng and garlic have anti-bacterial properties even greater than zinc, which may help account for their good reputation in alternative medicine circles. Green tea, the bitter stuff, has been shown to benefit its drinkers in a number of healthy ways. Drinking tabasco sauce is a popular method of relaxing among combat troops. Hot spicy foods release endorphins into the bloodstream to counter the internal burn. The endorphins provide a mild euphoria, which is interpreted by the body as feeling good. (One of the many reasons the Tex-Mex lifestyle tends to be more laid back.) Golden Seal and Siberian ginseng function as herbal stimulants, as well as anti-bacterials, when your lifestyle is depressing or just pooping you out. The research on algae is looking beneficial. Folic acid has been shown to be an extremely powerful buffer against heart disease.

Red wine kills most bacteria and some viruses because of its molecular structure, not alcoholic content. *Egri Bikaver,* a most excellent Hungarian dark red wine that is called "Bull's Blood," comes from some of the oldest continually producing vineyards in the Western world. Bull's Blood was beloved of Roman Emperors, Pan, Dionysus, and the SS. Due to the realities of the new capitalism, this wine can be had in the USA for less than eight dollars a bottle, and its presence is worth twenty times that. You can trust the vine, but I'm not certain of the water. The Communists never were real big on preventing pollution. Longevity studies of active octogenarians suggest a glass or two of wine a day keeps the undertaker away. The long-lived and active liked their veggies, salads, oatmeal, and maintained meaningful sexual relationships. Married folks tend to live longer than singles. Those who live long happily remain active in their communities.

Trust and Leadership

Trust. A leader of profound knowledge, regardless of the discipline, creates trust. Trust is more important than faith, or love, as it is based on reciprocity or the experience of competence. If you are going to be considered trustworthy, you must go beyond back scratching. Get help from people with knowledge, other leaders, and experts. Asking for help is not a sign of weakness, particularly when you need it and are able to identify who can actually help you. Returning the favor is where the real trust is engendered. Trust in business is based in competence. Trust in relationship is augmented by not calling in your dues at an inopportune time from the person who owes you a favor. It's a Mafia kind of thing. The best way to build trust is to live your word, do as you say, move from the heart, and be kind to others as you work on your own competence. Be knowledgeable and act in the best interest of your friend and customer. This is not rocket science.

A situation which limits your ability to respond with the truth as you understand it does not foment trust. For others, particularly leaders, to come to trust you often requires learning to balance your responses, particularly when discretion is involved over valor. In public life one should think carefully before speaking, for it is out of words that disputes arise. Choose to pursue a solution rather than place condemnation.

Trust is enhanced by reducing or driving out fear. Fear of failure, of looking foolish, losing one's job, anxiety in adventure, falling from grace, or into love, are all pretty scary. Few handle themselves well in new situations if they are scared or ignorant. Knowledge destroys the dwarf of ignorance, and driving out fear is like conducting a round-up of all the wild bulls, rumors of war, and gnashing of teeth, and getting them aligned in the direction of their true potential. Removing fear so people will problem-solve rather than place blame is truly a leadership skill that few master. It is difficult to get people who are frightened to trust each other, let alone get them to work together. It is important to study the concepts and actualize the behaviors that create trust. Isn't it strange that although people know it is easier to change themselves than to change others, they invariably elect to attempt to change others? (This is often mistakenly identified as leadership, especially in the enthusiastic.)

Problem-Solving as Solution Evaluation

Problem-solving is one of the primary abilities of successful leaders. There is a great deal of research data indicating that skill in problem-solving is a characteristic of those who rise to key executive positions. Problem-solving correlates significantly to achievement motivation but not to IQ, interestingly enough. Figuring out how to perform a particular martial art training technique is a physical manifestation of the process of good problem-solving. Think about it. Dr. Norman R.F. Maier, my mentor in Organizational Psychology, posited some heavily researched principles around problem-solving, creativity, and innovative thinking that were very useful to me, so I'll now pass them on to you. As far as I know, this is lecture material which he never published that we used in problem-solving seminars back in the early seventies before his death. Focus your attention on these principles if you want to succeed.

1. All innovative thinking is strange, or seems strange at first. If it were ordinary, everyone else would have thought of it. Innovative or creative equals new or different. If it is not different, it is not creative.

2. New ideas are rejected primarily for two reasons:
   a. People do not understand them, and therefore reject them;
   b. People do understand them, recognize they are no damn good, and reject them.

More new ideas are rejected for reason A than B. However, the second reason, B, is usually the reason given. If you are going to be a creative problem-solver, you must be alert and open to considering unusual ideas. If you want to be successfully creative you must work on conveying your ideas in ways that encourage understanding. Communication skills come from practice.

Maier had a formula, Q x A = EDM, which was a valuable tool for looking at numerous relationships in the world. I think it is as elegant as Einstein's Theory of Relativity. He applied it primarily to problem-solving, as he was a more rational man than I. The formula works like this: Q – Quality, A = Acceptance, EDM = Effective Decision-Making. It is used to evaluate solutions. (Or actions, or situations, or people, or organizations, or ideas. You get it.) Often problem-solving systems do not take acceptance into consideration, resulting in good solutions being discovered but not implemented. Quality can be thought of as "How well it works" and Acceptance as "How much do people like it." You can attach numbers from one to ten to either side of the equation. There are some low-quality ideas that have high acceptance and have been around for a very long time, as well as some high-quality ideas that will probably never get widely used in our lifetimes. The higher the number, the more effective the solution. Like this:

Q2 x A2 = EDM4   Low Quality times Low Acceptance equals "trickle down economics," somebody else's child, dog, or religion, "Scientific Creationism," child pornography.

Q9 x A2 = EDM18   High Quality times Low Acceptance
equals quarterly dental
examinations, quality health care
paid by major tax increases, doing
your daily dozen, no more fatty ice
cream, studying hard every night,
running marathons, sticking with
hard karate, paying for your child's
Ph.D. in 13th-century Middle
English.

Q2 x A9 = EDM18   Low Quality times High Acceptance
equals high-meat, low-veggie diet,
continuing smoking, pet rocks, flat
earth, the sun revolves around the
earth, some religious mythologies,
thinking tae kwon do will help you
in a real fight, our last five presiden-
tial elections. (You begin to see how
this works. It's fun.)

Q5 x A5 = EDM 25   Moderate Quality times Moderate
Acceptance equals two-party system
and most political races. Choosing
the lesser of two evils. Taking the
"gentleman's grade." My marriages
after the first five years.

Q9 x A9 = EDM 81   High Quality times High Acceptance
equals GI Bill, public schools away
from urban blight, the early space
program, airplanes, tai chi and
taijutsu, the ideas of W. Edward
Deming, Abraham Maslow, or
Douglas McGregor, Salk polio
vaccine, one's own children, etc.

Most people prefer to find solutions rather than identify
problems. There are good psychological reasons for this personal

bias. Problem identification often evokes defensive behaviors and can turn into a nasty negative business if the problems threaten the status quo. People involved in it are often viewed as being too critical; they make enemies, are regarded with suspicion, and generally are not met with pleasure. Furthermore, a problem once identified should be solved, and that means more work or guilt. Finding a solution, however, is rewarding, positive, and usually doesn't threaten others. If you want to point out a problem, you'll be more popular if you can also proffer a solution or two to soften the blow. Second solutions tend to work better than what you think of first, as the first choice is often conventional. If it were that easy, the problem would have already been solved. When you work with litigious people, it is often valuable to know the solution before asking the question. Being able to evaluate solutions in terms of quality and acceptance helps you to make better choices.

Most people like their ideas and solutions better than yours, regardless of your position, knowledge, or expertise. If you really want something to be done, be quick to release ownership of an idea to those who have to implement. Listening and asking questions are not usually recognized as important leadership communication skills. They are, and require practice. Asking "How do you see this problem?" often gives you new information as well as includes the other. Maier taught first-line supervisors to ask that question before providing solutions and got a thirty percent increase in production with no other intervention. You can "What if" people into finding a working solution if they haven't a clue. Work hard to help them to figure out what must be done, so that they will take ownership and champion the project. Not saying anything will often get you more and better information, as many people grow uncomfortable during silence and will begin to speak simply to fill in the dead air space. "Still waters run deep." "Speech is silver; silence is golden." Learning to shut up was terribly difficult for me, as I used to like to bandy words.

Teamwork

It is important to realize that the quick reaction, problem-solving, and consensus skills associated with martial artists, the ninja, business, and commando teamwork are relatively rare, as they are best nurtured by competition against established standards as in music, dance, theatre, and ongoing athletic teams. The British understood this well when they formed their Artist Brigades in World War I, which later became their World War II Special Boat Service and contemporary counter-terrorist SAS. SEAL training emphasizes small-group or squad-level teamwork. Skilled team leaders actively seek different viewpoints so they can expand their world view as well as create a more accurate assessment of reality for themselves and their team. Working with others is called cheating in the typical academic environment, but in reality that is how most quality products are produced in the real world.

Often organizations will actively seek and promote a "particular type." Ten or twenty years downstream this can result in reduced creativity because the people within the organization "think alike" and are often proud of their similarity. This can be seen easily in the conduct of both *ryu* and organizations. If group strengths are loaded toward conformity, change will be difficult to implement, as the membership will see it as a threat to the status quo. People in power who are insecure tend to select followers for dependency and approval seeking—such a group can lack decisiveness and will often follow the whims of a benevolent dictator rather than freeing themselves. If the group members' strengths are loaded toward acceptance of change, there is a danger of "risky shift" decision-making, and a tendency to be overly responsive to emotional appeals over scientific method. Adaptivity when perverted by needs for approval results in self-centered competitiveness, negative politics, and faddishness typical of modern organizations. If the group members are selected for assertiveness and objectivity they will often fail to make acceptable decisions, as they tend to ignore others' concerns. Skilled leaders encourage individual difference to prevent rigidity and imbalance in their teams, nurturing a norm of creativity.

For an organization to function creatively in a strategic manner, individuals must function on at least two levels. Its rather like the ninja *ura* (hidden) and *omote* (shown). Membership is based on shared or fundamental knowledge which are skills common to the whole group (the omote), and depth skills (ura), which are the particular expertise of a team member. The fundamental skills provide a shared experience that creates group cohesion and integrity, while the individual depth skills and diverse personalities rub together to encourage problem-solving and unique solutions, as long as the play is not destructive and is directed toward continuous improvement. Budo Taijutsu is a creative martial art. Edmund Burke, the eighteenth-century British parliamentarian, pointed out, "When bad men combine, the good must associate; otherwise they will fall, one by one, an unpitied sacrifice in a contemptible struggle... For evil to win, all that must happen is for good men to do nothing."

These principles apply to the manufacturing of products as well as the enhancement of people. A skilled leader is concerned with the growth and development of the group's membership, as the improvement of one benefits and develops the whole. You can hire experience and expertise, but not affection and loyalty. Affection and loyalty, like trust, are learned attitudes resulting from behavior. Often people tell me that their only positive group experience is in interacting with other members of their ryu or kwoon. That is a sad commentary on how business and education are often conducted in America.

Sex, Death, Sock and Soul

Mantak and Maneewan Chia's extensive and detailed books concerning the cultivation of chi through Taoist Esoteric Yoga may give you some strong clues as to how sex, energy, and spirit interact. Their work on sexual or healing love practice are the finest guides in the English language, and perhaps any language. If the idea of transforming aroused energy into total body orgasm strikes you as a fun goal worth pursuing in yourself or sexual partner, do I have to insist you should study on this? It is more fun than perfecting your side stomp kick, and may be more valuable in saving your life as well as attracting interesting play-mates. Sexuality and spirituality spring from the same physical location. I commented on this in the first book. If you followed my advice you are probably having a lot of fun and are the envy of all your colleagues and acquaintances by this time. Mantak Chia and his students of Taoist Esoteric Yoga have done good work in popularizing chi kung practice in a way that is under-standable and useful for Westerners.

On the energy level, the Chias hint at an experience of orgas-mic expression that can only be considered spiritual in nature. It is a real and repeatable experience and can exist on both sides of the mandala. To quote the Yellow Emperor's sex consultant, "Yang can only function with the cooperation of yin, and yin can only grow in the presence of yang" (Mantak Chia and Michael Winn, *Taoists Secrets of Love: Cultivating Male Sexual Energy*, Aurora, 1986). It is in the exchange of energy with your lover that one attains the valley orgasm that fills the bodies of the beloved. When that energy is pushed out through the head chakras into the Void to join with one's guiding spirits in chi kung meditation, a new relationship is formed. That linkage to higher power leads to insights and healing power which are non-ordinary. This is referred to by the ancients as "The Con-gress of Heaven and Earth" and is accomplished by uniting the body, soul, spirit, and universe through fully developing the positive while accepting the negative, which allows the origi-nal spirit to return to the Void. This is both a physical and men-tal practice which can only be accomplished through tempering the body. At some point the spirit will abandon the body, which will thoroughly convince you that there is life after death of the body. This usually results in a recognition of reincarnation and a rejection of fear of death. With practice one may become comfortable traveling into the Void and literally construct or achieve an existence in the subtle planes that in strange ways coexists with what we consider ordinary life or material existence. The ninja refer to this as "living the dual mandala." Be careful, for what you wish may manifest.

Senior Practitioners

Teachers of Ninpo vary greatly in their acceptance and understanding of the depth of the river in which they are immersed. I heard a joke at the Tucson Tai Kai concerning how many ninja it took to properly learn a new technique. Nine. Eight to videotape it from every angle, and one more to write a book! Occasionally people complain about who gets promoted and for what. From what I've seen, those who complain the loudest lack an understanding of the heart of the art. Others complain concerning the expense of seminars or promotion. I know of some who hold high ranks who have never received a billing under the rules of *giri*. Teachers decide what they charge. The market reflects the quality, eventually. I've talked with instructors who were refused promotion; they paid for tests and were not promoted, and felt they had been wronged. (Tough shit, you flunked! Go home, study up, and try again.) The Boss is interested in creating a more diverse group than simply fighters, and follows the principles of Budo and Ninpo.

Those who I have known to achieve greatness were seldom granted easy recognition of their skills or rewarded for their contributions, but instead have had to suffer scorn and rejection by the entrenched establishment. The new is always different. That is why it is considered new. It is a sad commentary on the human condition that the flames of endurance as a tool for forging swords that will not bend to defeat are often fueled by the jealousy of lesser beings who seek to defend their incompetence and lack of foresight. Kindness is often mistaken for weakness by the predator. Jealousy is a character defect and survival mechanism common to all primates and many other animals with enough smarts to want more loving attention.

Few Americans (or Japanese) are comfortable teaching *kyojitsu,* but enjoy teaching the physical skills. Hatsumi-soke teaches the *shinken* from a *kokoro* (Silence of the Heart) and physical perspective which makes it very difficult for his followers to understand or pick up. This is the traditional manner that preserves the hierarchy of learning in the Togakure Ryu. Shinken or kyojitsu is more of an individual thing and is really the domain of the grandmaster and possibly the Juyushi. If you don't see much of what I have described in your art or teacher, you will probably have to make a journey to find what you desire. I try to share as much of the magic as I can and can figure out. The Boss has far greater skills, particularly those that relate to art, healing, and taijutsu. I try to pick up what I can, whenever I see him. Kathy Glass, my editor, jokingly suggests my explanations "suffer from excessive clarity." These books, which The Boss supports, are our way of filling in the blanks for those who cannot find the higher art in their teachers.

Those shidoshi who specialize in teaching the true combat skills train incessantly. They are the holders of the combat methodologies coming out of their shihan, or The Boss. They are senior practitioners, but still have the youth and movement to convey the optimal expert technique. I've learned a lot from them. Kyojitsu is for the old boys' network. The Boss does something weird to you, and then you are supposed to figure out how he did it, and come back with your variation. Giri. If you can't ... shame on you. Like Confucius, the Boss shows you "one corner," and you are supposed to figure out the rest of the geometric. It is a favored teaching technique in the martial arts.

Intervention by the Bujin may become your only hope of participating. Taoists believe man's highest self is revealed through natural behavior. The siddhi are natural, but if you don't use them, you lose them. Keep playing.

Senior practitioners in the martial arts often have difficulty in realizing that their role may shift from the valued teacher of fighting skills to valued font of wisdom and strategy. Senior practitioners have the obligation to realize when their teaching role becomes less physical and more strategic. When one teaches it is tempting to quit working on one's own improvement and focus outward too soon. You can see that at the Tai Kai when the upper level belts don't have a clue as to how The Boss did a technique when they are asked to show their variation. They have allowed their cup to become full. You can easily see who has become predictable and comfortable in their art. Age does not necessarily correlate with wisdom. The Boss is relying more on the younger shidoshi who have spent more of their training years in Japan to act as his uke, along with those he brings from Japan, to prepare them for greater responsibility. The third generation of players are, for the most part, more harmonious than those of my generation. After all, most of us weren't raised on *Sesame Street* and *Mr. Rogers*. As a kid, my favorite comic was "Sgt. Rock," and all I wanted to be was a professional soldier, to the horror of my parents. Turning to the theatre in my teens was hardly an improvement, and if it weren't for the GI Bill and Penn State, I would never have achieved much of anything.

Shidoshi often go through a phase of thinking they are the Second Coming, and act like they are the only true source of taijutsu. It is a position to be pitied. They forget the sacrifice of their teachers. If they are only showing and not doing, they've missed the point of self-protection and The Boss' admonition to keep going. The real artist keeps playing—some of the real good stuff doesn't come out of the box until you've played for twenty years. Some of the shidoshi who went to Japan and stayed over there for a few years to study Ninpo and other martial arts have returned with incredible skills in Budo Taijutsu, and force us all to go back to the basics for another look as they hit the seminar circuit. Budo Taijutsu can be expensive to learn when you study with the best, but quality does not fade with time, and skills that are internalized are valued through eternity. Skills are best taught in a light-hearted and loving atmosphere.

The Boss wrote in *Sanmyaku*, "My life is always shrouded in the light and sounds my mentor [Takamatsu-soke] transmitted to me: yet it would be a mistake to think that the 'Hatsumi Masaaki Way' is the true way. The true way lies in the nine schools and several hundred Soke which I inherited. When your life follows this true path, it is important to accept remote control from a consciousness of natural justice, a consciousness of *Shinshin Shingan* [the mind and eyes of God]. I have come to see this over the last few years." He went on to write, "Bujinkan studies are like a Ph.D. course. Not, however, the kind of Ph.D. course which is fixed by the general society. It is important to maintain an attitude whereby you learn and grasp the great erudition alive in the world of Nature through your practice and training. I often tell buyu of the fifth dan and above that if you want to progress in the martial arts, practice in the dojo is not enough. Taking the living feeling with which you train inside the dojo, and putting it to use in society is also practice."

The ancient teachers of Zen and Chan recommended, "First awaken on your own, then see someone else." That is damn hard these days. The Yogic masters recommend practice with a positive and practical teacher who has experience of the divine feeling. Find a teacher (credible, licensed, with a sound reputation) of intelligence, not just faith, who makes you stretch, yet feel happy. Observe closely. If what you see seems false, move along. Remember what Gautama, the Sakyamuni Buddha, said about living up to it. There is no price you can put on the Way. And no way without self-development and protection. Paying a fraud for lessons in Ninpo, or any other form of spiritual development, is pounding sand down a rat hole. You quit showing up, you move up the road until you are out of harm's way. If they seem all-knowing, sweetness and light, run for your life. If they are eager to give you advice, and act like you should "kiss their ring and kneel to touch their hem," be very cautious. People are funny and complex. What appeals to me may not move you in the least.

Final Commentary

The principles of Budo serve as a guide for the warrior spirit. When a person without "religious feeling" achieves power, he or she can be a source of many problems. Kritias, a student of Socrates, became one of The Thirty Tyrants, and it was said of him, "When a man is freed from the bonds of dogma and custom, where will he run? He has gotten loose, of the soul if you like that word, or from whatever keeps a man on two feet instead of four. And now Kritias too is running on the mountains, with no more between him and his will than a wolf has." History, and particularly military history, teaches us that there is no worse combination than energy, ambition, and stupidity. The first two can be channeled into productive activities, but the third is incurable (Lo Q x Hi A = Lo EDM).

Some folks love studying old rituals and languages, and work hard to preserve traditions derived from a different reality. If you like that kind of mummy dust spread on your art, you may be more comfortable studying with someone who needs that kind of anal retentive stability. I have found that many of the old scrolls and *sutra* actually have false descriptions that only become apparent when you are having the actual experience. It's a little filter to eliminate the overly devout and non-practicing scholar. The preservation of mere words may also indicate nobody has actually done the deed for a very long time.

I like to know why something is done in a particular way and then move on, accepting or rejecting according to my experience and needs. I suggest you do the same.

My dentist told me reading a book by someone like me is the equivalent of reading the Bible. He's a nice man but a little naive. Kathy Glass informs me this statement is "a bit grandiose" but I like to think I'm more accurate in my translations having no political or religious viewpoint to extoll; I have tried to preserve a scroll-like utility to what I've written, being something of a magic-user. Some aspects of this book are very strange, even to me, but certainly no stranger than some other records concerning "religious feelings." (Virgin. Greek. innocent, unmarried, and/or humiliated, *not* hymen intacta or chaste as in English. Think about it. Joseph becomes a hero.) This book is all I really have to say about Ninpo, Budo, Bugei, and spiritual practice. I have included in this "scroll" guidance appropriate for surviving well in the twenty-first century environment. The world is changing and not all for the good, looking back will not prepare you for the world-wide-web of computer driven knowledge and magic that are becoming common threads in the fabric of our lives.

The reader should have realized by this time, what I have written has little to do with classical Togakure Ryu practice or Bujinkan Ninpo Budo Taijutsu. I can't profess to be a teacher of traditional taijutsu, Budo Taijutsu is only my hobby. I am a ninja master, more than some and less than others, but I do know who is real and who needs work. Ninpo is something I do for my own personal growth. For me it is the most consistent fun I have had in an interesting and varied life. While some see the Ryu as the Hell's Angels of the martial arts, and others see it as the ultimate in warrior experience and training, I think of my friends as members of something like a very ancient and demanding family-oriented bowling league where the game we all play has no rules other than those concerning self-protection.

Certain core traditions and standards of play are preserved for their value by the organization, but the individual players are left on their own to preserve or pass on what they think is useful in their particular environment, and the time limits on play are decided by survival and showing up. If people keep badgering me to write more, I shall ask the other masters to contribute to a collection of fiction and essays that relate to their experience of the Togakure Ryu. There are some interesting voices that have not yet articulated their experience in any public manner.

When I write about my experiences, I am doing it from the viewpoint of an anthropologist or transpersonal psychologist more than a martial artist. Think of me as an internal or *ura* specialist. There are others who can better teach you how to use the *omote* physical skills. Budo Taijutsu is, however, a miraculous catalyst for preparing one to appreciate the full range of human nature. Those who are fortunate enough to rise through the ranks of Bujinkan are privileged to participate.

Ye Olde Curiosity Shoppe: An Annotated Bibliography

The following books are all well worth reading and some of them will even blow your mind. I've tried to include ones that were fun to read, as well as challenging and useful, particularly if you are moving toward continuous improvement. If you've never been exposed to primary sources, this might even be enlightening for you. Kick back and put your local librarian to work. If you're one of those poor souls who usually doesn't read fiction, you might try some of the recommended writers I've enjoyed enormously over the years. They are listed at the end. For the task-oriented, it is not enough to be able to read words and understand the author's meaning. A real reader considers application to his or her life while absorbing the content. This is why all great leaders in the last few centuries were readers, and they also gathered diverse advisers of significant skills. True security can only be developed by looking within. In this age, if we are to prevent our destruction—not from war, but destruction of our econiche—it is important to create a society where spiritual wisdom is engendered, acknowledged, and communicated. A shift in consciousness cannot be sustained through ignorance. Even the primitive once and future King Arthur maintained his relationship with his living library Merlin. Once again I offer a romp for the reader who wants to become expert where many fail, because they don't know how to identify the leaders in a particular field, or to recognize good scholarship. Have a good read—it often correlates with a good life.

Transpersonal Psychology

Stanislav Grof (with Hal Zina Bennet, Ph.D), *The Holotropic Mind: The Three Levels of Human Consciousness and How They Shape Our Lives,* Harper San Francisco, 1993. Grof is considered one of the most brilliant minds in cutting-edge psychology. This book is easy to read, as Grof marshals an impressive interpretation of experiments, data, and personal experience to illuminate consciousness in its many natural but non-ordinary states. He provides descriptions derived from Freud, Jung, Harmon, Maslow, his government-sponsored LSD experiments in Czechoslovakia, and religious experiences East and West, and brings them together to create some fundamental insights that are accessible to all.

Bonnie Greenwell, *Energies of Transformation: A Guide to the Kundalini Process,* Cupertino, CA: Shakti River Press, 1990. The author is a former head of the Kundalini Research Network. This is the best scientific description and analysis of the kundalini experience in the English language.

Michael Murphy, *The Future Of The Body: Explorations Into the Further Evolution of Human Nature,* Los Angeles, CA: Tarcher, 1992. Examines the latent potentials and extraordinary abilities that are part of human capacities. Full of contemporary and historical examples that illuminate human potential. Murphy draws examples from religion, transpersonal psychology, and the martial arts. This is an important book.

Ken Wilber, *Sex, Ecology, Spirituality: The Spirit of Evolution,*

Boston & London: Shambhala, 1995. A great menacing fat book of over 800 pages of remarkable scholarly value. Wilber is the best syncretist writing today, and perhaps, ever. He creates order out of chaos. Order number 2072. Call 617-424-0228.

Emrika Padus, editor, *The Complete Guide to Your Emotions & Your Health: New Dimensions in Mind/Body Healing,* Emmaus, PA: Rodale Press, 1986. One of the best self-help texts in psychosomatic medicine. Full of useful information and techniques.

Stanislav Grof, *Beyond the Brain: Birth, Death, and Transcendence in Psychotherapy,* Albany, NY: State University of New York Press, 1985. Reading this extremely well-researched text may help you to understand the holotropic reality that is literally the home of the Bujin and a great deal more. Once you have learned how to be telepathic over distance and time as well as bilocated in the Void, this book will help you to understand your new relationship with an expanded reality.

C. D. Laughlin, J. McManus, and E. G. d'Aquili, *Brain, Symbol & Experience,* Boston, MA: New Science, Shambhala, 1990. This book is written for serious academics with a background in physical and psychological anthropology. The language used requires professional knowledge in three fields and the authors show no mercy for the neophyte. Very difficult reading, but right on.

Carl Jung, "Psychological Types," from *Collected Works,* Vol. Six, Princeton University Press, 1971. Jung was probably the greatest European psychologist and has a great deal of influence on transpersonal psychologists. He was a meditator, and a prolific writer. Much of what he wrote in this volume was channeled in meditation with a personality he called Philomen. He was erudite and wise, and I would have loved to meet him.

Richard & Bernice Lazarus, *Passion & Reason,* Oxford University Press, 1994. Short-and long-term cause and effect examination of many emotions. Evaluates stress and health research. Some studies indicate that emotions are not irrational but link thought and motive. Why not learn to use one's passions constructively?

Josie Hadley and Carol Staudacher, *Hypnosis for Change: A Practical Manual of Proven Hypnotic Techniques,* Oakland, CA, New Harbinger Publications, 1989. This is an excellent cookbook for the burgeoning hypnotist. Hypnosis is the basis of magic. The writers include history, rules, scripts, uses, how to, etc. It is the best guide for the beginner I've read, and includes many tips and helpful reminders for the skilled.

Robert Ornstein, *The Roots of the Self,* Harper San Francisco, 1993. Discusses how the 500-million-year-old structure of the brain affects our world view and self-development. Recent research as well as mind-blowing illustrations, jokes, legends, give us the patterns to understand the nurture/nature puzzle that results in individuation of the self. *The Healing Brain: A Scientific Reader* (New York: Simon and Schuster, 1987) is an excellent follow-up text that explores brain-mind-body relationships that pertain to health and illness.

John Welwood, *Challenge of the Heart,* Boston, MA: Shambhala, 1985. A philosophy of love is every bit as important as a philosophy of life. Intimacy is important to growth. You might contrast this book to Stanton E. Samenow's *Inside the Criminal Mind* (New York & Toronto: Time Books, 1984).

Gopi Krishna, *Living with Kundalini,* Boston & London: Shambhala Dragon Editions, 1993. This is the first modern description of the ancient kundalini process by someone with a scientific perspective. He was a true adventurer into the Void. His recommendations can save you from taking damage. Chapters Nineteen and Twenty sum up the personal research drawn from twenty years of experience. His commentary makes clear the value of integrating chi kung practice with kundalini. It is a shame that his call to research was dropped by the Indian government, but the organization (KRN) for studying the kundalini still exists.

Leadership Guides

Warren Bennis, *On Becoming a Leader,* Reading, MA: Addison Wesley, 1989. Actual research and profiles of successful leaders in the modern context. Much better than Machiavelli except when dealing with the more primitive exploiters of the business environment. Leadership in business is based on competence which builds trust. A real leader is able to develop others so the organization will survive his or her death.

John K. Clemens and Douglas F. Mayer, *The Classic Touch: Lessons in Leadership from Homer to Hemingway,* Homewood, IL: Dow Jones-Irwin, 1987. A good story teller has to know people and furthermore make them interesting. A rhetorical analysis of leadership ideals and failures.

Robert L. Wing, *The Art of Strategy: A New Translation of Sun Tzu's Classic, The Art of War, The World's Most Widely Read Manual on Skillful Negotiations and Lasting Influence,* New York & Sydney: Dolphin/Doubleday, 1988. Also *The Tao of Power: Lao Tzu's Classic Guide to Leadership, Influence, and Excellence,* New York & Aukland: Dolphin/Doubleday, 1986. Wing is the best translator of Eastern leadership texts for modern purposes that I've discovered. Thomas Cleary has also translated Sun Tzu, as has James Clavell and Samuel B. Griffiths.

Robert G. Henricks, translator, Lao Tzu, *Te-Tao Ching: A New Translation Based on the Recently Discovered Ma-wang-tui Texts,* New York: Classics of Ancient China, Ballantine

Books, 1989. This most ancient text resonates with the voices of the Bujin. There are subtle differences from the later translations that create major recognition in the knowing. It is amazing how the changing of a few words can completely alter meaning in such a well known and deeply studied work. This is the best text ever written on leadership application and behavior. It is the classic.

Meditation

Daniel Goleman, *The Meditative Mind: The Varieties of Meditative Experience,* Los Angeles, CA: Tarcher, St. Martin's Press, 1988. Hindu, Buddhist, Sufi, Jewish, Christian, TM, Tantric, Kundalini Yoga, Tibetan Buddhism, Gurdjieff's and Krishnamurti's methodologies, distinct levels of consciousness, the scientific studies, and the consequences to health. In short, all you need to know.

Taisen Deshimaru, *The Zen Way to the Martial Arts,* New York: E. P. Dutton, Inc, 1982. A Japanese master reveals the secrets of his samurai tradition. Meditation, massage, terminology, stories, and practice. A great book for younger martial artists. *Questions to a Zen Master,* New York: ARKANA, Penguin, 1985. An interesting book on the practice of zazen from the Soto sect and Sawaki lineage. A careful reading reveals the weakness in the system. Roshi Deshimaru taught in Europe and explains spiritual practice in a very practical manner.

Thomas Cleary, *Minding Mind: A Basic Course in Meditation,* Boston, MA: Shambhala, 1994. Lessons from seven famous masters' writing instruction manuals for their students. Densely packed with goodies for the serious student. Also *Buddhist Yoga,* Boston, MA: Shambhala, 1995. Good stuff.

Glenn J. Morris, *Meditative Mastery,* Eurotech Consulting, P.O. Box 489, Fenton, Michigan, 48430. Eight one-hour cassette tapes to guide the individual from beginner at sitting to mastery of moving meditation. Contains dozens of exercises, eight audio tapes, and a workbook in a three-ring binder for $129.95. Used with groups in many dojo and kwoon. Includes guidance for chi kung.

Animal Consciousness, Shamanism, and Angels

Ted Andrews, *Animal Speak: The Spiritual & Magical Powers of Creatures Great & Small,* St. Paul, MI: Llewellyn Publications, 1994. All mythologies have a garden tale of when humans and animals could speak with one another. This book includes a comprehensive dictionary of animal, bird, reptile, and insect symbolism useful for those who desire a better understanding of spiritual ecology and work to establish a relationship with a totemic animal or insect.

Drs. Carl Sagan and Ann Druyan, *Shadows of Forgotten Ancestors,* New York: Random House, 1992. This book is extremely useful in achieving an understanding of our real distance from animal nature. It presents important ideas with clarity. There is a video.

Donald R. Griffin, *Animal Minds,* University of Chicago Press, 1992. This book brings together much of what we know about animal cognition. There has been a lot of research in the last ten years concerning the nature and potential of animal minds. The communication signals of animals provide a "window" on their thoughts and feelings, and scientific analysis may soon tell us more about what animal cognition is really like. Norman R.F. Maier's work showed clearly that animals are much smarter than we tend to credit them, as practically any farmer's wife will report if you ask. *Secret Garden* (New York: Simon & Schuster,1992) by David Bodanis, and *The Beastly Book: 100 of the World's Most Dangerous Creatures* (Englewood Cliffs, NJ: Prentice Hall General Reference, 1993) by Jeanne K. Hanson will greatly add to your understanding, as will anything by primatologist Jane Goodall.

Holger Kalweit, *Shamans, Healers, and Medicine Men*, Boston: Shambhala, 1992. Translated anthropological descriptions of primarily American Indian—particularly Inuit—practice. Interesting viewpoints that are similar to Ninpo.

Gary Doore, *Shaman's Path: Healing, Personal Growth, and Empowerment*, Boston: Shambhala, 1988. An excellent collection derived from anthropological observation of the practice and utility of shamanistic methods. Includes some very useful techniques.

Jose and Lena Stevens, *Secrets of Shamanism: Tapping the Spirit Power Within You*, New York: Avon New Age Non-Fiction, 1988. The designation "nonfiction" may not be totally accurate, but there are many fun exercises to try out in this book, which with a little bit of creativity on your part will take you past the authors' original intent.

Morton Kelsey, *Dreamquest: Native American Myth and the Recovery of Soul*, Rockport, MA: Element, 1992. The author is a Jungian therapist, Episcopal priest, and theology professor examining the tales of the Seneca. He opens a window to a nature reality that includes spirits of good and evil. These are the Indians I grew up near and played football against as a boy in Kane, Pennsylvania. I also spent some time with Jicarilla Apache as a young man recovering from my "education abroad" courtesy of the US Army.

P.M.H. Atwater, *Beyond the Light: What Isn't Being Said About Near Death Experience*, New York & Toronto: Birch Lane Press, 1994. Sometimes visions of Hell and other interesting interactions with various boogies are granted to NDE experiencers. Some of the after-effects of NDE are similar to the kundalini but seem more mundane. Interesting research that isn't getting much attention beyond pop interpretation.

Malcolm Godwin, *Angels: An Endangered Species*, New York: Simon and Schuster, 1990. From the ancient book of Enoch to UFO research and consciousness scientists, this book filled with illustrations and descriptions, might give you a clue or two concerning those you meet when you penetrate into neighboring dimensions.

Daniil Andreev, *Roza Mira (The Rose of the World)*, Moscow: Inoi Mir, 1992. Andreev spent his years in the Gulag meditating and writing down his map of the metaphysical universe. It is a multi-layered strange one. If you don't read Russian, Alexei Bogdanov wrote an article about Andreev for *Gnosis* magazine in the spring of 1994.

Alternative Medicine

Daniel Goleman and Joel Gurin, eds, *Mind Body Medicine: How to Use Your Mind for Better Health*, Yonkers, NY: Consumer Reports Books, 1993. In league with the Fetzer Institute, the authors have compiled a collection of studies from the United States' top medical centers. Provides scientific basis for many alternative medical solutions to health problems.

Deepak Chopra, *Ageless Body, Timeless Mind: The Quantum Alternative To Growing Old*, New York: Harmony Books, 1993. A trendy title for when ancient wisdom and modern science flow together to create strategies for living a long and fruitful life. Useful information from the pen of a practical medical practitioner.

Stephen T. Chang, *The complete book of acupuncture*, Berkeley, CA: Celestial Arts, 1976. A thorough reference and guide, including energy flow, meridians, diagnostics, and specific techniques. *The Great Tao,* San Francisco: Tao Publishing, 1987. Everything you ever wanted to know about Taoism and health from a historical and secular perspective. A great book, almost as much fun to work with as Chang's *Tao of Sexology: The Book of Infinite Wisdom*, San Francisco: Tao Publishing, 1986. Ignore his advice concerning chi kung and AIDS.

Rodale Editors, *Training the Body to Cure Itself: How to Use Exercise to Heal,* Emmaus, PA: Rodale Press, 1992. The Rodale people have always been very helpful in presenting do-it-yourself health information that is medically sound. Lots of good ways to stretch and keep the old bones from falling apart when you are playing with the younger athletes.

Mantak & Maneewan Chia, *Chi Nei Tsang: Internal Organ Chi Massage,* Huntington, NY: Healing Tao Books, 1990. This book has many little surprises as well as health tips that make for much safer chi development. *Awaken Healing Light of the Tao,* Huntington, NY: Healing Tao Books, 1993. The classic guide. Mantak Chia has written many useful books on the subject of chi kung, and his methods work. He writes well for both sexes, and his applications have martial and mystical merit even though he emphasizes medical applications.

Michael Reed Gach, *Acupressure's Potent Points: A Guide to Self-Care for Common Ailments,* New York: Bantam New Age Books, 1990. Keys to pressure points, excellent line drawings, pictures, and instructions. Simple techniques that relieve most common ailments and put you in charge of the process. It doesn't take much imagination to see the dim mak applications.

Linda G. Rector-Page, N.D., Ph.D, *Healthy Healing: An Alternative Healing Reference,* Ninth Edition, Sonora CA: Healthy Healing, 1992. A really complete general reference to alternative preventative medicine. Extremely well organized and useful. Deals with food therapy, vitamins and minerals, herbal therapy, and bodywork. Combine with acupressure and chi kung, and your healing skills will take quantum leaps. Organic techniques have a long history of success, and the popularity of such alternatives as homeopathy and chiropractic is based on empiricism by the consumer.

David Hoffman, *The New Holistic Herbal,* Shaftesbury, Dorset & Rockport, MA: Element, 1993. Herbology is important to your health if you follow alternative medical practice. Full of viable information. Another useful source is Eric Mandell's *Herbal Bible* (New York & Singapore: Simon and Schuster, 1992).

Sexual Practice

Douglas Wile, *The Art of the Bedchamber: The Chinese Sexual Yoga Classics Including Women's Solo Meditations,* Albany, NY: SUNY Press, 1992. The book is divided in two parts. The first lays out the theory and development, ethos, sexual practices, medical applications, thematic expressions, etc. The second gives the reader translations of a wide variety of texts with detailed explanations. This book significantly advances Western knowledge and interpretation.

Thomas Cleary, *Immortal Sisters,* Boston, MA: Shambhala, 1989. Cleary's translation of this classic Chinese text and insights show clearly that there were female Taoist adepts from the fourth to the twelfth century. Reading this after Mantak Chia will connect many esoteric practices for the astute reader. Taoist roots of some ninja practices should jump right out at you, particularly the emphasis on secrecy.

Mantak Chia, Maneewan Chia, and Michael Winn, *Taoist Secrets of Love: Cultivating Male Sexual Energy,* New York: Aurora, 1986. Reveals how to use energy and orbit work with a partner. Many useful exercises. *Healing Love Through the Tao: Cultivating Female Sexual Energy,* Huntington, NY: Healing Tao Books, 1986. The best book concerning chi development for women. You wannabe a superwoman? You'll need more energy than you get from a Mr. Goodbar. Ovarian kung fu. Go for it.

Strategy (Heiho and Bugei)

Thomas Cleary, *Thunder in the Sky: On the Acquisition and Exercise of Power,* Boston, MA: Shambhala, 1993. When you read "Master of the Demon Valley" a text that obviously influenced Lao Tzu, you will find the forerunner of Ninpo complete with reference to spider knowledge. This is the first scroll of The School Wrested from the Nine Demon Gods. Its an esoteric gold mine if you have mastered your practice of chi kung. *Wen-Tzu: Understanding the Mysteries*, Boston, MA: Shambhala, 1992. More commentary on Lao Tzu and the Tao that has never been published in the West until Cleary translated it. The commentary on strategy is right on. Cleary's translation of *The Book of Balance and Harmony* (New York: North Point Press, 1988) provides a 13th-century map to the "Isle of the Immortals."

Shi Ming (trans. by Thomas Cleary), *Mind Over Matter: Higher Martial Arts,* Berkeley, CA: Frog, Ltd., 1994. This book should be in your library if you are trying to understand the effects of chi. A very clear delineation of the viewpoint of refined consciousness attained through the higher level martial arts. It doesn't tell you how or why, but it is a pretty good map of what can be there.

Benjamin Franklin, *Selections From Poor Richard's Almanac,* New York: Avanel Books, 1982. Ben Franklin could put more wisdom into an adage, maxim, or epigram than most writers can put in a book.

Shifu Nagaboshi Tomio (Terence Dukes), *The Bodhisattva Warriors,* York Beach, ME: Samuel Weiser, Inc. 1994. Symbols, consciousness, history, Mikkyo Buddhism, Shaolin, all the interesting mystical stuff and mummy dust laid out in an easily understood and useful description.

Miyamoto Musashi, *The Book of Five Rings,* Boston & London: Shambhala Dragon Editions, 1993. A new translation by

Thomas Cleary which includes the extremely valuable book on sword strategy, *Family Traditions on the Art of War* by Yagyu Munenori. Some of Munenori's comments on swordsmanship will seem very familiar, if you've studied with The Boss. Musashi is revered as a master of painting, sculpture, metal working, swordsmanship, and strategy, but he is not well understood. Cleary's translation is the best I've read in English and his commentary adds value. This is *Walden* for the samurai, according to my young friend Matt Smith.

A. L. Sadler, *The Code of the Samurai: The Spirit That Drives Japan*, Rutland, VT & Tokyo: Tuttle, ninth printing, 1993. Daidoji Yuzan wrote this chivalric code after serving under six different shoguns. He lived in interesting times and his commentaries on survival behavior are easily generalized to modern living conditions. Yuzan's concepts are more accepted than *The Hagakure*. He was the samurai equivalent of the famed ronin Miyamoto Musashi.

Karl F. Friday, *Hired Swords: The Rise of Private Warrior Power in Early Japan*, Palo Alto, CA: Stanford University Press, 1992. Traces the evolution of military practice from the seventh through twelfth centuries in Japan before the samurai coalitions. There are many divergences from much of the received history concerning warrior ways and families. The elite of the provinces were the protectors of the imperial courts. This book casts a different light on the "ninja" roots for a diligent scholar willing to search behind revision.

Stephen K. Hayes, *The Ninja and Their Secret Fighting Art*, Rutland, VT: Tuttle, eighth printing, 1994. The book that started The Ninja Boom improves with age, especially after you've come to know some of the folks described. There is a lot of well presented good solid information for the practitioner of Ninpo in this book.. *The Ancient Art of Ninja Warfare: Combat, Espionage, and Traditions*, Chicago, IL:Contemporary Books, 1988. Hayes at his best. Traces concepts and techniques to the source. *Ninja Realms of Power*, Chicago, IL: Contemporary Books, 1986, is a primer revealing basic interpretations of ninja lore and traditions.

Robert L. Spencer, *The Craft Of The Warrior*, North Atlantic Books, 1993. A collection of meaningful readings on the theme of warrior disciplines concerned with the development of harmony and compassion. Surveys practices ranging from meditation to NLP. A good overview for the beginner seeking enlightenment in contemporary practice.

James T. Evans, *Where Liberals Go To Die: The End of Let's Pretend*, Houston, TX: Commonwealth Publishing, 1994. I usually disagree with the author's identification of causes, being liberal more than conservative, but I have grown to appreciate his solutions. He is a well-known legal and political figure in Texas. His chapter on insensitivity training and the asking of hard questions is particularly worth contemplating.

Dave Lowry, *Sword and Brush*, Boston & London: Shambhala, 1995. Lowry is an excellent source of information concerning Budo. Some of his explanations will create consternation in the more rigid practitioner, but I find him accurate from my experience. This book explains many terms important to the martial artist in a Japanese system as well as esoteric traps, practice, and meaning.

Chungliang Al Huang and Jerry Lynch, *Thinking Body, Dancing Mind: Taosports for extraordinary performance in athletics, business, and life.* The chapter on affirmations is drivel but the rest of the book is excellent.

Michael D. DeMarco, editor, *Journal of Asian Martial Arts*, Media Publishing Co., 821 West 24th St., Erie, PA, 16502. Scholarly articles from primary research, substantial interviews, and book reviews. Another interesting source of reliable material when you have to look someone up is Corcoran and Farkas' *The Original Martial Arts Encyclopedia* (Los Angeles, CA: Pro-Action Publication, 1993).

Religion and Mythology

Geoffry Parrinder, ed, *World Religions: From Ancient History to the Present,* New York: Facts on File Publications, 1971. This was a gift from Karim Abu Shakra to clue me into Islam so I wouldn't freak my Muslim students so much. It is an excellent overview of the religious mind across cultures.

Larry Dossey, M.D., *Healing Words: The Power of Prayer and the Practice of Medicine,* San Francisco: Harper Collins, 1993. A book to consider carefully, as the documentation is extraordinary.

Arthur Cotterel, *The Macmillan Illustrated Encyclopedia of Myths and Legends,* New York: Macmillan Publishing Co, 1989. Its helpful to have a bio of the opposition when you work with archetypes. Some archetypes even look like their pictures and statues when they appear in your meditations. Rather than scratch your head and wonder what the hell that was, you can look it up. Positively cosmic.

Anthony S. Mercantante, *World Mythology and Legend,* New York: Facts on File, 1988. When you want to know what a goddess can actually do, this is a great little source of information.

John White, *Kundalini: Evolution and Enlightenment,* New York: Paragon House, 1990. In depth presentation of well researched essays concerning the many controversial aspects of the search and results of attaining higher consciousness. Contains traditional views, Personal accounts, research explorations, and advice.

Alain Danielou, *Gods of Love and Ecstasy: The Traditions of Shiva and Dionysus,* Rochester, VT: Inner Traditions, 1992. Ancient religions can provide many insights into modern theology. Shiva is a god of creativity and associates easily with Western concepts concerning acceptance of personal choice.

Frank J. Tipler, *The Physics of Immortality: Modern Cosmology, God and the Resurrection of the Dead,* Boston, MA: Anchor Books, 1995. This is a book that will wilt your perception. Tipler's proof ignores non-Christian resurrection but aside from ignoring the population problem opens the door to the spirit world with minimal mumbo-jumbo. The Divine Comedy crashes the party at the Omega Point.

Taking Care of Yourself and Family

The Sivananda Yoga Center (Lucy Lidell), *The Sivananda Companion to Yoga,* New York: Fireside Simon and Schuster, 1983. A complete guide to the physical postures, breathing exercises, diet, relaxation, and meditation techniques of this school of Yoga. Get into the breath chapters and the meditative chapters before taking on the asanas. If you can maintain a meditative state while stretching yourself into new territory, you'll find many interesting challenges in Yoga.

Mr. Garth A. Clarke, *A Coach's Kit for Modified Soccer,* Monroeville, PA: Pennsylvania West Soccer Association, 1993. I've known Garth for nearly thirty years. He is a great coach, and his techniques for getting all the players to play will help the coach of any sport. I spent a lot of time on the bench (five years) and know how discouraging that can be for a youngster. He also includes chapters on getting the community involved.

Steven Bernola and Glenn J. Morris, *Butokuden Dim Mak,* Eurotech Consulting, P.O. Box 489, Fenton, Michigan, 48430. Thirty-eight points of blight that will create energy blocks and hematomas. Drawn from Chinese kempo, hoshin-roshiryu jujutsu, Bujinkan Ninpo, isshinryu karate, hwarang-do, and Nihon Karate Jujutsu. A workbook for those who want to master Death Touch. Details location, nerve and vascular damage, timetables for practice and striking, and the rarely presented resuscitation points.

Joanne and Stephanie Oppenheim, *The Best Toys, Books & Videos for Kids: The 1995 Guide to 1000+ Kid-Tested, Classic and New Products—for ages 0–10,* San Francisco: Harper Perennial, 1994. You can't start too young. We all need help. Two pots on the kitchen floor doesn't cut it anymore.

Tom Brown, Jr., with William Owen, *The Search,* New York: Berkley Books Non-Fiction, 1982. Tom is a bit goody-two-shoes in his fictional presentation of self, but what he describes can be done and is a lot of fun. Many American ninja go to his tracking and fire-starting seminars.

Strategic Organizational Guides

Douglas McGregor, *The Human Side of Enterprise,* New York & Tokyo: McGraw Hill, 1960. The classic work concerning motivation. Practically everything written on this topic from the business perspective is derivative of McGregor.

Tom Peters, *Thriving On Chaos,* New York: Alfred A Knopf, 1988. A pretty good description of the tools and techniques necessary for survival over long periods in a turbulent world market.

Alvin and Heidi Toffler, *Creating A New Civilization,* Atlanta, GA: Turner Publishing Inc., 1994. This is the book that has been shaking up the politicians. It seems to be a pretty good wake up call for those who have foundered in the third wave. There is no escape from change. If your company hasn't made some effort in achieving and implementing some of the concepts discussed, it is highly probable you'll get to experience the ride of the samurai and fate of the dinosaur.

Thomas Cleary, *The Japanese Art of War: Understanding the Culture of Strategy,* Boston: Shambhala, 1991. May help you to achieve a deeper understanding of Japanese strategy and tendency to treat business as war. His commentary on Zen is particularly helpful.

Maryann Keller, *Rude Awakening: The Rise, Fall, and Struggle for Recovery of General Motors*, New York: Morrow, 1989. Ms. Keller is an observer of the car industry. She knows everyone, and is sometimes a little too kind in describing their folly. She does not, however, fall into the trap of accepting their viewpoint, which warped the analysis of General Motors by Dr. Rosabeth Kantor in her book *The Change Masters*. Knowledge without integration and application is only academic.

Dr. Norman R.F. Maier, *Problem Solving Discussions and Conferences*, New York: McGraw Hill, 1963, and *Psychology in Industrial Organizations*, 5th ed, Boston: Houghton Mifflin, 1982. Gertrude Casselman Verser writes with Norm's voice. He may be dead but this book illuminates his thinking far better than the older editions, which had elements he disliked but included for the editors. This is the Norm that I remember. He was the greatest organizational psychologist who ever lived and based all his observations scientifically.

Mr. Robert Levering, *A Great Place to Work: What Makes Some Employers So Good (And Most So Bad)*, New York: Random House, 1988. If you are going to work for somebody, then spend some time learning what to look for when selecting a company. There are companies that can crush the soul of any honest person, given enough time.

Miscellaneous Resources

The Moulton Alabama CNCKI chi kung institute (Their tapes are still available at 800-824-2433.) I recommended in the first book seems to have developed into Pacific Rim Publications in Santa Clara, California, first under Master Roger Hagood, and now some people I don't know. Pacific Rim is a fine source of videos and publications concerning martial art practice. They publish three martial art magazines on a quarterly basis. *Qigong/Kung Fu* which includes chi kung (qi qong) information, for those who follow Chinese traditions. *Mudo/Dojang* is for Korean stylists. Their *Budo/Dojo* magazine reflects Japanese traditional martial arts and often has very interesting articles even though I often find myself in disagreement with how some of the information is presented.

Favorite Authors

Fiction Writers: Kenneth Roberts, C.J. Cherryh, John D. McDonald, Ursula K. Leguin, Louis L'Amour, Tom Clancy, Andre Norton, Rudyard Kipling, Tony Hillerman, Jack Chalker, James Clavell, Joan Brady, Joe Haldeman, Michael Crichton, Dick Francis, Larry Niven & Jerry Pournelle, Jonathan Kellerman, Julian May, Norman Spinrad, Sue Grafton, Roger Zelazny, and Anne Rice. They'll hold your kids' or your attention.

Poets: John Ciardi, e e cummings, Robert Frost, Rumi, Langston Hughes, Basho, Rainer Maria Rilke, Edgar Lee Masters, and Emily Dickinson have stood the test of time, fad, and fashion, creating wonderful characters as well as producing interesting insights.

About the Author

Glenn J. Morris is a member of The World Head of Family and Sokeship Council as soke of the Hoshinroshiryu, and was elected to the World Martial Arts Hall of Fame. In 1993 he was given the rank of *hachidan* (eighth-dan black belt) in Bujinkan Ninpo Budo Taijutsu. Dr. Morris was granted the title *Oshihan* (major teaching master) by the Board of Directors of the Bunbu-Ichi Zendo Budo/Bugei Remmei, and the honorary title of *Kyoshi* (senior practitioner or knight) by the Yi Tsung. He has been ranked *rokudan* (sixth-dan black belt) in Nihon Karate Jujutsu. He was personally given a shidoshi's license in Bujinkan Ninpo by Grandmaster Masaaki Hatsumi, Soke and thirty-fourth linear grandmaster of the oldest surviving mystery school of combatic strategy in the world. Togakure Ryu ninjutsu has an unbroken lineage extending back to the eleventh century. Ninja are revered by those who know them well for their spiritual abilities, longevity, and harmonious lifeways under duress.

Dr. Morris earned his bachelor's degree in General Arts and Science and master's in Speech at Penn State, and his Ph.D. in Communication, Rhetoric, and Public Address at Wayne State. He completed a Doctorate of Science in Psychology with Eurotechnical Research University. Dr. Morris has been a psychological consultant to business and industry for twenty years, as well as a member of faculty at Penn State; Wayne State; Univ. of Michigan; Univ. of Windsor, Canada; Hillsdale College; and Jackson Community College. He has written, taught, and designed training programs in leadership development for Meijer's Thrifty Acres, Upjohn Corporation, Hillsdale College, Exxon, Texas Utilities, and General Motors Engine Division. He is a specialist in experiential training, problem-solving, team development, selection and development, cross-cultural strategy, diagnostics, interpersonal communication skills, and stress management. He is vice president of human resource development for Pacific Biotech Inc. of Houston, which specializes in the research and development of treatments for viral-related cancers and immune disorders, as well as research for Oilex, Inc., in oil recovery and environmental clean-up. He lives in Houston, Texas, with Aree Marquis and their daughter.

Dr. Morris has or has had professional memberships in the American Association for the Advancement of Science, Association for Transpersonal Psychology, Association for Humanistic Psychology, The Speech Communication Association, The International Society for the Study of Subtle Energy and Energy Medicine, Chinese National Chi Kung Institute, Foundation for Shamanistic Research, Kundalini Research Network, Institute of Noetic Sciences, International Association of Counselors and Therapists, and The National Guild of Hypnotists.